Archaeomagnetic Dating

Archaeomagnetic Dating

Edited by Jeffrey L. Eighmy and Robert S. Sternberg

THE UNIVERSITY OF ARIZONA PRESS   TUCSON

The University of Arizona Press
Copyright © 1990
The Arizona Board of Regents
All rights reserved

Manufactured in the United States of America
⊛ This book is printed on acid-free, archival-quality paper.

94 93 92 91 90   5 4 3 2 1

LIBRARY OF CONGRESS CATALOGING-IN-PUBLICATION DATA

Archaeomagnetic dating / edited by Jeffrey L. Eighmy and Robert S.
  Sternberg.
       p.   cm.
    Includes bibliographical references and index.
    ISBN 0-8165-1132-2
    1. Archaeological dating. 2. Archaeometry. I. Eighmy, Jeffrey
  L. II. Sternberg, Robert Saul.
CC78.A73   1990
930.1'028'5–dc20   90-11110
                                                                 CIP

British Library Cataloguing in Publication data are available.

Dedicated to our families

Contents

About the Contributors

KENNETH J. BERRY
Department of Sociology, Colorado State University,
Fort Collins, Colorado 80523

JEFFREY L. EIGHMY
Department of Anthropology, Colorado State University,
Fort Collins, Colorado 80523

J. HOLLY HATHAWAY
Department of Anthropology, Colorado State University,
Fort Collins, Colorado 80523

ALLEN E. KANE
Pike and San Isabel National Forests,
1920 Valley Drive, Pueblo, Colorado

GEORGE J. KRAUSE
Department of Anthropology, Colorado State University,
Fort Collins, Colorado 80523

RICHARD C. LANGE
Arizona State Museum, University of Arizona,
Tucson, Arizona 85721

RANDALL H. MCGUIRE
Department of Anthropology, State University of New York
at Binghamton, Binghamton, New York 13901

PAUL W. MIELKE, JR.
Department of Statistics, Colorado State University,
Fort Collins, Colorado 80523

BARBARA A. MURPHY
Arizona State Museum, University of Arizona,
Tucson, Arizona 85721

GARY P. SMITH
Bureau of Land Management, P.O. Box 36800,
Billings, Montana 59107

ROBERT S. STERNBERG
Department of Geology, Franklin and Marshall College,
P.O. Box 3003, Lancaster, Pennsylvania 17604-3003

DANIEL WOLFMAN
Office of Archaeological Studies, Museum of New Mexico,
P.O. Box 2087, Santa Fe, New Mexico 87504

JEN HAUR YU
Elf Exploration, Inc.,
1000 Louisiana, Suite 3800, Houston, Texas 77002

Preface

Archaeomagnetic dating refers to the dating of archaeological features and artifacts by comparing the magnetic information recorded in these materials with known changes in the earth's magnetic field. Although changes in either the direction or strength of the geomagnetic field can be used for archaeomagnetic dating, use of the former is more common. It is to the problem of archaeomagnetic direction dating in the Americas that this volume is addressed, with specific geographic emphasis on North America and Mesoamerica.

Some archaeologists feel that a concern for problems of dating has occupied too much of this discipline's attention. Archaeologists are urged to go beyond problems of chronology and subsistence to the study of social archaeology (Redman et al. 1978). Indeed, a continuing debate in archaeology centers on which of various research strategies will produce the most accurate and comprehensive understanding of the social life that produced the archaeological record (Schiffer 1976; Spriggs 1984; Butzer 1982; Redman et al. 1978). Given this widespread concern among modern archaeologists for the behavioral and social referents of archaeological data, a book detailing research in one of the archaeological dating techniques might seem irrelevant or outmoded. We think not.

The pertinence of a book of this nature to current processual and "social" archaeology stems from the role that dating theory plays in linking archaeological observation to systemic interpretations (Dean 1978:224). Both temporal and spatial control are essential for documenting the archaeological context against which behavioral models are tested. As behavioral questions become more detailed and as debate about the efficacy of competing behavioral research strategies emerges, the quality of temporal control also becomes significant.

Although chronometric control is not intrinsically interesting to the anthropologically trained archaeologist, it is essential to all prehistoric archaeology. Therefore, the quality of archaeomagnetic dating should be of more than passing interest to all archaeologists.

Although this book has been prepared with the goals of the archaeologists in the forefront, most of the discussion and results herein should also be of interest to geophysicists. Archaeomagnetism is an inherently interdisciplinary field, combining aspects of both archaeology and the geophysical discipline of paleomagnetism. Independently dated archaeomagnetic results, along with other paleomagnetic results from recent sedimentary and igneous rocks, extend the historic record of direct observations of the geomagnetic field back into prehistory. Similarly, archaeologists use established records of this secular variation to determine archaeomagnetic dates. The goals of these two groups should be seen as complementary rather than conflicting. The archaeologists who supply the geophysicist with archaeomagnetic samples that are already dated by some other technique may later benefit from the secular variation curve derived from those samples.

The general organization of the book is as follows. Part 1, the Introduction, discusses the geophysical underpinnings of archaeomagnetism. Part 2 deals with the general methodological problems faced by any archaeomagnetic study—sample collection, laboratory measurement and analysis, and treatment of the data. Part 3, on experimental archaeology, presents the findings of some field and laboratory studies that advance and refine our understanding of the archaeomagnetic method. Part 4 summarizes results on archaeomagnetic secular variation and archaeomagnetic dating that serve as useful case histories. We have also included the raw data sets from these individual studies but have placed them in the appendix to avoid interrupting the narrative. Part 5 is a single concluding article that gives a perspective on where the study of archaeomagnetism stands today. Because many references are common to several of the articles, a single bibliography has been compiled for the entire volume.

In dealing exclusively with the subject of archaeomagnetism, this book should give the reader an overview of the archaeomagnetic technique. As a compendium of research papers, however, this volume is not intended to be as complete or as continuous as a textbook. We recommend that the interested reader fill in these gaps by reading among the other articles and books referred to herein.

Choosing between the various systems of units for magnetic quantities has always been a vexing problem. Geomagnetists and paleomagnetists traditionally used Gaussian CGS (cm, g, and s) units. In 1960 the General Conference on Weights and Measures gave formal approval to the Système International d'Unites, or SI units. Geophysicists have been rather sluggish in changing over to this new standard but are now encouraged, and sometimes required, to do so by most geophysical societies and journals. We have thus adopted SI units as the standard for this volume, even though most archaeomagnetists think, and some archaeomagnetists still work, in CGS units. The relation between the two most common quantities in archaeomagnetism are as follows:

Quantity	SI Unit	Gaussian CGS Unit
Magnetic induction	1 tesla (T)	10^4 gauss (G)
Magnetic moment per volume	1 ampere/meter (A/m)	10^{-3} gauss

Strictly speaking, the magnetic field strength (usually denoted as the H-field) is distinct from magnetic induction (the B-field). The relationship between these two quantities is $B = \mu H$, where μ is the magnetic permeability, and the units of the H-field are in oersteds. The distinction between B and H fields is not always important in CGS units, because these two quantities are numerically equal when measured in air, where the magnetic permeability is 1. This is not true in SI units, where $B = \mu H$, with the units of H being amperes/ meter (A/m), but the value of the permeability of free space is $4\pi \times 10^{-7}$. A similar confusion exists with the magnetic moment per unit volume, which in CGS is numerically equal to the magnetization, while in SI it is not. Shive (1986) discusses the use and misuse of common paleomagnetic units. Payne (1981) also gives a complete set of tables for converting magnetic quantities between CGS and SI units. In the present volume, the numerical magnetic quantities are given in terms of magnetic induction and magnetic moment per volume. The reader will find, however, that these quantities are also loosely referred to as the magnetic field strength and magnetization (also as the strength or intensity of magnetization), respectively.

The contributions in Part 4 depend on independently dating virtual geomagnetic poles. We view the documentation and publication of these dated poles as another important contribution of this book.

For the convenience of those interested in using these data, we have placed them as a uniform set of tables in an appendix at the end of the book. We would like to thank Sharilee Counce for compiling the appendix tables from data provided by contributors to this volume, and the College of Arts, Humanities and Social Sciences, Colorado State University, for a faculty research grant to support the compilation.

PART 1

Introduction

Introduction

Because many of the readers of this book will be archaeologists, we have taken the liberty to presume a familiarity with the essentials of archaeological methodology and research goals. We have in this introductory section included a single article by Sternberg that gives the geophysical basis for the archaeomagnetic method. Archaeologists in the position of providing archaeomagnetic samples can best help geophysicists by having at least a general awareness of the goal of secular variation studies. The archaeologists as users of archaeomagnetic dates must also have some knowledge of archaeomagnetism to best appreciate its strengths and weaknesses. Besides providing this overview, the article also places archaeomagnetism in the context of other dating techniques, categorizing it as a regional pattern-matching technique and showing its structural similarity to other techniques such as dendrochronology.

CHAPTER 1

The Geophysical Basis
of Archaeomagnetic Dating

ROBERT S. STERNBERG

Chronometric techniques in archaeology are inherently interdisciplinary, requiring the expertise of the physicist, the chemist, the geologist, and the biologist to extract the information necessary to determine a date. But only the archaeologist can determine the contextual meaning of that date, and developing and testing these techniques require material and information that only the archaeologist can provide. Successful archaeomagnetic research depends on input from both geophysics and archaeology and is in turn capable of providing useful information to both disciplines. Thus, even the archaeologist who is merely using archaeomagnetic dates should have an understanding of the fundamentals of archaeomagnetism. Only by understanding how archaeomagnetic dating works and what its limitations are can the archaeologist best interpret the information provided by archaeomagnetic dates and develop realistic expectations for how these dates can be incorporated into a research design.

The purpose of this introductory chapter is to provide a brief overview of the geophysical basis of archaeomagnetic dating. This involves a discussion of the geomagnetic field, the ability of archaeomagnetic materials to act as geomagnetic tape recorders, and the relevant techniques of paleomagnetism. The chapter also presents a general classification scheme for chronometric methods in order to emphasize the two major tasks in archaeomagnetic dating: constructing a secular variation curve and interpreting dates based on that curve. This scheme is useful in highlighting the complementary goals and needs that the geophysicist and the archaeologist bring to archaeomagnetic research.

For more complete discussions of these topics, including the relevant mathematical equations and extensive lists of references, the interested reader may consult several sources: for geomagnetism and paleomagnetism, Irving (1964), McElhinny (1973), Merrill and McElhinny (1983), Tarling (1983), and Rikitake and Honkura (1985); for rock magnetism, Nagata (1961), O'Reilly (1984), Stacey and Banerjee (1974); and for methodology, Collinson (1983), and Collinson et al. (1967). Creer et al. (1983) present a compendium of secular variation results from archaeomagnetic and limnomagnetic studies. Discussions of archaeomagnetic dating can be found in most books on archaeometry—for example, Aitken (1974), Bucha (1971), Michels (1973), Fleming (1976), and Parkes (1987). Critical evaluations of archaeomagnetic dating and discussions of more specific problems can be found in Eighmy et al. (1980), Wolfman (1984), and articles in this volume.

GEOMAGNETISM, ROCK MAGNETISM,
AND PALEOMAGNETISM

Geomagnetism

Geomagnetism, the study of the earth's magnetic field, is one of the major branches of geophysics. The study of the main (internal) part of the geomagnetic field is primarily concerned with the morphology of the field, its secular variation, and the origin of the field.

The magnetic field can be described at any point on the earth's surface by a vector indicating the direction and strength of the field (Fig. 1.1). This vector can be completely described by three magnetic elements: the declination, inclination, and field strength. The declination is the angle between geographic north and the horizontal component of the magnetic field vector. The inclination is the dip of the total field vector with respect to the horizontal, with a positive inclination indicating a dip below the horizon. The field strength is the magnitude of the total field vector. A typical geomagnetic field strength of 50 μT (μ = micro) can be compared with the field found near a small ceramic magnet of about 2000 μT.

The pattern of these elements over the earth's surface specifies the structure of the field. Contour maps of the values of magnetic declination, inclination, and total field strength (Figs. 1.2, 1.3, and 1.4) indicate that much of the field can be attributed to a dipole field, which is also the characteristic field shape around a bar magnet. The dipole field is completely specified by the orientation of the axis and the strength of the dipole moment. If the dipole axis were parallel to

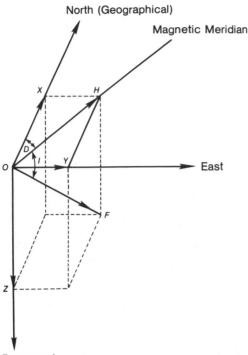

North (Geographical)

Magnetic Meridian

East

Downward

Figure 1.1. The magnetic elements used to describe the magnitude and direction of the magnetic field at any point on the earth's surface. *D*, declination (degrees); *I*, inclination (degrees); *F*, total field strength (T, or teslas); *H*, horizontal component of field strength (*T*); *X, Y, Z* (north, east, and downward components of field strength, *T*).

the rotation axis of the earth (axial dipole), contour lines for inclination and total field strength would parallel lines of latitude, and declination would be everywhere equal to 0°. Inclination would vary from −90° (vertical and pointing outward) at the south geographic pole to 0° (horizontal) at the equator and to +90° (vertical and pointing inward) at the north geographic pole. The field strength would be twice as strong at the poles as at the equator. The deviation of the real field from this pattern is due in part to the fact that the best-fitting dipole is inclined by 11° with respect to the rotation axis, cutting the earth's surface at coordinates 79° N, 109° W (the Queen Elizabeth Islands in Canada) in the northern hemisphere. The present dipole moment is 7.9×10^{22} Am^2 (Fabiano et al. 1983).

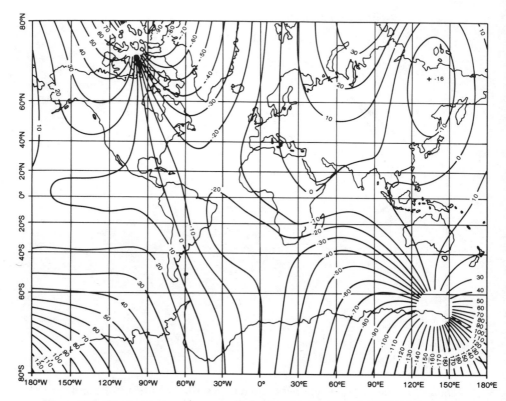

Figure 1.2. Contour map of magnetic declination for epoch 1980.0 (after Fabiano et al. 1983).

The dipole pattern is further perturbed by the nondipole component of the geomagnetic field. This is just that part of the field left over after the best-fitting dipole has been removed. The nondipole field causes regional perturbations of the dipole field (Figs. 1.5, 1.6). Thus, both a global dipole pattern in the geomagnetic field and a regional nondipole variation are observed. These patterns can be described in great detail for the present-day field, utilizing direct measurements from magnetic observatories (about 200 worldwide) and satellites. The dipole and nondipole fields are mathematically represented by spherical harmonic analysis, which represents a least-squares fit on the surface of a sphere. The coefficients of this analysis for recent epochs are given in Fabiano et al. (1983).

Differences between magnetic vectors from two different geographic sites occur due to both the dipole and nondipole fields. The

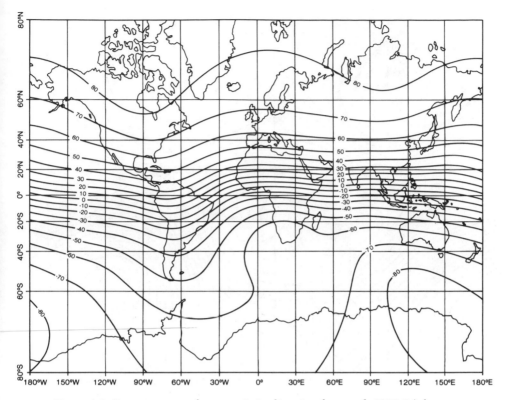

Figure 1.3. Contour map of magnetic inclination for epoch 1980.0 (after Fabiano et al. 1983).

intersite change in the dipole field can be corrected for by calculating virtual geomagnetic poles (VGPs), or by transforming directions to a common site through their VGPs. This is just a mathematical transformation that translates the declination and inclination at a given site into the geographic coordinates of the equivalent dipole axis. The term *virtual* indicates that this pole is different from the best-fitting dipole axis, which is determined by using a global data set. Even after this transformation, VGPs from different sites differ because of the existence of the nondipole field. Shuey et al. (1970) find that for epoch 1965.0, two directions transformed through the VGP still typically differ by 0.29° for every degree (111 km) of geographic separation between sites in the north-south direction, and by 0.15° for every degree of geographic separation in the east-west direction. This is why master archaeomagnetic records derived in one region

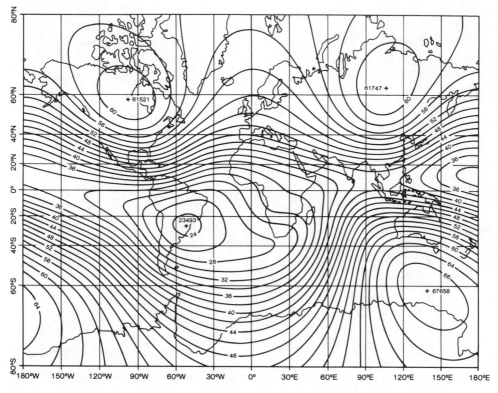

Figure 1.4. Contour map of total magnetic field strength for epoch 1980.0 in units of nT $(10^{-9}$ T) (after Fabiano et al. 1983).

become increasingly less applicable the farther one gets from that region and why it is necessary to compile new records for regions separated by distances over which the nondipole field exhibits appreciable change. If the accuracy for an archaeomagnetic direction is about 5° (Eighmy and Hathaway 1987), the above figures suggest that a given master record is most useful out to a distance of about (5°/.29°) × 111 km ≈ 2,000 km from the center of the given region.

The magnetic field undergoes temporal as well as spatial variation. The temporal change of the internal field, with time scales on the order of decades to several millennia, is called the secular variation. Both the strength and direction of the total field change due to changes in strength and direction of both the dipole and nondipole components. Consequently there is a global signature to the secular variation but also significant regional differences. Again, present-day patterns of secular variation are readily obtained from direct observations of the field at different locations. Figure 1.7 shows the longest secular variation record based on direct measurements of field direction. During the period from 1600 to 1950, inclination near London has varied by 8° and declination by 35°.

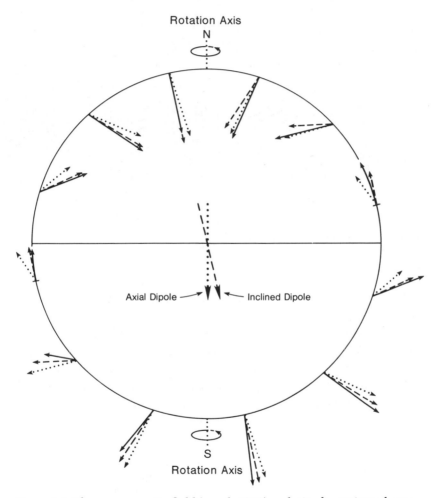

Figure 1.5. The geomagnetic field (epoch 1945) vs. latitude, projected onto the plane for meridian 290° east. The dotted lines are for the best-fitting geocentric axial dipole; the dashed lines are for the best-fitting geocentric inclined dipole; the solid line is for the actual magnetic field. The field strength at the surface is proportional to the length of the line, and the inclination is the angle below horizontal (after Cox and Doell 1960).

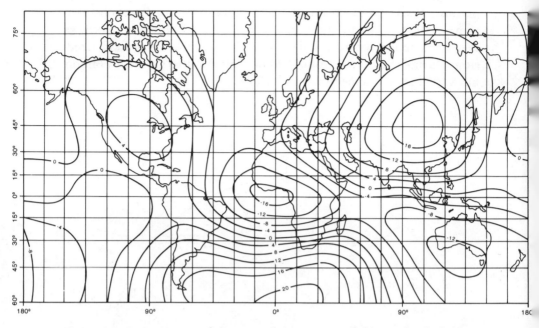

Figure 1.6. Contour map of the vertical component of the nondipole field, units of 10^{-6} T (after Parkinson 1983).

Two modes of secular variation appear in the historical record. The first is the westward drift of the nondipole field at a rate of about 0.2°/yr. This can be seen in maps of the nondipole field from different epochs as the peaks in the nondipole field drift noticeably westward over time. The direction of drift can also be inferred from the secular variation record derived at a single site. When using Bauer (1896) inclination vs. declination plots for the directions, as in Figure 1.7 for London, or VGP plots of the same data, a clockwise looping generally indicates a westward-drifting source (Dodson 1979). The other predominant secular variation pattern is the nearly linear 8% decrease in the dipole moment during the last 150 years (Fig. 1.8). In addition, the dipole axis has also been drifting westward, and features of the nondipole field have grown and decayed over time. Archaeomagnetic data are critical for determining whether these recent patterns or distinctly different modes of secular variation are evident for prehistoric time.

One ultimate goal of the geomagnetist is to understand the origin of the magnetic field. Although this was almost a complete mystery as recently as 40 years ago, geophysicists now believe that dynamo theory can explain the existence and behavior of the field. According to this theory, the magnetic field is continuously regenerating itself due to electromagnetic interactions between the field and the electrically conducting fluid in the outer core of the earth. Geomagnetic dynamo theory, however, is extremely complex and is not yet able to predict the detailed behavior of the magnetic field. McFadden's (1984) analysis of paleointensity data suggests a time constant for the dipole moment of 2,000 years. By looking at physical parameters of the earth's core, Yukutake (1968) calculated a free decay time of the nondipole field that can be as long as 7,000 years. As a complement to the work of the theorists, data on archaeomagnetic secular variation during the past few thousand years have the potential for contributing greatly to our understanding of dynamo processes.

Rock Magnetism

Ferromagnetic minerals are able to retain a remanent (permanent) magnetization even after the magnetic field that caused the magneti-

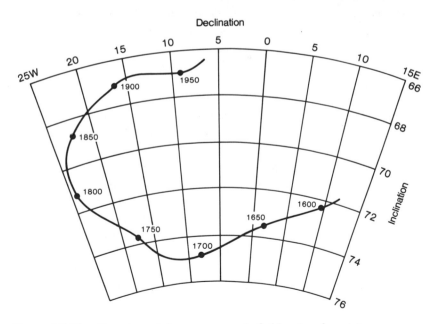

Figure 1.7. The direction of the geomagnetic field at London at 5-year intervals, smoothed from the original observations (after Malin and Bullard 1981).

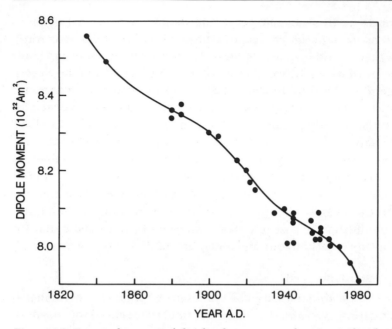

Figure 1.8. Recent decrease of the dipole moment, showing individual determinations and the trend (after Merrill and McElhinny 1983).

zation is removed. A stable remanent magnetization thus acts as a magnetic tape recording of the ancient magnetic field of the earth, even though that field has since changed in both direction and magnitude. Rock magnetism encompasses the study of ferromagnetic minerals, the physics of how grains of these minerals become magnetized, and the processes by which rocks (which include a large number of grains) acquire a remanent magnetization. A knowledge of rock magnetism is necessary for the proper interpretation of paleomagnetic results. For example, the mineral(s) carrying the remanent magnetization and the mode(s) by which the magnetization was acquired can suggest what event(s) in the geologic history of the rock caused the magnetization to be acquired. This can be significant because the direction of the paleomagnetic field varies during the lifetime of the rock, and the direction recorded depends on the timing of the event(s) when the recording occurred.

Similar questions are also relevant in archaeomagnetic studies, where baked clay objects such as hearths and ceramics are used. Most of the remanence in these objects is typically a thermoremanent magnetization (TRM) acquired during a heating event to several hundred degrees Celsius. Heating above the Curie point of the ferromagnetic minerals completely erases all remanence and leads to the acquisition of a total thermoremanent magnetization. On the other hand, heating to a temperature less than the Curie point may not erase all previous remanence and results in the acquisition of a partial thermoremanent magnetization (PTRM). The TRM actually becomes stable in a particular grain only after it has cooled through its blocking temperature, which is less than or equal to the Curie temperature, depending on grain size and shape. If the last heating of the archaeomagnetic feature was above the Curie point, the primary magnetization represents this event. However, if there have been repeated heatings of the object to temperatures below the Curie point, the total magnetization can represent the integrated effect of these heatings.

Different modes of magnetization can further obscure the primary component of magnetization. When a specimen is first brought into the laboratory, its natural remanent magnetization (NRM) is the vector sum of the primary magnetization, presumably a TRM or PTRM for archaeomagnetic features, and all subsequent secondary components acquired by whatever mechanism. A chemical remanence (CRM) can be acquired if chemical alteration of the magnetic mineralogy occurs—by precipitation of hematite cement in a sedimentary rock, for example. Lightning strikes can produce an isothermal (IRM) or anhysteretic (ARM) remanence. Some viscous remanence (VRM) is almost always acquired as less stably magnetized grains become remagnetized parallel to the present-day field. It is usually possible to remove these secondary components of magnetization via magnetic cleaning, but an investigation of the rock magnetism of a suite of specimens is always useful in bolstering an interpretation of when and how the various components of magnetization were acquired.

The most important magnetic minerals in rocks and archaeological features are magnetite and hematite. Their Curie temperatures are 580° C and 680° C, respectively. These minerals are actually end members of solid solutions of titanomagnetite and titanohematite minerals (Fig. 1.9). The titanomagnetites can oxidize toward the

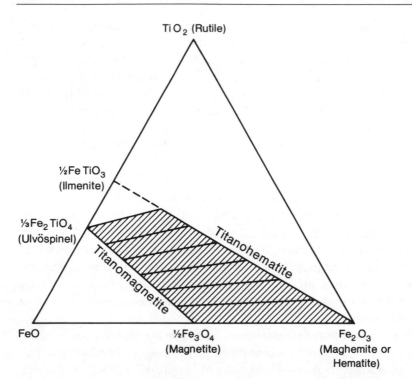

Figure 1.9. Ternary diagram for the Fe-Ti-O system. The important solid solution series of ferromagnetic minerals are the titanomagnetites (magnetite–ulvospinel) and titanohematites (hematite–ilmenite). The composition of the titanomagnetites changes during oxidation parallel to the solid lines toward the titanohematite series (from Stacey and Banerjee 1974).

titanohematite series so that the region on the Fe-Ti-O ternary diagram that is bounded by these solid solution series comprises ferromagnetic minerals whose properties vary as a function of composition. Grain size and shape, as well as mineralogy, can also have a significant effect on magnetic properties. In addition, the grains that carry the remanence are not necessarily the same as the grains that are responsible for the bulk magnetic properties of the sample. The complete rock magnetic picture becomes rather complicated! A variety of techniques can be used to study these magnetic properties in the paleomagnetic laboratory, and other types of examination, such as petrography or X-ray diffraction, can also be useful.

Paleomagnetism

Paleomagnetism is the study of the ancient magnetic field of the earth. Such a study is possible because rocks can act as magnetic recorders. This rock magnetism can be stable over geologic time, increasing the temporal coverage of the magnetic field by a factor of about ten million beyond what the observatory data provide. The direction of the paleomagnetic field can be determined from oriented specimens of *in situ* rock. Although most paleomagnetic research has dealt with directions, paleointensities (strengths of the ancient field) can also be determined. As with the present-day field, good geographic coverage of the paleomagnetic field is needed to examine the morphology of the dipole and nondipole fields. For example, Thompson and Barraclough (1982) combined historic observations of the field with archaeomagnetic results to produce spherical harmonic analyses of the field at 50-year intervals since A.D. 1600.

Paleomagnetic studies have provided a more complete picture of the nature of secular variation. Not only is this useful for understanding the geomagnetic field, but these variations can also be related to changes in other geophysical parameters. For example, the strength of the dipole field has varied by about ± 50% over the past 10,000 years. The flux of charged cosmic rays into the upper atmosphere is inversely related to the dipole moment. This change in flux causes the production rate of carbon 14 to vary by a factor of about 10%, with a concomitant variation in atmospheric radiocarbon concentration (Sternberg and Damon 1979). This violates one of the basic premises of radiocarbon dating, and it is the primary reason why radiocarbon ages must be calibrated into calendric ages.

Another particularly dramatic type of paleomagnetic behavior quite distinct from secular variation is the magnetic polarity reversal, whereby the dipole field inverts by 180° so that the north magnetic pole becomes the south magnetic pole and vice versa. The last well-documented reversal occurred 700,000 years ago, although there is evidence for shorter-lived reversals that may have occurred about 100,000 and 40,000 years ago. As a benefit to anthropology, the dating of sedimentary strata using magnetic polarity stratigraphy has proved useful in studies of hominid evolution and Paleolithic cultures.

Perhaps the most significant contribution of paleomagnetism to geology is its application to the study of continental drift and plate tectonics. The paleomagnetic directions recorded by many rocks do not agree with the directions expected at their present locations for a dipolar field. Because the field has always been predominantly dipolar and the dipole axis is on the average coincident with the earth's rotation axis, this discordancy implies that the rock (and continental block it rests on) have moved relative to the rotation axis since the rock became magnetized. To focus on the dipole field it is necessary to average out the secular variation that is the focus of most archaeomagnetic research. Sites from a single rock formation must span a sufficiently long period (typically about 10,000 years) to average out the secular variation so that a true paleomagnetic pole, as opposed to a virtual geomagnetic pole, can be determined.

Archaeomagnetism can be classified as a subfield of paleomagnetism. The term archaeomagnetism has been applied to both paleomagnetic studies utilizing archaeological materials and to paleomagnetic studies (on rocks as well as archaeological materials) covering archaeological time. In most cases the distinction is not important. Archaeomagnetism is useful in extending our knowledge of secular variation back into protohistoric and prehistoric time. The dating precision of archaeological materials is rather high by geologic standards, and the TRM that archaeological features acquire generally yields a reliable spot recording of the ancient field. Once the secular variation record has been determined from independently dated features, it can serve as a reference or master curve for archaeomagnetic dating.

Other records of secular variation are complementary to archaeomagnetic records. Rapidly deposited sediments can provide a nearly continuous record of paleomagnetic directions covering many thousands of years. Individual horizons can be dated using radiocarbon or tephrachronology. Problems may occur with the orientation of sediment cores, and the detrital remanent magnetization (DRM) of sediments does not always record the field direction as reliably as the TRM of archaeomagnetic features. Carefully selected sites can yield good secular variation records. For example, Verosub et al. (1986) present results from Fish Lake, Oregon, that are congruent with contemporaneous archaeomagnetic results from the American Southwest. In principle, secular variation curves based on DRM could also serve as master curves for archaeomagnetic dating, and archaeological sediments could be archaeomagnetically dated if they contained a reliable magnetization.

Volcanic rocks also carry TRM and can provide secular variation data. For example, historically dated lava flows from Mount Vesuvius (Hoye 1981) and Mount Etna (Tanguy et al. 1985) have provided important secular variation data for Europe. Champion (1980) used flows dated by ^{14}C in the western United States to investigate Holocene secular variation. Holcomb et al. (1986) used radiocarbon-dated Hawaiian flows to define a secular variation curve, which they then used for dating other flows. This procedure for secular variation dating is quite similar to archaeomagnetic dating. Holcomb et al. (1986) raise several issues pertinent to archaeomagnetism in their thoughtful analysis.

Paleomagnetic Methodology

The major steps involved in any paleomagnetic study are sample collection, laboratory measurement, and statistical analysis. The collecting locale in paleomagnetism is called a site, representing an instant in geologic time. A number of independently oriented specimens (usually 6 to 12 for archaeomagnetism) are collected at each site. Orientation is done using a level and either a magnetic or sun compass. The sun compass is preferable because it orients in geographic coordinates and is not subject to anomalies in the local magnetic field caused by the geology of the area or perhaps by the magnetization of the feature being sampled. With oriented specimens, the direction of magnetization measured relative to specimen coordinates in the lab can be transformed to magnetic direction relative to geographic coordinates in the field. If the feature has remained *in situ* since the magnetization was acquired, this in turn represents the direction of the archaeomagnetic field.

Magnetization is measured in the laboratory with a rock magnetometer (not to be confused with field magnetometers used for magnetic surveying). Two types are in common use today. Cryogenic magnetometers utilizing principles of superconductivity are extremely sensitive and can measure specimens rapidly. Laboratories that have "cryogenics" often schedule considerable downtime for the instrument because it requires liquid helium, which is rather costly. The spinner magnetometer is less sensitive and takes more time (but still usually less than two minutes) to measure an individual specimen. Spinners are sensitive enough for archaeomagnetic specimens, and they can be kept in constant operation without additional problems or expense.

Proper laboratory procedure also includes magnetic cleaning using thermal or alternating-field (AF) demagnetization. This procedure attempts to remove secondary components of magnetization acquired by the sample subsequent to the original, primary component. Secondary components must be removed to reveal the direction of the primary component, which is presumably parallel to the archaeomagnetic direction of interest. This is feasible because the secondary component is generally less stable magnetically than the primary component. Thermal demagnetization involves heating the sample to a given temperature and then cooling it in a zero magnetic field, thus erasing the magnetization in grains with lower blocking temperatures than the heating step. In AF demagnetization, the sample is subjected to a sinusoidal magnetic field with an envelope that linearly decays from the peak field to zero. This randomizes the magnetization in all grains that can be affected by the peak field. An AF demagnetization "step" of 15 mT means that the peak field of the decaying sinusoid was 15 mT. As a generalization, it is appropriate to use AF demagnetization when the remanence is carried by titanomagnetites (which have low magnetic coercivities) and thermal demagnetization when the remanence is carried by titanohematites (which have high coercivities). AF demagnetization is customarily used in archaeomagnetism, where the secondary magnetization is likely to be VRM and the ferromagnetic mineralogy is usually titanomagnetite.

To evaluate the magnetic stability of the remanence, it is customary to subject at least one pilot specimen to progressive demagnetization at a number of peak AF fields and/or temperatures. The remanence is remeasured after each step. These demagnetization results are commonly plotted on vector endpoint diagrams (Roy and Park 1974; Zijderveld 1967), an example of which is shown in Figure 1.10. These diagrams present two graphs that show how the endpoints of the total magnetization vector and the horizontal component of magnetization change as a function of the demagnetization step. The graph for the total vector plots the vertical component of magnetization against the horizontal component. The angle between the horizontal axis and a line connecting any point to the origin is thus the inclination for that step. The distance of the point from the origin is proportional to the strength of the total magnetization vector. The graph for the horizontal component plots the north component of magnetization against the east component. The angle between the

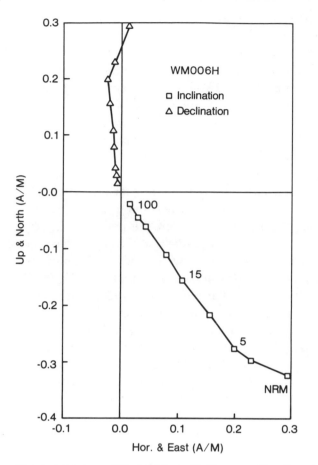

Figure 1.10. A modified Zijderveld diagram. The direction changes upon initial demagnetization, stabilizes by the second demagnetization step (5 mT), and remains stable through the final step (100 mT). At the optimal demagnetization step (15 mT) chosen for this feature, $D = 354°$, $I = 48°$, and $J = 0.189$ A/m.

north axis and a line connecting any point to the origin is the magnetic declination for that demagnetization step. The distance of a point from the origin is proportional to the strength of the horizontal component of magnetization. While secondary components of magnetization are being removed, these plots show the change of inclination and/or declination. After the secondary components have been removed, both plots show linear trends toward the origin, the direction of primary magnetization remaining constant as the strength of magnetization decreases.

The results from the pilot specimens are used to select the optimal demagnetization step at which the remaining specimens should also be demagnetized. For both the NRM and this optimal step, the results from the individual specimens are averaged to get a mean archaeomagnetic direction for the feature and an associated estimate of precision for this direction. Fisher (1953) developed special statistical methods for working with directions, which as vector quantities obey different statistical distributions from scalar quantities. The directions are often plotted on stereographic projections, with declination plotted from 0° to 360° around the perimeter of the stereonet and inclination plotted from 0° to 90° from the perimeter inward. The mean vector direction for a group, like the individual specimen directions, plots as a single point on the stereonet. The precision with which this mean direction is known is indicated by either the precision parameter k or the angular radius of the 95% cone of confidence, α_{95}. This cone of confidence subtends an angle of α_{95} degrees about the mean vector direction and maps out as a circle of radius α_{95} on the stereonet (Fig. 1.11). Better precision is reflected in a higher value for k and a lower value for α_{95}. Both measures of precision initially improve with the number of specimens collected, but they improve less dramatically once the number of specimens exceeds seven (Tarling 1983). This provides a basis for the typical number of 6 to 12 specimens collected for archaeomagnetic studies.

When transforming the average direction to its equivalent VGP, the α_{95} is transformed to an equivalent oval of confidence about the VGP location. The semiminor axis of this oval (dp) lies on the great circle between the geographic site and the VGP, and the semimajor axis (dm) is in a perpendicular direction.

Paleointensity

Archaeomagnetic specimens can be used to determine field intensity as well as direction. Because paleointensity studies do not require oriented specimens, pottery can be used. The term archaeomagnetic dating conventionally refers to the use of field direction, but several studies have used paleointensity data to provide dating information on archaeological material (Aitken et al. 1981; Barbetti 1976; Shaw 1979; Sternberg and McGuire 1981a). The extant archaeointensity

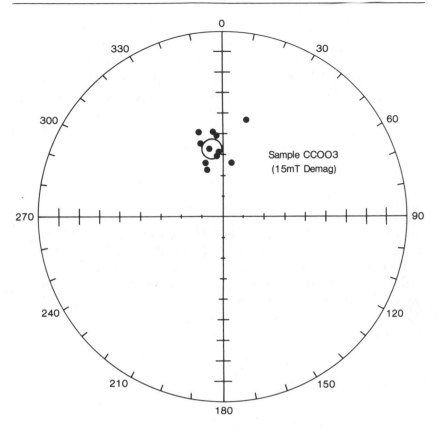

Figure 1.11. A stereographic projection of archaeomagnetic directions. The solid circles represent directions of magnetization for individual specimens. The center of the open circle represents the mean direction for this feature ($D = 351°$, $I = 57°$). The circle about the mean is the projection of the cone of confidence ($\alpha_{95} = 4.7°$).

data for North America are summarized in DuBois (1989) and Sternberg (1989a).

Absolute paleointensities can be determined only for samples that carry a thermoremanent magnetization. Theoretical and experimental investigations of TRM have shown that the strength of TRM is linearly proportional to the strength of the field in which the TRM is acquired. Thus, $J_{paleo} = k_{TRM} \times B_{paleo}$, where J_{paleo} is the strength of magnetization acquired in the ancient field of strength B_{paleo}. The constant of proportionality k_{TRM} is a complex function of the magnetic mineralogy and cannot be directly determined. If the specimen is heated in the laboratory, however, it acquires a magnetization of $J_{lab} = k_{TRM} \times B_{lab}$. J_{paleo} and J_{lab} can be measured, and B_{lab} is also known. Thus, if the magnetic mineralogy has not changed (k_{TRM} remained constant), $B_{paleo} = J_{paleo}/J_{lab} \times B_{lab}$. The magnetic mineralogy, however, may have altered *in situ* since the sample acquired its primary TRM or as a result of laboratory heating to a high temperature. The paleointensity experiment is thus done by stepwise heating to progressively higher temperatures. If alteration has occurred, it usually becomes evident, and data from the unaltered temperature interval can be used to infer the paleointensity (Thellier and Thellier 1959a, 1959b; Thomas 1983a).

To summarize, the theory and techniques of archaeomagnetism are derived from paleomagnetic methodology, but there are some aspects of each phase of archaeomagnetic research that are not characteristic of other types of paleomagnetic work. Because archaeomagnetism results from the interaction of cultural activity and the physical environment, controlled experiments can be used to address many questions concerning the archaeomagnetic method. The papers in this volume, by investigating some of these questions, make a significant contribution to both the archaeomagnetic and paleomagnetic literature.

A CHRONOMETRIC FRAMEWORK
FOR ARCHAEOMAGNETIC DATING

Absolute dating techniques in archaeology can be divided into two basic types, rate-dependent processes (or clocks) and pattern matching. Within each type there are dating techniques that are useful worldwide and those useful on regional scales only. Thus we can set up a matrix for these techniques as follows:

	clocks	patterns
global	GC	GP
regional	RC	RP

The letters in each block represent the first letters of the applicable categories.

For the rate-dependent processes, the clocks may tick due to radioactive decay within a sample (e.g., potassium-argon and radiocarbon dating), the effects of radioactive decay on sample properties (thermoluminescence, fission-track), or other types of progressive physicochemical change within the sample (obsidian hydration, amino acid racemization). These three types of clock tend to exhibit, in the order listed, an increasing dependence on sample characteristics or environmental parameters. For radioactive decay techniques, the decay rate is a nuclear process independent of environmental conditions, so the clock always ticks at a constant rate. Thus, knowing the decay rate for the relevant radionuclide allows the technique to be used anywhere in the world (GC techniques). For the other clocks, the rate can vary with location, material, and time. Rates must then be evaluated separately for each study (RC techniques). It is not always easy to determine the rates at which these clocks run, but once accomplished, dates can be determined in a reasonably straightforward fashion. The specific quantity being measured is scaled by the rate at which it is produced.

Pattern-matching techniques require that much effort be put into determining the pattern of change, or master record, for the phenomenon whose variation is being investigated. A method is also needed to determine for what period of time the measurements agree with the master record. These techniques can be further distinguished by whether the nature of the pattern is binary, representing an alternation between two states, or continuous, whereby a physical parameter exhibits continuous variation as a function of time. For instance, paleomagnetic reversal stratigraphy involves the globally synchronous phenomenon of geomagnetic field reversals. Data from around the world can be used to compile the pattern of polarity reversals. The rocks used to compile this master record must be dated by some other technique. This record can then be used to date rocks from any geographic area (GP technique). The magnetic field has either a normal or a reversed polarity, so this is a binary technique. Enough reversals must occur in an uninterrupted sequence of rocks to produce a stratigraphic pattern of reversals that can be unambiguously matched to the temporal pattern of the reversal time scale.

Dendrochronology, on the other hand, is a binary regional pattern-matching (RP) technique. It depends on the response of tree-ring growth to regional climatic variability. The characteristic ring-width pattern must be determined from trees growing in the same climatic zone, and dating by that pattern is valid only for that zone. Tree-ring dating is binary in that one is looking at the width pattern of alternating layers of earlywood and latewood. Enough wood must be present so that the pattern of annual rings can be unambiguously matched against the master tree-ring growth record.

Although the determination of raw radiocarbon ages in ^{14}C years is a GC technique, the calibration of ^{14}C years to calendar years falls under the rubric of a GP method. The fluctuation of the amount of radiocarbon in the atmosphere systematically affects all ^{14}C dates from a particular epoch. Atmospheric radiocarbon varies continuously with time, so the calibration is also a continuous function of time. In a continuous GP technique, a single evaluation (a raw ^{14}C age) is matched against the continuous function representing the master record (calibration curve) to produce a date (calibrated ^{14}C age).

Finally, we come to archaeomagnetic dating, which is a continuous regional pattern-matching (RP) technique. The direction of the geomagnetic field is continuously shifting due to secular variation. Because of the nondipole field, each region yields a distinct record of secular variation. Archaeomagnetic dates are inferred by comparing the archaeomagnetic direction recorded by a single feature or group of features to the regional secular variation record.

COOPERATION IN ARCHAEOMAGNETIC RESEARCH

The process of archaeomagnetic dating can thus be broken down into two components. The first task is to determine the pattern of secular variation. The second is to use this record to interpret the archaeomagnetic date by matching a particular archaeomagnetic direction with this pattern. (Details of both types of analysis are presented in this volume.) In a sense, these two components are of primary interest to the paleomagnetist (as geophysicist) and the archaeologist, respectively. The archaeomagnetist, if we define one to be a scientist engaged in archaeomagnetic research, lies somewhere along the continuum between these two end members. Regardless of their position on this continuum, archaeomagnetists, to be most effective, must have some awareness of the needs and goals of both the paleomagnetist and the archaeologist. From my perspective as a paleomagnetist, I would like to conclude with a few remarks concerning how the archaeologist can help meet the goals of the paleomagnetist engaged in archaeomagnetic research.

The primary geophysical goal of the paleomagnetist engaged in archaeomagnetic research is to recover the record of secular variation. This, along with similar records from other regions, can be used to make inferences about the structure of the archaeomagnetic field and the nature of secular variation. To compile such a record for a particular region, one needs a sufficient number of well-dated archaeomagnetic features distributed over the region and time period of interest. The dates required pertain to the time when the primary remanence was actually acquired. In most cases this will be the last intense firing of the object. For a hearth, this may just predate the abandonment of the room or site. If the hearth were subsequently re-heated to several hundred degrees Celsius, however, the remanence would be reset and the date of interest would be this later event. This would be the case whether the reheating was cultural, due to reoccupation of the site, or natural, due to a fire at the site. Thus the date that the paleomagnetist needs to know refers to when the remanence was acquired, which does not necessarily correspond to the date when the feature was built. It may also bear an even less direct relationship to the events that can be directly dated in the room or at the site (Dean 1978). For example, a tree-ring date for room construction may predate the time when the remanence was acquired by the number of years the room was occupied. Thus the archaeologist must be aware of the meaning of the date needed by the paleomagnetist. An attempt should be made to communicate to the paleomagnetist what chronometric methods were involved in determining this date, what assumptions were made, and what is the total uncertainty of the estimated date.

The paleomagnetist may need samples from sites or periods of time not of immediate interest to the archaeologist. Archaeomagnetic samples are generally collected from archaeological sites that are currently being excavated. This collecting strategy is convenient, but it is usually not known at the time the samples are collected how well they will eventually be dated. An alternative strategy would be to return to well-dated sites that have previously been excavated and locate remaining features that can be sampled. The archaeologist should recognize that these well-dated features, perhaps troublesome to collect at the time, may one day help to provide an archaeomagnetic date at another site that is not as well dated. This approach has already proved useful in the Southwest (Sternberg 1982). This region encompasses mountains and plateaus, where tree-ring dating is possible, and also desert, where available species of trees are too complacent to provide good tree-ring dates. It is especially desirable to obtain archaeomagnetic samples from the upland regions, where good tree-ring dates are more readily available. The secular variation curve can thus be calibrated using more accurate and precise dates and can later be used to derive archaeomagnetic dates for less well dated sites in the desert.

The paleomagnetist may also desire secular variation data for periods of time when the archaeologist does not ordinarily require archaeomagnetic dates. This might be the case for historic and protohistoric data. The southwestern secular variation curve of Sternberg and McGuire (this volume) extends from A.D. 700 to 1450. Direct observations of the field began in the Southwest in about 1850. It would be highly desirable from the geophysicist's perspective to fill the gap in the secular variation record from A.D. 1450 to 1850. If the archaeological community supports the development of the master curve for this period, the secular variation record will be available should an archaeomagnetic date for the period become desirable.

Secular variation curves can be tested by comparing archaeomagnetic dates with other chronometric dates. This has been useful in evaluating versions of the southwestern secular variation curve. Again, the assistance of the archaeologist is necessary to obtain dates that can be meaningfully compared. Features that are judged to be coeval on archaeological grounds can also be used to evaluate the fidelity of the archaeomagnetic recorder.

What is really needed for the optimal use of archaeomagnetic research, then, is not just the casual interaction of paleomagnetists and archaeologists but cooperation between providers and users of archaeomagnetic dates. The best archaeomagnetic work is done when the scientists involved in a project have an appreciation for both disciplines and their respective goals. This enables the maximum amount of information to be recovered both for secular variation analyses and for the interpretation and use of archaeomagnetic dates.

PART 2

Methodology

Introduction

Each of the chapters in this section discusses an important component of the archaeomagnetic method. Eighmy, in Chapter 2, describes field collecting procedures. Although central to quality archaeomagnetic research, collecting techniques are rarely written up in detail. Despite much thought over the years, alternative sample collection methods that are generally useful, significantly faster, and/or less tedious (and less wearing on the collector's knees and back) have not been forthcoming. The time and care required in sample collection may mean that only a limited number of potential features from a site can be sampled.

One of the benefits of the recent flurry of archaeomagnetic research is that some conclusions can be drawn based on statistical analyses of the resulting larger data sets. One of the most sobering conclusions drawn from the data of Lange and Murphy (Chapter 3) is that appropriate training of collectors by archaeomagnetic specialists significantly improves results. It had been hoped that archaeomagnetic samples could be routinely collected by archaeological field crews in the same way that dendrochronological and radiocarbon samples are collected. Lange and Murphy's conclusion, however, is that archaeomagnetists may have to maintain more direct control over the collection process.

In Chapter 4, Yu discusses some laboratory techniques that can be used to gain a better understanding of the nature of the magnetization of the archaeomagnetic samples and possibly to preselect samples that will give better results. Rock magnetism has played an integral role in paleomagnetic studies' goal of understanding the mineralogy, processes, and timing involved in the acquisition of remanent magnetization. Studies such as Yu's should provide similar insight for archaeomagnetists.

Apart from absolute dating, making statements about contemporary events may prove to be a significant application of the archaeomagnetic method. This relative dating technique could be used even when a master curve of secular variation is not available. Mielke, Berry, and Eighmy (Chapter 5) present the basis for a nonparametric statistical comparison of sample directions that could be used for tests of sample contemporaneity. Their methods are also applicable to the problem of absolute dating, whereby an archaeomagnetic direction is compared to a series of directions constituting a secular variation curve.

Sternberg and McGuire (Chapter 6) describe techniques for constructing archaeomagnetic secular variation curves and for dating archaeomagnetic samples. Their quantitative methods provide an alternative to the traditional graphic techniques used for archaeomagnetic curve construction and dating.

CHAPTER 2

Archaeomagnetic Dating: Practical Problems for the Archaeologist

JEFFREY L. EIGHMY

Over the past twenty years a fairly uniform strategy of archaeomagnetic sample collecting has emerged among North American archaeologists. Although Eighmy (1980a), Rodgers (1978), Windes (1978), and others have described this strategy and although elements of the process have clear antecedents in the paleomagnetic and archaeomagnetic collecting techniques of Europe and Asia (Thellier 1967; Watanabe 1959:27–30), it is important to include a description of the process in this first book-length treatment of North American archaeomagnetism. A detailed description of the process as it has evolved in North America is important because references to the process in published articles are too brief for critical evaluation and because archaeologists using this book as an introduction to archaeomagnetism should have a clear understanding of the sample-collecting procedures.

The collecting strategy now in use in the United States was first introduced by the geophysicist Dr. Robert L. DuBois. While at the University of Arizona, DuBois became aware in the early 1960s that the Southwest could provide the best time control for establishing ancient master records of magnetic field changes in North America. Therefore, when the opportunity arose to measure the thermoremanence of well-dated archaeological features, DuBois began collecting ancient archaeomagnetic secular variation data (Weaver 1967). DuBois modified a method for collecting archaeomagnetic samples developed by Watanabe (1959) in Japan and Aitken (1974) and Thellier (1967) in Europe. *In situ* pieces of burned archaeological features were isolated in square pedestals with one diagonal running roughly north-south. Over this pedestal DuBois would place a square brass mold seated in a collar of ordinary modeling clay. With an orienting instrument made in Japan, he would simultaneously level and slightly turn the mold by pushing into the clay, so that its top was perfectly horizontal and one diagonal pointed due magnetic north. DuBois would then fill the mold with plaster, encasing the piece of burned material. Experimenting with several types of plaster, he found a type that was hard and nonmagnetic. The sides and top of the plaster cube served to orient the specimen, because each top had no dip and the diagonals were running north-south and east-west. Six to eight of these specimens served as an archaeomagnetic sample.

The procedure DuBois introduced in North America worked well. He was able to collect samples that produced extremely reliable estimates of paleodirections. Subsequent modifications in the procedure have served not so much to improve collection accuracy as to make the technique more widely available.

SAMPLE COLLECTION

One of the first modifications in the technique was the replacement of the orientation device built specifically for archaeomagnetism with the more common pocket transit. Horizontal control of sample direction does not require that the sample be oriented in a predefined direction, only that its actual orientation be known. Therefore, rather than cutting specimen diagonals pointing north-south and east-west, samples are cut in any convenient orientation, and this orientation is measured with a hand-held pocket transit. Vertical control is still maintained with levels, but instead of levels mounted on the old orienting device, simple cross-test levels can be used. Besides requiring less esoteric equipment, these modifications have the advantage of allowing specimen direction to be determined solely by the location and orientation of the best burned material instead of by the necessity of orienting the specimen north-south. With these modifications, both horizontal and vertical control can still be easily maintained to within 30 minutes of arc.

A more recent modification is in cube size. At the time DuBois began working, laboratory magnetometers could not be obtained commercially; therefore DuBois built his own (astatic) magnetometer. It was designed to accommodate 1.7-inch cubes. Today, several companies are making reliable and sensitive magnetometers, but few of them will accept the 1.7-inch design. Commercial magnetometers are designed for use by geophysicists, whose rock core samples are held in 1-inch holders. As a result, many labs otherwise capable of analyzing archaeomagnetic samples cannot do so when the larger 1.7-inch cubes are used. Apparently accuracy is not affected when specimens are cut for the 1-inch cubes (see Smith, this volume), and the smaller size has the double advantage of fitting modern magnetometers while requiring less burned area for an adequate sample.

Despite these modifications, the essential features of the collection procedure have changed little in the past fifteen years. The more detailed discussion of collecting procedures to follow will include most of the important past and present modifications in the collecting technique. Before the detailed discussion begins, however, it will be helpful to introduce a few definitions so that the discussion of collection procedures will be less ambiguous:

> Specimen. A piece of burned material collected *in situ* with vertical and horizontal control and constituting one archaeomagnetic reading. Paleomagnetists usually refer to a specimen as a sample (see Sternberg 1982:22–23).
> Sample. Several specimens from a burned feature.
> Cube. A plaster-encased archaeomagnetic specimen.
> Mold. A nonmagnetic metal form for casting cubes.

The archaeomagnetic sampling procedure can best be approached as a series of common questions faced during collection. These questions begin with the evaluation of the potential of a given burned feature and proceed through the technical problems encountered during actual collection.

Is the Feature Worth Collecting?

As mentioned in the introductory chapter, most remanent magnetism in clay is acquired at temperatures of around 400–500° C. Besides temperature, however, the quality of an archaeomagnetic sample is influenced by the percentage of clay, the clay mineralogy, and the homogeneity of the material and firing. Archaeomagnetic collections at hundreds of sites suggest that most archaeological soils have sufficient ferromagnetic material to acquire a good thermoremanence. Fine-grained material (<0.5 mm) maintains remanence better than coarse, large-grained material (Hathaway, Smith, and Krause, this volume), and homogeneous samples are better than nonhomogeneous ones (clay with rock, organic, or cultural inclusions). Despite the fact that the exact effects of temperature, texture, and clay mineralogy await further study, at some point the collector should assess the archaeomagnetic potential of the burned feature. Field collectors should find the following observations and suggestions useful.

Texture. One of the first important determinations to make is the amount of clay present in the feature. Clay is an extremely fine-grained (0.002 mm) microscopic material. Because of its size, estimating clay content in the field is extremely difficult. Soil texture is defined on the basis of sand (0.05–1 mm), silt (0.002–0.05 mm), and clay content. A deposit with at least 45% clay is called a clay soil, so that a prehistoric potter's clay deposit can be much less than pure clay. The minimum amount of clay necessary for a good archaeomagnetic sample is unknown, but percent clay correlates positively with the retention of thermoremanent magnetism over long periods of time. Hathaway (1982b) has recently shown that sandy and silty matrices acquire a better remanence but that apparently clay material retains its thermoremanent directional information better after hundreds of years. In choosing an archaeomagnetic sample, it is important, therefore, to try to assess the texture of the sample material. Field techniques for describing texture are less than perfect but do provide a means of standardizing communication between archaeomagnetic field collectors and laboratory personnel. The collector should first select a representative piece of material and send it back to the lab with the archaeomagnetic sample. To convey information about sample quality, there is no substitute for having an actual specimen in the lab.

Second, the collector should try to judge the clay content in the field. Although clay is ubiquitous in the archaeological context, few archaeologists have had to estimate the clay content of soil rigorously. Most archaeologists are aware that a majority of soils contain some clay, but they are unaware of the tremendous regional variation. In forest zones (acid soils), for example, the upper 25 cm of modern soil profiles may be noticeably leached of clay and iron. Many modern soils of the Great Plains and Southwest have clay containing already oxidized iron, giving them the familiar reddish-brown cast (Hunt 1975:176–194). On archaeological sites the cultural deposits filled with trash, organic material, and ash often have less clay than the subsoil, but in some instances cultural activity has actually increased the clay content of features, as when hearths, floors, and walls were intentionally plastered with clay material (Limbrey 1975:328–330).

Archaeologists should try to judge the clay content of the chosen feature as accurately as possible. They should examine the material (using unfired portions) when it is dry. Clay grains cannot be seen with the naked eye; all macroscopic grains are either sand or silt. It is likely that, since sand is the most easily observed component, the description of the material will be based largely on the sand content. Clay grains are so small that when mixed with water they muddy it. With particles less than 0.24 mm, water molecules actually interfere with the rate of fall and as a result the particles tend to stay suspended for long periods of time. Sand falls to the bottom rather quickly, and silt filters through after some time. Although a water test can detect the presence of clay, it seldom allows for a field estimation of the relative proportion of clay. If, however, a soil sample is dissolved in water and the water clears up quickly (within 2 minutes), it is unlikely that it contains much clay.

A more useful field exercise for identifying grain size is to moisten the soil until it is plastic and observe its characteristics. If the lump can be molded easily into various shapes without breaking, it probably contains at least 25% clay; if the lump can be formed into a strong thread with a pin point, then it probably contains at least 30% clay; and if a thin ribbon formed from the material can be bent into flexible shapes without breaking, then it is likely composed of at least 40% clay. Sandy soil feels gritty. Clay feels greasy and sticks to the fingers when wet. It dries slowly and when dry, it is hard and lumpy. Silt dries quickly, does not stick to the fingers when wet, and with wear turns to a fine powder faster than does clay.

If all clay in the feature uncovered by the excavation is fired, physical examination of the prefired material described above is impossible. The collector then has to rely on a physical examination of the postfired material alone. Examination of the fired material can be useful in assessing the mineralogy of the feature and the extent of firing.

Mineral Content. It is nearly impossible to determine in the field the exact mineralogy of a sample. Only the presence of hematite (Fe_2O_3) can be identified with relative certainty. When fired in air, the ferromagnetic contamination of most soils turns orange, pink, or red as the rate and extent of oxidation increase and hematite is formed (Hathaway 1982b). Oxidation is also accelerated by increased temperatures, but color changes are less perceptible; therefore, burned material with an orange color change indicates the presence of some but not all forms of ferrous material. Such an orange color change is highly significant evidence as to the archaeomagnetic possibility of a feature. Features burned in a reducing atmosphere producing magnetite (Fe_3O_4) can also give excellent results. In fact, the magnetization of magnetite is some 200 times stronger than that of hematite. The problem here is to distinguish magnetite from normal charcoal-stained surfaces. When formed, magnetite produces a black color that can appear identical to many dark unburned soils. Possibly the best way to distinguish the formation of magnetite is a dark color change in the soil, decreasing away from the fired surface. Thus, color change becomes extremely important in assessing the presence of magnetic minerals.

Degree of Burning. In evaluating a potential archaeomagnetic sample, the collector should choose material that appears to have been burned hotter than 400° C (Hathaway 1982b:89). As with clay content and mineralogy, in the field there is no way to know the exact firing temperature of a feature. Controlled experiments using various hearth and fuel types are badly needed, but in the interim the collector must rely on tentative impressions from a few experimental archaeomagnetic hearths and sketchy data from the study of pottery firing. In general it is safe to assume that the soil immediately on the surface of fire hearths, burned rooms, and ovens has likely been exposed to temperatures sufficiently high for archaeomagnetic dating.

Anna O. Shepard (1954:Figs. 4–6) measured the temperature of 11 large, open fires used for firing pottery. Maximum temperatures for the fires ranged between 675° and 950° C and were usually reached within 40 minutes to an hour. Although pottery fires tend to be larger than cooking or heating fires, it is possible that these smaller fires reached similar temperature maximums. The clay under these fires, however, probably does not get this hot. In three experimental hearths, the temperature of the soil 0.5 cm below and behind the hearth surface reached only 450° C (Krause 1980), and in four "hot" hearths (Hathaway 1982b) the temperature at 1 cm was less than 75% of what it was at 0.25 cm below the surface. The absolute temperature of Hathaway's four hearths 0.25 cm below the surface aver-

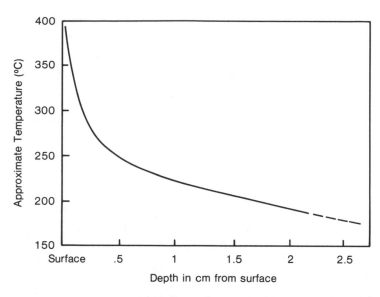

Figure 2.1. Temperature falloff as a function of depth from hearth surface.

aged about 250° C. In both these experimental situations, the hearths were fired at temperatures judged to be hotter than "normal" cooking or heating fires. Our experiments indicate that temperature falls off rapidly with increasing depth (Fig. 2.1).

Hardness. Firing at any temperature increases the hardness of an underlying clay feature. Therefore, an important observation in selecting suitable samples is their hardness. Unfortunately, exact estimates of firing temperatures based on a hardness test alone cannot be decisive, because hardness is influenced by a number of factors other than temperature. Primary among these factors is the nature and concentration of clay. A sandy material fired to 900° C is still friable, but some unfired clay when dry can be as hard as a fingernail (Matson 1971:Tables 3, 4). Only with clay content held constant can hardness be used as a reliable test of firing temperature.

An important factor to keep in mind while judging hardness is the moisture content of the sample. Sample material that remains hard when soaked is much more likely to be hard as the result of high-temperature firing. Dry unfired clay can be quite hard, as any archaeologist who has let his or her excavation floor dry out for a couple of days can testify. When wet, however, such unfired floors return to their usual soft, sticky character. Fired clay, on the other hand, remains hard even when wet. A wet, predominantly clay fired feature should have a hardness of at least 1 on the Mohs hardness scale. This does not mean that softer features are useless. Most archaeomagnetic samples come from a softer matrix, simply because few are predominantly clay. Burned materials that remain hard when wet are good possibilities for archaeomagnetism, however, because they indicate two things: a high clay content and intense firing.

A final observation relative to firing is color change. This section has mentioned color change due to the oxidation formation of hematite or the reduction formation of magnetite several times. Color change is also useful when considering the extent of firing. Note that the point revolves around color change, not just an orange or black color. If the surface of a burned feature has a color change from the surrounding subsoil which gradually penetrates 2 to 5 cm deep, then a hot fire is indicated. The contrast in color and color change is a surer indication of firing than a simple uniform bright orange color because the origin of such widespread oxidation is uncertain. The depth of the color change is positively correlated with the degree of firing and sample quality.

Summary. Clay content, color change, and hardness are interrelated factors. Together they provide the primary evidence available to the archaeologist in deciding whether a feature is worth collecting for archaeomagnetic purposes. When they are used in conjunction, reasonable estimates of the potential of a feature can be made. Additional characteristics that indicate good sample quality are the absence of cracking in the burned surface and the absence of indications of shifting, settling, or slumping. Burned roof fall and redeposited burned wattle and daub should not be considered.

In its dealings with the CSU archaeomagnetic lab, the Dolores Archaeological Program developed a five-point system for the field evaluation of archaeomagnetic samples (Table 2.1) (Hathaway and Eighmy 1982:18). Class 1 samples are those judged most likely to have a good thermoremanent direction, and class 5 are those least likely to have a good direction. The system proved useful during the first year of implementation (class 1 and 2 samples yielded archaeomagnetic dates in 67% of the cases, while class 4 and 5 samples dated in only 50% of the cases), but the system can be further refined. For example, clear differences existed between fired hearths

Table 2.1. Evaluation of Archaeomagnetic Samples

Factors	Class 1	2	3	4	5
Color change	distinct color 1 cm + thick (usually oxidation)		spotty color change; 0.5 cm thick		no color change
Hardness/ preparation	hard, solid; surface well prepared, i.e., coping-plaster		hard but unprepared surface		soft; no preparation; surface is not smooth
Erosion/ weathering	very little apparent weathering; uncracked	I N T E R M E D I A T E	some cracking and/or erosion of sample area	I N T E R M E D I A T E	cracked and hard; slumped or eroded
Texture (clay/sand silt)	20% or more clay content		granular/sandy, but 10–20% clay content		very sandy; 0–10% clay content
Intrusions	none to very few intrusions		some intrusions		excessive intrusions
Collection quality	good, solid pedestals; no unstable specimens		some unstable specimens		friable situation; specimens are all a little unstable due to soil conditions

and fired walls. A total of 91% of all fire-hardened walls (of all classes) was successfully dated, but only about 60% of all hearths and floors were datable (Hathaway and Eighmy 1982:43–45).

How Many Specimens Should Be Collected?

Once it has been determined that a feature is of archaeomagnetic potential, the next series of decisions revolves around taking the sample. Since the ancient direction cannot be measured in the field, a way must be devised to take the feature to a laboratory for measurement. These specimens must be collected in an oriented fashion, because the entire method depends on directional information. Any collecting procedure is bound to suffer from inherent error. To minimize the significance of this error, it is best to collect several specimens from the hearth. The average of the several readings is a much more precise estimate of the true archaeomagnetic direction.

There is no set number of measurements to make, but increasing the sample size from 1 to 4 specimens can increase the precision of estimating the true mean direction of a burned feature (all other factors held constant) by 75%. An increase from 5 to 8 specimens adds only an 8% increase to the precision, and beyond 10 specimens, only very small increases in precision are achieved (Tarling 1971:79). Generally, eight good specimens are considered minimally adequate, while very little is gained by going beyond 12 carefully collected, oriented specimens.

Is the Burned Area Large Enough to Sample?

Some experience with archaeomagnetic sampling is helpful at this stage because the amount of burned area necessary for an archaeomagnetic sample depends on the shape of the burned area, the cube size, and collector competence. As a result, establishing a minimum size is difficult. Collecting on a horizontal surface requires more burned area to sample than collecting on a vertical surface. These two collection modes are discussed in greater detail below, but all that is meant is whether the burning is on a horizontal surface (e.g., a floor) or a vertical surface (e.g., a wall face or a firepit rim). If a horizontal surface such as a floor is burned, much of the burned floor must be cut away in order to isolate a specimen. When a vertical face is burned, however, less burned area is destroyed in cutting specimens. Rough estimates of the area needed (assuming no sample area is destroyed during collection) is 170 cm^2 horizontal surface per 12 specimens for 1-inch cubes and 470 cm^2 for 1.7-inch cubes.

What Special Tools and Equipment Are Necessary?

Nonmagnetic Molds. The most important but most difficult item to obtain is one or more archaeomagnetic molds. The size and construction of these molds must be accurate because the orientation of the specimen depends on the shape of the cube cast by the molds. In the lab the plaster cubes made during the collection of the feature are placed in a magnetometer. The encased specimen is not broken out but remains inside during all laboratory processing. Magnetometers are designed to take a cube. If they are not perfectly square, the field orientation of the specimen cannot be maintained. The squareness of a cube ultimately depends on the squareness of the mold used in casting the cube, so a well-made mold should be used.

The mold should be made of nonmagnetic material such as aluminum or brass. High-quality stainless steel is supposed to be nonmagnetic, but any molds made from steel must be tested thoroughly to assure that they are and remain completely nonmagnetized. Any good machine shop can manufacture these molds, or the molds can be obtained from an archaeomagnetic lab. Most commonly, ¼-inch angle stock is used if the angle is precisely 90°. Brass is stronger, more expensive, and heavier than aluminum. Commercial brass screws can be used in both aluminum and brass molds.

Nonmagnetic Plaster. Plaster used to cast the cubes must be a variety that sets up hard so that it can be held tightly by the lab equipment. It must also be nonmagnetic. DuBois has experimented with various types of plaster and finds that, typically, Hydrocal White Cement, made by U.S. Gypsum, is much less magnetic than the samples themselves. During the refinement of the plaster, however, magnetic particles can contaminate a batch, or the deposit may have naturally occurring magnetic contamination. Therefore each bag should be checked in the lab for magnetic inclusions. This test can be done physically by trying to extract macroscopic iron particles with a strong magnet or by casting up a cube of plaster and measuring its magnetic moment. If the magnetization is negligible or can be cleaned by low-level demagnetization (≤ 10 mT), then the bag is safe to use.

Cross-Test Level. Cross-test levels by L. S. Starrett (#136) are accurate to <30 minutes of arc. Any comparable level is acceptable, but be aware that in some levels the glass containing the air bubble is slightly convex, making it easy to level and therefore less precise. Glass in the Starrett level is completely flat, resulting in a very sensitive level. To give an idea of its sensitivity, if half the bubble or less lies outside the center area, it would be less than half a degree off horizontal.

Pocket Transit. Most archaeological field supplies include a good pocket transit, and one is essential for archaeomagnetic collection. Secure a pocket transit that measures azimuth, has a 360° rose, and does not have a dampened needle.

Archaeomagnetic Collecting Form. Well in advance of the field collection, the collector should construct or acquire an archaeomagnetic collection form. This form is sent to the lab along with the sample and provides the lab with information necessary for sample measurement and analysis. The minimum information on the form should include sample identification, site location, local declination, collector's name, project director and address, feature identification, feature description, estimated age, specimen orientations, and a sketch map of the collection. An example of a collection form is provided in Figure 2.2.

Modeling Clay. Ordinary modeling clay is another essential item. The clay is used in leveling the molds and sealing the bottom when plaster is poured. The equivalent of a small handful of clay for each sample collected will be needed.

Miscellaneous Tools and Equipment. Hacksaw blades (18 pts/inch) are highly recommended. Their uses are numerous in any sampling situation, and with good, hard, burned features they are essential. An awl is necessary for cube marking and is sometimes useful in specimen cutting. A rubber mixing bowl and spatula are handy for mixing plaster. Pliers or screwdrivers are often necessary in taking the molds apart, and light oil is used to oil the molds for easy cube removal. Nonmetallic water containers are preferable. The amount of water necessary depends on whether the feature is to be soaked before collection. If collected dry, carry at least one liter of water per sample for mixing with the plaster. If soaking is planned (see below), carry about 10 extra liters per feature. Heavy paper bags or boxes to carry samples are useful. Large kitchen knives with straight blades are useful in cleaning and shaping cubes. Brushes, trowels, pencils, tape measures, and various small digging tools also come in handy.

Planning the Collection

Before actual sampling begins, the collector will make a series of significant decisions. Often these decisions are automatic, but it is important to discuss them in order to make the archaeomagnetic novice more fully aware of all contingencies and options. Collection strategy varies greatly, depending on whether the burned surfaces are horizontal or vertical. Horizontal surfaces usually include firepit

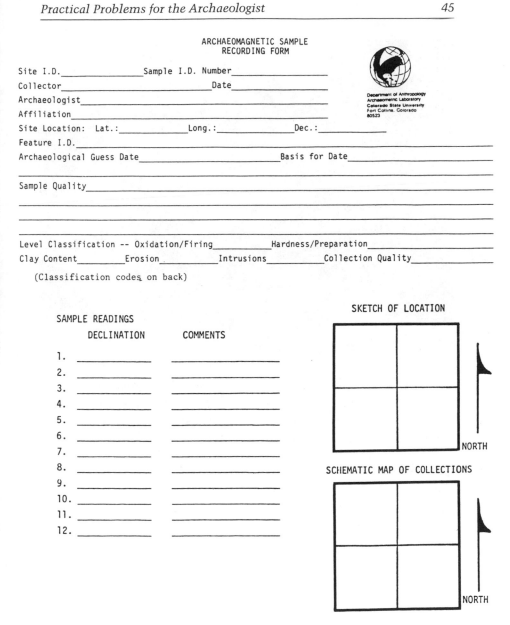

Figure 2.2. An example of an archaeomagnetic field collection form.

Figure 2.3. Trenching behind a hearth rim.

bottoms and burned floors or living surfaces. Vertical surfaces include burned walls or firepit rims. Collecting a burn on a horizontal
surface is more straightforward. The most intensely fired areas
within the burn should be located and collected first. Less well
burned material should be collected only after the best material is
gone. A clean, flat surface close by can be used to receive samples as
they are collected and cleaned. A large sheet of plastic is helpful in
keeping the collection area clean and organized.

Vertical surfaces require slightly more preparation. The collector
should locate the best linear section or sections of the burn with a
total length of between 40 and 70 cm and decide generally where the
specimens will be cut. If the vertical surface is a hearth rim, she or
he should begin trenching around the back of the rim with a pick or
trowel. This "moat" should be about 6 to 9 cm across, about 6 cm
deep, and 3 to 5 cm away from the rim surface, leaving a thick ridge
standing upright (Fig. 2.3). If the feature is to be dampened, the collector should fill the hearth and moat with water and wait while the
water soaks thoroughly in and through the feature. After soaking at
least a couple of hours, with the soil just damp, the hearth rim is
ready for collection.

Figure 2.4. Trenching behind a burned wall surface.

A burned wall is prepared in generally the same way as a hearth rim. The wall should be caved away to just above the target area. A trench 6 to 9 cm wide should be dug 3 to 5 cm behind the wall face (Fig. 2.4). If the wall consists only of large rocks covered with burned plaster, these rocks can be carefully removed from behind, leaving a vertical ridge of plaster veneer standing *in situ*. If the collection is to be dampened, fill the trench with water, splash/pour water over the burned surface, cover with plastic, and let stand at least two hours.

The collector should be alert to the possibility of wall tilting and slumpage (Harold 1960). At one site, 5MT0023, Hathaway collected separate walls in 6 different pit houses. She could detect no tilting or movement in the walls prior to collection, but in several cases she found significant differences in the sample directions (Table 2.2). These observations, however, cannot be taken as a recommendation to avoid collecting wall samples, because in another set of observations, wall samples fared somewhat better than floor and hearth samples (Table 2.3).

Next, the specific locations of the first series of specimens should be identified. Depending on collection skill and number of molds available, two or three specimens may be collected at a time. Collect-

Table 2.2. Comparison of Pairs of Archaeomagnetic Samples from the Same Burning but on Different Pit House Walls

	First Wall			Second Wall		
Sample	Dec.	Inc.	α_{95}	Dec.	Inc.	α_{95}
5MT0023-46	4.85	50.50	2.64	9.42	55.98	2.66
5MT0023-56	3.54	50.87	3.87	6.22	54.99	6.24
5MT0023-61	4.91	58.39	2.42	3.56	55.86	3.11
5MT0023-98	358.27	54.91	3.26	3.22	49.19	2.25
5MT0023-10	7.51	68.91	7.79	357.55	58.83	2.40
5MT0023-10	10.89	51.70	1.98	9.17	51.00	1.94

SOURCE: Colorado State University Archaeomagnetic Reports; on file in CSU Archaeomagnetic Laboratory.

Table 2.3. A Comparison of the Collection Situation and Productivity of Archaeomagnetic Samples

Collection Situation	No. of Samples	No. Dateable[a]	Percent Dateable
Fire-hardened walls	11	10	91%
Central pit house hearths	24	17	71
Exterior hearths	22	10	46
Fire-hardened floors	2	1	50

SOURCE: Hathaway and Eighmy 1982:45
[a]Number dateable is the number of samples with small α_{95}s and falling close to the master Southwest virtual geomagnetic pole curve. For a definition of a virtual geomagnetic pole curve, see Sternberg and McGuire, this volume, chap. 6.

ing two or three specimens speeds up the collection procedure but complicates collection and measurement strategy. Therefore, beginners should collect one specimen at a time until they have a "feel" for the process—particularly the plaster set-up time. If more than one cube is to be cast at a time, however, the samples should be located as far apart as possible. Collectors should not try to collect two or three adjacent specimens at the same time. They will inevitably run into problems when, for example, attempts to measure the direction of one cube are hampered by the proximity of the adjacent mold.

Figure 2.5. Specimen cutting on a horizontal surface.

How Is an Archaeomagnetic Sample Collected?

An archaeomagnetic collection is best conceived of as a cycle that is repeated until the desired number of specimens is collected. What follows is a description of the basic cycle, which can be broken into nine steps. An actual collection consists of several cycles. A novice collector should proceed deliberately.

Cutting Specimens. The first step in the cycle is specimen cutting. The object is to isolate a small pedestal of burned material without disturbing its orientation. If the burned surface is on a floor, a small square either 2 or 3 cm on a side (depending on mold size) should be marked off and the surface cut along the sides of this square and extending about 3 cm beyond the square. The square will eventually be the top of the pedestal. Next, cut a trench around all four sides of the square large enough to accommodate the molds acquired for the collection. For either mold size the trench should be at least 3 cm wide but not unnecessarily large, because extra cutting will only destroy more potentially collectible burn. Long exit channels can be cut from one or more of the trenches to help with cleaning away dirt (Fig. 2.5).

Figure 2.6. Specimen cutting on a vertical surface.

If the surface is vertical and the moat has already been prepared, carefully begin shaving the back of the ridge until it is either about 2 or 3 cm thick (depending on mold size). Next, make crosscuts on the narrowed ridge, with 2 or 3 cm of space between them. This is the beginning of the pedestal itself. Do not plan to thin the ridge down by shaving the vertical (front) burned surface, since this is likely to be the best material. Expand the crosscut to the appropriate thickness and depth (Fig. 2.6).

Cutting should always be done in a wide trench. A common tendency is to attempt to cut a deep, narrow trench next to the pedestal. The problem with this strategy is that if, during the cutting stroke, a large sand grain or small pebble dislodges, the loose pebble will wedge between the blade and the specimen, knocking it over.

Another common mistake is to begin by cutting a large pedestal, with the idea of shaving it down to size. This approach has the disadvantage of requiring a lot of cutting after the pedestal is free of its matrix on all four sides. A better approach is to determine the appropriate pedestal size at the outset and cut it to size from the beginning strokes. The pedestal wall should be cut as straight up and down as possible. Small pebbles and rocks are common, and the best approach to them is to cut around them until they loosen and fall away—even if the pedestal shape is altered somewhat. Pedestals do not have to be square, although a square is optimal, because it will include the most burned material in a cube.

The depth of the trench also depends on the type of molds available. The 1-inch molds require pedestals about 2.5 to 3 cm high. Larger molds require trenches 3.4 to 4 cm deep. The trench should be as level as possible all the way around the pedestal. Under some soil surface conditions, picking with an awl or small dental spoon is preferable to sawing with a saw blade. The collector should carefully pick away at the material until a 2-cm trench has been cleared all the way around the pedestal.

What Happens if the Specimen Moves? Slight vibration is inevitable during collection and does not ruin a specimen, but an *in situ* piece of the hearth is needed, so if the specimen permanently shifts position, it should not be considered a reliable part of the sample. Cutting specimens without breaking or moving them is probably the greatest concern of the beginner, but with practice, specimen cutting can be accomplished with relative ease. It is advisable to keep a finger always resting lightly on the specimen to stabilize it and to help detect when the specimen pedestal is getting weak.

Positioning the Clay Collar. The clay should be molded into a 0.5-cm roll and formed into a square the same size as the mold. This collar is placed around the base of the pedestal. Collections made on horizontal surfaces present no problems when placing the collar, but vertical surfaces have one side of the pedestal with no base. There are two ways of solving this problem. One is to form an artificial shelf out of modeling clay and overlap this shelf around the base of the front of the pedestal. This shelf should be fairly massive and sturdy because it will eventually have to support a mold under slight pressure.

A second option is simply to shovel in a little back dirt and build up an artificial dirt base in front of the surface. The core of this mound can be rock, but rocks alone are difficult to level. Screened back dirt is easy to work and easy to smooth out level with the rest of the base. Hearths can be partially refilled with dirt back up to the specimen base line. With a dirt platform, a normal collar roll can be placed around the pedestal. Experience suggests that the dirt platform solution is best.

Oiling and Positioning the Mold. A collection kit usually contains only a few molds so that during the collection it is usually necessary to remove cubes from molds before the plaster has thoroughly set up. To ensure that the cubes do not break upon removal, it is best to oil the molds slightly. Only one or two drops of oil are needed, and the oil should be spread into all corners and onto all sides. Too much oil in the molds might run and alter the shape of the plaster cast, and it is often a mistake to oil the molds too early, because the oil collects unwanted dust and dirt.

The oiled mold can be placed over the pedestal and on top of the clay collar. The mold should rest roughly level, with none of the pedestal protruding. The collector should be alert to the position of the specimen in the mold. Space should exist between the mold and all four sides of the specimen so that there is enough room to pour the plaster.

Leveling the Mold. It is now time to place the cross-level on top of the mold. By gently pressing the mold into the clay collar, the mold can be leveled. If the weather is hot, the clay turns extremely plastic and leveling becomes difficult. When the leveled mold sets on the clay collar too long under intense sun, it may begin to sink off level as the clay slowly softens. In hot weather, keep the clay out of the sun until the last minute, and try to level the mold and pour the plaster quickly. The clay could even be kept in water or under a water-soaked rag. In cold weather, the other extreme can be a problem. For obvious reasons, cold, hard clay is difficult to work.

Mixing and Pouring Plaster. The rubber bowls used in ceramic work are excellent for mixing the plaster and water. The collector should mix about 1 part water with 1.5 parts plaster. When mixed, this should have the consistency of cream. It is mixed most easily by pouring the water into the plaster in the bowl. The plaster should be poured into the cubes as quickly as possible. After the plaster begins to set, do not try to add more water, because the plaster can go into suspension and when poured into the mold can create a "fluff cube" (Windes 1978:5). Fluff cubes are soft, must be treated with special care, and should be avoided.

When pouring the plaster, collectors should at first only partially fill the mold (Fig. 2.7) and then check for leaks around the bottom of the mold. Leaks are common but can be stopped by simply sprin-

Figure 2.7. Pouring plaster. Note the cross-test level at right.

kling some fine-grained, dry dirt against the leak. The dirt will ab-
sorb moisture quickly, cause the plaster to set immediately, and stop
the leak. Slightly overfill the mold, though plaster should not pour
over the sides, especially the side from which you will eventually
measure the bearing. The plaster should sink at the mold corners;
these depressions can be filled by daubing a little more plaster with
a finger.

Reading Cube Azimuths. The collection is now at a critical moment. After the plaster has been allowed to set for a few minutes, it
should be tested to see if it is hard enough to allow measurement of
the cube bearing without moving the cube. It is difficult to predict
how long to wait, because this depends on weather conditions. The
length of time varies between 2 and 10 minutes, but the plaster
should not be allowed to get too hard because it becomes almost
impossible to work after it is set. After reading the cube direction it
is necessary to clean off excess plaster, and this is extremely difficult
after the plaster sets. Hydrocal White, for instance, has a hardness of
nearly two when dry. When ready for reading, the plaster should be
firm but penetrable with a sharp metal tool.

Figure 2.8. Taking a magnetic declination reading.

At this stage, the area should be cleared of all metal objects, such as digging tools, vehicles, and metal canteens. It should be safe to place small tools and canteens 2 m away, but vehicles should be kept at least 30 m away. With the area cleared of metal, the collector can place the pocket transit against one side of the mold. He or she should hold the pocket transit flush and level (bull's eye) to read the azimuth (Fig. 2.8).

It has become standard practice to set the local magnetic declination on the pocket transit to zero rather than attempt to adjust it to true north. It is important to know the local declination, but the declination correction is easily and more accurately made in the lab. To measure the azimuth of the mold side from magnetic north, the 90° side of the pocket transit can be placed against the mold and the degree mark (to the nearest ½° or 30 min) under the north-tending end of the compass needle read. It makes no difference which side of the mold is read as long as the side read is eventually marked on the cube.

It may take a while to get a reading while the pocket transit is simultaneously level and flush. The collector should therefore get into a comfortable position. She or he should not try to hold the compass with unsupported hands and arms but should rest them on solid ground near the mold side to be measured while the fingers move the pocket transit against the mold. The collector can now bend close to the compass to read the azimuth. The reading should be rechecked until its direction is certain. The reading should immediately be recorded on an archaeomagnetic field data sheet.

Cleaning and Marking the Cube. After reading the declination and after the plaster has set stiffly, the cube is ready to be cleaned. By holding the mold firmly with one hand, the excess plaster that protrudes over the top of the mold can be shaved off. A large knife with a straight cutting edge is useful here (a curved cutting blade will likely cut into the cube, creating one concave face). Alternatively, the back of a saw blade can be used. Regardless of the instrument used, deep slices should be avoided because the plaster tends to lose chunks when thick cuts are made.

Before removing the specimen and cube, the top should be marked so that the edge measured for bearing can be identified. The easiest method is to scribe an arrow in the top of the cube along the edge and in the direction measured. DuBois and many of those he trained mark the corner from which the azimuth was read. If the mold moves after measurement, there is no need for alarm unless the cube and/or specimen move inside the mold. As long as all three move together, directional control of the encased specimen is still maintained.

The cube can now be safely extracted from the feature. If the sample is of a sandy soil, the unconsolidated pedestal breaks easily. In such a case the cube can simply be picked up. If, however, the pedestal is of hard clay, it may be so firmly attached at the base that attempting to pick up the mold will cause the pedestal to pull out of the plaster cube. This can be avoided by pushing a knife, trowel, or awl tip up to the pedestal base and sharply striking the back of the tool, causing the specimen, cube, and mold to break off and tumble away together. The collector should not try to hold the mold too tightly, because the blow might move the specimen inside the plaster; they should be allowed to fall together.

Once it has been removed, it is important to finish cleaning the cube immediately. Again, the plaster will be getting hard. The bottom should be cleaned first, and for this the broken saw blade will come in extremely handy. The back of the blade can be used to clean out the plaster and pedestal base to about 3 mm below the bottom of the mold. The top of the cube should then be shaved completely level with the mold top. Next the sample and specimen identification can be scribed on the cube top. Two types of identification conventions are commonly used. The first convention uses the site number, numbers each sample set taken at that site consecutively (in the center), and numbers each specimen in the sample set consecutively (in the lower left). The second convention, originally designed by DuBois, uses a date and specimen number. Using this convention, samples taken on the same day must be given different (arbitrary) dates.

Pouring the Base. The cycle is almost complete for the first cube. Before removing the cube, however, its base must be capped with plaster. The collector can overfill the base with a little plaster, and after it is firm, shave the base flat. Normally it is more convenient to pour the base with plaster mixed during the next cycle, as this saves time and plaster.

Removing the Cube. After the bases are firm and the collection cycles have proceeded to where no unfilled molds remain, cubes from the first cycle can be removed. Normally the molds must be unscrewed entirely, but the cubes can be removed easily and cleanly with a little tap. While the molds are in two halves, they can be cleaned of plaster and dirt. It is best not to combine the sides from different molds; they should be put back together just as they were. To finish drying, the cube can be placed in a clean place for the rest of the day. The chunk of burned material is now encased in a cube with a known orientation.

SAMPLE COMPLETION

The collection cycle should be repeated until the desired sample size has been achieved. The specimens, particularly the last few, will still be damp and should be allowed to dry for a couple of days before final packing. Drying will be more thorough if the specimens are turned several times during the period. After the specimens are dry, the sample is ready to send to the lab, but before they are shipped, important information needs to be gathered to be sent with the sample. This information is most conveniently gathered while in the field and recorded on an archaeomagnetic data sheet like the one illustrated in Figure 2.2.

Besides directional information for each specimen, any unusual observation about specimen collections should be noted (e.g., movement, relatively more or less oxidation/reduction, extraneous inclusions, and proximity of metal). Also, the sample's quality should be described in detail. The lab will want to know details about color change, soil texture, and hardness, and an age estimate would be helpful. All this should be recorded at the time of collection.

The present-day declination is also an important piece of information to include. The most accurate way to determine the *general* site declination for sites in the United States is to call the National Geophysical Data Center of the National Oceanographic and Atmospheric Administration in Boulder, Colorado, and request a "declination at a point" for the site latitude and longitude. The center can provide an up-to-date reading of the declination for a region based on continental maps of declination. Alternatively, the declination can be taken from USGS topographic maps. The published declination for a map is supposed to relate to the center of the mapped area during the year the map was published. If the map is old, a correction factor may have to be added to obtain the current declination. If the average annual rate of change is not known for the mapped area or local magnetic anomalies are suspected, it is best to check the declination at the point where the collection takes place. Determining the local declination may be particularly important if there is reason to believe that some very localized geologic structure or recent cultural activity is influencing the local geomagnetic field. Most large-scale magnetic anomalies are mapped, but not all small or recent (cultural) ones are known. The only way to be absolutely sure that the site declination is the same as that reported by the National Geophysical Data Center or the USGS for the region is to check it.

Calculating Site Declination

Two methods for determining local declination can be recommended: Polaris and topographic observation. A third technique, solar observation, is not as accurate and requires special protective devices that are uncommon in the normal archaeological field kit.

Accurate solar observation is difficult because the sun moves rapidly and because its image through the lens system of a transit is too large to center easily.

The Observation of Polaris. Although the Polaris method of determining local magnetic declination necessitates a late-night trip to the collection site, it has the advantage of being the most accurate method. To sight Polaris, a transit, flashlight, and recording paper are needed. The transit (leveled) should be set up on the site as close to the collected surface as possible. The upper and lower base plate should be locked at 0°. The two plates should be rotated until the 0° marks rest directly under the north end of the magnetic needle. After loosening the upper plate from the lower, Polaris can be sighted. It may be convenient to shine a flashlight obliquely into the transit while focusing the cross hairs. Polaris can usually be identified with certainty as the last star in the handle of the Little Dipper. Its elevation angle above the horizon is equal to the site latitude from which the sighting is being made.

A good approximation of the local magnetic declination can be read from the upper plate's compass rose, which should now rest under the compass needle close to the local declination or, more accurately, by reading the vernier angle between the upper and lower base plates. This method provides only an approximation of the local declination because Polaris itself does not lie directly along the earth's axis of rotation but actually appears to rotate slightly (less than 1°) around this axis. To adjust for this rotation, it is necessary to record the latitude, longitude, date, and time of day. This information, when combined with standard observations recorded for the Greenwich Meridian and obtained from a current ephemeris (the *American Ephemeris and Nautical Almanac* or the *Solar Ephemeris* of the Keuffel and Esser Company), can be used to correct for the position of Polaris. With a fix on Polaris, the local magnetic declination can be calculated accurately. A much larger error is likely to be introduced by inaccurate sighting. To compensate for this problem, Polaris should be sighted at least five times and the readings averaged.

Topographic Observations. A second method of deriving local declination is to compare the true bearing of prominent topographic features from a good topographic map with the observed magnetic bearing of those features. This system is less attractive because it may rely on the very maps being checked, but if the object is to find the present magnetic declination for an area with old but accurately drawn maps, then the method may provide acceptable results. It has the advantage of being applied during normal daylight hours but requires an area with some topographic relief and long (>1 mile) lines of sight. Necessary equipment includes a transit, a protractor, a straightedge, and a topographic map.

First, several distant features that can be pinpointed should be located on a map. Then, with the protractor and straightedge, calculate the true bearing of these points from the site location. (These angles may not be the same as grid angles.) The true-north arrow to the north-south grid line can be compared to check for any necessary correction of grid north to true north. Next, use a transit to determine the magnetic bearing to these points. The difference between the true bearing and the magnetic bearing is a rough approximation of the local magnetic declination. With five or more sightings, mechanical and sighting errors can be averaged out and a reliable mean calculated.

Avoiding the Declination Problem Altogether. Tarling (1971:59) argues that the fastest and most accurate lightweight orienting instrument is the sun compass. The sun compass is more accurate because a true bearing can be calculated independently of a magnetic needle and of the problems inherent in magnetic directions. Tarling (1975:191) believes that the magnetic orientation method is particularly suspect on archaeological sites because large fired features such as burned floors, pit houses, kivas, and kilns are often so strongly magnetized as to cause significant local variation in the field. Thus, knowing the magnetic declination of a site may not be sufficient, and a magnetic declination for each burned feature may have to be determined. Obviously, more work on this important practical problem is in order, but in any case, routine use of a sun compass is hampered by the fact that commercial availability is limited. Several controlled experiments have failed to demonstrate the superiority of the sun compass over the pocket transit in collecting isolated fire hearths (Hathaway 1982b; Krause 1980). The same studies have shown, however, that the sun compass is another accurate way of calculating magnetic declination. Although a sun compass is simple to design and make, the average archaeologist generally does not have either the time or the inclination to construct a sun compass. When using a sun compass to orient archaeomagnetic specimens, note not only the angle of the sun's shadow but also the time, date, and location of the collection for later calculation of the cube's direction.

DEALING WITH THE ARCHAEOMAGNETIC SPECIALIST

The relationship between archaeometric specialists and archaeologists has often been a sterile one. Interaction between the two groups has generally followed a pattern in which specialists receive field samples, perform a mysterious analysis, and report the results back to the archaeologist. Archaeomagnetism is no exception. Traditionally, an archaeologist collects (or has collected) an archaeomagnetic sample, it is sent to a lab, and a resultant date is returned. The problem with this type of archaeologist-archaeomagnetist interaction, as with any specialty, is that, on the one hand, the lab results may not be what the archaeologist presumed or expected, or on the other hand, the lab results can contain much more potential information than the archaeologist appreciates. These problems are part of the much more general problem in archaeology of underestimating the complexity in moving from archaeological data to inference about past human social behavior. Oversimplified assumptions about the relationship between archaeological observation and the context of ancient social systems hinder detailed reconstruction of prehistoric social systems and understanding of human social behavior. The archaeological and behavioral referent of archaeomagnetic analysis is more complex and can be more productive than current practice allows. The solution to the problem is to discard old habits of interaction and increase and improve the quality of communication between archaeomagnetists and archaeologists. Getting the most out of archaeomagnetic analysis depends on asking the right questions, and answering some of these questions requires a precise understanding of either the basic archaeomagnetic observation or the cultural significance of the data.

The Archaeological Context of an Archaeomagnetic Sample

To begin with the archaeological context, note that even the most common and basic question asked of the archaeomagnetists—What is the date of my sample?—is inadequate by itself because the question confuses archaeomagnetic observation with interpretation. A program of archaeomagnetic analysis is first of all a process of physi-

cal examination to determine the most stable component of remanent magnetism. This information can be compared with master records of secular variation for temporal interpretation. The direction
of this stable component is the fundamental datum produced in laboratory analysis, and this directional information, established in the
archaeological context, should be of initial interest to the archaeologist. Temporal interpretation of this direction may change as master
curves are refined and made more regionally specific, but the measurement of direction will not change. If archaeologists have been
given only a date for their archaeomagnetic samples and if alterations or refinements in the master curves occur, as is inevitable,
then they will have no way to reinterpret their samples relative to
the improved information. This predicament would be analogous to
a problem already experienced in radiocarbon dating. For years,
radiocarbon labs returned temporal interpretations rather than data
to archaeologists. The fundamental data in radiocarbon analysis consist of the ratio of stable to unstable carbon isotopes. The temporal
interpretation of this ratio depends on a number of things, one of
which is the original concentration of atmospheric carbon. Normally, a radiocarbon report consists of a date based on some assumption about atmospheric carbon. But what if, as has in fact happened,
the variable amount of atmospheric carbon during past epochs comes
to be known with greater precision? The answer is that the dates
have to be calibrated and the basis for the reinterpretation specified.
It would be less ambiguous if radiocarbon results were simply published first as lab results, as some measure of the isotope ratio, and
second as the current interpretation of the temporal significance of
that value. Subsequent reinterpretations are made much easier by
having the fundamental data available.

The first question, then, that an archaeologist should ask of an
archaeomagnetist is, What is the direction of my sample's stable remanent magnetism? By specifying the stable component, the archaeologist is in effect requesting the sample to be magnetically cleaned of
low-level unstable magnetic noise. It is important to know the level
of demagnetization in case future analysis is contemplated. The resulting magnetic direction should reflect the direction of the earth's
field at the time the feature was last intensely heated.

The sample direction should be expressed as a mean direction and
an associated α_{95} angle of confidence. The size of the angle depends
on the degree of clustering of individual specimen directions and the

number of specimens collected. The internal consistency of the specimen directions depends on the intensity of firing, the quality of the collection, and soil texture. Because of the importance of good internal agreement between specimens, it should be obvious why the factors of soil texture, firing, and collection accuracy are so important in the sample evaluation and collection stages.

Careful field notes are important for this stage of analysis because, if in the course of laboratory processing it becomes obvious that a specimen is inconsistent with the others and field notes indicate that it was, for example, shaky or unfired, then such an "outlier" can safely be discarded. A better, truer representation of the actual direction of the remanent magnetism will then be provided by the results of the remaining specimens.

A lab report from the archaeomagnetist should therefore contain a summary of sample treatment and the final processing results. These directional results should indicate the number of specimens used from the sample, the definition and identity of outliers, the intensity of magnetization, the mean inclination, the mean declination, the precision parameter (k), the α_{95}, the latitude of the virtual geomagnetic pole (VGP), the longitude of the VGP, the error (dm) in estimating pole latitude, and the error (dp) in estimating pole longitude (see Sternberg, this volume, for a definition of these terms).

Communication about the archaeological context of an archaeomagnetic sample should go both ways. Not only should archaeologists expect certain information from archaeomagnetic specialists, but also they should provide complete archaeological context information in order to insure complete exploitation of archaeomagnetic data. Carefully designed and completed archaeomagnetic data sheets help to assure adequate archaeological context information. It is essential, for example, to know whether the sampled feature has remained in place since being fired. Further, the archaeological context information provided by archaeologists has been and continues to be of great service to archaeomagnetists. Master-curve construction continues. Only a small portion of the United States has securely dated master records. Knowledge gained from independently dated archaeomagnetic samples helps speed and expand the construction of the master curves.

The archaeomagnetic lab report should provide the archaeologist with information from which a temporal interpretation can proceed.

In this report the archaeologist will have a direction of magnetization and the location of an ancient pole, along with the error parameters associated with estimating this location. This information can be compared to archaeomagnetic master curves to assign a date. At first glance, deriving a date is simply a matter of noting where the VGP of the sample strikes an appropriate master curve. Interpreting the temporal range of an archaeomagnetic collection from a virtual geomagnetic pole and an oval of confidence is, however, more complicated. (For contrasting approaches, see Sternberg and McGuire, this volume, chap. 6, and Wolfman, this volume, chap. 14.) The range is greater or less, depending on how the curve passes through the oval at that point and how closely the oval of confidence falls to the curve. Because the master VGP curve crosses itself and the sample VGP seldom falls directly on the curve, many sample locations produce two or more possible dates based on archaeomagnetic evidence alone. Only independent information concerning the chronological context of a sample allows one to choose a preferred interpretation. Age determination is also ambiguous when the VGP location falls far from the curve. Even when the extreme cases are ignored, many samples plot close enough to be suggestive but not close enough to be firmly dated.

The Systemic Context of an Archaeomagnetic Date

To this point, the chapter has been written as if the results of archaeomagnetic analysis refer to the last intense firing of a feature. Although not a thoroughly tested assumption, the last firing is likely (and is most commonly assumed) to be the event measured by an archaeomagnetic date (Smith 1981), and for convenience, what follows assumes that this is so. But because knowing which event (i.e., the first, last, or a combination of all firings) is actually being dated is of critical importance to archaeologists, more experimental work in determining the exact systemic reference of an archaeomagnetic direction is badly needed (Hathaway 1982b:110). Until this experimental work is done, the exact systemic context of dates will remain uncertain.

Even assuming the most likely outcome of future research—that is, that the archaeomagnetic date refers to the last firing—systemic interpretation of this date is neither uncomplicated nor a simple mechanical process. To determine the systemic referent of an archaeomagnetic date, it is necessary to determine which firing is involved. For example, during the collection of many hearths, the collector will find that the excavated hearth is only the last of a series of repaired and rebuilt burned surfaces. Care must be exercised to avoid collecting specimens from different phases of the hearth and to relate the hearth actually sampled to room remodeling or to the sequence of occupation surfaces. Systemic interpretation can be further complicated if the room, occupation surface, or site was burned. If the event of interest is the burning of the site, or if the fire coincides with an event of interest (like abandonment) and the archaeomagnetic sample clearly came from this burning, then interpretation is simple. If, however, the relationship of site or room burning to site or room abandonment is not absolutely clear, then it should not be assumed that the archaeomagnetic date relates to site or room abandonment. The date refers only to when the site was burned, an event that may have occurred long after abandonment.

If the appropriate conditions were present, even the remanent magnetism of the rim of a fire hearth may not relate to the last time the hearth was used for heating or cooking but rather to the room burning. A very interesting situation exists for the archaeomagnetist when a last hearth burning is protected—that is, covered with ash, as in the base of the hearth, or covered with fill before the room was subsequently burned. Here the systemic implications of the event measured are clear. A hearth sample would represent the last cultural use of the room (room abandonment), and the burned room sample would represent the final destruction of the habitation area.

ACKNOWLEDGMENTS

This chapter is a substantial revision of portions of Eighmy (1981), which includes a fuller treatment of some topics. Copies of the 1981 publication can be obtained by writing Chief, Interagency Archaeological Services, U.S. Department of the Interior, National Park Service, Washington, D.C. 20240. The author gratefully acknowledges the support [Purchase Order No. A35024(78)] of Interagency Archaeological Services in Denver.

CHAPTER 3

A Discussion of Collection Factors Affecting the Quality of Archaeomagnetic Results

RICHARD C. LANGE AND BARBARA A. MURPHY

In order to achieve the full potential of archaeomagnetic dating, samples must ultimately be collected routinely on archaeological projects. This should be done regardless of the presence of other means of chronological control, such as radiocarbon or tree-ring samples. At one level, this allows an independent means of cross-checking dates on those sites that do have radiocarbon or tree-ring dates. At a more general level, these other samples can be used to refine and build secular variation, or master, curves. As archaeological excavations continue in the desert Southwest, archaeomagnetic samples will inevitably be recovered from contexts that are presently either poorly documented or not covered at all by the master curves. Associated radiocarbon or tree-ring dated materials can help extend and refine the archaeomagnetic curves but only if the archaeomagnetic samples are taken.

The two curves currently in use at the University of Arizona are the Sternberg/McGuire southwestern virtual geomagnetic pole (SWVGP) curve (Sternberg 1982 and this volume), and the Eighmy VGP (EVGP) curve. The SWVGP curve is based on samples from 73 *in situ* archaeological features and covers the period A.D. 700–1450. Sternberg adapted the Eighmy VGP curve from data Eighmy supplied for the period A.D. 600–950. The curve used by Colorado State University's Archaeometric Laboratory covers roughly the same period of time as the SWVGP curve.

This paper deals with some problems, their causes, and possible solutions related to field sampling, laboratory analysis, and final dating interpretations that are part of the process of archaeomagnetic dating.

THE DATA

The primary data in this paper are the results of analyses of 301 samples collected by 36 samplers or sampling teams on 25 projects conducted by 14 institutions, agencies, or groups (Table 3.1). Most of the samples were collected from archaeological sites in southern Arizona, others were collected elsewhere in Arizona, and a few in southern New Mexico.

All but seven of the samples were analyzed by personnel from the Arizona State Museum during the period January 1, 1980, to March 31, 1984. The seven samples (project designations AM, NS, and RR) were analyzed in previous research conducted by Robert S. Sternberg and Randall H. McGuire, culminating in Sternberg's (1982) dissertation. Archaeologists requested that these seven samples be redated using the new techniques and curves, so they have been included with this data set.

The Arizona State Museum, in cooperation with the Paleomagnetism Laboratory, Department of Geosciences, University of Arizona, provided the archaeomagnetic dating interpretations for samples reported here. When the analyses were done, the Paleomagnetism Laboratory had both a spinner magnetometer and a cryogenic magnetometer. Samples were measured on the cryogenic magnetometer when possible; only those samples too strongly magnetized for it were analyzed on the spinner magnetometer. Technical descriptions of the magnetometers and demagnetizer used in the analyses are available in Sternberg (1982).

Brief descriptions of the projects from which the samples were collected are given in Lange and Murphy (1989) and include sample designations, site name and number, locational data for the site, project dates, institution, archaeologist, relevant references to the site or project, number of samples taken, and number of samples analyzed. Dating interpretations are also given in Lange and Murphy (1989), based on the 1982 versions of the SWVGP and EVGP dating curves. Standard archaeomagnetic results from the samples' analyses are also presented in Lange and Murphy (1989). A discussion and further description of the nature of paleomagnetic results may be found in standard paleomagnetism texts, such as Irving (1964), McElhinny (1973), and Tarling (1971).

Such results are indispensable to the development and full understanding of archaeomagnetic dating interpretations (McGuire et al. 1980). The archaeomagnetic data should therefore be presented routinely along with any archaeomagnetic dating interpretations in archaeological reports. Presenting such results permits the full evaluation of VGP curves, the refinement of curves, and the reinterpretation of dates as revised curves are developed by future researchers.

Archaeologists should be aware that archaeomagnetic analyses initially produce not the dates, which they are most interested in, but rather a set of archaeomagnetic data. The dates are interpreted by comparing the pole latitude and longitude (Plat and Plong) and the semimajor and semiminor axes of the 95% oval of confidence about the pole position (*dm* and *dp*) to the known path of the geomagnetic pole. Variables affecting the quality of the results from archaeomagnetic analyses can be investigated by examining the archaeomagnetic data set, in particular the α_{95} angle. The α_{95} is the angle subtended by the 95% cone of confidence about the mean pole direction. The α_{95} value is used here to define the quality of the results from a sample—the smaller the α_{95}, the better the sample.

DISCUSSION

Field sampling—that is, the recovery of archaeomagnetic specimens—is a crucial step in obtaining reliable archaeomagnetic results. For purposes of discussion, sampling can be divided into five factors: the project, the sampler or sampling team, the sample, the feature type, and environmental characteristics. There is, of course, overlap among these variables, and many problems are a function of many factors all working at once.

The first step in this study was to look at the 301 samples on a project-by-project basis. The 25 projects are represented by from 1 to 178 analyzed samples (Table 3.1). The largest number of samples analyzed from a project came from the Hohokam site of Las Colinas (178 samples), followed by 17 samples each from the Phoenix Townsite Project (sample designation SS) and the Los Morteros Project (sample designation LM). The average α_{95} values for all of these projects range from 1.0° to 12.3° and as a set average 5.1°. In an effort to limit the effect of an individual sample, we have reexamined the eight projects that had five or more samples. The α_{95} values for this set range from 2.9° to 12.3°, with an average of 5.3°. On a project-by-project basis,

Table 3.1. Projects and Samples Reported

Proj. Desig.	Project Name	Institution	Samples Taken	Samples Analyzed
AC	Ash Creek	ASU	10	10
AM	Adobe Mitigation	MNA	—	1
AR	Anamax-Rosemont	ASM-CRMD	15	9
BW	Blue Wash	AAS-Cave Creek	1	1
CH	Chodista'as	UA	1	1
FP	Florence Prison	BLM	1	1
FT	Salt-Gila Aqueduct	ASM-CRMD	15	14
HS	Henderson Site	UM	6	6
LC	Las Colinas	ASM-CRMD	178	178
LM	Los Morteros	ASM-AS	17	17
MP	Midvale Park	PCC	2	2
NR	Nan Ranch	TxA&M	3	3
NS	Nat'l Semiconductor	ASM-CRMD	—	5
OM	Ord Mine	MNA	5	5
OW	Oraibi Wash	ASU	2	2
PR	Powers Ranch	ASM-CRMD	4	4
PV	Salt-Gila Aqueduct	ASM-CRMD	3	3
RR	Rabid Ruin	ASM-CRMD	—	1
SD	Salt-Gila Aqueduct	ASM-CRMD	4	4
SG	Salt-Gila Aqueduct	ASM-CRMD	12	9
SS	Phoenix Townsite	SSI	17	17
UA 1&2	Abused Ridge	ASM-CRMD	2	2
UA 3	Matty Cnyn-Archaic	ASM-CRMD	1	1
UA 4	Ash Terrace	CACA	1	1
UA 5	Como Site	ASM-AS	1	1
UP	Udall Park	ASM-CRMD	1	1
VS	Volunteer Site	AAS	1	1
WS	Wood Site	AAS-Sedona	2	2

INSTITUTIONS

AAS	Arizona Archaeological Society
ASM-AS	Arizona State Museum, Archaeology Section
ASM-CRMD	Arizona State Museum, Cultural Resource Management Division
ASU	Arizona State University, Office of Cultural Resource Management
BLM	U.S. Bureau of Land Management
CACA	Central Arizona College, Aravaipa
MNA	Museum of Northern Arizona
PCC	Pima Community College
SSI	Soil Systems, Inc.
TxA&M	Texas A&M University
UA	University of Arizona, Department of Anthropology
UM	University of Michigan, Museum of Anthropology

Not Run Past NRM	Average α_{95}	Number of Samplers
1	3.7	1
—	6.2	2
5	7.0	2
—	3.9	4
—	5.6	6
—	1.8	2
—	5.4	3
—	2.9	1
2	3.5	6
—	3.3	10
—	1.0	2
—	8.2	2
—	2.5	1
—	4.2	1
—	6.2	2
—	8.6	2
—	4.9	2
—	2.7	1
—	8.8	1
1	5.4	4
—	12.3	2
—	7.4	1
—	8.8	1
—	5.0	2
—	2.5	2
—	1.9	1
—	2.9	1
—	2.8	2

the α_{95} values are influenced by the nature and quality of the features being sampled and by the sampler. Thus, project-by-project, it may be possible to identify problem areas in the Southwest with unsuitable soils or other variables and to identify samplers who do not do quality work.

Another possible source of the variation among projects is local magnetic anomalies. Local anomalies are not, however, likely to be reflected in the α_{95} values. These anomalies can affect very limited geographic areas and often cannot be detected with a Brunton compass alone. A sun compass is a good way to test for them. For example, sun compass readings were taken during the recovery of many of the Las Colinas samples. Measured declinations ranged from 7.20° to 15.95°, with an average of 12.54°. The 1973 USGS quadrangle shows a declination of 13.5°. All of the most extreme Las Colinas variability was directly attributable to elements introduced into the site by modern houses: power lines, metal pipes, and fence posts.

In 1984 the authors visited 12 sites where sampling had occurred on five projects and took comparative Brunton and sun compass readings. The results were within the range of error of the field measuring equipment (approximately $\pm 1°$). This eliminated natural anomalies as a reason for poor results on those projects. Unfortunately, it is impossible to determine whether human-induced magnetic problems such as wheelbarrows, trucks, or shovels were near enough to distort the magnetic field.

The next variable examined was the sampler. Each individual sampler and sampling team was given an alphabetic letter code. Table 3.2 lists the samples by project along with the type of feature the sample came from, the sample's α_{95} value, and the sampler code. Table 3.3 lists the sampler along with the number of samples each had taken, the average α_{95} value, and the standard deviation and variance of the α_{95} value.

The number of samples taken by the 36 individual samplers and teams ranged from 1 to 93. Two of the samplers accounted for over 50% of the 301 samples taken (174). Without these two samplers, the number of samples taken ranged from 1 to 19. There is no difference in the average α_{95} values if the samples taken by these two samplers are removed from the data set. There is a difference, however, in the range of α_{95} values. The α_{95} values for the full set range from 1.2° to 18.6°. A total of 19 of the 35 samplers and teams took only one sample apiece, and 6 samplers took 2 to 4 samples. The range of average

Table 3.2. Samples, Features, and Samplers

Sample	Feature Type[a]	α_{95}	Sampler Code	Sample	Feature Type[a]	α_{95}	Sampler Code
AC001		—	AN	FT014		10.3	AJ
AC002		1.6	AN	FT015		4.0	BI
AC003		1.6	AN	HS001		4.4	AZ
AC004		5.5	AN	HS002		1.3	AZ
AC005		6.0	AN	HS003		2.4	AZ
AC006		2.6	AN	HS004		2.6	AZ
AC007		5.2	AN	HS005		4.9	AZ
AC008		3.9	AN	HS006		2.0	AZ
AC009		3.5	AN	LC001		8.4	BM
AC010		3.3	AN	LC002		2.5	BM
AM001		6.2	BN	LC003		3.5	AW
AR001		—	AJ	LC004		2.7	AW
AR002		9.9	AJ	LC005		3.8	AW
AR003		—	AJ	LC006		2.9	AW
AR004		10.3	AJ	LC007		2.8	AW
AR005		—	AJ	LC008		3.1	AW
AR006		—	AJ	LC009		2.1	AW
AR007		3.2	AJ	LC010		1.7	AU
AR008		—	AJ	LC011		2.4	AU
AR009		4.7	AJ	LC012		4.7	AU
BW001		3.9	BW	LC013		3.0	AU
CH020		5.6	BY	LC014		1.5	AU
FP001		1.8	BA	LC015		1.7	AU
FT001	2	2.4	BJ	LC016		2.0	AU
FT002	2	3.4	BJ	LC017		4.5	AO
FT003		7.4	BJ	LC018		4.6	AO
FT004		2.8	BJ	LC019		4.0	AO
FT005	1	1.4	AJ	LC020		2.7	AU
FT006		4.8	AJ	LC021		2.2	AO
FT007		3.2	AJ	21A–F		1.6	AO
FT008		5.6	AJ	21G–L		2.4	AO
FT009		8.8	AJ	21M–R		1.5	AO
FT010		7.6	AJ	LC022		5.7	AU
FT011	2	—	AJ	LC023		3.5	AO
FT012		5.0	AJ	LC024		3.2	AO
FT013		8.6	AJ	LC025		3.1	AU

[a]Key to feature type:

blank	hearth		
1	floor	4	burned pit
2	horno	5	wall
3	crematory	6	sediment

Table 3.2. Continued

Sample	Feature Type[a]	α_{95}	Sampler Code	Sample	Feature Type[a]	α_{95}	Sampler Code
LC026		3.6	BA	LC065		3.9	AO
LC027	2	1.9	AU	LC066		14.8	AU
LC028		2.0	BA	LC067		3.4	AU
LC029		2.2	AV	LC068	4	8.7	AO
LC030		3.3	AU	LC069	4	5.6	AO
LC031	1	15.0	AO	LC070	4	3.3	AU
LC032		5.1	BA	LC071	4	2.6	AO
LC033		3.6	AV	LC072		2.2	AU
LC034		1.2	AV	LC073		2.5	BA
LC035		6.9	AU	LC074	2	1.7	BA
LC036		3.5	AV	LC075		4.2	AO
LC037		1.9	AV	LC076		4.8	AU
LC038	5	2.7	AU	LC077	2	6.4	AU
LC039		6.6	AV	LC078		3.3	AO
LC040		3.4	AU	LC079		3.0	AU
LC041		3.3	AV	LC080		4.2	AO
LC042		3.0	AU	LC081		2.2	AU
LC043		2.6	AV	LC082	1	4.7	AO
LC044	5	2.0	BV	LC083		2.0	AU
44A–H		4.1	BV	LC084		3.1	AV
44I–P		1.7	BV	LC085		1.2	AU
44Q–X		2.2	BV	LC086		1.9	AV
LC045		2.1	AU	LC087		2.8	AV
LC046		1.8	AU	LC088	6	7.7	AU
LC047		5.8	AO	LC089		1.5	AV
LC048		3.1	AO	LC090		1.9	AU
LC049		4.2	AU	LC091	1	2.4	AU
LC050		2.7	AU	LC092	4	2.5	AU
LC051		3.7	AO	LC093		2.5	AU
LC052		1.4	AO	LC094	1	3.1	AU
LC053		2.9	AU	LC095		1.8	AU
LC054		2.5	BA	LC096		2.0	AU
LC055		3.9	AU	LC097		2.5	AU
LC056		4.9	AO	LC098		1.7	AU
LC057		3.8	BA	LC099		5.7	AU
LC058		2.2	AU	LC100	3	2.1	AU
LC059		3.6	AO	LC101		1.1	AU
LC060		3.7	AV	LC102		2.7	AU
LC061		3.3	AU	LC103	4	5.1	AU
LC062	4	8.9	AO	LC104		2.4	AU
LC063		2.7	BA	LC105		1.8	AU
LC064		2.8	AU	LC106	2	—	AU

Sample	Feature Type[a]	α_{95}	Sampler Code	Sample	Feature Type[a]	α_{95}	Sampler Code
LC107		3.0	AU	LC149	6	8.4	AU
LC108		1.3	AO	LC150	6	5.3	AU
LC109		4.9	AO	LC151	6	9.6	AU
LC110		2.6	AO	LC152		1.8	AU
LC111	3	2.9	AO	LC153		4.3	AU
LC112	1	4.4	AO	LC154		3.0	AO
LC113		2.8	AO	LC155	5	3.4	AU
LC114		2.7	AO	LC156	4	3.8	AO
LC115		2.3	AO	LC157		4.2	AU
LC116		3.3	AO	LC158		3.2	AU
LC117		1.9	AO	LC159		2.8	AU
LC118		3.8	AO	LC160		2.2	BA
LC119		3.8	AO	LC161	4	7.0	BA
LC120		3.8	AO	LC162	2	2.3	AU
LC121		4.2	AO	LC163	2	1.6	AU
LC122		3.2	AO	LC164		1.8	AO
LC123		3.0	AO	LC165		2.6	AO
LC124		1.8	AO	LC166		1.7	AU
LC125		2.1	AU	LC167		2.4	AO
LC126		1.8	AU	LC168	4	5.4	AU
LC127		2.3	AO	LC169		2.4	AU
LC128		2.1	AU	LC170		5.4	AO
LC129		1.8	AU	LC171		5.1	AO
LC130		3.8	AU	LC172		1.5	AU
LC131		1.8	AO	LC173		2.7	AO
LC132		2.3	AO	LC174		4.0	AU
LC133		1.8	AU	LC175		5.1	AO
LC134		2.7	AO	LC176		2.3	AU
LC135		2.8	AO	LC177	1	3.5	AU
LC136		2.8	AU	LC178	4	7.0	AU
LC137		2.4	AU	LM001	3	1.2	BO
LC138	4	10.1	AO	LM002	4	1.2	BP
LC139		2.2	AO	LM003		3.0	BQ
LC140	4	5.2	AU	LM004	1	2.8	BR
LC141		3.4	AU	LM005	1	5.0	BS
LC142		2.4	AO	LM006		3.8	BA
LC143	6	5.1	AU	LM007		3.7	BA
LC144	6	5.8	AU	LM008	1	10.0	BA
LC145	6	5.3	AU	LM009		2.7	BA
LC146	6	6.9	AU	LM010		3.2	BA
LC147	6	6.1	AU	LM011	5	3.6	BZ
LC148	6	7.2	AU	LM012	1	6.6	CA

Table 3.2. Continued

Sample	Feature Type[a]	α_{95}	Sampler Code	Sample	Feature Type[a]	α_{95}	Sampler Code
LM013		2.9	AU	SG002		5.7	BG
LM014	2	1.9	AO	SG003		10.3	AR
LM015	2	1.5	BA	SG004		10.5	BL
LM016	2	1.6	AU	SG005		—	AJ
LM017	2	1.8	AO	SG006		5.2	AJ
MP001	4	0.9	AU	SG007		2.3	AJ
MP002	4	1.1	AO	SG008		3.5	AJ
NR008		16.1	CE	SG009		3.5	AJ
NR009		4.4	CE	SS001		42.8	BH
NR010		4.0	CE	SS002		9.1	AB
NS001		1.4	AS	SS003		14.8	AB
NS002		4.5	AS	SS004		9.5	AB
NS003		2.7	AS	SS005		3.8	AB
NS004		1.5	AS	SS006		6.7	AB
NS005		2.2	AS	SS007		3.6	BH
OM001		5.5	AD	SS008		1.4	BH
OM002		3.1	AD	SS009		5.2	AB
OM003		1.5	AD	SS010	1	2.3	AB
OM004		7.5	AD	SS011		6.6	AB
OM005		3.4	AD	SS012		8.1	AB
OW001		2.0	BB	SS013		23.7	AB
OW002		10.3	BC	SS014		11.3	AB
PR001		17.1	AU	SS015	4	14.2	AB
PR002		8.0	AO	SS016		19.5	AB
PR003		7.8	AU	SS017	1	26.5	BH
PR004		1.4	AO	UA001		12.0	AJ
PV001		9.2	BE	UA002		2.9	AJ
PV002		3.2	BF	UA003		8.8	AO
PV003		2.4	BF	UA004		5.0	BO
RR001		2.7	AS	UA005		2.5	BA
SD001		10.7	AW	UP001		1.9	AF
SD002		8.5	AW	VS001		2.9	AO
SD003		3.0	AW	WS001		3.3	AU
SD004		13.1	AW	WS002		2.2	AO
SG001		2.0	BG				

Table 3.3. Sampler Averages

Sampler	Group	Number of Samples	Average α_{95}	Standard Deviation	Variance
AB	II	13	10.4	6.2	38.9
AD	II	5	4.2	2.3	5.4
AF	I	1	1.9	—	—
AJ	II	19	5.9	3.2	10.2
AN	II	9	3.7	1.6	2.6
AO	I	63	3.6	1.9	3.7
AR	II	1	10.3	—	—
AS	I	6	2.5	1.1	1.3
AU	I	93	3.7	2.6	6.7
AV	I	13	2.9	1.4	1.9
AW	II	12	4.8	3.8	14.1
AZ	II	6	2.9	1.4	2.0
BA	I	18	3.5	2.1	4.5
BB	II	1	2.0	—	—
BC	II	1	10.3	—	—
BD	II	1	5.0	—	—
BE	II	1	9.2	—	—
BF	II	2	2.8	0.6	0.3
BG	II	2	3.8	2.6	6.8
BH	II	4	18.6	19.7	389.6
BI	II	1	4.0	—	—
BJ	II	4	4.0	2.3	5.3
BL	II	1	10.5	—	—
BM	II	2	5.4	4.2	17.4
BN	II	1	6.2	—	—
BO	I	1	1.2	—	—
BP	I	1	1.2	—	—
BQ	II	1	3.0	—	—
BR	II	1	2.8	—	—
BS	II	1	5.0	—	—
BV	I	1	2.0	—	—
BW	II	1	3.9	—	—
BY	II	1	5.6	—	—
BZ	II	1	3.6	—	—
CA	I	1	6.6	—	—
CE	II	3	8.2	6.9	47.2

NOTE: Those samplers listed as code "BA" and below are sampling "teams" consisting of two or more persons. Persons who have been involved in sampling but who have not worked alone are not listed in the table; this group consists of 22 persons, whose codes are AA, AC, AE, AG, AH, AI, AK, AL, AM, AP, AQ, AT, AX, AY, BK, BT, BU, CB, CC, CD, CF, and CG.

Table 3.4. Statistical Comparisons of Sampler Averages

a. Individual Samplers vs. Sampling Teams

α_{95} Value	Individuals	Teams	Test Result
<6.0	201	40	$\chi^2 = 0.8488$, $df = 1$; not
≥6.0	40	12	significant $(p > .10)$

b. Group I vs. Group II Samplers (Individuals and Teams)

α_{95} Value	Group I	Group II	Test Result
<6.0	178	62	$\chi^2 = 22.229$, $df = 1$;
≥6.0	21	32	significant $(p < .0005)$

c. Comparison of Sample Averages of α_{95} values

	Number of Samples	Average α_{95} Value	Standard Deviation
Group I	199	3.52	2.24
Group II	94	6.34	5.98
TOTAL	293	4.42	4.06

α_{95} values for the eleven remaining samplers (from 5 to 93 samples taken) is reduced to a range of 2.5° to 10.3°.

A simple chi-square test shows that individual samplers and sampling teams perform equally well (Table 3.4a); that is, there is no significant difference in the results. Proper training, however, is essential for good results. The statistics presented in Table 3.4 clearly show the differences between Group I and Group II samplers. For purposes of the comparison presented here, Group I was formed of those samplers directly associated with the University of Arizona Paleomagnetism Laboratory. Group II is composed of samplers not directly trained by experienced samplers and of samplers with no connections to the UA lab (see also Table 3.3). Often these samplers are second- or third-generation trainees, that is, they did not receive training directly from someone familiar with the full range of field and laboratory practices. In both groups, samplers have been lower-level project personnel or consulting specialists brought to a site specifically to take samples. In some cases the samplers could be considered both specialists and lower-level personnel.

The quality of the individual samples causes more variability than any of the other factors, with α_{95} values ranging from 0.9° to 42.8° (see Table 3.2). Several samples were judged to be so poor that their analyses were never completed (analyses should probably not have been completed on the 42.8° sample, SS001).

One of the obvious factors affecting sample quality is the type of feature that was sampled (Table 3.5). First and most obvious, the feature must be composed of soil and/or plaster that has been subjected to heat and has remained in place, with two notable exceptions being samples of suspended sediments (from reservoir strata, samples LC088 and LC143–151) and experimental attempts to use the paleointensity of unoriented ceramic materials to measure their ages (Sternberg 1982).

The types of features and their associated α_{95} values are considered in several ways in Table 3.5. Table 3.5a lists the types of features sampled, the number of each type of feature sampled regardless of α_{95} values, and the average α_{95} value. Table 3.5b lists the same infor-

Table 3.5. Average α_{95} Values by Feature Type

	Feature Type[a]						
	Floor	Pit	Horno	Wall	Crema-torium	Reservoir	Hearth
a. All samples regardless of α_{95} value							
Number of samples	13	17	12	4	3	10	237
Average α_{95} value	6.8	5.4	3.2	2.9	2.1	6.7	4.3
b. Samples with α_{95} values ≤10.0°							
Number of samples	10	15	12	4	3	10	221
Average α_{95} value	3.1	4.6	3.2	2.9	2.1	6.7	3.5
c. Percentages of samples with α_{95} values ≤10.0°							
Percentage	77	88	100	100	100	100	93

[a]All are burned except the reservoir features.

mation but only for samples with α_{95} values of 10.0° or less. Table 3.5c gives the proportion of samples of each feature type that falls into the 10.0°-or-less category. Samples with an α_{95} value of 10.0° or more generally indicate features that should not have been sampled and samplers who need better training in recognizing and taking "good" samples or, not totally in jest, samplers who should find alternative work.

Samples from burned floors can produce less reliable results than samples from other types of features (Table 3.5). This is perhaps due to disturbance of such surfaces (through compaction or other distortion) during excavation of the feature. If greater care is taken not to walk on floor surfaces during excavation, floors should produce more reliable results, assuming that those floors that produced an α_{95} value of 10.0° or greater were distorted during excavation.

If at all possible, features to be sampled should not be excavated until immediately prior to sampling. Moisture is thus preserved, making them easier to cut. Also, the integrity and stability of the features are better preserved. If they must be excavated more than a day or two before sampling, features should be immediately refilled or reburied with damp soil and well covered with plastic and soil to prevent the drying out, cracking, and shifting of parts of the feature.

In general, it appears that the features that were fired the hottest (hornos, walls, and crematories) produce the best results, although the data may be slightly misleading due to the relatively small number of features sampled in two of the categories. These data also discredit the notion that a feature must have plaster to be able to be sampled and dated. Further evidence for this is found in the field forms, where there are numerous descriptions of hearths with little or no plaster.

Support was found for observations made by Hathaway (1982b), Krause (1980), and Smith (1981) of the vertical stratification of intensities of magnetization related to variable heating from top to bottom in a feature during firing. The rim or top edge of hearths seems to be preferable to the lower sides, bottom, or collar areas back from the edge.

Samples from burned soil matrix rather than true plaster can produce results as reliable as samples from features with true plaster. Usually the burned soil features are hornos and burned pits, where temperatures may have been generally higher than in the plastered firepits or hearths.

On a specimen-by-specimen basis from a single feature, samples recovered from plastered areas vary in intensity and often even in direction from samples recovered from burned soil areas. If possible, all samples from a feature should be removed from one material type. Choose samples from areas most likely to have been exposed to the greatest heat rather than those easiest to cut.

The suspended-sediment samples can produce results (the average α_{95} value is less than 7°), but clearly the results are not as reliable as samples recovered from a burned feature.

The final point for consideration is the effect of environmental factors, both prehistoric and modern. There are some unusual samples, including one probably struck by lightning (LC106). The magnetization of this sample is more than an order of magnitude stronger than any other archaeomagnetic sample analyzed by the University of Arizona laboratory. While it was radically altered, three other samples, all 5 m or less away, appear to have been unaffected (LC110, about 5 m; LC112, about 5 m; LC170, about 2.5 m).

One potential problem is the possibility of local magnetic anomalies. The features themselves may distort the magnetic field during firing and therefore affect the direction of remanent magnetization in the samples (see Tarling 1971). Pebbles and rocks in the plaster matrix, especially those of volcanic origin, may also affect the specimens' magnetization. These may, of course, have affected the features prehistorically. Historically, lightning strikes may severely distort the local field and alter the magnetization of a feature. Vehicles, wheelbarrows, shovels, and metal toolboxes may have affected the compass by being too close during sampling. Factors such as ground subsidence—and in some settings, strong electromagnetic fields—may also have altered the direction of remanence of a feature.

Further care should be taken to look for potential problems in the field. Comparative orientation measurements using sun compass readings are a simple means of controlling for some of these. It may be necessary to cut open sample cubes to conduct a better analysis of the soil, clay, and mineral content of particular samples.

CONCLUSION

The authors have learned much about field sampling by also conducting the laboratory work. Differences in sample intensity can be matched directly to the field observation of differences in soil coloration and composition. Also apparent in the laboratory analyses is the range of variability in direction and intensity produced by sampling various portions of a feature. We do not believe, however, that personal experience in the lab is a necessary prerequisite to getting good results.

We do suggest that training for samplers be sought from archaeologists or specialists aware of all the aspects of archaeomagnetic dating. Such training alone does not guarantee good results, of course. Experience and, because of the extremely labor-intensive nature of sampling, a patient, compulsive, perfectionist mentality are also essential. An awareness of the requirements of archaeomagnetic dating greatly assists specialists or well-trained field samplers in getting the best results.

Overall, two factors clearly contribute to achieving good archaeomagnetic results. The first is the proper training of samplers, with a stress on the need for careful recovery of the samples and the selection of the most appropriate materials. The second is the protection of features during and after excavation to ensure maximum integrity and stability.

The use of archaeomagnetic dating is increasing as a chronometric tool for archaeologists. Great care and more effort are required to ensure that trained personnel take the samples in accordance with current standards. It is also essential to bring about a better understanding among archaeologists of the process, capabilities, and limitations of archaeomagnetic dating. Perhaps most critical is the need to gain greater technical knowledge of the beast we are studying. Experiments such as those by Hathaway (1982b), Krause (1980), and Smith (1981) concerning soil and clay content, firing temperatures of features, magnetic distortions, and techniques for extracting samples in the field are necessary and should be encouraged.

CHAPTER 4

Some Thermal Magnetic Qualities of Baked Clay

JEN HAUR YU

Since the 17th-century work of William Gilbert, we have obtained most of our information about the geomagnetic field by direct recording at magnetic observatories (Gilbert [1600] 1958). These data cover only the past 400 years. Fortunately, paleomagnetism provides the means to extend the record of the magnetic field back into remote geologic time. Permanent magnetism is a natural property of rocks. The total remanent magnetization of a specimen when it is brought into the laboratory, due to all natural sources, is called the natural remanent magnetism (NRM). The magnetic component acquired when the rock was formed is called the primary component of the NRM. Subsequent secondary components of NRM may be added by a variety of processes, including reheating, weathering (Manley 1956; Robertson and Hastie 1962), lightning (Cox 1961; Graham 1961; Matsuzaki et al. 1954), and time. The resulting secondary components may be a thermoremanent magnetization (TRM), chemical remanent magnetization (CRM), isothermal remanent magnetization (IRM), or viscous remanent magnetization (VRM). The part of the NRM of geophysical interest is the primary component, which is usually the most magnetically stable (Irving et al. 1961).

The purpose of this study is to analyze the primary and secondary components of the NRM of baked clays by using thermal demagnetization and by comparing the thermal demagnetization of NRM with the thermal demagnetization of a laboratory-induced TRM (Thellier 1938; Thellier and Thellier 1959b; Wilson 1961). Thermal demagnetization, like alternating-field (AF) demagnetization, is a type of magnetic cleaning. In thermal demagnetization, a specimen is heated in the laboratory to a temperature below the Curie temperature of the magnetic minerals and then cooled back down to room temperature. The heating-cooling cycle is carried out in a zero magnetic field. All the magnetic grains in the specimen with blocking temperatures less than or equal to the peak heating temperature are demagnetized, or magnetically randomized. Magnetization in grains with higher blocking temperatures is not affected.

The samples used here are baked clays that had been fired in ancient time at a temperature above their Curie temperature; thus the primary component of NRM of these samples is a total TRM (Folgerhaiter 1899). Effects of reheating, lightning, and magnetic anisotropy are studied by experimental application in the laboratory and by theoretical computations to establish some typical thermal demagnetization curves. By comparing these curves with the actual thermal demagnetization curves of the samples, the origin of different magnetic components contained in the NRM can be inferred. This may make it possible to identify samples containing a minimal amount of secondary remanence for use in archaeomagnetic studies.

LABORATORY EXPERIMENTS

Description of Samples

All the baked clays used in this study were associated with burned rooms or hearths collected from North, Central, and South America, and from Egypt. A total of 62 specimens from 22 samples was cut into 1.8 cm cubes.

Experimental Apparatus

Three pairs of Helmholtz coils were used to cancel out the earth's magnetic field during thermal demagnetization. Inside this field-free space, a fourth pair of Helmholtz coils was used to produce any necessary artificial magnetic field for imparting a laboratory TRM to the specimens. A nonmagnetic oven in the center of the Helmholtz coils was used to heat the specimens. Its temperature was controlled by a thermocouple to within $\pm 1°$ C of the desired temperature. During an experiment, the drift of the magnetic field within the furnace was no more than ± 25 nT. A typical heating-cooling cycle for the furnace is shown in Figure 4.1. To allow the entire volume of the specimen to reach the desired temperature, the desired heating temperature was maintained in the furnace for 30 minutes. Magnetization of the specimens was measured on a Princeton Applied Research Model 2 Spinner Magnetometer, which can measure

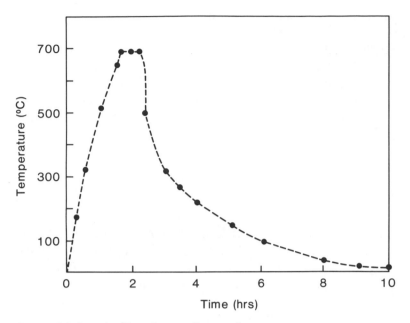

Figure 4.1. A typical heating-cooling cycle.

a magnetic moment as weak as 0.01 Am^2. A magnetic susceptibility bridge (the Geophysical Specialties Company Model MS-3) was used to measure magnetic susceptibility.

Thermal Demagnetization and Laboratory-Induced TRM

In Wilson's method (Wilson 1961), a specimen is heated in a zero magnetic field to a specific temperature T, then cooled to room temperature T_o. This procedure is repeated at progressively higher temperatures until the Curie temperature T_c is reached. The residual NRM (RNRM) of the specimen is measured on the spinner magnetometer at room temperature after each successive heating-cooling cycle has been completed. Then the specimen is heated above T_c and cooled in the presence of an artificial laboratory field of 50 μT to impart a total TRM, and the same thermal demagnetization process is repeated to observe residual TRM (RTRM) as a function of temperature. During thermal demagnetization, both RNRM and RTRM decrease as a function of temperature.

In the Thelliers' method (Thellier and Thellier 1959a), the specimen is heated to temperature T and cooled to room temperature T_o

in a lab field of 50 μT. The remanent magnetism $J(T)$ measured at T_o is thus the vector sum of $RNRM(T)$ and $PTRM(T)$, the partial TRM (PTRM) acquired by the specimen while cooling from T to T_o in the artificial field. The same heating treatment is applied again after rotating the specimen 180° relative to the applied field. After this heating-cooling cycle, the measured magnetization is $J'(T)$. After the double heating, the RNRM and the PTRM can easily be calculated from the measured values of $J(T)$ and $J'(T)$ as

$$\overline{RNRM}(T) = \tfrac{1}{2}[\overline{J}(T) + \overline{J}'(T)]$$

$$\overline{PTRM}(T) = \tfrac{1}{2}[\overline{J}(T) - \overline{J}'(T)]$$

where the bars over the variables indicate that they are vectors, and vector addition must be used. The same procedure is then repeated by raising the temperature T stepwise at increments of 50° C until the temperature is above the T_c of the specimen (about 700° C). Whereas RNRM decreases as a function of temperature, PTRM increases with temperature because it involves a thermal remagnetization of the specimen.

Reheating Effects and Secondary PTRM

Theoretical calculations as well as experimental tests were made to consider the effects that reheating would have on the magnetization of specimens. The theoretical calculations assumed that the specimen had originally acquired a total TRM after heating above the Curie temperature, followed at some later time by the acquisition of a PTRM during a reheating event to a temperature T below the Curie temperature in a field F_r. The angle between the directions of the original NRM (J_o) of the specimen and the field F_r is α. Then the vector magnetization after reheating is

$$\overline{J}_n(T) = \overline{RNRM}(T) + \overline{PTRM}(T),$$

where $J_n(T)$ is the remanent magnetization after reheating to T; $RNRM(T)$ is the remaining NRM after reheating from T_o to T; and $PTRM(T)$ is the PTRM acquired during cooling from T to T_o in field F_r. Once again, the bars indicate vectors. Using the law of cosines, the magnitude of $\overline{J}_n$ will then be

$$\overline{J}_n(T) = [\overline{RNRM}(T)^2 + \overline{PTRM}(T)^2 - 2 \times \overline{RNRM}(T) \times \overline{PTRM}(T) \times \cos \alpha]^{\tfrac{1}{2}}.$$

During a reheating, the RNRM gradually diminishes as higher temperatures are reached. Conversely, the PTRM in the direction of the applied field increases as higher temperatures are reached. The direction of the total magnetization in the specimen gradually rotates from the NRM direction toward the direction of the applied field.

An example of what would be observed as a result of specimen reheating is illustrated in Figure 4.2. Figure 4.2a shows the RNRM- and PTRM-vs.-temperature curves for specimen 18.01, normalized by the NRM. The PTRM was acquired in a lab field of 50 μT. Also shown is the direction of the RNRM as a function of temperature, which demonstrates that the direction remained stable until the Curie temperature of magnetite (580° C) was approached, even as the strength of the RNRM decreased. Figure 4.2b is a cross-plot of the RNRM- and PTRM-vs.-temperature curves for the Thelliers' method. Each point on this curve represents the results for a particular heating step in the laboratory thermal demagnetization (of RNRM) and remagnetization (of PTRM) experiments. Although not the emphasis of this paper, it should be noted that the magnitude of the slope of this curve multiplied by the value of the lab field gives the paleointensity of the earth's magnetic field at the time the original NRM (assuming it was a total TRM) was acquired (Thellier and Thellier 1959a, 1959b). Wilson's method produces a similar curve for paleointensity analysis except that the slope is positive.

Using these experimental data and the equations above, one can calculate what would result from a natural reheating and PTRM acquisition for this specimen. Figure 4.2c shows the normalized RNRM curves as a function of temperature that would be observed for this specimen if a secondary PTRM had been superimposed on a primary total TRM. The reheating is assumed to have been to a temperature of 350° C, and various angles between the NRM and PTRM are indicated by the different curves, which merge at the reheating temperature of 350° C. A thermal demagnetization curve that looked like one of these would thus be suggestive of the presence of a secondary PTRM, with a reheating temperature of 350° C. This inference might also be made from the changing direction of magnetization up to 350° C, after which the direction would remain stable and parallel to the primary TRM. Figure 4.2d shows what would be expected if the RNRM decay were cross-plotted against the acquisition of a laboratory PTRM, using the Thelliers' method. (Note that this lab

PTRM is distinct from the secondary component of NRM, which is a naturally induced PTRM.) Again, the form of the curve is indicative of a secondary PTRM as a component of the NRM, due to a reheating to 350° C, at a particular orientation relative to the NRM. These results assume that the primary TRM and secondary PTRM were both acquired in the presence of an ambient field strength of 50 μT. If the reheating occurred decades or centuries after the original TRM was acquired, substantial changes in the strength of the geomagnetic field would be another variable in the problem.

Figure 4.3 shows experimental RNRM-PTRM results using the Thelliers' method for a specimen that had received (in the laboratory) a primary total TRM and secondary PTRM. These results and others agree well with the model predictions (Fig. 4.2d). This suggests that the theoretical calculations are generally valid and can be used to make inferences regarding secondary magnetization due to reheating.

Lightning Effects and Secondary IRM

The outer few feet of a rock surface can be strongly and irregularly magnetized due to lightning strikes (Graham 1961; Hallimond and Herroun 1933). Roquet (1954) studied the stability of IRM by applying thermal demagnetization and showed the thermal demagnetization curves for both TRM and IRM imparted in the lab to a dispersed magnetite powder (Fig. 4.4). The IRM is less stable than the TRM, particularly the TRM in weak fields (42 μT) equivalent to that of the earth's field. Kobayashi (1959) reached a similar conclusion.

For a lightning-struck specimen, the resultant magnetism, $M(T)$, after thermal demagnetization to temperature T is

$$\overline{M}(T) = \overline{RNRM}(T) + \overline{IRM}(T),$$

Figure 4.2. Illustrations of specimen heating (specimen 18.01): (A) the RNRM- and PTRM-vs.-temperature curves, normalized by the NRM (the solid dots are for the RNRM, and the open dots are for the RTRM); (B) a cross-plot of the RNRM- and PTRM-vs.-temperature curves for the Thelliers' method; (C) the normalized RNRM curves as a function of temperature that would be observed for this specimen if a secondary PTRM ($T = 350°$ C) had been superimposed on a primary total TRM (the angle between the TRM and PTRM is the parameter); (D) the results that would be expected if the RNRM decay of (C) were cross-plotted against the acquisition of a lab PTRM.

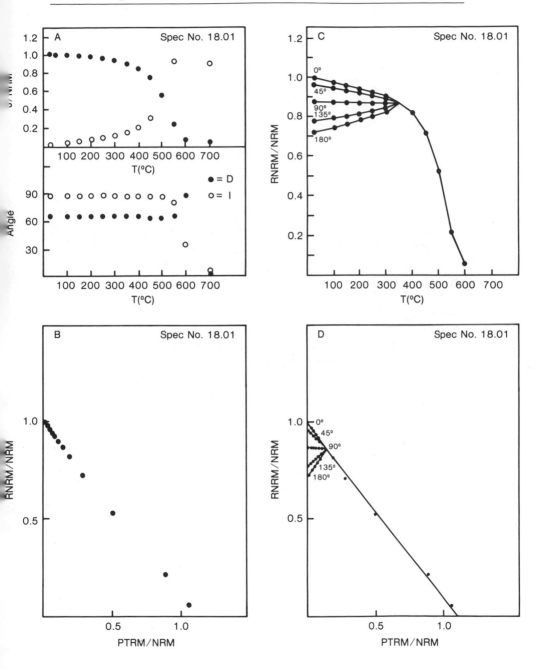

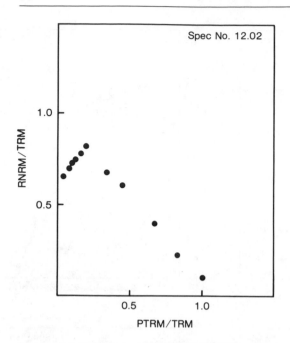

Figure 4.3. Experimental RNRM-PTRM results using the Thelliers' method for a specimen that had received (in the laboratory) a primary total TRM and a secondary PTRM. The PTRM was acquired by heating to 350° C and applied at an angle of 180° to the TRM.

where $RNRM(T)$ is that part of the primary TRM remaining after thermal demagnetization to temperature T, and $IRM(T)$ is that part of the IRM remaining after being thermally demagnetized to T. In my theoretical calculation, the RNRM-vs.-temperature and PTRM-vs.-temperature curves (Fig. 4.2a) of specimen 18.01 are used as a basis. Then the demagnetization curve of the IRM produced in an 88 mT field (Fig. 4.4) is superimposed on that of specimen 18.01, assuming that the intensity of IRM is that of the NRM. The results of the theoretical RNRM-vs.-temperature curves are shown in Figure 4.5a for various angles between the NRM and IRM directions. When the angle is less than 90°, the thermal demagnetization curves are characterized by a rapid drop-off at the lower temperatures due to the easily demagnetized IRM. When the angle is more than 90° (i.e., the TRM and IRM are in opposite directions), the magnetization first increases as the IRM is preferentially demagnetized and then decreases as the TRM is demagnetized. Note that the thermal demagnetization curve of a lightning-produced IRM is generally smoother than that for a secondary PTRM.

Figure 4.5b shows the RNRM-PTRM curve for the lightning effect when the angle between the TRM and IRM is 45°, plotted according to the Thelliers' method. For Wilson's method, the RNRM-PTRM curves would have a similarly anomalous shape.

In conclusion, the lightning effect does change the normal demagnetization curves, and it biases the results for paleomagnetic usage. Thermal demagnetization can be used to discern the presence of a lightning-induced IRM.

Magnetic Susceptibility and Monitoring of Thermochemical Reactions

Magnetic susceptibility is a measure of the tendency of a material to be magnetized by an external magnetic field. Susceptibility refers to induced magnetization, which, unlike remanent magnetization, disappears when the external field is removed. The magnetic suscep-

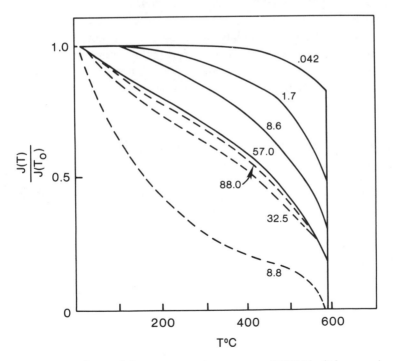

Figure 4.4. Thermal demagnetization curves of TRM (solid curves) and IRM (dashed curves) produced in various fields (values given in mT).

tibility bridge was used to measure the susceptibilities of 16 specimens in three orthogonal directions before and after every heating-
cooling step. This instrument neither measures nor is affected by
remanent magnetization. If the magnetic mineralogy of specimens
changes chemically during the heating treatment, the susceptibilities change correspondingly. Hence, variation of susceptibility during the heating process hints at the occurrence of chemical reaction.
For the 16 specimens, the median change in the magnitude of magnetic susceptibility between room temperature and 600° C was 6.1%,
with the largest change being 28%.

Anisotropy is another important rock magnetic property (King and
Rees 1962; Stone 1963). The degree of anisotropy can be expressed as
the ratio of the maximum to minimum susceptibilities along the
three axes. The TRM acquired by an anisotropic rock is expected to
be deflected toward the direction of easy magnetization (maximum
susceptibility). Uyeda et al. (1963) found that the amount of deflection is directly related to the anisotropy, and if the anisotropy is
more than 5%, the deflection becomes significant and cannot be neglected. Because the primary magnetism of baked clays usually is a
TRM, it is important to consider the anisotropy effect. For the 16
specimens measured, the median anisotropy of magnetic susceptibility was 17%, with a maximum value of 80%. These results suggest
that anisotropy is a factor that should be considered in archaeomagnetic investigations.

THERMAL DEMAGNETIZATION CHARACTERISTICS
OF ARCHAEOMAGNETIC SPECIMENS

We have seen that several parameters can be used to test the nature of
the NRM and to identify the presence of secondary magnetization.
The most important parameters are susceptibility, the direction of
magnetization, and the shape of thermal demagnetization curves.
The specimen studies show that after the heating process is complete, all the specimens can be divided into six groups (see Fig. 4.6):

Figure 4.5. Lightning effects and secondary TRM: (A) the theoretical
RNRM-temperature curve of lightning effect (the parameter is the angle
between the TRM and the lightning-induced IRM); (B) a theoretical
RNRM-PTRM curve for an angle of 45° between the TRM and IRM (the
straight line is the normal curve).

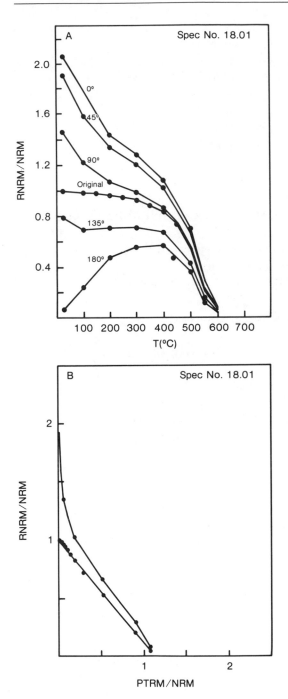

Group 1 specimens
  Constant susceptibility and direction
  Smooth RNRM-temperature curve
  Linear RNRM-RTRM or RNRM-PTRM curve
Group 2 specimens
  Varied susceptibility, constant direction
  Smooth RNRM-temperature curve
  Concave downward RNRM-RTRM or RNRM-PTRM curve
Group 3 specimens
  Varied direction, constant susceptibility
  Smooth RNRM-temperature curve
  Concave downward RNRM-RTRM or RNRM-PTRM curve
Group 4 specimens
  Varied direction, unmeasurable susceptibility
  Irregular RNRM-temperature curve
  Irregular RNRM-RTRM or RNRM-PTRM curve
Group 5 specimens
  Varied direction, constant susceptibility
  Bent RNRM-temperature curve
  Two straight lines in RNRM-RTRM or RNRM-PTRM curve
Group 6 specimens
  Varied direction, constant susceptibility
  Smooth RNRM-temperature curve
  Smooth upward RNRM-RTRM or RNRM-PTRM curves with a
    rapid drop-off at the beginning of the heating process

DISCUSSION

Group 1 represents an ideal case for paleomagnetic study. RNRM-vs.-temperature curves of NRM and laboratory-induced TRM have a similar shape; this means that the primary magnetization is a TRM. Also suggestive of the lack of secondary components are the constant susceptibility and direction, smooth RNRM-vs.-temperature curves, and linear RNRM-RTRM or RNRM-PTRM curves. Specimens from Groups 2 and 3 exhibited chemical reactions during the

Figure 4.6 (pages 93–98, following). Thermal demagnetization characteristics of specimens from Groups 1 through 6: (A) the RNRM-temperature curve; (B) a comparison of RNRM- and RTRM-vs.-temperature.

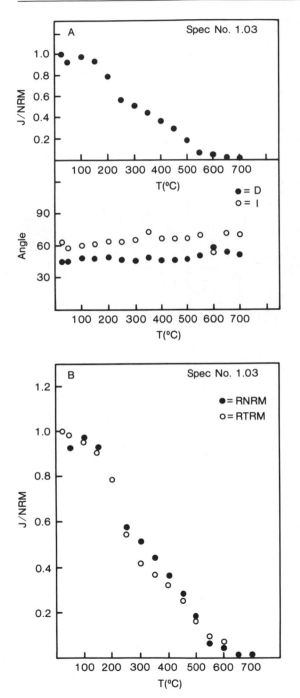

Group 1

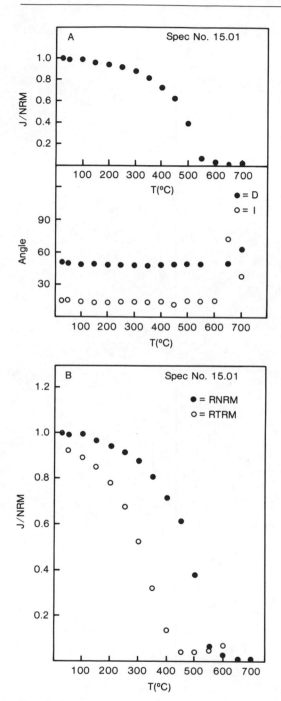

Group 2

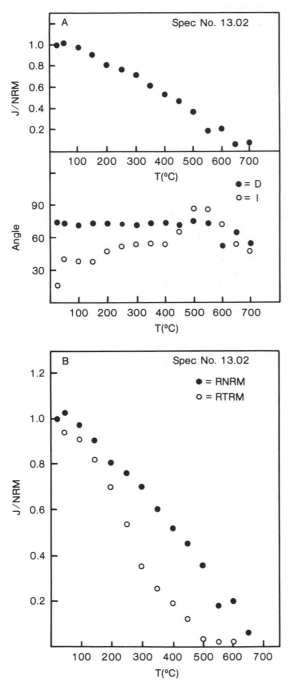

Group 3

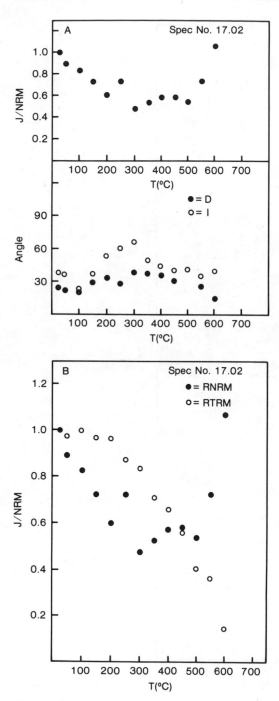

Group 4

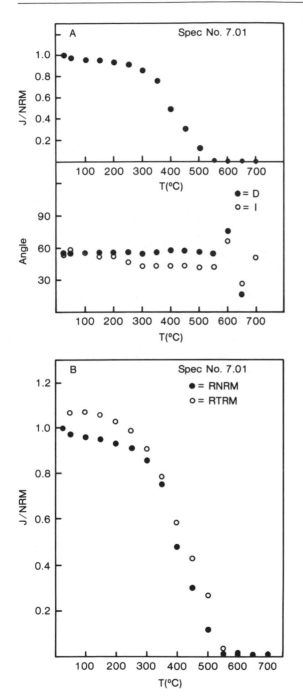

Group 5

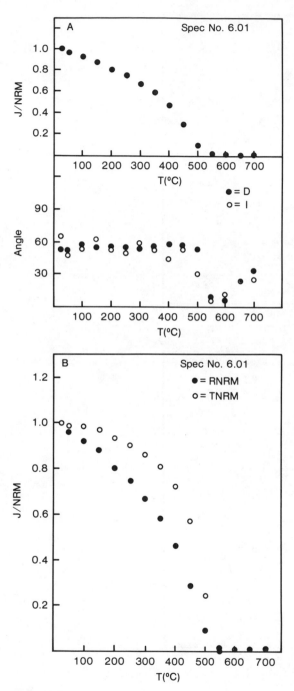

Group 6

heating process in the laboratory. Chemical reaction may only cause a change of the magnitude of magnetization, in which case it can be easily detected by the change of susceptibility (for instance, Group 2). If chemical reaction alters the direction of magnetization, this is shown by the change of direction (Group 3). For Groups 2 and 3, the demagnetization curve of laboratory-induced TRM is below that of NRM, so this chemical reaction probably is a process of oxidation of magnetite to hematite, the latter having a weaker magnetization. Their RNRM-RTRM or RNRM-PTRM curves, which exhibit a concave downward shape, could also be used as an indicator of chemical reaction.

Group 4 specimens are more complicated. Because the susceptibility is too small to be measured by the susceptibility bridge, two interpretations are possible for this group. First, if susceptibility does change during the heating process, this group could be interpreted as having undergone chemical reaction during the heating treatment. On the other hand, if susceptibility does not change, the behavior may be due to the imposition of VRM. The RNRM-vs.-temperature curve shows two temperature intervals in which magnetization increases: one from 300° to 450° C, the other from 500 to 600° C (the point at 250° C is judged to be spurious). These two changes may be due to the removal of secondary components, which probably resulted from VRM due to storage in the laboratory or *in situ* exposure to the present magnetic field. The magnitude of the NRM for this group is small compared to the others, which decreases the reliability of results. The low NRMs correlate with the low susceptibilities.

Group 5 (in this case, specimen 7.01) shows its direction change until 300° C. The RNRM-vs.-temperature curve bends at 300° C, and the degree of bending implies that the specimen had been reheated at an angle of 90°. The intersection of two straight lines in the plot of RNRM-RTRM also confirms the reheating effect and the reheating temperature of about 300° C. All the specimens in this group were probably refired to a certain temperature below their Curie temperature and at a different angle than the primary TRM.

Group 6 specimens show the change of direction through the whole heating process, but the shape of the RNRM-vs.-temperature curve is still smooth. The RNRM-vs.-temperature curve of the laboratory-induced TRM is above that of the NRM, which is the opposite of Groups 2 and 3. Therefore, this abnormal shape is not caused by chemical reaction. The RNRM-RTRM curve presents a concave upward shape and has a rapid drop-off at the beginning of the heating process; these phenomena are characteristic of IRM and suggest that the specimen was probably struck by lightning.

This classification scheme for archaeomagnetic specimens provides a framework for the selection of useful specimens for archaeomagnetic direction and paleointensity studies. Thermal demagnetization can identify the various secondary effects but is especially effective in removing secondary components resulting from reheating. Among these six groups, Group 1 would be the most useful for paleomagnetic study.

CONCLUSION AND APPLICATION

The aim of thermal demagnetization is selective demagnetization, first of those components with low blocking temperatures and then of components with higher values, in order to investigate the blocking temperature range in which the useful magnetic components reside (Irving 1964). Although all model experiments were carried out on a short time scale and in an imperfect imitation of natural conditions, they provide a general framework of ideas within which the identification of the secondary components of magnetization can proceed, and they allow an appropriate demagnetization treatment (thermal or alternating-field) to be suggested.

The minimum criteria for selecting useful specimens and enhancing the prospect of reliable results are as follows:

(1) When collecting samples, determine whether they are weathered or unweathered, judging by color, hardness, or other evidence of oxidation or hydration, and only collect unweathered samples. This helps to minimize both VRM and CRM.

(2) In the laboratory, measure the susceptibility of specimens and choose only isotropic specimens. Anisotropic specimens are not useful for studying the direction of the ancient field, because the magnetization would be deflected toward the easy magnetization direction.

(3) By conducting thermal demagnetization and observing the changes of susceptibility, direction, and the shape of thermal demagnetization curves, the secondary effects—such as chemical reaction, reheating, and lightning—can be identified. Then the most useful specimens, which have a primary TRM and have not been disturbed by secondary effects, can be selected for paleomagnetic studies.

Following the above criteria would improve the reliability of pale-omagnetic data and would also allow the identification of secondary effects. In addition, the RNRM-vs.-temperature curve can supply some interesting physical information about mineral constituents as identified by their Curie temperatures. In this study, most specimens contain only one magnetic mineral, which is either magnetite ($T_c = 578°$ C) or hematite ($T_c = 675°$ C). Some specimens contain two magnetic minerals that show up on the thermal demagnetization curves such as for specimen 1.03 (Fig. 4.6, Group 1). The spectrum of blocking temperatures is also related to grain size (DuBois 1962). Finally, the firing temperature of baked clays may also be estimated from thermal demagnetization data (Aramaki and Akimoto 1957). Thus archaeomagnetic specimens provide us with information not only on secular variation but also on certain aspects of prehistoric technology.

ACKNOWLEDGMENTS

The author is especially grateful to Dr. Robert L. DuBois for directing this work. His help, advice, and suggestions were invaluable in the completion of the research. The author would also like to express his gratitude to Dr. Jim Lawson and Dr. John S. Wickham for their comments, and to Dr. Charles W. Harper for his suggestions during the study. The project was supported by the Archaeomagnetic Laboratory and the School of Geology and Geophysics at the University of Oklahoma. The author is grateful to Roberta Rambin for her typing and editing and to all personnel drafting the figures, particularly Jeanette Blubaugh.

CHAPTER 5

A Permutation Procedure
for Comparing Archaeomagnetic
Polar Directions

PAUL W. MIELKE, JR., KENNETH J. BERRY,
AND JEFFREY L. EIGHMY

In archaeomagnetic research it is often necessary to draw two or more samples of specimens from their respective archaeological features (such as *in situ* walls, floors, kilns, ovens, and hearths) and to test to determine if the magnetic directions of the features are identical. For example, archaeomagnetists often need to know if similar archaeomagnetic dates (i.e., polar directions) were produced by the same thermal event. In addition, as the volume of archaeomagnetic work increases, it is important to know whether directional differences obtained from instruments of different laboratories and/or types are comparable. The problem in all its manifestations arises because (1) archaeological materials imperfectly record and preserve magnetic direction, (2) magnetometers are unable to measure remanent magnetism perfectly, and (3) usually it is not possible to measure the entire archaeological feature of interest. Repeated measurements on large sample sets reduce the uncertainty in estimating an ancient direction, but when two or more samples produce different magnetic directions, the question remains as to whether the sample differences in estimated magnetic directions are due merely to sampling and measurement error or instead reflect actual differences among the archaeological features from which the samples were drawn.

The F-test, first proposed by Watson (1956), is widely used in archaeomagnetic research to address the problem by testing the hypothesis that two or more archaeological features possess identical magnetic directions. Unfortunately, the F-test is limited in its applicability by a number of requirements that are often difficult to satisfy (see Engebretson and Beck 1978; Larochelle 1967a, 1967b; Onstott 1980; Watson 1956; Watson and Irving 1957; Watson and Williams 1956). In particular, the F-test requires (1) that both populations possess equal precision parameters (i.e., homogeneity of variance) and (2) that the directions of magnetism follow a normal probability density function on a sphere (Fisher 1953). In addition, the F-test utilizes a squared-distance measure that may give disproportionate importance to outliers. Because of these requirements, application of the F-test should be limited to situations in which the requisite conditions can be satisfied. Note that, for example, such uncontrollable variables as variation in grain size, variation in magnetic mineralogy, and instrument noise—all of which are common in archaeomagnetic research—may cause unequal variances in samples that are of comparative interest.

Presented here is a rigorous permutation procedure for evaluating directional differences among two or more archaeological features. This permutation procedure requires neither equal variances nor normality, and it permits analyses of two or more samples that may be of equal or unequal size.

THE PERMUTATION PROCEDURE

Watson's (1956) approach to comparing magnetic directions is to compare the sample mean directions statistically. If the assumptions are satisfied (e.g., equal variances and normality), then large mean sample differences imply directional differences among two or more features. In contrast, the permutation procedure is based on the within-sample average of the arc distances between surface points on a sphere, where a surface point is merely the location at which a direction of magnetism intersects the earth's surface and is calculated from the remanent magnetism of a single specimen from an archaeological feature. In archaeomagnetic applications the surface points are described by the latitude and longitude of virtual geomagnetic polar locations. Although the permutation method can compare sample directions (i.e., declination and inclination) as easily and accurately as surface points (Mielke 1984, 1986; Mielke and Berry 1982), in this application sample directions are converted to virtual geomagnetic polar locations because this is the most common method among archaeologists for comparing archaeomagnetic samples.

Let $\Omega = \{\omega_1, \ldots, \omega_N\}$ designate a finite population of N specimens. In the case of archaeomagnetic research, surface points are determined for each specimen from the directions of magnetism (see Irving

1964:43–44). Let the latitude (λ_s) and longitude (ϕ_s) of the collection site be known, and let the declination (D_i) relative to the meridian of the site (ϕ_s) and the inclination (I_i) of a specimen (ω_i) be determined $(i = 1, \ldots, N)$. Then the latitude (λ_i) and longitude (ϕ_i) for the surface point associated with specimen ω_i $(i = 1, \ldots, N)$ are given by

$$\lambda_i = \sin^{-1}[\sin(\lambda_s) \cos(\psi_i) + \cos(\lambda_s) \sin(\psi_i) \cos(D_i)]$$
$$(-90° \leq \lambda_i \leq +90°) \text{ and}$$
$$\phi_i = \phi_s + \sin^{-1}[\cos(\psi_i) \sin(D_i)/\cos(\lambda_i)]$$
$$(0° \leq \phi_i \leq 360°) \text{ when } \cos(\psi_i) \geq \sin(\lambda_s) \sin(\lambda_i), \text{ or}$$
$$\phi_i = \phi_s + 180° - \sin^{-1}[\cos(\psi_i) \sin(D_i)/\cos(\lambda_i)]$$
$$(0° \leq \phi_i \leq 360°) \text{ when } \cos(\psi_i) < \sin(\lambda_s) \sin(\lambda_i),$$

and where the colatitude, ψ_i, is given by

$$\psi_i = \cot^{-1}[\tfrac{1}{2}\tan(I_i)]$$
$$(0° \leq \psi_i \leq 180°).$$

The Cartesian coordinates (x_i, y_i, z_i) for the surface associated with specimen ω_i $(i = 1, \ldots, N)$ are obtained from

$$x_i = \rho \cos(\lambda_i) \cos(\phi_i),$$
$$y_i = \rho \cos(\lambda_i) \sin(\phi_i),$$

and

$$z_i = \rho \sin(\lambda_i),$$

where ρ is the radius of the sphere and is given by

$$\rho = (x^2 + y^2 + z^2)^{\frac{1}{2}}.$$

Let $S_1, \ldots, S_g$ represent an exhaustive partitioning of the N specimens comprising Ω into g disjoint samples, let n_i be the number of specimens in the ith sample, and let $\Delta_{j,k}$ be the arc distance between the surface points associated with specimens ω_j and ω_k, i.e.,

$$\Delta_{j,k} = \rho\gamma_{j,k},$$

where $\gamma_{j,k}$, the angle in radians between the surface points associated with specimens ω_j and ω_k, is given by

$$\gamma_{j,k} = \cos^{-1}[(x_j x_k + y_j y_k + z_j z_k)/\rho^2].$$

The test statistic of interest, δ, is then defined as

$$\delta = \sum_{i=1}^{g} \frac{n_i}{N} \zeta_i,$$

where

$$\zeta_i = [\sum_{j<k} \Delta_{j,k} G_i(\omega_j) G_i(\omega_k)] / \binom{n_i}{2}$$

is the average of the arc distances between the surface points associated with the ith sample $(i = 1, \ldots, g)$, $\sum\limits_{j<k}$ is the sum over all j and k such that $1 \le j < k \le N$, and

$$G_i(\omega_j) = \begin{cases} 1, \text{ if } \omega_j \in S_i, \\ 0, \text{ otherwise.} \end{cases}$$

Thus defined, δ is the weighted within-sample average of the arc distances between corresponding surface points on a sphere where the weight (n_i/N) is the proportional contribution of the number of specimens in the ith sample. Utilizing δ, consider H_0: the *a priori* samples $S_1, \ldots, S_g$ correspond to a random distribution of the surface points $\omega_1, \ldots, \omega_N$ to the g samples, with fixed size structure $n_1, \ldots, n_g$, versus H_1: the distribution is not random. If H_0 is rejected, there is evidence of a meaningful difference in surface-point locations among the g samples. The one-sided lower-tailed probability value p corresponding to a realized value of δ,

$$p = P\{\delta \le \text{realized value of } \delta | H_0\},$$

provides a measure of the effectiveness of the *a priori* classification of specimens to samples. Next to be considered are the procedures to obtain values of p for a realized data set.

Under H_0, the underlying permutation distribution of δ dictates that each of the

$$M = N! / \prod_{i=1}^{g} n_i!$$

possible allocation combinations of the N specimens to the g samples with fixed size structure will occur with equal probability. The mean, variance, and skewness of δ under H_0 are respectively designated by μ_δ, σ_δ^2, and γ_δ. If δ_j signifies the jth value among the M possible values of δ, then

$$\mu_\delta = \frac{1}{M} \sum_{j=1}^{M} \delta_j,$$

$$\sigma_\delta^2 = \frac{1}{M} \sum_{j=1}^{M} \delta_j^2 - \mu_\delta^2,$$

and

$$\gamma_\delta = (\frac{1}{M} \sum_{j=1}^{M} \delta_j^3 - 3\mu_\delta\sigma_\delta^2 - \mu_\delta^3)/\sigma_\delta^3.$$

Computational techniques to obtain μ_δ, σ_δ^2, and γ_δ for a realized set of data are described elsewhere (Mielke 1984; Mielke et al. 1976, 1981). Incidentally, the results of this permutation procedure do not depend on ρ, and it is therefore convenient to deal with a unit sphere (i.e., $\rho = 1$).

Because the calculation of p based on obtaining all M possible values of δ is not computationally feasible even with fairly small samples, an approximation of the permutation distribution of δ under H_0 is required. The standardized test statistic given by

$$T = (\delta - \mu_\delta)/\sigma_\delta$$

is approximately distributed as the Pearson type III distribution (Mielke 1984; Mielke et al. 1981). In particular, the Pearson approximation compensates for the fact that the permutation distribution of δ under H_0 is often skewed in the negative direction (i.e., $\gamma_\delta < 0$).

APPLICATION

In archaeomagnetic/paleomagnetic research, it is often necessary to draw two or more samples of specimens from their respective archaeological/geological features and test to determine whether the magnetic directions of the samples are from a common population of directions. To demonstrate the utility of the permutation procedure for evaluating directional differences, consider the following application drawn from archaeomagnetic research.

Archaeomagnetic collection involves removing 0.5-inch cubes of burned archaeological features (encased in one-cubic-inch plaster molds) to a laboratory for measurement of remanent magnetization.

The orientation of each specimen is determined *in situ* before removal. Archaeomagnetists are interested in knowing whether the normal orienting technique using a magnetic compass is accurate. It is possible that local magnetic anomalies may influence the accuracy and/or precision with which a magnetic compass will record a specimen's orientation.

A sun compass orients a specimen independently of local magnetic fields, but a sun compass that is usable in the field is inoperable on cloudy days or in shady locations, and the definition of the shadow cast by a sun compass prohibits the determination of directions finer than 0.5° of arc. Therefore, a test was devised to see whether the two collecting instruments produce identical results for independent samples drawn from a small, isolated hearth. In this application, the entire rim of an experimentally fired hearth yielded a total of 20 specimens. The latitude and longitude of the hearth were $\lambda_s = 40.03°$ N latitude and $\phi_s = 251.24°$ E longitude. Unrestricted randomization by a coin toss determined whether each specimen's orientation was measured by the sun compass or the magnetic compass. Eight (n_1) specimens were measured with the magnetic compass (S_1) and 12 (n_2) specimens were measured with the sun compass (S_2). The directions of all 20 specimens were measured on a spinner magnetometer after magnetic cleaning at 15.0 mT. Values for I, D, x, y, and z for each specimen from the sun compass and magnetic compass samples are presented in Table 5.1. The permutation procedure yields a test statistic $T = -1.7863$ and associated probability value based on the Pearson type III distribution of $p = 0.0611$. This value suggests the possibility that the two instruments are not providing the same results and indicates that additional tests of the accuracy and precision of the two types of collecting instruments should be considered.

SUMMARY

The permutation procedure described above is free from the limiting assumptions of homogeneity of variance and normality that other tests require. The above example compares samples collected with two different instruments: a magnetic compass and a sun compass. The permutation procedure can be used, however, in various applications. The F-test (Watson 1956) may be dramatically affected by the kinds of variance differences and/or departures from normality encountered on a routine basis, and its uncritical adoption is associated with serious hazards (e.g., incorrect p values, which may lead to faulty conclusions [Mielke 1986]). The proposed permutation procedure is not hindered by the limiting requirements associated with the F-test and yields appropriate results for drawing subsequent conclusions.

Table 5.1. Spinner Results and Coordinates for Magnetic Compass and Sun Compass Samples from an Experimental Hearth after Demagnetization at 15.0 mT

	I	D	x	y	z
Magnetic compass					
1	63.892534	353.823818	−0.103226	−0.069757	0.992209
2	68.539084	358.322075	−0.082925	−0.187875	0.978686
7	65.824629	6.620646	0.026960	−0.160119	0.986729
10	39.311705	358.559969	0.076044	0.296205	0.952092
11	64.479298	351.039389	−0.138844	−0.074336	0.987520
12	59.250287	344.550616	−0.198901	0.048493	0.978819
15	68.932574	343.522396	−0.237928	−0.162247	0.957636
19	63.976796	356.161276	−0.076284	−0.079166	0.993938
Sun compass					
3	59.814995	4.425123	0.051272	−0.030976	0.998204
4	58.675287	3.736358	0.050845	−0.006866	0.998683
5	59.278579	349.759477	−0.131591	0.035557	0.990666
6	63.606032	2.779853	0.003118	−0.097052	0.995274
8	67.726197	353.333329	−0.129960	−0.153875	0.979507
9	66.554675	343.988973	−0.226876	−0.106020	0.968136
13	57.522915	12.484115	0.167661	−0.034946	0.985225
14	66.250308	7.751968	0.034913	−0.174285	0.984076
16	60.509894	6.636072	0.072802	−0.054861	0.995836
17	56.107320	5.126743	0.086118	0.030657	0.995813
18	64.849730	7.774427	0.048456	−0.145260	0.988206
20	62.873623	13.110091	0.125879	−0.134123	0.982937

Techniques for Constructing Secular Variation Curves and for Interpreting Archaeomagnetic Dates

ROBERT S. STERNBERG

AND RANDALL H. MCGUIRE

Archaeomagnetic dating involves the comparison of an archaeomagnetic direction determined from one or more features with a secular variation record of the archaeomagnetic field. Although this sounds straightforward, two problems that we will address here have received insufficient attention in the archaeomagnetic literature. First, given a data base of independently dated archaeomagnetic results, how should the secular variation curve be constructed? Second, once this record is available, how should the archaeomagnetic date be interpreted? We will discuss techniques used by other investigators and by ourselves. Our own procedures have evolved toward (1) a technique for curve fitting that considers the errors inherent in archaeomagnetic data; (2) a resulting secular variation curve with mean directions and associated confidence intervals for the curve; (3) a dating technique that accounts for uncertainties in both the curve and the feature to be dated; and (4) methods that are quantitative and replicable.

SOURCES OF ERROR IN ARCHAEOMAGNETIC DATA

As elaborated upon by other papers in this volume, an archaeomagnetic datum consists of a measure of the direction of the earth's magnetic field recorded by a feature at the time it was fired. This direction can be represented by a unit vector commonly specified by two parameters: declination (D) and inclination (I). In archaeomagnetic studies, this direction is often transformed to an equivalent virtual geomagnetic pole (VGP), which is also a unit vector, specified by pole latitude and longitude. It should be emphasized that although the magnetic direction or VGP can be specified by two scalar quantities, the fundamental quantity of interest is a vector and ideally should be treated as such when analyzing the data.

In general, we are concerned with systematic errors, which affect the accuracy of the mean archaeomagnetic direction, and random errors, which affect the precision. The mean archaeomagnetic direction for a particular feature is determined by averaging the directions from the eight or so specimens collected, using Fisher (1953) statistics. One measure of the dispersion of these directions is the α_{95} angle, which corresponds to the 95% cone of confidence (two standard errors) about the mean direction.

The dispersion of directions can be handled in two ways. First, individual archaeomagnetic directions (for individual specimens) can be transformed to VGPs, and Fisher statistics can be applied directly to these poles. The resulting cone of confidence is denoted by its A95 value. Second, the mean direction can be calculated from the specimen directions and then transformed to an equivalent pole. In this case, the circle of confidence about the mean direction is mapped into an oval of confidence about the mean pole. Strictly speaking, whether Fisher statistics should be applied to directions or poles depends upon which variable follows the Fisherian distribution. In both archaeomagnetism and paleomagnetism, Fisher statistics have more often been applied to specimen directions before transformation to the pole.

Other papers in this volume address the issue of the accuracy and precision of the archaeomagnetic method. This is also discussed in Wolfman (1984). Analyses of paleomagnetic accuracy and precision have been carried out for recent Hawaiian lava flows by Doell and Cox (1963) and Holcomb et al. (1986). Although igneous rocks have somewhat different magnetic characteristics from archaeomagnetic features, other points in these paleomagnetic discussions closely parallel issues of concern in archaeomagnetism. Here we will qualitatively review some of the aspects of archaeomagnetic data that affect their accuracy and precision as recorders of the magnetic field direction.

The secular variation curve we want to construct will be used as a master record upon which to base subsequent archaeomagnetic dates. This curve will contain noise (imprecision) from four sources: (1) dispersion of specimen archaeomagnetic directions within a feature, (2) dispersion of feature mean archaeomagnetic directions, (3) the nondipole field over the geographic area covered by the curve, and (4) uncertainty in the ages corresponding to the feature directions.

The first two sources arise because hearths are not perfect recorders of the archaeomagnetic field. In a specimen acquiring TRM, there is a strong bias toward magnetizing grains in a net direction parallel to the ambient field, but a smaller random component is also acquired (Irving et al. 1961). This component is not parallel to the ambient field; consequently, neither will the direction of the total TRM vector be exactly parallel to the ambient field direction. Furthermore, moving a feature subsequent to its acquisition of remanence can affect the results. Such movement can occur due to trampling of the feature either before burial or after excavation; driving vehicles over the feature before excavation; or subsidence, which is common in the Southwest due to the withdrawal of groundwater. The cracks frequently found in hearths are suggestive of feature shifting.

Dispersion of directions also occurs because collecting and measuring samples introduce random and possibly systematic error. Errors can occur during sampling due to faulty compasses or incorrect readings as a result of anomalous magnetic fields. In the lab, the secondary components of magnetization may not be completely removed by demagnetization, and the demagnetization process itself can introduce spurious components of remanent magnetization.

It would be desirable to construct a secular variation curve for an area approximately the size of the American Southwest. This makes it more likely that a sufficient number of features covering a substantial span of time will be available to determine the curve, and it allows any local anomalies in the magnetic field or other problems specific to a site to be recognized and averaged out. The nondipole portion of the geomagnetic field, however, may still be significant on such a scale, and it will introduce from 1 to 2° of imprecision into the secular variation curve for the region (Eighmy et al. 1978; Shuey et al. 1970; Sternberg and McGuire, this volume, chap. 12). Although greater density of data may reduce the effect of the first two sources of error, a point of diminishing returns is reached that is largely due to the nondipole field.

An archaeomagnetic secular variation record is based on archaeomagnetic directions determined for features of known age. The age required for the archaeomagnetic feature corresponds to the date at which the remanent magnetization was acquired. In terms of Dean's (1978) model for archaeological dating, the remanence acquisition is the target event that we want to date for the purpose of constructing a master curve. Assuming that a hearth may be used until a room is abandoned, this target event is sometimes thought to correspond approximately to an abandonment date for the room or site. Unfortunately, remanence acquisition is rarely a reference event (i.e., a potentially datable event) that can be directly dated by some other chronometric technique. Only in the case of organic material recovered from a hearth or burned room could a tree-ring or ^{14}C date have reference events closely associated with the target event of remanence acquisition. More typically, our target event is different from the dated events at a particular site, examples of the latter being room construction as determined by a tree-ring date for a roof beam, or the manufacture of a particular type of pottery inferred by seriation and cross-dating. In these cases, bridging events connect the event actually dated to the target event of remanence acquisition. Thus uncertainty is introduced into the estimate of the date of remanence acquisition by errors in the techniques used to date the reference event and by errors in the archaeological inferences used to bridge the hiatus between the reference and target events. For example, if a site is dated by intrusive ceramics, error in the date assigned to the firing and remanence acquisition of a hearth depends on uncertainties about when that pottery type was manufactured, when it was brought to the site in question, and what the temporal association was between that event and the time that the hearth actually acquired its remanence. Thus the "independent" dates needed to construct the secular variation curve are not independent dates in the sense of Dean (1978) because they are not independent of archaeological systematics. The problem of accurately and precisely inferring the date of remanence acquisition is also a limiting factor in the reconstruction of secular variation.

In our study of southwestern secular variation (Sternberg and McGuire, this volume, chap. 12) all chronometric information supplied by project archaeologists was carefully examined before assigning a date corresponding to the desired target event of remanence acquisition. These dates were conservatively assigned; that is, we resisted the temptation to assign overly precise age ranges where they were not warranted. We also found it important to confirm dates for archaeological sites that were still being excavated or for which work had only recently been completed. Preliminary chronometric information provided at the time the archaeomagnetic samples were collected was frequently augmented or modified by subsequent work at the site.

We have treated the age ranges for our features as uniform probability distributions; the true age of firing when the feature acquired its remanence is considered to be equally likely anywhere in the range and having zero probability of being outside the interval. We believe this assumption is reasonable in view of the combination of dating techniques and archaeological arguments used to infer the dates of remanence acquisition. A Gaussian distribution for the age range would overemphasize the likelihood of the age's being near the center of the range.

CONSTRUCTING THE SECULAR VARIATION CURVE

Previous Methods

The problem of constructing an archaeomagnetic secular variation curve is similar to that of constructing a paleomagnetic apparent polar wander (APW) path. As with archaeomagnetic VGPs, each paleomagnetic pole within the APW path has an assigned age, along with errors in both independent and dependent variables (time and direction, respectively). Different paleomagnetic phenomena and time scales are involved in the two types of curves. Secular variation arises from rearrangements of fluid motion in the earth's core over a period of years or decades. Apparent polar wander involves the motion of the rock and the continent it rests on relative to the geographic pole since the magnetization was acquired (continental drift), occurring over a significant period of geologic time. To observe APW at a site, the effects of secular variation must first be nullified by averaging paleomagnetic results from an interval of time representing several thousand years.

Thompson and Clark (1981) discussed the problem of fitting polar wander paths to paleomagnetic data, noting the different methods that have been used. Freehand APW paths have been drawn when paleomagnetic data were sparse and are appropriate under such circumstances. As more data become available, mathematical smoothing is generally used. When sufficient data are available, mean vectors can be computed using Fisher statistics for individual time intervals. As still more data accrue, running means can be applied to successive or overlapping periods of time. Thompson and Clark's smoothing technique, using cubic splines and a weighted least-squares approximation, allows for weighting of the data according to the paleomagnetic precision. Reduced weight is given to outlying observations. The resulting APW curve consists of vector means with associated 95% confidence limits calculated at equally spaced points in time.

Archaeomagnetists have also used a variety of techniques in constructing secular variation curves. Freehand curves have been drawn by Wolfman (1973, 1982, and this volume, chaps. 14, 15), DuBois (1975a, 1975c), Thellier (1981), and Hathaway et al. (1983). As with the APW data, this technique is probably the only one that can be used when data are sparse, and the resulting curve does not necessarily contain serious error. We believe, however, that freehand curves should be abandoned as data become more abundant and objective smoothing techniques can be used. The development of the Arkansas curve (Wolfman 1982) illustrates how subjectivity may influence the drawing of curves. The Arkansas curve looks very much like a previously developed curve for the American Southwest (DuBois 1975c). Indeed, one would hope that there was a resemblance between these two curves, because secular variation should be similar in areas that are close to one another. The Arkansas curve, however, was drawn in exact agreement with the southwestern curve for several periods of time. The 1500-km displacement between source areas is enough that the nondipole field should cause at least some difference between the respective VGP paths. Random errors in the data would also preclude two independently derived curves from being exactly the same. Objectively derived curves based on the Arkansas data and a new southwestern data base (Sternberg 1982; Sternberg and McGuire, this volume, chap. 12) still exhibit good agreement, but the patterns are now somewhat different from the earlier freehand curves. When data are sparse, it may be justified to rely on preexisting curves as a guide in drawing freehand curves, but too much reliance on this method may lead to the self-reinforcement syndrome. This idea was employed in a different context by Watkins (1972) to indicate that once a geomagnetic excursion (a short-term, rapid change in paleomagnetic direction) has been postulated, attempts to corroborate it have a tendency to do so even if the original detection of the event was spurious.

As more archaeomagnetic data accumulate for a region, improvements can be made to the freehand-drawing method of preparing secular variation curves. The temporal distribution of the data can vary due to the occupation history of the area, the periods of occupation being covered by archaeological excavation, and the ability to date archaeomagnetic features from the various periods. Thus it may be possible to average archaeomagnetic data for certain periods before there are enough data to justify smoothing over the entire time range of interest. This approach has been used by Hathaway et al. (1983).

Holcomb et al. (1986) proceeded in a similar fashion in a study of secular variation using Hawaiian lava flows. They initially grouped by age the flows that have been historically or radiocarbon dated and then computed average directions and α_{95}s for these time intervals. They refined their analysis by incorporating results from undated lava flows into the secular variation curve. They first sorted the flows into contemporaneous groups using the criteria (in decreasing importance) of geologic evidence, ^{14}C dates (for dated flows), and the magnetic directions themselves. The average directions for these groups are then ordered into a secular variation curve using the criteria (in decreasing importance) of geologic evidence (stratigraphy), the group-average ^{14}C dates, and Occam's razor. Geologic evidence is favored over the ^{14}C dates because of problems of accuracy and precision in the dates. An example of the use of Occam's razor is the preference for simple (smooth) curves over more complicated (jerky) secular variation curves. The incorporation of the undated flows not only helps to constrain the secular variation curve but also sets limits on magnetic dates for these flows.

We believe that the approach of Holcomb et al. (1986) can be useful in the delineation of secular variation if judiciously applied. Wolfman (1982) has adopted a similar approach to the construction of archaeomagnetic secular variation curves. This tends to de-emphasize the information provided by independent dates for each feature, emphasizing instead the ordering of the magnetic directions themselves. The appropriateness of this emphasis may depend on the chronology of a particular culture region. Wolfman draws his secular variation curve through individual feature directions, however, rather than through the average of several contemporaneous features. This is less than ideal in view of the inaccuracy of individual archaeomagnetic directions, although it does avoid the problem of evaluating the contemporaneity of archaeomagnetic features on archaeological grounds.

The Moving-Window Method

As discussed above, the secular variation record is based on data containing some error in both the independent variable of time and the dependent variable of magnetic direction. The secular variation curve itself thus contains error due to these sources. The method we have used for constructing the secular variation curve incorporates these sources of error to produce a curve that includes confidence limits for each point on the curve.

Data occurring at evenly spaced, discrete points in time are often smoothed with running means. For example, monthly indications of meteorological phenomena might be smoothed with a four-point running mean, where the mean of four successive points is plotted at the midpoint. This operation tends to suppress month-to-month fluctuations and to emphasize seasonal or annual variations. Of course, archaeomagnetic data do not occur at evenly spaced points in time, so the analogous operation is the use of moving windows. With the moving window, all data falling within a window of time are averaged together. The window is then moved by a certain increment and another average computed. The result is a series of discrete points, generally plotted at the window midpoints. For directional data, Fisher statistics can be used to compute the interval averages. This method, which Tarkhov (1964) first suggested in the archaeomagnetic literature, has also been used for smoothing archaeomagnetic data by Burlatskaya (1972) and Kovacheva (1980). It may be used to construct archaeomagnetic secular variation curves when the data sets are sufficiently dense, though it is only applicable to independently dated features.

We have modified the moving-window smoothing technique to account for the uncertainties in both age and magnetic direction of the data (Sternberg 1982; Sternberg and McGuire 1981b). Harrison and Lindh (1981, 1982) have applied similar steps to APW paths. The explicit treatment for the age uncertainty is not encompassed in other smoothing techniques discussed by Thompson and Clark (1981). Harrison and Lindh (1982) have shown that consideration of this factor can lead to significant modifications of APW (or VGP) paths. To treat the age error, we weight each datum according to the overlap of its age range with the window. If the probability distribution of the age range is uniform, as we have assumed, this weight is just equal to the fractional overlap of these spans of time. The fractional overlap is the amount of time represented by the overlap of the window and the age range divided by the age range. For example, consider the window of time A.D. 1000–1100. A feature with an age range totally within this window (e.g., A.D. 1000–1100, 1000–1050, 1070–1080) would be given a weight of 1.0. A feature with an age range totally outside the window (e.g., A.D. 900–1000 or 1300–1325) would be given a weight of 0.0. A feature with an age range partially inside and partially outside the window would be given a weight between 0.0 and 1.0 equal to its fractional overlap. For example, a feature with age A.D. 950–1050 is given a weight of 50/100 = 0.5; a feature with age A.D. 850–1050 is given a weight of 50/200 = 0.25; a feature with age A.D. 925–1025 is given a weight of 25/100 = 0.25; and a feature with age A.D. 900–1300 is given a weight of 100/400 = 0.25. Thus, the age range and its uncertainty for each datum are explicitly included in this smoothing technique. Freehand curves, on the other hand, depreciate independent chronological information by following a path along which the VGPs seem to fall, without regard for their assigned ages.

The data can also be weighted to account for error in the dependent variable, magnetic direction. The data should be weighted by their paleomagnetic precision parameters. This weighting reduces the influence of the features with less precisely determined archaeomagnetic directions. It is not then necessary to preselect an arbitrary cutoff precision for acceptable archaeomagnetic results. For a very precise parameter, the Fisher statistical distribution approaches a two-dimensional normal distribution. In this case, the precision parameter becomes equivalent to the inverse of the population variance. For observations with different precisions, weights should be inversely proportional to the variances of the corresponding observations (van der Waerden 1969:110). Thus the total weighting factor for an individual feature, accounting for uncertainty in both age and direction, becomes $w_i = f_{ij} k_i$, where f_{ij} is the fractional overlap of the ith feature with the jth window and k_i is the precision parameter for this ith feature. A useful characterization of the data density within the jth window is given by the effective data density N_j, where $N_j = \Sigma f_{ij}$, or the sum of the fractional overlaps of all the data points within that window.

The effect of this smoothing technique depends on the errors in the data, the density of the data, the window size, and the increment between successive windows. If the window is too big, smoothing is excessive and meaningful information is lost. All data with age ranges totally within the window receive equal weights of 1.0 regardless of the relative precision of the dates. On the other hand, if the window is made too small, too little information is contained within any one window. Smoothing is thus insufficient, and noise in the data is not completely filtered out. In principle, the method of cross-validation (Clark and Thompson 1978; Stone 1974; Thompson and Clark 1981) could be used to determine the optimal window length. In lieu of this, Tarkhov (1964) suggested that the window lengths be similar to the age ranges for the individual data. The window length can also be a variable, increasing for periods when data are more sparse. Successive windows can be overlapped to yield more points along a smoother curve. Overlapping also reduces the importance of the starting date chosen for the initial window. Successive points will not, however, be completely independent of one another if windows overlap. This is also evident in Figure 12.5b of Sternberg and McGuire (this volume), in which A95s of successive points on the secular variation curve overlap, indicating that any two neighboring directions on the curve are not significantly different from one another.

We have followed these guidelines in testing various windowing schemes for our southwestern data base (Sternberg 1982; Sternberg and McGuire, this volume). We considered window lengths of 25, 50, and 100 years, corresponding to the peaks in the age-range distribution (Sternberg and McGuire, this volume, Fig. 12.3). The interval between successive windows was half the window length. The final windowing configuration utilized a 100-year window from A.D. 700 to 1050 where the data were sparse (median N_j = 2.74; Sternberg and McGuire, this volume, Table 12.2) and a 50-year window from A.D. 1000 to 1450 where the data were more dense (median N_j = 5.74). These windows were chosen to give the curve a combination of smoothness and resolution. The method was applied to the VGPs, although the precision parameters for the mean feature directions were used for precision weighting. The VGPs generated from successive windows were simply connected with straight lines to generate the VGP path (Sternberg and McGuire, this volume, Fig. 12.5). Each VGP along the secular variation curve has an associated 95% cone of confidence, which is denoted as A95 when applied to poles rather than the magnetic directions. The final secular variation curve was not overly sensitive to changes in window length or increment, indicating that the observed pattern was indeed due to secular variation and was not an artifact of the smoothing process.

Tarkhov (1964) originally applied the moving-window smoothing technique to paleointensities, which are scalar data. Weighted interval averages for scalars can be computed using equations based on Gaussian distributions for observations of unequal precision (van der Waerden 1969:110). For directional data, Fisher statistics conventionally assign equal weight to all data. The initial equations for conventional Fisher statistics are

$$R_x = \Sigma l_i, \quad R_y = \Sigma m_i, \quad R_z = \Sigma n_i$$

where l_i, m_i, n_i are the directional cosines of the ith direction and R_x, R_y, and R_z are the component sums along the x, y, z axes for the N results being averaged. Following from these,

$$R = (R_x{}^2 + R_y{}^2 + R_z{}^2)^{\frac{1}{2}}$$

$$D = \tan^{-1}(R_y/R_x) \qquad\qquad I = \sin^{-1}(R_z/R)$$

$$k = \frac{N-1}{N-R} \qquad \alpha_{95} = \cos^{-1}[1 - \frac{N-R}{R}(20^{1/N-1}) - 1]$$

where R is the resultant vector length, D is the mean declination, I is the mean inclination, κ is the precision parameter, and α_{95} is the semi-angle subtended about the mean direction by the 95% (two standard errors of the mean) cone of confidence. When applied to poles rather than directions, declination is replaced by the pole longitude, inclination by the pole latitude, and α_{95} by A95.

Sternberg (1982) modified the equations of Fisher statistics to allow for variable weighting of the data. The component sums can be written as

$$\hat{R}_x = \frac{\Sigma w_i l_i}{\Sigma w_i}, \quad \hat{R}_y = \frac{\Sigma w_i m_i}{\Sigma w_i}, \quad \hat{R}_z = \frac{\Sigma w_i n_i}{\Sigma w_i}$$

where w_i is the weight for the ith result and $\hat{R}_x$, $\hat{R}_y$, and $\hat{R}_z$ are now weighted sums. Following the same development as for the unweighted case,

$$\hat{R} = n(\hat{R}_x{}^2 + \hat{R}_y{}^2 + \hat{R}_z{}^2)^{\frac{1}{2}}$$

$$D = \tan^{-1}(\hat{R}_y/\hat{R}_x) \qquad\qquad I = \sin^{-1}(\hat{R}_z/\hat{R})$$

$$k = \frac{N-1}{N(1-\hat{R})} \qquad \alpha_{95} = \cos^{-1}[1 - \frac{1-\hat{R}}{\hat{R}}(20^{1/(N-1)}) - 1)]$$

where $\hat{R}$ is the unit vector in the direction n specified by D and I. These equations are analogous to those for the unweighted case if we regard R for the unweighted case as equivalent to $N\hat{R}$ for the weighted case. The weighted equations have the desirable property of reducing to the unweighted equations when all the weights w_i are equal to one another. It is also noteworthy that a precision parameter and angular uncertainty, as well as a mean direction, can be determined with these equations. This calculation of confidence limits allows for statistical comparison of the curve with other results. This forms the basis for our method of interpreting archaeomagnetic dates.

The moving-window technique is not inherently resistant to the presence of outliers. That is, if a feature has an archaeomagnetic direction discordant with directions of contemporaneous features, and if the precision of that feature is reasonably good (small α_{95} or high k), it will significantly affect the mean direction for that interval. The smoothing method of Thompson and Clark (1981) is resistant to outliers in that outlying observations are automatically given less weight as part of the smoothing process. We have accounted for outliers by using separate tests to identify them (Sternberg 1982; Sternberg and McGuire, this volume), and discarding them from the data set before smoothing. To minimize the possibility of spuriously increasing the precision of the secular variation curve, we were conservative in our rejection of outlying observations. It may also be possible to incorporate the more resistant/robust statistical approaches employed in Van Alstine and de Boer (1978) and Van Alstine (1980) into a moving-window technique.

Previous suggestions that archaeomagnetic secular variation curves should be represented by a band of finite thickness (Eighmy et al. 1978, 1980; Wolfman 1979) rather than simply a line can be quantified with this smoothing method by the interval A95s. Figure 6.1 shows the dependence of the interval A95 values on N_j for three data sets that we have smoothed (this volume, chap. 12). The value of A95 depends inversely on N_j and reaches a fairly constant value of A95 = 1.5° to 2° for $N_j > 7$. This suggests the optimum amount of data needed per window to generate a secular variation curve: N_j should be greater than seven or so to achieve maximum curve precision, while a significantly greater density of data will not have a correspondingly significant effect on the precision of the curve. The lower limit of A95 is similar to the α_{95} for a single archaeomagnetic feature. Burlatskaya and Nachasova (1978) have previously indicated

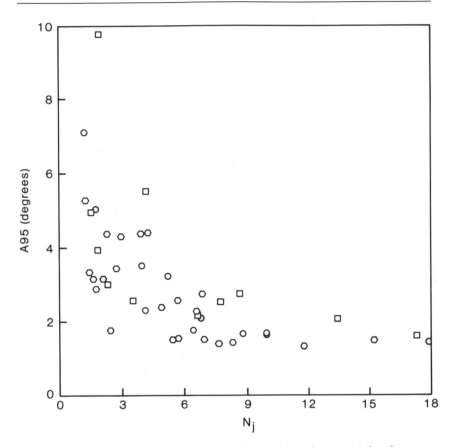

Figure 6.1. The interval A95 values vs. effective data density N_j for the corresponding windows. The moving-window smoothing method was applied by Sternberg and McGuire (this volume, chap. 12) to the data of Sternberg and McGuire, this volume, chap. 12 (hexagons); Eighmy et al. 1983 (squares); and Wolfman 1982 (circles).

that the precision and accuracy of the secular variation curve are comparable to those of the individual features. The precision of the curve is ultimately limited by the accuracy of the archaeomagnetic recorders and the dispersion introduced into regional results by the nondipole field. Assuming no systematic errors, the accuracy of the curve should increase with the density of the data. A rapid secular variation occurring on a time scale less than or equal to the window length, however, is not resolvable.

The statistical nature (interval mean directions with confidence intervals) of the secular variation curve allows comparison with similarly constructed secular variation curves, individual archaeomagnetic results, and theoretical models of secular variation. This now provides us with a rigorous method for interpreting archaeomagnetic dates.

INTERPRETING ARCHAEOMAGNETIC DATES

Although the general approach for deriving an archaeomagnetic date by comparing an archaeomagnetic direction with the secular variation record is intuitive, the exact mechanics by which this is done have not always been explained. General treatments of archaeomagnetic dating (Bucha 1971; Fleming 1976; Michels 1973; Tarling 1975) circumvent this issue. More specific discussions are included in Wolfman (1979, 1982, 1984), and in Eighmy et al. (1980).

Graphic Methods

Archaeomagnetists in the United States have used graphic techniques to interpret archaeomagnetic dates. As is the case for freehand secular variation curves, this method of interpretation has its role as a secular variation curve is being developed for an area. Once a smoothed secular variation curve and associated confidence intervals have been derived, however, a more rigorous statistical method for interpreting dates becomes possible.

In the graphic technique, the secular variation curve is plotted along with the archaeomagnetic direction and confidence interval of the feature to be dated. Confidence intervals have not been associated with the curve itself for this method of interpretation. It has also been the convention to plot the directions as VGPs, although declination vs. inclination plots could also be used. To interpret a date, the oval of confidence for each feature is compared with the secular variation curve. Ideally, this is simply a matter of noting where the path of the curve cuts through the oval. The mean date would correspond to the point on the curve most closely approaching the center of the oval. The 95% confidence interval for the date would be defined by the two points where the oval intersected the curve. Estimating the actual dates involves measuring distances along the curve from the nearest dated points on the curve (usually century marks) and interpolating between these points.

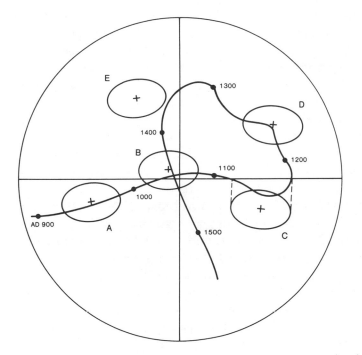

Figure 6.2. Situations encountered in the interpretation of archaeomagnetic dates.

Figure 6.2 schematically illustrates some of the problems involved in the chronological interpretation of archaeomagnetic data using the graphic approach. The curve and VGPs are hypothetical, but they illustrate several situations that we have encountered with graphic interpretation. Case A is a relatively clear case in which a mean date and a standard error would appear to represent the age range adequately. The curve passes almost directly along the semimajor axis of the oval. Case B shows a situation that would produce two alternative dates, each of which would have different error estimates because the curve cuts the short axis of the oval in one case and the long axis in the other. For case C, the age range represented by the intersection of the curve and oval is small. If the mean VGP is further removed from the curve, however, this should imply a less precise date, not a more precise one. Our procedure for such cases was to estimate the date by projecting the total length of the oval onto the curve. For case D, the error in the date would be asymmetrical about the mean date because the curve cuts the short axis of the oval first, then follows the long axis. Finally, case E represents a case in which we would make no interpretation of a date, because the oval is not cut by the curve at all. Due to this variety of relationships and the impossibility of making probabilistic statements concerning the error factors on archaeomagnetic dates interpreted through the graphic technique, some archaeomagnetists (Eighmy et al. 1980; McGuire et al. 1980) proposed that such dates should be interpreted as age ranges, not as means with standard errors. This draws less attention to the importance of the central date.

In DuBois and Wolfman (1970b) and Wolfman (1979, 1982), the authors also find archaeomagnetic dates by graphic proximity to the VGP curve. Age uncertainties are found by dividing the feature *dm* (the semi-major axis of the oval of confidence) by a typical rate of VGP motion along DuBois's curve, given as 0.1°/yr. Thus the age uncertainty is $\pm 10 \times dm$. Note, however, that this rate is twice the typical rate on the Sternberg-McGuire curve (this volume). Using the slower rate of VGP motion alone would multiply the error of interpreted dates by a factor of two.

There are two problems with the graphic technique. First, this methodology implicitly assumes that there is no error in the curve. This is clearly untenable. As discussed above, the secular variation curve is constructed from measurements that include errors in direction and errors in dating. Drawing a simple line through the centers of these ovals does not take into account these errors. Furthermore, the location of the VGP to be dated does not always relate to the curve in an obvious way. Thus the confidence interval for the interpreted date is unduly optimistic. We have been unable to develop an interpretational technique using the graphic method that we feel allows for this error to be included in the estimation of dates. Wolfman (1982) increases the age range of the archaeomagnetic date to account for the uncertainty in the curve by adding five years onto both ends of the age range. Although this is better than making no correction at all for the uncertainty of the curve, it is an ad hoc solution to the problem. The second problem with the graphic method is that it is subjective, allowing different investigators to interpret different dates from the same data. It would appear difficult to establish rigorous conventions for interpreting dates using this method.

A Statistical Method

Sternberg (1982) presented a new method for calculating archaeomagnetic dates that relies on a statistical test rather than a graphic comparison. It is objective and repeatable, and it accounts in a rigorous way for the uncertainty of the secular variation curve. This method involves the common test of comparing two paleomagnetic directions, each having a mean and standard error. It requires a secular variation curve composed of discrete points, each having an associated confidence interval. A curve generated by the moving-window smoothing technique can thus be used for this dating method.

The problem of interpreting an archaeomagnetic date is one of statistical inference whereby two sample means are compared, with the true population variation unknown. This procedure is discussed in most elementary statistical textbooks (e.g., Lentner 1972:182). In interpreting an archaeomagnetic date using this method, we make a point-by-point comparison of the VGP to be dated with each point on the secular variation curve. The archaeomagnetic date is derived from those points on the curve that cannot be said to represent a different population than is represented by the VGP for the specific feature we are trying to date. The archaeomagnetic date corresponds to the total age range for all such adjacent points on the curve. Multiple dates are possible if two discontinuous sets of points on the curve provide dates.

For each interval of time represented on the curve by a discrete point, we first test to see whether the precisions corresponding to the VGP and point on the curve are comparable (i.e., from the same or different populations). We then make a second test against the null hypothesis that the directions for the feature and for the point on the curve are the same, with the alternative hypothesis that the two directions are not the same. To make these tests, we need a test statistic and a level of significance for the test. The test statistics must pertain to directions or vectors, so they are based on Fisher statistics. For the VGP to be dated, the angle $B95 = \sqrt{dm \cdot dp}$ is calculated (Harrison and Lindh 1982). B95 is analogous to the A95 angle, but it is calculated from the semimajor (dm) and semiminor (dp) axes of the oval of confidence. The equivalent circle of confidence described by B95 has the same area as the oval of confidence described by dm and dp. From the equations given above for the unweighted case, B95 can then be used to obtain equivalent values of R and k, which are required for the statistical tests. The test statistic for the comparison of precisions is the F-test of Watson (1956). If the precisions are not significantly different at the 5% significance level, they are assumed to be samples from the same population. The directions can then be compared using the F-test of McFadden and Lowes (1981:Eq. 25). If the precisions are significantly different, no exact test to compare directions can be made. An approximate test can be used which assumes that the sample precisions are equal to the values for the two populations (McFadden and Lowes 1981:Eq. 23). It may also be possible to replace the separate precision and direction tests with a single permutation procedure, as discussed by Mielke et al. (this volume).

A 5% significance level is a common choice for statistical tests, especially in paleomagnetism. In making such statistical tests, rejecting the null hypothesis is the stronger statement. We can then say that the directions are indeed different unless a 5% Type II error has been made. If the null hypothesis cannot be rejected, all we can say is that there is no evidence that the null hypothesis is not true. For an interval that dates, what this method really says is that there is no evidence at the 5% significance level that the two directions are different.

It is, strictly speaking, more appropriate to speak of these dates as 5% significance level dates rather than 95% confidence interval dates. The connotation of both statements is the same, but significance levels pertain to the statistical problem of hypothesis testing (which we are doing for each point on the curve), while confidence intervals pertain to the problem of interval estimation (which we are not really doing on a point-by-point basis). The gist of this method, however, is to find that interval of time on the curve for which the magnetic direction is not different from our unknown. Therefore, if this procedure for determining the archaeomagnetic date is clear, it is reasonable (if not completely rigorous) to refer to such archaeomagnetic dates as 95% confidence intervals.

An approximate graphic test of the consistency of two directions can be used to visualize the statistical tests outlined above. If there is overlap between the oval of confidence for the VGP to be dated and the circle of confidence for a point on the curve, then it is likely that these directions are not statistically different from each other at the

5% significance level. If the oval and circle do not overlap, then the directions are likely to be significantly different.

The archaeomagnetic date is the union of all continuous intervals of time on the secular variation curve for which the directions are not significantly different from the VGP being dated. The final precision of the date is governed by the configuration of the curve, the precision of the curve, and the location and precision of the VGP to be dated. Because the angle between points on the curve for successive intervals may be rather small, a typical archaeomagnetic date encompasses the time range of several points on the VGP curve. The most precise archaeomagnetic date that can be obtained thus corresponds to the length of a single window interval used to generate the secular variation curve. For the southwestern VGP path of Sternberg and McGuire (this volume), 50-year age ranges are the best that can be obtained. Even these will only occur at times when secular variation is more rapid, such as A.D. 1075 when the VGP swings out suddenly to a distinctly low latitude. VGPs falling in this area and to the outside of the curve sometimes date to only this single interval of time. This 50-year range is similar to the minimum age range of 40 years postulated by Eighmy et al. (1980) even though they did not explicitly account for the uncertainty in the curve. Otherwise, age ranges of 100 to 200 years at the 5% significance level are typical. Although this is far inferior to tree-ring dates, it is comparable to ^{14}C dates with 95% confidence intervals.

Archaeologists may note that our technique does not yield as precise results as are sometimes claimed for archaeomagnetic dates. Tarling (1975), DuBois (1975b), and Wolfman (1982) suggest that archaeomagnetic age ranges of 5–25 years are possible. These estimates are based primarily on the α_{95} values of the features to be dated and assumed rates of secular variation. The archaeologist engaged in the perpetual quest for the perfect dating technique must be aware that the accuracy and precision of an archaeomagnetic date depends not only on the measured results for the feature being dated but also on the secular variation curve and the method used for interpretation. An archaeomagnetist might report more precise (seemingly better) dates because of a particular method of interpretation rather than more precise (actually better) work.

It is worth noting that there are some marked similarities between the problems of calibrating radiocarbon dates and archaeomagnetic

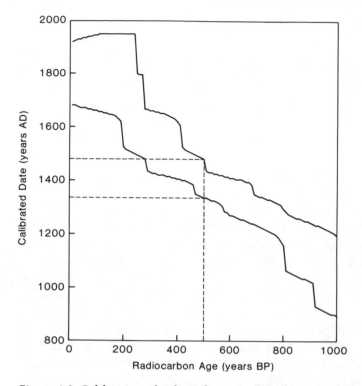

Figure 6.3. Calibration of radiocarbon ages (based on Klein et al. 1982: Table 2 for ^{14}C ages with measurement uncertainties of ± 50 years, using a half-life of 5,568 years). The original tables also give calibrations for uncertainties of ± 20, 100, 150, 200, and 300 years. The mean radiocarbon age (horizontal axis) calibrates into a calibrated date range (vertical axis), which represents a 95% confidence interval. The example shows that a radiocarbon age of 500 ± 50 before present calibrates to a calendric age range of A.D. 335–480.

dating. A concerted effort has been made in recent years to develop a consensus within the radiocarbon community as to how dates should best be calibrated. Klein et al. (1982) have published a series of calibration tables as a result of the 1979 Workshop on Calibrating the Radiocarbon Time Scale. Some of our attitudes toward the problem of archaeomagnetic dating have been shaped by the conclusions of this workshop.

The pattern for calibration of ^{14}C dates is established by determining ^{14}C dates for dendrochronologically dated tree-ring samples and plotting tree-ring, or calendar, age as a function of ^{14}C age. In principle, a ^{14}C date is calibrated by entering the calibration curve with the raw ^{14}C age on one axis and reading the corresponding calendar age off the other axis. Figure 6.3 illustrates the calibration procedure. This process is complicated by the facts that individual ^{14}C determinations contain random counting errors and that the calibration curve itself has an inherent error due to errors in the data that make up the curve. Thus the calibration involves a complicated interaction between the raw ^{14}C age, the shape of the calibration curve at that time, and the size of the error bars on both the ^{14}C age and the curve. Two recommendations by Klein et al. (1982) concerning ^{14}C calibration represent a break with previous practice. First, they recommend that calibrated dates be given in terms of age ranges rather than a central date with a ± error. Second, they recommend that calibrated ^{14}C dates now be given as 95% confidence intervals rather than 67% confidence intervals. Both these recommendations for a more conservative statement of ^{14}C dates have been followed in our recommendations for the interpretation of archaeomagnetic dates.

SOME ADDITIONAL NOTES
ON THE INTERPRETATION OF DATES

Date Reporting

The user of an archaeomagnetic date must be concerned with and should expect more information than the date itself (McGuire et al. 1980). First, a summary of the raw paleomagnetic measurements should be provided. This is what is actually measured in the laboratory for the particular feature of interest. Second, the secular variation curve used in making the interpretation should be cited. Third, the method of interpretation used to derive the date should be given. The raw data allow dates to be reinterpreted using different methods or master curves. Unfortunately, these standards were not met in much of the archaeomagnetic research in the United States prior to 1980.

The paleomagnetic results should include

1. the site's latitude and longitude
2. the number of individual samples collected, the number used to compute the results, and the reasons why any samples were deleted before computation
3. the mean inclination and declination derived for the feature
4. the α_{95} value for the sample directions

5. the precision parameter k for sample directions
6. the VGP position corresponding to the mean direction
7. the semimajor (dm) and semiminor (dp) axes of the oval of confidence about the mean VGP
8. the demagnetization treatment used
9. the mean NRM magnetization of the feature.

Publishing archaeomagnetic dates without the paleomagnetic data from which they are derived is inadequate, for three reasons: (1) it does not allow for independent evaluation of the interpreted dates; (2) it does not allow the dates to be revised to conform with revisions of the secular variation curve, which inevitably occur as additional independently dated archaeomagnetic results accumulate; and (3) it does not provide those researchers investigating the nature of the secular variation curve with the basic data needed.

In the cases of Champion's (1980) dating of Sunset Crater lava flows and Wolfman's (1977) dating of Hohokam pit houses, we were able to calculate revised archaeomagnetic dates (Sternberg 1982; Sternberg and McGuire, this volume) using our new secular variation curve and interpretation method. This was possible because the paleomagnetic data were published. It cannot be done in cases in which only archaeomagnetic dates have been released. Although over 200 archaeomagnetic features have been sampled in Chaco Canyon and approximately 80% yielded dates (Windes 1980), the paleomagnetic data have never been published. The availability of these data, in conjunction with our new secular variation curve, would be especially important, in view of the discrepancy between these archaeomagnetic dates and abundant tree-ring dates in Chaco Canyon (Sternberg and McGuire, this volume, chap. 12; Windes 1980). As we argued in McGuire et al. (1980), archaeomagnetic dates are of little value without the pertinent paleomagnetic data.

Sternberg (1982) was also able to calculate revised secular variation curves from Arkansas data (Wolfman 1982), Mesoamerican data (Wolfman 1973), and data from the Dolores Program (Hathaway et al. 1983) because the raw data and associated independent dates were published as tables. It was thus possible to smooth the various data sets in a similar manner and make statistical comparisons of the resulting curves. Although some of DuBois's preliminary data were graphed (Watanabe and DuBois 1965), they have never been tabulated in a format useful for other investigators.

Multiple Interpretations

As pointed out in association with Figure 6.2, multiple archaeomagnetic date ranges are possible because of the folding back of the secular variation curve upon itself, and this is the case regardless of the method of interpretation employed. We strongly believe that all such archaeomagnetic interpretations should be reported, with equal archaeomagnetic validity assigned to each. The archaeologist may then interpret these options in light of other information, and it is perfectly reasonable to do so. Frequently only one of the possibilities makes sense for the archaeological context of that feature. The selection of one of these intervals over any other, however, is an archaeological interpretation of the multiple possibilities provided by the archaeomagnetic information.

It should also be kept in mind that the extant secular variation curves cover only a limited period of time. For the Southwest, the Southwestern curve (Sternberg and McGuire, this volume) runs from A.D. 700 to 1450; DuBois's (1975a, 1975b) from A.D. 600 to 1500; and Hathaway et al.'s (1983) from A.D. 700 to 900. Direct observations of the magnetic field began in the mid nineteenth century and have continued to the present. It is not currently possible to infer archaeomagnetic dates outside these periods, although it may well become possible as the secular variation curves are extended. Because the curve has certainly folded back on itself even further in the past, features with true dates outside the limits of the curve may yield spurious dates within the range of the present curves, or they may not date at all. Likewise, archaeomagnetic dates encompassing the end points of the current secular variation curve should be regarded as open-ended on that side.

No Interpretation

Returning to the analogy between archaeomagnetic dating and radiocarbon calibration, one significant difference is that archaeomagnetic dates are based on vectors, while ^{14}C calibration is based on scalar quantities. In addition, the plot of calibrated ^{14}C date vs. radiocarbon age (Fig. 6.3) is nearly monotonic, while the archaeomagnetic VGP oscillates around the geographic pole. Thus, any ^{14}C age (unless it is outside the range of the calibration curve) yields a calibrated date. On the other hand, a particular archaeomagnetic feature may not date (i.e., its direction may be significantly different from all points on the secular variation curve). Assuming the validity of the master curve, this situation implies an inaccurate recording of the magnetic field direction by the feature to be dated. This situation could also arise if the age of the feature were outside the period of time covered by the secular variation curve.

Coeval Archaeomagnetic Results

To ensure accuracy for ^{14}C dating, counting statistics are averaged together from several runs of the same sample. It is also desirable to compare and average ^{14}C results from coeval samples to account for problems such as contamination with systematically young or old carbon. Coevalness must then be judged by criteria other than the ^{14}C dates themselves, such as the archaeological context. In archaeomagnetism, it has been customary to collect 8 to 12 specimens per feature, corresponding to the multiple ^{14}C runs. When coeval features have been sampled, however, individual dates have generally been reported for each feature. Archaeomagnetic results are also subject to systematic and random errors (e.g., demagnetization may not completely remove secondary components of magnetization). These errors could be identified or averaged out if directions from coeval features were averaged together, and the archaeomagnetic date could be inferred from the final average. Again, coevalness must be judged on independent archaeological or chronometric evidence. The time span corresponding to "coeval" should be based on the resolution desired for the archaeomagnetic dates and would depend on the questions that the archaeologist is trying to answer. The directions for the coeval features could be treated in the same way as individual sample directions are presently handled. These feature directions, obtained from averaging specimen directions within each feature, can then be averaged themselves.

If it is suspected that two or more features may date to a time not represented by the curve, archaeomagnetism may still be useful as a relative dating technique. Directions of two or more features can be compared to see if they are significantly different from one another. This is almost a test for coevalness of the features. The difference between the directions depends on the resolution of the archaeomagnetic method and the rate of secular variation of the magnetic field. This rate itself is variable over time. Known rates of secular variation, however, could be used to attach some temporal meaning to the comparison of magnetic directions. Such a comparison of magnetic directions without the inference of a chronometric age might be useful for certain archaeological problems even when the features were thought to date to an interval of time represented by the curve. Downey and Tarling (1984) have used this approach to correlate the archaeomagnetic directions and intensity in destruction levels of Minoan Crete with paleomagnetic directions and intensities of specific ash horizons of the Santorini volcano.

Direct comparison of archaeomagnetic directions of coeval features can also be useful in evaluating the archaeomagnetic method. After all, coeval features should yield the same magnetic direction. Thus it would prove useful to the archaeomagnetist for the archaeologist to document the evidence for coevalness of the various archaeomagnetic features at a site. Another means of evaluating the validity of archaeomagnetic dates is by comparing them to other, independently derived chronometric information for the same feature, such as a ^{14}C date on charcoal from a hearth or tree-ring-dated intrusive pottery in the room. When such comparisons can be made, it is important for the archaeomagnetist to know how such independent dates compare.

CONCLUSION

This paper has described the nature of archaeomagnetic data and some of the consequent issues that must be dealt with in the construction of a secular variation curve and in the interpretation of archaeomagnetic dates. Archaeomagnetic data do contain errors, and these are important to consider. Subjective methods of curve construction and graphic methods of dating are appropriate when the archaeomagnetic data base is relatively sparse, but as more data accumulate, other methods can be brought into play. We have developed analytical, objective, replicable methods that seem to reflect the true strengths and limitations of the archaeomagnetic method.

We would like to stress that our differences with past and present archaeomagnetic methodology do not challenge the basic validity of the archaeomagnetic dating technique. We do believe that the approach has occasionally been oversold in the past and that its precision has been exaggerated. Therefore, it is not surprising that some archaeologists have become skeptical of the technique, especially when the validity of previous dates is questioned. We urge our colleagues to have faith, for only through further cooperation and the collection of necessary material will the technique be further improved. As more research is done, there will inevitably be further changes in secular variation curves and possibly in methodology as well. As long as the archaeologist has the basic paleomagnetic information, however, such revisions can be used to recalculate archaeomagnetic dates. A greater understanding of the limitations of the archaeomagnetic method should also lead to a greater appreciation of its strengths.

ACKNOWLEDGMENTS

This work was supported by National Science Foundation grants EAR77-22340 and EAR79-19726, and by the State of Arizona.

PART 3

Experimental Archaeomagnetism

Introduction

Ethnoarchaeology has been extremely beneficial in understanding social processes, the technology of material culture, and the properties of the resulting materials. For example, Sternberg (1982) discusses some of the relevant ethnoarchaeological data for understanding the remanent magnetization acquired by archaeological ceramics, including general pottery-making techniques and actual temperatures measured during specific pottery firings. To our knowledge, there is no equivalent set of observations for the hearths and similar *in situ* archaeomagnetic features that are the focus of this volume. This gap will be partially filled, however, by experimental archaeomagnetism. In this section we present studies that examine several of the variables likely to affect the archaeomagnetic method as experienced in archaeological features in the Americas.

Two chapters look at questions regarding collecting techniques. Although large, strongly magnetized archaeomagnetic features such as kilns generate magnetic fields that can appreciably deflect a compass needle, Hathaway and Krause (Chapter 7) reassure us that for almost all of the archaeological features collected in North America, the magnetic compass is a satisfactory orienting device. Smith (Chapter 8) finds no reason to fault the general shift toward the collection of smaller cubes.

Chapters 8 through 11 also examine the "rock" magnetic questions of how magnetization is acquired by an archaeomagnetic feature. Smith, again in Chapter 8, finds that remanence is primarily acquired during the last high-temperature heating. In Chapter 9, Hathaway examines the impact of cultural practices with regard to hearth use (temperature and length of use) on archaeomagnetic results. Hathaway, Smith, and Krause (Chapter

10), combining the results from their separate studies, conclude that any of the common archaeological soil matrices can record magnetic field directions with acceptable precision. In Chapter 11, Hathaway uses petrographic examination and the thermomagnetic qualities of experimentally fired baked clays to look at the important question of the mode of remanence acquisition in these features. Partial thermoremanent magnetization is apparently augmented by a chemical remanence. It will be interesting indeed to see if future experimental work can identify variables or combinations of variables that consistently lead to better (or worse) archaeomagnetic results.

CHAPTER 7

The Sun Compass
Versus the Magnetic Compass
in Archaeomagnetic Sample
Collection

J. HOLLY HATHAWAY AND GEORGE J. KRAUSE

In archaeomagnetic field collections, a specimen's orientation must be established relative to true north. Therefore, when using a magnetic orienting instrument, it is critical to establish the current local declination at a collecting site. The magnetic declination printed on United States Geological Survey quadrangle maps provides local information on the declination; these values, however, are often 20 or 30 years out of date. Assuming a 0.2° per year change in the magnetic declination (Yukatake 1967), this adds up to a 6° difference over a 30-year period. Unless these maps are current, they cannot be used to establish the local declination. For generalized trends, USGS National Oceanic and Atmospheric Administration maps like that of Fabiano and Peddie (1975) may be consulted. Such maps provide isogonic lines of declination for the United States along with generalized rates of change, thus enabling the derivation of the current field declination for a site. In some instances, however, these maps are not accurate enough for archaeomagnetic purposes. Differences of up to 2° from the published declination have been noted in some areas (Hathaway and Eighmy 1982). Local geological sources may be the cause of some major distortions in the field. Tarling (1971:59) suggests that a deviation of as much as 30° can be expected between sun and magnetic compass readings in igneous terrain. A more accurate method for obtaining the current local declination is to sight Polaris with a transit on a clear, dark night at the site. The field value obtained should be corrected for the seasonal variability of the star's location in the sky (generally less than 1° difference). This correction can be established with the aid of an ephemeris for the appropriate year. To avoid mechanical and sighting errors, several sightings should be collected on different nights. The averaged values provide a reasonably accurate magnetic declination for the site, inclusive of any local distortions caused by geological sources or other magnetic influences in the area (e.g., historical debris).

Although the methods described above may provide operationally accurate estimates of the current local field declination, none of the methods accounts for smaller variations possibly caused by field distortions surrounding a burned archaeological feature. Because burned features have a thermoremanent magnetization, their magnetic fields may be systematically different from that of magnetically weak surrounding soils. Further, the magnetic field of the feature may increase the dispersion among specimens through a self-refracting effect (Aitken and Hawley 1971; Hoye 1982). Magnetometer surveys in southwestern Colorado (Burns 1981; Weymouth and Huggins 1983) have shown that some archaeological features (e.g., burned pit structures) produce magnetic field distortions (anomalies) on the order of 25 to 50 nT, enabling detection and location of the burned archaeological features prior to excavation. Clearly, these anomalies, if strong enough to affect a magnetic compass, have the potential of producing directionally biased information for samples recovered near or within them.

One solution to this problem is to avoid using magnetic orienting devices in the field and instead to use a sun compass for collecting specimen azimuths. The sun compass, however, is not as unrestricted in its use as is the magnetic compass, as cloudy days and shady collection areas (in pits or caves) limit its applicability.

Experiments were conducted on sets of test hearths in two areas in northeastern and southwestern Colorado to establish the effects of small burned features on the magnetic compass and the effectiveness of the sun compass. The principal advantage in firing experimental hearths lies in having known reference directions (present-day declination and inclination) against which to compare sample data. Fifteen hearths were constructed, fired, and archaeomagnetically sampled using the two orientation methods; 18 samples (216 specimens, 12 specimens per sample) were recovered from these hearths. The differences in azimuths for each specimen, based on the values calculated from the sun compass readings and the observed field values of the magnetic compass, were determined to see if a feature effect could be observed.

DATA COLLECTION

The experimental hearths were dug, fired, and archaeomagnetically sampled. Twelve of the hearths were located in southwestern Colorado in the Dolores River Valley; the remaining three hearths were situated in northeastern Colorado near Fort Collins. The experiments were conducted during the summers of 1979 and 1980. The hearths constructed were basin-shaped, unlined, and approximately 0.5 m in diameter and 0.2 m in depth. To maintain strongly burning fires, wood fuel was added in approximately 2.5-kg bunches every 10 to 20 minutes. Firing temperatures were monitored by means of a potentiometer; thermocouples placed about the hearths enabled temperatures to be recorded at various soil depths and locations. Pertinent information on the firing characteristics of each hearth is available in Hathaway (1982b) and Krause (1980). The temperature at the rim varied from 397° C to 814° C among the 15 hearths.

After the hearths cooled, the archaeomagnetic samples were recovered. Only one sample was obtained from hearths 1 through 12; two samples were recovered from hearths 13 through 15, one from the rim and one from the base. Both sun compass and magnetic compass azimuths were collected for each specimen. The magnetic compass values were obtained in the standard manner (Eighmy 1980b) by reading the azimuth angle along the east side of each aluminum mold after the mold was leveled and the plaster poured. The sun compass orientations were obtained after the mold was leveled but before the plaster was poured. The sun compass was designed by J. L. Eighmy and G. J. Krause of Colorado State University specifically for archaeomagnetic purposes. The instrument consisted of a circular aluminum platform with a 360° protractor mounted on top. Underneath the platform was a square aluminum block with two perpendicular flanges extending down approximately 2 cm. The block was mounted along the cardinal directions and calibrated due north (0°) on the protractor. Calibration was estimated at 0.5°. A vertical pin 7 cm high was mounted in the center of the protractor. The device was placed on top of the molds with the perpendicular flanges flush with the south and east edges of the molds (Fig. 7.1). The angle of the sun's shadow cast by the vertical pin was recorded in the field along with the exact (standard) time and date of collection. The field data were used to calculate the specimen's orientation relative to true north.

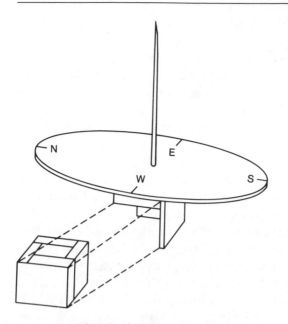

Figure 7.1. Sketch of a sun compass, showing how it is positioned over the specimen form for directional measurement.

These values were obtained with the aid of solar ephemeris tables according to the formula presented in Tarling (1971:59):

$$AZ = 180° + \tan^{-1} \frac{-\sin LHA}{\cos LAT \times \tan SD - \sin LAT \times \cos LHA}$$

where AZ is the azimuth of the shadow, $\tan^{-1}$ is the arc tangent, LAT is the site latitude, LHA is the local hour angle, and SD is the sun's declination.

DATA ANALYSIS

The approximate magnetic declination and inclination of the two collection sites are according to Fabiano and Peddie (1975):

	Declination	Inclination
Dolores River Valley	13.1°E	64.1°
Fort Collins	12.4°E	67.9°

The mean sample azimuth differences and standard deviation for the sun compass and magnetic compass values for the experimental hearths are listed in Table 7.1. It is apparent from the values in column 2 that the observed magnetic declination at the Dolores site(s) (11.5° E) is over 1.5° different (westerly) from the Fabiano and Peddie (1975) map approximation of the estimated declination value, whereas the average of the Fort Collins values (12.4° E) generally confirms the published declination. The more westerly declination for Dolores was later confirmed by Polaris sightings in 1981 (11.1° E average) and collections of sun compass/magnetic compass azimuths for prehistoric samples from the Dolores Archaeological Program sites (more than 700 cases). The magnetic declination in the Dolores area for 1980 was finally established at 11.55° E (Hathaway and Eighmy 1982), 1.6° west of the published value.

Although some variability between the current declination value and the mean sample azimuth differences is noted among the 18

Table 7.1. *Mean Sample Azimuth Differences Between Magnetic Compass and Sun Compass Measurements*

Sample No.	Mean Sample Azimuth Difference	Standard Deviation	Mean Sample Azimuth Difference Less Local Declination
Dolores (local declination: 11.5°)			
1	12.6° E	1.26	1.1° E
2	13.2° E	0.83	1.6° E
3	11.5° E	0.97	0.0°
4	11.8° E	0.89	0.3° E
5	11.8° E	0.85	0.3° E
6	11.1° E	0.62	0.4° W
7	11.4° E	1.60	0.1° W
8	10.6° E	1.10	0.9° W
9	9.3° E	3.31	2.2° W
10	11.0° E	0.97	0.5° W
11	11.6° E	1.23	0.1° E
12	11.0° E	1.50	0.5° W
Fort Collins (local declination: 12.4°)			
13	12.6° E	1.05	0.2° E
14	12.6° E	1.18	0.2° E
15	12.5° E	0.93	0.1° E
16	10.8° E	1.01	1.6° W
17	11.8° E	1.43	0.6° W
18	12.0° E	1.15	0.4° W

Table 7.2. NRM Sample Results Based on Magnetic Compass Measurements

Sample No.	Mean Sample Declination	Mean Sample Inclination	Mean Sample Intensity (A/m)	α_{95}
1	12.57	64.47	1.34	1.57
2	10.05	65.54	0.65	1.38
3	8.78	64.53	0.29	2.16
4	11.99	64.28	1.28	1.32
5	9.90	66.06	0.26	1.95
6	12.90	64.47	0.17	2.16
7	10.14	62.43	0.48	2.05
8	11.92	64.92	0.22	2.89
9	11.12	63.67	0.14	2.70
10	13.25	65.24	0.16	3.08
11	15.23	65.88	0.08	3.09
12	7.79	65.00	0.04	4.09
13	14.46	69.29	1.54	3.87
14	20.38	72.12	9.37	3.22
15	13.05	69.08	0.71	2.35
16	32.69	71.38	0.61	7.82
17	13.17	68.44	0.61	3.30
18	357.95	69.14	0.75	10.20

samples, generally less than 0.5° deviation is apparent (see Table 7.1). Only sample 2 has a mean sample azimuth difference statistically significant at the 5% level. The samples exhibiting more than 0.5° deviation (samples 1, 2, 8, 9, and 16) do not appear to be related to site location, sampling area (base or rim), or the magnetic intensity of the feature (see Table 7.2). The sample with the largest deviation (sample 9), however, does have a much higher standard deviation, indicating a problem with sampling techniques or other sampling errors.

The natural remanent magnetization (NRM) of the samples was determined on a Schonstedt spinner magnetometer. The measured NRM for each sample was processed based on the two sets of field azimuths. For comparability among results and because only slight changes were noted after demagnetization of these recent firings, only the NRM results are considered in this analysis. For demagnetized results, see Hathaway (1982b) and Krause (1980). The calculated remanent directions, levels of confidence, and mean sample intensities are provided in Tables 7.2 and 7.3. A comparison of the α_{95} values resulting from the two sets of azimuth values suggests very

Table 7.3. NRM Sample Results Based on Sun Compass Measurements

Sample No.	Mean Sample Declination	Mean Sample Inclination	Mean Sample Intensity (A/m)	α_{95}
1	13.61	64.51	1.34	1.75
2	11.65	65.54	0.65	1.36
3	9.06	64.56	0.29	2.27
4	12.40	64.26	1.28	1.32
5	10.09	66.06	0.26	1.97
6	12.46	64.46	0.17	2.14
7	9.49	62.47	0.48	2.23
8	11.00	64.96	0.25	3.00
9	8.67	63.72	0.14	2.86
10	11.55	65.30	0.16	3.26
11	15.15	65.91	0.08	3.19
12	7.24	65.01	0.04	4.11
13	14.35	69.32	1.54	3.92
14	20.80	72.12	0.93	3.22
15	13.09	69.11	0.71	2.42
16	30.92	71.45	0.61	7.88
17	12.62	68.47	0.61	3.38
18	357.22	69.15	0.75	10.20

little difference in confidence levels between the magnetic compass and sun compass orientations; the largest net difference between the two sets of α_{95} values is less than 0.2°. This small difference is in sharp contrast to the large difference in α_{95} values, which vary by almost 9.0° among the 18 samples (15 different hearths), which may relate to differences in the physical qualities (e.g., soil texture, iron content, firing temperatures, and lengths of firing) of the features (Hathaway 1982b; Krause 1980).

The NRM directions calculated from the sun compass and magnetic compass azimuths are plotted in Figures 7.2 and 7.3. The magnetic compass orientation results deviate no more from the reference location than do the sun compass orientation results. As one might expect, however, the features (samples) exhibiting the largest α_{95} values and lowest mean sample intensities have the most divergent remanent directions (i.e., those directions farthest from the reference location). The samples farthest from the reference location (samples 14, 16, and 18) were recovered from the base of hearths 13 through 15.

Studies conducted by Hathaway and Eighmy (1982) for the Dolores Archaeological Program compared the mean sample differences between the sun and magnetic azimuths of samples closely associated with intensely burned areas (e.g., burned pit structures) and samples isolated from intensely burned areas (solitary campfires or hearths in unburned structures). These studies showed little difference between the two groups, indicating that even in situations in which intense magnetic anomalies (measured by proton precession magnetometer, up to 50 nT) are present, thermally induced magnetic 'anomalies' typical of the southwestern Anasazi cultures are not sufficient to affect the magnetic compass readings significantly.

SUMMARY

The 18 experimental samples collected by magnetic and nonmagnetic orientation methods revealed very little effect on the magnetic compass values as a result of small magnetic field distortions within small burned features. Although this general conclusion is substantiated by other studies of the Anasazi cultures, other features occur-

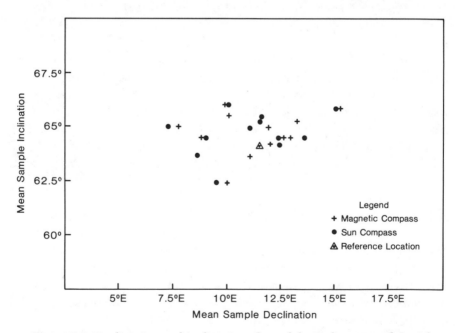

Figure 7.2. Declination and inclination plots of the Dolores samples with the reference direction.

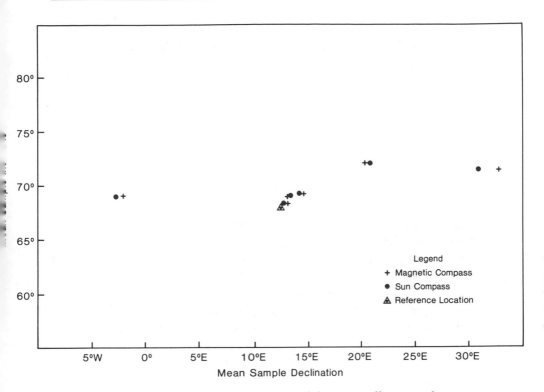

Figure 7.3. Declination and inclination plots of the Fort Collins samples with the reference direction.

ring in the greater Southwest (e.g., Hohokam hornos) may produce magnetic fields capable of affecting the magnetic compass or causing self-refraction. Both the sun compass and the magnetic compass produce comparatively accurate *in situ* specimen azimuths, with the proviso that in the case of the magnetic compass, the current local declination is accurately established. The collector should be aware, however, that small variations in the generalized magnetic patterns depicted on continental scale maps are possible. Consequently, when using a magnetic compass for archaeomagnetic collection, the collector should verify the published value by some independent method in the field. Two good ways of establishing accurate local magnetic declinations are through sun compass/magnetic compass specimen orientation differences or through sighting Polaris with a magnetic instrument.

CHAPTER 8

Cube Size and Refiring as Factors that Influence Archaeomagnetic Results

GARY P. SMITH

The objective of archaeomagnetic dating is to determine the age of a good thermoremanent magnetic direction. Although this objective has met with success, questions remain among archaeomagnetists as to whether current methods and assumptions best allow them to reach their objective. Two cube sizes are currently in use in the collection of archaeomagnetic samples, and it is important to determine whether the two sizes produce equally precise results. Also, it has often been tacitly assumed that the archaeomagnetic data recovered from a hearth were produced by the last thermal event in hearth use (e.g., Hathaway 1982b). For several reasons, this assumption may not be valid. These two problems were investigated by measuring the remanent magnetism in experimental hearths fired in the present-day magnetic field.

EXPERIMENTS

First Experiment: Cube Size

Robert DuBois, who initiated archaeomagnetic research in the United States, conducted his studies with magnetometers he built himself that accommodated 1.7-inch collection cubes. Since that time, however, geophysicists and other scientists interested in paleomagnetic research have standardized the cube size at 1 inch, and most commercial magnetometers are produced to this specification. Today, these two cube sizes are used by archaeomagnetists despite the fact that no one has addressed the issue of whether the two sizes produce equally good directional results in similar circumstances.

In theory there should be little difference between the results produced by the 1.7-inch cube and those produced by the 1-inch cube.

The magnetic particles responsible for remanent magnetization are quite small and numerous even in small amounts of soil. Still, disagreement exists over the appropriate cube size. Bucha (1971) contended that smaller specimens have a greater chance of even firing as opposed to larger specimens. Conversely, smaller specimens may accrue relatively larger errors in recording the past geomagnetic field and in the collection process. Thellier (1967) recommended the use of larger samples weighing on the order of 1 kg. He found that collection errors can be reduced by as much as 1° and also suggested that accuracy in depicting the past geomagnetic field may be improved by the use of larger samples. It follows, then, that the smaller samples may not be as precise and may reflect significant noise in the baked feature's magnetic direction.

To determine whether the results produced by the 1-inch cube differ from those produced by the 1.7-inch cube, an experiment was designed to collect hearths using both cube sizes to see if directional results (i.e., declination and inclination) produced by the 1.7-inch cubes are significantly more precise and accurate than those produced by 1-inch cubes.

Second Experiment: Reheating

Paleomagnetic theory suggests that all previous thermoremanence from a hearth is erased once that hearth has been reheated to a temperature exceeding the temperature of all previous firings (Irving 1964:24; Tarling 1971:16).

Reheating experiments on hearths have been conducted prior to this investigation. Grisso (1978) investigated second heatings that generated a secondary magnetization. In this case, the investigator demonstrated that second but lower-temperature reheatings could be identified by thermal demagnetization. Thus, when thermally demagnetized, the average declination of the samples, D, showed progressive changes toward the original D values. The progressive changes in D indicated that the reheating was a secondary component of the total magnetization.

Yu (1978 and this volume, chap. 4) conducted reheating experiments on baked clay. The investigator heated specimens to 700° C and then allowed them to cool to room temperature in a 50 μT field to acquire a total thermoremanent magnetization (TRM). Then the specimens were reheated to varying temperatures below 700°, with each specimen subject to a field deflected from the original direction by different degrees. When the samples were thermally demagnetized, Yu was able to isolate and delineate the second heatings.

As a result of Grisso and Yu's experimental work with reheated archaeological material, we know that secondary partial thermoremanent magnetizations (PTRMs) of archaeomagnetic samples can be isolated from an original TRM (Yu 1978:109). Further, the lower-temperature reheatings are indicated by a progressive change toward the original directions (Grisso 1978:57). Because of the role that chemical remanent magnetization (CRM) and viscous remanent magnetization (VRM) play in the acquisition of a remanent magnetization, however, the precise effect of reheating below Curie temperatures is unknown. This question is important because it is unlikely that the hearths surrounding most prehistoric campfires reached temperatures above 550° C (Krause 1980:34). Recently it has been suggested that if a low-temperature hearth is repeatedly reheated to approximately the same temperature, there will be an accumulation of high-temperature VRM (Sternberg et al. 1980).

We now need to ask, What is the thermoremanent result of repeated refirings at temperatures below the Curie point of hematite and magnetite? If Sternberg et al. (1980) are correct, the total magnetic direction of a hearth reused for long periods of time may be an integrated result of several reheatings. For hearths used less than 10 years, the result would be negligible, because geomagnetic variation for such a short period is small, but in long-period reuse the problem can be significant. Hearths that were in use for over 20 years may have a complicated remanent magnetization requiring extensive magnetic cleaning.

In order to clarify this issue, experimental hearths were reheated above an original firing temperature but still below 600° C in a magnetic field different from that during the original heating. If the final PTRM declination and inclination were unaffected by the original PTRM direction, the results would suggest that the highest-temperature last firing, not necessarily some integrated combination of heatings, produced the primary remanence.

EXPERIMENTAL DESIGN

To test the hypotheses, movable "hearths" were built in a rectangular container constructed of wood. On the floor of the container,

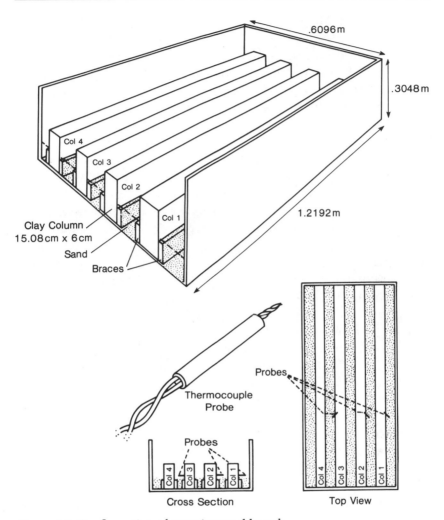

Figure 8.1. Configuration of experimental hearth.

wooden support braces in sets of two were placed to secure four linear "hearths" (Fig. 8.1). The braces ran the length of the container, with the paired braces 6 cm apart.

The hearths were composed of commercial clay mixed with sand, silt, and water and formed into clay columns (henceforth the hearths will be referred to as columns). The combinations of clay, sand, and silt were mixed in proportions that approximate some natural conditions of clay-lined hearths. As a result, comparisons can be made with some well-prepared archaeological hearths. Sand was then added throughout the container to insulate the wooden platform.

Temperature is a crucial factor in the acquisition of magnetic ther- moremanence and is especially important for these experiments. The temperatures reached during the first firing must be high enough to permit at least a partial thermoremanent magnetization. Further- more, the temperature of the second firing must exceed the highest temperature recorded in the first firing in order to test the second- firing remagnetization.

As a consequence, before the clay columns were allowed to dry, three thermocouple probes were inserted in columns 1, 2, and 3. The thermocouple probes were made of a copper-constantan wire that could measure temperatures up to 1,000° C. The probes were then attached to a Leeds-Northrup Potentiometer located about 2 m from the hearth. This instrument records temperature in degrees centi- grade above the ambient temperature. The ambient temperature dur- ing the firing was obtained from a nearby outdoor thermometer. The probes were positioned so that the temperature recorded reflected the temperature of the columns, not the fire. The probes were in- serted 5 cm into three of the columns, each probe being 76 cm from the north side of the container. After the probes were inserted, the wet columns were allowed to dry several days before the first firing.

First Firing

Prior to the firing of the hearths, the container was turned toward magnetic north and leveled. Orientation and leveling of the box were done to simplify the reheating experiment. A total of 18 kg of fuel was placed on the columns in increments of 2.25 kg every 30 min- utes. Temperature was recorded every 15 minutes. The highest tem- perature reached during the first firing was 346.5° C.

In order to minimize the effect of variation in clay composition and firing, the collection of sample specimens was guided by a ran- dom sample design (see Smith 1981:41–45). Two sample sets from each column, one with large molds and one with small molds, were collected, for a total of eight sample sets. They were numbered 1 through 8 (2, 4, 6, and 8 were small-cube samples). The maximum size of a sample was 12 specimens.

Second Firing

The primary purpose of the second firing was to conduct the reheat- ing experiments. In order to look at the effect of the second firing, the hearth container was turned 90° to the west and refired. A comparison of declination and inclination values from both firings should show whether the PTRMs from the first firing remained. Again, as with the first firing, the hearth container was leveled. If the second firing completely erased the magnetization from the first firing, the magnetic remanence should again be close to magnetic north.

The same amount of fuel was used for this firing, but this time the fuel was placed on the uncollected remaining third of the hearth to ensure that the temperatures reached during this firing exceeded those of the first firing. The temperatures were recorded at 15-minute intervals, with a high temperature of 544° C.

Collection of samples from the second firing was largely determined by available space. Four samples were removed, one sample per column. One-inch molds were used in collecting these four samples. The samples were numbered 9 through 12.

Once all the samples were collected from the hearth, they were measured for their natural remanent magnetization on a spinner magnetometer. All samples were thermally demagnetized. No secondary components of magnetization could be identified; therefore, NRM results are used for comparison throughout the study (Smith 1981:57–60).

RESULTS

The laboratory results are presented in Table 8.1. These results were evaluated in two ways. First, the median pole positions were plotted on a polar projection and the difference in location between each sample's average VGP and reference pole position was observed. Samples were compared using plotted pole positions instead of declination and inclination values, although declination and inclination values for this single-locality experiment could have been as easily used. Second, a permutation-based test statistic, MRPP, was employed to test whether sets of specimen direction were likely to have been drawn from the same population. The technique is based on the median location of a set of directions on the surface of a sphere and avoids some of the problems associated with using means (Berry et al. 1982; see also Mielke et al., this volume).

Experiment One: Cube Size

When the samples from the 1.7-inch cubes (samples 1, 3, 5, and 7) and the samples from the 1-inch cubes (samples 2, 4, 6, and 8) were

Table 8.1. NRM Sample Results

Sample Number	Number of Specimens		Dec	Inc	Lat	Long	α_{95}	dp	dm
	Collected	Used							
1	12	12	24.78	64.37	71.13	319.15	7.88	10.09	12.61
2	12	12	29.75	64.84	67.66	318.68	5.13	6.65	8.26
3	12	12	20.00	62.39	74.81	325.99	7.47	9.09	11.65
4	12	12	13.40	68.04	75.78	291.69	4.88	6.87	8.18
5	11	11	18.38	59.11	75.96	341.26	6.41	7.16	9.58
6	12	12	20.12	65.78	73.73	310.53	4.00	5.31	6.51
7	10	10	15.34	65.22	76.98	308.12	6.78	8.87	10.97
8	10	10	15.09	61.71	78.45	327.67	6.12	7.31	9.46
9	9	9	14.69	66.66	76.36	300.00	5.74	7.81	9.47
10	12	12	16.69	65.76	75.84	307.12	2.91	3.87	4.75
11	12	12	14.19	62.58	78.90	321.84	2.03	2.48	3.17
12	12	12	15.20	71.19	71.64	283.30	4.66	7.10	8.13

plotted on a polar projection, the 1-inch cubes appeared to be closer to the calculated reference pole position for three out of four of the columns. In two of those three cases, however, the 1-inch cube and the 1.7-inch cube pole positions were very close (Fig. 8.2).

In the statistical comparison of the 1.7-inch cube with the 1-inch cube, the samples were paired by column. In column 1, a comparison of specimens in sample 1 (1.7-inch cubes) with those in sample 2 (1-inch cubes) yields a probability value of .598, suggesting that the difference between sample 1 and sample 2 is not significant either in terms of direction or overall sample scatter. From column 2, sample 3 (1.7-inch cubes) and sample 4 (1-inch cubes) were also compared, and the probability of significant difference is .444. This value indicates no significant difference in sample direction or in the scatter of individual specimen direction. When sample 5 (1.7-inch cubes) and sample 6 (1-inch cubes) from column 3 were compared, however, a significant difference was found. The probability value is .037, and the difference is due to both direction and scatter. Sample 6, in other words, has a tighter clustering of individual specimen directions and is closer to the reference pole position. The locational difference can be observed in Figure 8.2, where sample 6 is much closer to the reference pole position and quite displaced from sample 5. In column 4, sample 7 (1.7-inch cubes) and sample 8 (1-inch cubes) are not significantly different in either direction or scatter. The probability that the difference in location between the two samples was due to something other than chance is only .544.

Experiment Two: The Reheating Investigation

Differences between the first and second firing were considered by combining the samples from the first firing into one group (samples 1 through 8) and the second firing (samples 9 through 12) into another group. Thus an average latitude and longitude were calculated for each firing (Fig. 8.3). The first firing yielded a location of 74.3° N, 319.3° E. The same procedure was used with the second firing, and the median location was 76.6° N, 308.0° E. As Figure 8.3 indicates, the second firing is closer to the reference pole position. The question remains whether this difference is due to actual directional differences or to dispersion of individual specimen directions. Accord-

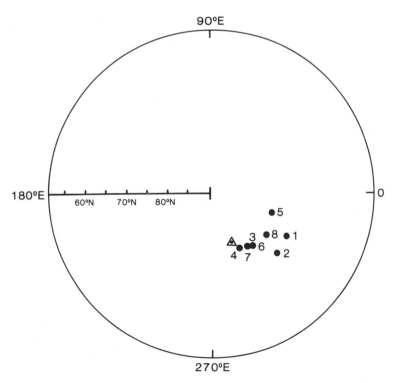

Figure 8.2. Polar projection of reference pole position with samples 1–8.

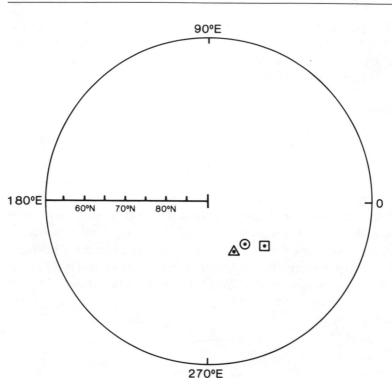

Figure 8.3. A comparison of reference pole position with first and second firing groups. The circle indicates the second firing, and the box the first firing.

ing to the MRPP test statistic, there was a probable difference in both direction and scatter. Second-firing samples were closer to the reference pole position and had less scatter in specimen direction than first-firing samples (a probability value of .011).

SUMMARY

The results of the experiments do not give any reason to change existing archaeomagnetic methodology. In the first experiment, only one case showed any significant statistical difference (between samples 5 and 6) in direction and scatter. In this case the smaller cube size appeared more precise and accurate, but one case is hardly sufficient to recommend one size over the other. These data provide no basis for recommending the larger cube size. Until further comparative data are available, the 1.7-inch cube and the 1-inch cube can be used with equal confidence.

In the second experiment it was hypothesized that a hearth originally heated below the Curie temperatures of magnetite and hematite upon reheating to a higher temperature but still below the Curie temperatures will produce a PTRM whose direction will be unaffected by the original PTRM direction. The results of the investigation appear to support the hypothesis, for two reasons. First, the VGP position of the second firing was closer to the reference pole position (MRPP indicated a significant difference between the first and second firings). If the second firing had been affected by the first firing, the second firing would have been farther away as a result of rotating the hearth a full 90° to the west. Second, Grisso (1978) found that during thermal demagnetization there is a progressive change in declination toward the declination of the original firing. This change was not observed when the experimental samples were thermally demagnetized (Smith 1981:56–62). Apparently, the PTRM acquired during the second firing replaced the PTRM of the first firing.

Thus the most important conclusions to be drawn from this experimental work are that, under the firing temperatures and soil conditions used in this experimental design, no proof could be found that (1) larger cubes are better than smaller cubes, or that (2) previous firings significantly affect the final sample direction. In terms of current archaeomagnetic methods, it is reassuring to know that (1) archaeomagnetic data do appear to relate generally to the latest firing if that firing exceeded the temperature of preceding firings, and that (2) both mold sizes can produce good archaeomagnetic samples.

CHAPTER 9

Firing Temperature and Time as Variables Affecting the Quality of Archaeomagnetic Results

J. HOLLY HATHAWAY

Archaeomagnetic dating is becoming an important method for the temporal control of archaeological sites in the United States (Aitken 1974; DuBois 1975c; Eighmy et al. 1980; Wolfman 1979). Because the applications and techniques of archaeomagnetism are relatively recent additions to archaeology, many problems exist that need to be resolved before accurate, reliable data can be recovered from archaeomagnetic samples. A problem recognized during extensive archaeomagnetic studies of Anasazi ruins in southwestern Colorado (Hathaway 1982a) was to identify the limits within which archaeomagnetic samples have a good chance of producing useful directional and, consequently, temporal information. The variety of burned media identified in the archaeological record ranges from very well fired (almost vitrified in some cases) to poorly heated matrices, as in the case of temporary campfires. The archaeomagnetic results within these extremes vary enormously. Well-fired features are capable of producing superior archaeomagnetic results with α_{95} values under 2.0°, while less well heated matrices can be problematic and may produce results that are only marginal (3.5° to 10.0° α_{95} values) or poor (α_{95} values over 10.0°). In order to provide some basis for evaluating hearths and other burned matrices in the field, a study was conducted which examined two variables, firing temperature and length of firing, as factors affecting the quality of archaeomagnetic sample results.

According to paleomagnetic theory (Irving 1964; Nagata 1961), the magnetic remanence acquired by a burned medium does not obtain a total thermoremanent magnetization (TRM) unless temperatures of the magnetic minerals' Curie point (T_c) are reached (in this paper, 580° C—the T_c of magnetite—will be used). Lower temperatures result in a partial TRM, the magnitude of which is directly related to the maximum temperature achieved in the matrix. Unlike igneous rocks, however, the temperatures of prehistoric hearths probably rarely attained temperatures sufficient for a total TRM (Hathaway 1982b; Krause 1980; Sternberg 1982). Additionally, due to the nature of wood fires, the temperatures attained by the matrices were probably not evenly distributed, resulting in an inhomogeneous acquisition of the partial TRM. Theoretically, additional reheatings at similar temperatures should not improve the magnetism acquired, although a remagnetization of those magnetic grains affected within the temperature range should occur. It was suspected, however, that a sustained utilization of hearths at lower temperatures would result in a more homogeneous magnetization of the material and thus a stronger signal for eventual archaeomagnetic recording.

MATERIALS AND METHODS

To test the effects of firing temperature and length of firing on archaeomagnetic quality, twelve hearths were constructed in the Dolores River Valley in southwestern Colorado. The hearths were constructed to resemble the size and shape of hearths recognized from Anasazi cultures uncovered in the valley (Hewitt 1983:111; Schlanger 1983:86). The hearths were 0.5 m in diameter, 0.2 m deep, and basin-shaped.

The hearths were built in four soil texture types, two classified as loams (one with higher proportions of clay), one classified as sandy loam, and one as clay. Three hearths were dug in each area (see Hathaway et al., this volume, chap. 10, for specific hydrometer results). One hearth from each area was fired for a three-hour period at temperatures exceeding the T_c; the remaining two hearths in each area were fired at temperatures below the T_c (approximately 400° C). One of the lower-temperature hearths from each area was heated over a three-hour period, and the other lower-temperature hearth was heated on five separate occasions for three hours. Thermocouple wires were inserted into the hearth matrices in order to monitor and record the hearth temperatures during firing. The maximum hearth temperatures were obtained from a thermocouple located just below the top of the north wall of the hearths and exposed to the flame (thermocouple 5). Seven other thermocouples were placed about eight hearths (1, 3, 4, 6, 7, 9, 10, and 12) to measure the temperature differences within the soil matrix and the variation in temperature from the base of the hearth to the top rim. Thermocouples 1, 2, 3, and 4 were all located approximately 1 to 2 cm below the top rim—3 and 4 on the north side of the hearth, 1 on the southwest side, and 2 on the southeast side. These thermocouples were located between 0.25 cm and 2.0 cm back from the wall of the hearth (recessed into the soil matrix and away from direct flame). Thermocouples 6 and 7 were recessed into the soil approximately 0.5 cm at 6 to 7 cm and 10 to 11 cm from the top of the hearth on the north side, respectively. Thermocouple 8 was located on the bottom of the hearth and was exposed to the flame (see Hathaway 1982b for the precise locations of the thermocouples). Temperatures recorded from thermocouple 5 were used for regulating hearth temperatures during firing.

The hearths were fired using wood fuel (primarily *Pinus edulis*). The hearth temperatures were recorded in approximately five-minute intervals. An average high temperature was calculated from the recorded temperatures of each hearth. The average high temperature represents the mean value of the 10 highest temperatures recorded for each firing; the 10 highest temperatures from each of the 5 firings from the reheated hearths were combined and averaged; the result thus represented the average temperature over 50 measurements. This value was used to average out the occasional high-temperature spikes during firing and to exclude the lower values characteristic of the beginning and end of the firings. This value is believed to be a meaningful representation of the temperatures maintained by the hearths over most of their firing periods.

Archaeomagnetic samples were collected from all of the hearths after the firings were completed. The sampling techniques included recovery of 12 individual 2.5-cm specimens from each hearth. Orientation of the *in situ* positions was obtained by recording the azimuth of one cube side with a magnetic pocket transit.

The archaeomagnetic samples were measured for their NRM. Demagnetized results from these samples are presented in Hathaway (1982b); NRM results are used in this study because the demagnetized results were only slightly different from the NRM results (especially in remanent direction). Three sample parameters were established as indicators of archaeomagnetic sample quality: the α_{95} value, the mean sample intensity value, and the mean sample remanent direction. Smaller α_{95} values and larger intensity values were thought to represent better archaeomagnetic quality. Sample remanent directions that approximated the true reference direction (as

Table 9.1. The Average High Temperature Recorded at Thermocouple Locations for Experimental Hearths, in Degrees Centigrade

Hearth Desig.	Thermocouple Number							
	1	2	3	4	5	6	7	8
1	376°	353°	324°	413°	630°	259°	188°	283°
2					365			
3	218	226	197	277	413	290	373	481
4	652	489	424	542	702	409	216	279
5					390			
6	385	348	249	301	396	360	333	550
7	416	565	313	401	688	331	135	418
8					375			
9	272	233	195	283	383	313	224	498
10	361	413	393	444	651	376	234	342
11					385			
12	194	266	234	274	409	257	201	483

apparent from Dolores, Colorado), especially when taking into account the confidence radius (α_{95}), were considered to be good-quality samples. The reference location—78.02° N, 293.74° E—is the virtual geomagnetic pole position corresponding to the present-day field direction. Local magnetic declination was determined based on the difference between sun and magnetic compass specimen azimuths (see Hathaway and Krause, this volume, chap. 7). Local magnetic inclination was determined from projected 1980 values of the United States Geological Survey map *Magnetic Inclination in the United States: Epoch 1975.0* (Fabiano and Peddie 1975).

RESULTS

The calculated average high temperatures for each hearth are listed in Table 9.1. The temperatures recorded (the average high temperature) from hearths 1, 4, 7, and 10 all reached or exceeded the T_c. The remainder of the hearths averaged lower temperatures, around 400° C. The thermal gradient throughout the individual hearth matrices was considerable; temperature differences of up to 500° C are noted. The hottest areas recorded for the high-temperature hearths and for the low-temperature hearths are different. The hotter hearths

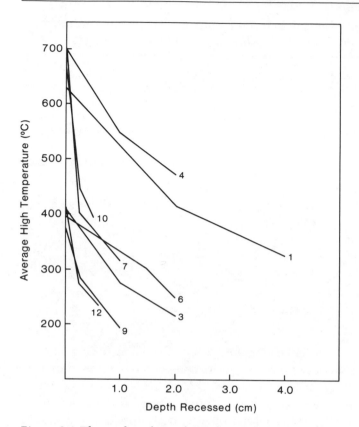

Figure 9.1. Thermal gradient through soil matrix in single-fired hearths. The parameter is the hearth number.

(as measured from the rim) were relatively cool on the bottom, whereas the cooler-temperature hearths were much hotter on the bottom than on the rim of the same hearth and also hotter than on the base of the high-temperature hearths. The unusually low temperatures at the base of the hot firings are attributed to the buildup of ash due to the greater amount of wood needed to maintain such high temperatures.

The thermal gradient in the soil matrix was evaluated by comparing the average high temperature of thermocouples 3, 4, and 5 on the appropriate hearths. The temperature drop from the exposed thermocouple (5) to thermocouples recessed into the matrix is shown in Figure 9.1. Part of the temperature variation by depth is probably due to variable placement of the thermocouples in the hearths' matrices.

The temperature gradient of all soil textural compositions, however, is quite marked, and most of the temperature change occurs within 0.5 to 2.0 cm of the surface. Because the relatively cool temperatures at depths beyond 2 cm result in a reduction of magnetization, based on the law of partial thermoremanent magnetization (Nagata 1961:160), these data suggest that even in very hot firings a *total* TRM is probably not being acquired by the entire matrix recovered for an archaeomagnetic sample (normally 2.5 cm).

The NRM directional results obtained from each sample are shown in the Appendix, Table A-5. In each case, the sample mean direction, when viewed with the oval of confidence, includes the reference direction. A negative correlation between intensity and α_{95} values is noted (see Hathaway et al., this volume); the higher the intensity values, the lower the α_{95} values.

The NRM intensity values of some prehistoric samples collected in the Dolores Archaeological Program were determined from 27 contexts of Anasazi origin. Three contextual groups were reviewed: exterior surface hearths, probably utilized occasionally at low temperatures; pit structure central hearths, probably utilized extensively at moderate temperatures; and burned pit structure walls, heated once, presumably at very high temperatures. Over a set size of 9 for each group, the averages of the mean sample intensities of the groups are: surface hearths, 6.29×10^{-3} A/m, with a standard deviation (SD) of 2.39×10^{-4} A/m; central structure hearths, 1.15×10^{-2} A/m, with an SD of 1.15×10^{-3} A/m; and structural walls, 8.83×10^{-3} A/m, with an SD of 3.18×10^{-3} A/m. The intensities of even the strongest of the three groups (central structural hearths) are comparable to only the low-temperature, single-fired hearths. As none of the prehistoric features approaches the intensities of the high-temperature hearth samples, the prehistoric features may not have been getting as hot as the experimental hearths. It is likely, then, that the experiments conducted do not represent the absolute lower range of firing temperatures occurring in the prehistoric cultures of the Dolores Valley.

By pairing the recorded firing temperatures of once-fired hearths (average high temperature) with the archaeomagnetic NRM results from the respective samples, the effect of firing temperature on archaeomagnetic quality can be evaluated. Figures 9.2 and 9.3 illustrate these relationships. The correlation coefficients and regression lines are provided on the figures. The results indicate a positive correlation

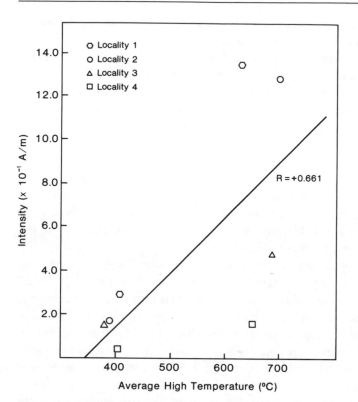

Figure 9.2. NRM mean sample intensity as a function of firing temperature.

between archaeomagnetic sample quality, as measured by increasing magnetization and decreasing α_{95} values, and firing temperatures.

A comparison of the length of firing of low-temperature hearths and NRM results (Figs. 9.4 and 9.5) indicates that sustained hearth use is only weakly related to archaeomagnetic quality. In all textural cases, however, results from hearths that were repeatedly fired were somewhat better than those from singly fired hearths.

SUMMARY

The firing experiments and subsequent archaeomagnetic sampling show that archaeomagnetic quality can improve with higher firing temperatures and that the length of firing can have some positive effect on the quality as well. Also, it is apparent that features attaining temperatures as low as 400° C provide adequate archaeomagnetic sample results. The firing temperatures achieved at the surface of the hearths decreased rapidly within the soil matrix so that only a thin veneer of magnetized material was produced. Temperatures at the base of the hearths depended on the firing temperatures of the hearth; higher temperatures at the rim correspond to *lower* temperatures at the base and vice versa. This is attributed to the greater amount of ash buildup in high-temperature hearths, which provided a layer of insulation from the heat.

A comparison of the experimental sample results and prehistoric Anasazi sample results indicates that the prehistoric features were fired at temperatures even cooler than those of the low-temperature hearths in the experimental group. It is suggested, therefore, that the majority of the prehistoric features sampled in the Yellowjacket and Dolores districts (Kane 1983) have acquired a partial rather than a

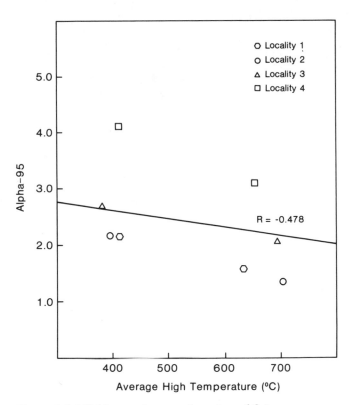

Figure 9.3. NRM α_{95} value as a function of firing temperature.

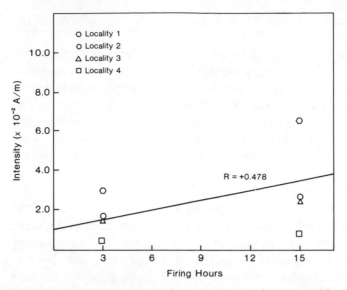

Figure 9.4. NRM mean sample intensity as a function of firing time among hearths fired at low temperatures.

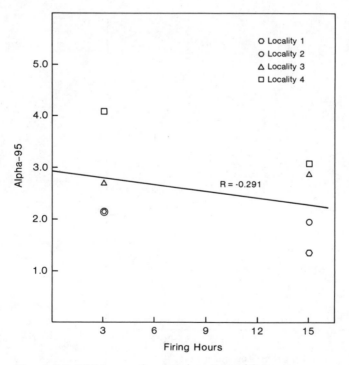

Figure 9.5. NRM α_{95} value as a function of firing time among hearths fired at low temperatures.

total TRM. The features utilized over longer periods (e.g., central pit structure hearths) represent a more homogeneous acquisition of remanence throughout the feature, which may result in slightly better results than those for similarly heated temporary-use hearths.

The collector of archaeomagnetic samples should be wary of features used minimally and with marginal evidence of burning. The most likely features to yield precise archaeomagnetic dates are those used continually over long periods or features that have obviously been raised to very high (greater than 400° C) temperatures.

CHAPTER 10

Variation in Soil Texture and Its Effect on Archaeomagnetic Sample Quality

J. HOLLY HATHAWAY, GARY P. SMITH,
AND GEORGE J. KRAUSE

There has been a great deal of research concerning the acquisition of remanent magnetization in magnetic minerals (e.g., Barbetti et al. 1977; Dunlop 1972; Liebermann and Banerjee 1971; Sigalas et al. 1978; Stacey and Banerjee 1974). Little of this work, however, has been directed toward examining soil textural variation as it relates to the acquisition of remanent magnetization in archaeomagnetic features and how it affects archaeomagnetic results. Although most soils contain sufficient amounts of ferromagnetic minerals for the acquisition of remanent magnetization (Michels 1973:131; Tarling 1975:186), other factors may be important. Bucha (1971:61) suggests that soils that are compact and porous produce the best archaeomagnetic results. According to Eighmy (1980b:20), clay soils provide the best material for archaeomagnetic results from prehistoric features. The apparent basis for these findings may be explained by a greater tendency for the inclusion of single domain (SD) and pseudo–single-domain (PSD) grains rather than multi-domain (MD) grains in finer-grained soils (e.g., clay-based soils) (Tucker and Thomas 1983). The behavior of MD and SD/PSD grains is very different (McElhinny 1973), and much of paleomagnetic thermoremanent theory is based on the predominance of SD and PSD grains.

THE EXPERIMENTS

The investigations conducted by Krause (1980), Smith (1981), and Hathaway (1982b) were controlled firings in a known magnetic field (current local field). The VGPs corresponding to the current local magnetic field direction were established for Fort Collins, Colorado (Krause 1980; Smith 1981), to be 76.6° N, 290.4° E, and for Dolores, Colorado (Hathaway 1982b), to be 78.0° N, 293.7° E. For both areas the field direction was determined by sun compass measurements for declination and the United States Geological Survey map *Magnetic Inclination in the United States: Epoch 1975.0* (Fabiano and Peddie 1975) for inclination. Firing temperatures were monitored and controlled by a potentiometer, with several thermocouple wires placed at the surface of the hearths or inserted into the soil at depths from 0.5 to 2.0 cm, depending upon the experiment. The temperatures achieved in the hearths at a soil depth of 0.5 to 1.0 cm ranged from moderate (325° C) to very hot (650° C). The hearths heated by Krause tended toward the lower-range temperatures (425° C average); Smith's hearths tended toward midrange temperatures (550° C average); Hathaway's hearths were of varied temperatures (4 hearths were of lower temperatures [350° C], and the other 8 hearths were of mid- to upper-range temperatures [500–650° C]; see Hathaway, this volume, chap. 9).

The experiments conducted by Smith (1981) were constructed on a movable platform with four long columns of soil composed of varying percentages of clay and sand. Soil texture was controlled by mixing different proportions of sand and commercial ceramic clay (Red Mountain). Krause's and Hathaway's hearths were dug into native soils of various textures near Fort Collins, and Dolores, Colorado, respectively. Soil samples for all of the hearths were submitted to the Colorado State University Soils Laboratory for hydrometer analysis of sand, silt, and clay percentages. Smith's material was also tested for percent of gravel inclusion (the fraction over 2 mm). The textural percentages for each hearth or column are presented in Table 10.1. The range of percentages of sand and clay among the 19 hearths varied widely, in some cases exceeding 50%.

After the firing experiments were completed and the material was completely cooled, archaeomagnetic samples were recovered from the hearths. Sampling followed standard procedures for the United States (Eighmy 1980b): 12 specimens were collected for each sample except Smith's hearth 9 (designated S9), for which only 9 specimens were recovered due to a lack of collecting material. The experiments conducted by Smith and Krause included the collection of more than one sample per hearth (for which only one set per hearth is used in this study). This was an attempt to minimize the effects of other variables so that any variation due to soil texture could be more easily isolated. Smith's studies included the collection of large (4.3 cm) and small (2.5 cm) molds from each column. After the initial firing

Table 10.1. Grain Size Percentages for the Experimental Hearths

Hearth Desig.[a]	Percent Sand	Percent Silt	Percent Clay	Percent Gravel	Textural Category
K1	30%	28%	42%	—	Clay
K2	78	14	8	—	Sandy loam
K3	27	27	46	—	Clay
S9	30	18	49	3	Clay
S10	43	14	37	6	Clay loam
S11	57	10	25	8	Sandy clay loam
S12	70	6	13	11	Sandy loam
H1	38	44	18	—	Loam
H2	35	44	21	—	Loam
H3	31	45	24	—	Loam
H4	59	31	10	—	Sandy loam
H5	61	27	12	—	Sandy loam
H6	55	21	24	—	Sandy clay loam
H7	43	35	22	—	Loam
H8	45	32	23	—	Loam
H9	41	33	26	—	Loam
H10	28	28	44	—	Clay
H11	17	30	53	—	Clay
H12	17	29	54	—	Clay

[a]The K designation represents data from Krause 1980; S, data from Smith 1981; and H, data from Hathaway 1982.

and collection with large molds, the platform was turned 90°, the columns were refired, and samples were collected using small molds (also used by Krause and Hathaway). Because three groups of samples recovered from the same column differ noticeably, the best group— the refired samples (9–12)—was selected for this study. Krause's studies included the collection of samples from the hearth rim and the hearth base. Again, due to the noticeable difference in the two groups, the better group—the rim samples (1–3)—was used.

The archaeomagnetic samples were run on a Schonstedt spinner magnetometer to measure the natural remanent magnetism (NRM). Demagnetized results for all samples are available in Krause 1980, Smith 1981, and Hathaway 1982b. Because the demagnetized results were not significantly different from the NRM results (especially in direction), the NRM results are used exclusively in this paper. Three of the sample parameters were considered to be important indicators of archaeomagnetic quality: the α_{95} value, the mean sample intensity value, and the mean sample pole location. An α_{95} value reflects the degree of specimen direction clustering around the mean sample direction. Small values indicate tighter clustering around the mean and hence better archaeomagnetic quality. As indicated in studies by Hathaway and Eighmy (1982), the intensity value tends to correlate negatively with α_{95} values for prehistoric samples; thus, higher intensity values should correspond to better archaeomagnetic quality (e.g., smaller α_{95} values). Finally, because the samples were recovered from hearths fired in a known magnetic field (i.e., local current fields for Dolores and Fort Collins), the arc distance between a sample's mean pole location and the observed reference location was calculated. The smaller the arc distance, the better the sample quality was believed to be.

ANALYSES AND RESULTS

The NRM results for each of the 19 samples are found in the Appendix, Table A-5. The very large difference in intensity values between Smith's samples and the samples of Hathaway and Krause is believed to be partially due to hotter firing temperatures attained more homogeneously throughout the columns of soil. The intensities of Smith's first firings (i.e., lower firing temperatures) are quite a bit lower than the refired samples and are more consistent with the intensities obtained by Hathaway and Krause. The calculated arc distances between the local geomagnetic pole positions and the mean sample pole positions are provided in Table 10.2. The NRM polar plots of the 19 samples are illustrated with their respective reference pole positions in Figures 10.1 and 10.2. Generally, the mean sample plots have α_{95} value ranges that include the reference locations.

The correlations between the sample/soil parameters and the arc-distance/α_{95} parameters are presented in Table 10.3. Due to the small number of samples in Krause's and Smith's experiments, no statistical significance can be drawn from their correlations. Nevertheless, the Krause/Smith data are considered for their descriptive potential.

As expected, sample intensity and α_{95} values in Hathaway's group of samples are negatively correlated, and there is less than .001 probability that an r of $-.745$ would result if the variables are in fact not negatively correlated. The trend in Smith's data is also negative, but

Table 10.2. Arc Distances of Experimental Sample Remanent Directions to the Reference Pole

Sample Desig.[a]	Sample α_{95}	Arc Distance from Actual Pole Location
K1	3.87°	2.45°
K2	2.35	1.82
K3	3.30	1.02
S9	5.74	2.27
S10	2.91	4.05
S11	2.03	6.95
S12	4.66	5.36
H1	1.57	0.80
H2	1.38	2.13
H3	2.16	2.02
H4	1.32	0.40
H5	1.95	2.82
H6	2.16	1.02
H7	2.05	2.35
H8	2.88	1.08
H9	2.70	0.65
H10	3.08	1.83
H11	3.09	3.41
H12	4.09	2.84

[a]The K designation represents data from Krause 1980; S, data from Smith 1981; and H, data from Hathaway 1982.

Krause's three samples trend in the opposite direction. The correlation between α_{95} and arc distance trends in a positive direction for all three data sets. That is, as α_{95} gets larger, the VGP tends to plot farther from the reference pole position, though in none of the data sets does this correlation rise to a statistically significant level.

Figure 10.1. The polar plots of samples from Smith's (plus signs) and Krause's (circles) hearths.

Figure 10.2. The polar plots of samples from Hathaway's hearths.

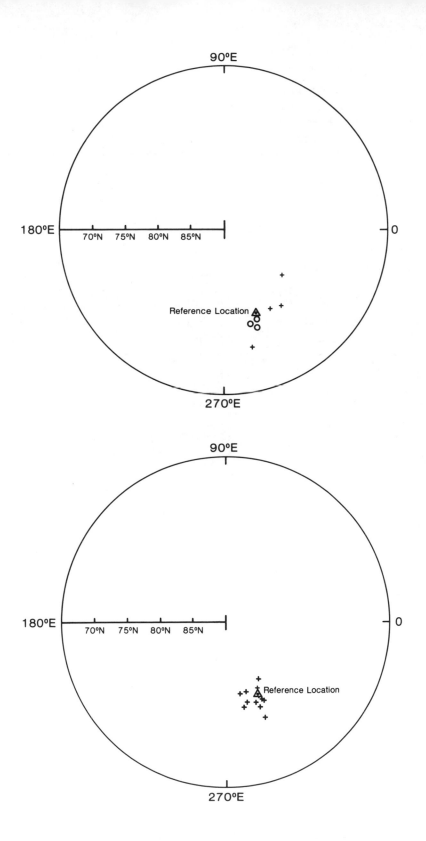

Table 10.3. Correlation Coefficients for Experimental
Sample Results

Case[a]	X Var.	Y Var.	r
Krause	Intensity	α_{95}	+.7214
Smith	Intensity	α_{95}	−.1090
Hathaway	Intensity	α_{95}	−.7449
Krause	α_{95}	Arc Dist.	+.1648
Smith	α_{95}	Arc Dist.	+.3105
Hathaway	α_{95}	Arc Dist.	+.4489
Krause	Intensity	Arc Dist.	+.8020
Smith	Intensity	Arc Dist.	−.6428
Hathaway	Intensity	Arc Dist.	−.5727
Krause	Sand	Arc Dist.	+.2225
Smith	Sand	Arc Dist.	+.8830
Hathaway	Sand	Arc Dist.	−.6500
Krause	Silt	Arc Dist.	−.1501
Smith	Silt	Arc Dist.	−.8792
Hathaway	Silt	Arc Dist.	−.0863
Krause	Clay	Arc Dist.	−.3057
Smith	Clay	Arc Dist.	−.8792
Hathaway	Clay	Arc Dist.	+.4799
Krause	Clay	Intensity	+.3236
Smith	Clay	Intensity	+.8985
Hathaway	Clay	Intensity	−.6058
Krause	Sand	Intensity	−.3645
Smith	Sand	Intensity	−.8997
Hathaway	Sand	Intensity	+.3650

[a]Krause: $N = 3$; Smith: $N = 4$; Hathaway: $N = 12$.

Hathaway's set also shows a statistically significant ($p < .02$) relationship between intensity and arc distance: the more magnetized samples are likely to plot closest to the reference locations. The trend in Smith's data is similar, although Krause's data reveal a trend with a positive correlation.

Hathaway's set shows an unexpected relationship between soil texture and arc distance. Sample VGPs plotting closest to the reference location tend to be low in clay content and high in sand content. The correlation between sand and arc distance is statistically significant ($p < .02$). The trends in the small Smith and Krause sets are as expected, but sample sizes are small.

These data reveal no strong relationship between soil texture and intensity. Correlation trends (sand vs. intensity; clay vs. intensity) tend to be inconsistent among the data sets and to rise to significant levels in only one case. In Hathaway's 12-sample set, samples with high clay content actually tended to be less intensely magnetized ($p < .02$).

Perhaps the most interesting result produced by these studies is the correlation between soil texture and α_{95} (Figs. 10.3 and 10.4). In all three data sets, the correlation between clay content and α_{95} tended to be positive, and that between sand content and α_{95} tended to be negative. In Hathaway's large data set, these correlations are statistically significant at the .001 and .02 levels respectively. These

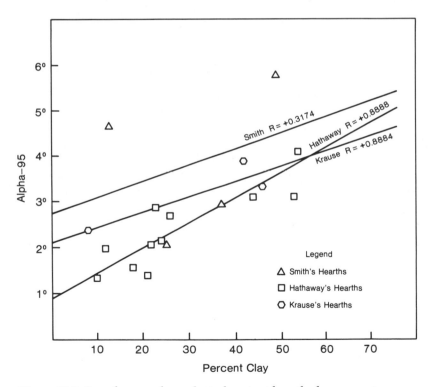

Figure 10.3. Sample α_{95} values plotted against hearth clay percentages.

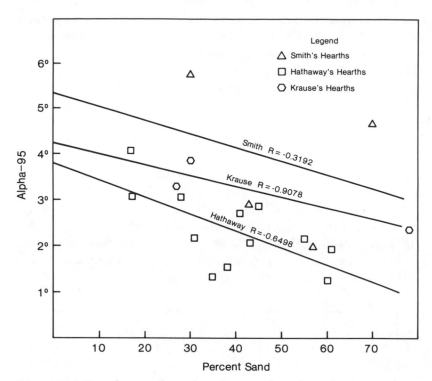

Figure 10.4. Sample α_{95} values plotted against hearth sand percentages.

results are interesting because the correlation trends do not support conventional archaeomagnetic wisdom.

Based on years of experience, conventional archaeomagnetic wisdom holds that samples with high clay content (as opposed to high sand content) produce the best clustering (smallest α_{95}s) of specimen directions (Eighmy, this volume). In one analysis of prehistoric archaeomagnetic samples (Hathaway and Eighmy 1982:47–56), sandy soils did not provide better archaeomagnetic samples with smaller α_{95} values. Further, in the Hathaway and Eighmy study, no trend could be observed in the correlation between clay content and α_{95} to support the observation from the experimental hearths that features with a greater proportion of clay tended to produce worse results. Thus, while the more sandy soils in the experimental hearths seem to be able to acquire a remanent magnetism as well as, if not better than, the more clayey soils, there is no evidence that after hundreds of years the more sandy soils maintain a more precise record of their remanent direction.

CONCLUSION

It is reassuring for the archaeomagnetist to note a positive correlation in the experimental sample results between the precision of the acquired remanent direction (as measured by α_{95}) and the arc distance between the reference pole position and the VGP location. These results support an important assumption of archaeomagnetism: that samples with more precise mean directions reflect more closely the field direction at the time of acquisition of the remanence. At the same time, however, the results suggest that the quality of the acquisition of remanent magnetism in sandy soil matrices can be as good as, if not better than, the acquisition of remanent magnetism in clay soils. At least for soils with a sand fraction $\leq 70\%$ and a clay fraction $\geq 10\%$, the acquisition of remanent magnetism is clearly no greater a problem than it is for more clayey textures.

Comparing these results on the acquisition of remanent magnetism in experimental hearths with limited results on the retention of remanent magnetism (from archaeomagnetic samples) after burial for hundreds of years is instructive. The limited quantitative description (Hathaway and Eighmy 1982) reveals that sandy soils are no better at retaining remanence of a high quality (i.e., small α_{95}, higher intensity, and VGP close to the reference location). In fact, years of experience with archaeomagnetic samples suggest that soils with greater clay content usually produce better archaeomagnetic results. Taken together, the two sources of data (experimental hearths and burned archaeological features) suggest that while sandy soils can acquire a remanent magnetism as good as that of clay soils, the clayey soils are better able to maintain their remanence over hundreds of years. Thus it is the maintenance of remanence rather than the acquisition of remanence that makes the clayey matrices better archaeomagnetic prospects.

CHAPTER 11

Determining the Source of Remanence in Archaeological Soils: A Microscopic Study of Heated and Unheated Soils

J. HOLLY HATHAWAY

Archaeomagnetism is based on the fact that after an archaeological feature such as a hearth is burned, a record of the geomagnetic field remains. When the burning was a single event or when the feature was used over a short period of time, interpreting the age of the burning is relatively simple. However, when a feature was utilized over long periods of time (>10 years) or when it was reused at a much later date, establishing the time at which the primary magnetic remanence was acquired is essential for proper interpretation. Determining when in the use life of a hearth the primary remanence was acquired can be a problem because magnetic remanence may be acquired in a variety of ways, and the resultant natural remanent magnetism (NRM) may represent a chemical and thermal composite of several firing events. It is therefore important to identify the source or sources of remanence in multiple-use features so that the proper event will be recognized and dated.

Three original sources of magnetic remanence are considered important when dealing with incinerated prehistoric features: a total thermoremanent magnetization (TRM), a partial thermoremanent magnetization (PTRM), and a chemical remanent magnetization (CRM). TRM is acquired during the cooling of iron oxides through and below their respective Curie temperatures (T_c). The remanence attained over any one temperature interval below the Curie point is referred to as a partial TRM (Nagata 1961). The majority of a total TRM is attained at temperatures within 200° of T_c (Irving 1964:26). As suggested in studies by Hathaway (1982b) and Krause (1980), the temperatures attained within the soil of small prehistoric hearths are unlikely to have reached temperatures sufficient for a total TRM.

CRM may also contribute to the total magnetization acquired during the heating and cooling of an archaeological feature. CRM is acquired during the growth of a ferromagnetic mineral in the presence of an external magnetic field. CRM may occur as a very small (superparamagnetic) grain grows past a critical volume or as a mineral alters in structure to produce a ferromagnetic mineral. Although CRM can be acquired at temperatures below the T_c of the minerals involved (Strangway 1970:46), it exhibits a TRM-like behavior (McElhinny 1973:60). Kobayashi (1959:116) suggests, however, that CRM remanence may be as low as 10% of the TRM in the same mineral. The oxidation of magnetite to hematite is a common example of this CRM process. In the archaeological situation, the oxidation of magnetite to hematite and/or the growth of new hematite grains is evidenced by the change of the native soil color to the orange-red soils that frequently surround burned features (Hathaway and Eighmy 1982). Because each of these processes results in remanent magnetization and because they may be acquired at different times during the use history of a fired prehistoric feature, a precise archaeomagnetic interpretation must identify the appropriate firing event.

MATERIALS AND METHODS

Distinguishing among the different sources of magnetic remanence might be accomplished in several ways. Two analyses are considered here. First, a microscopic study of the magnetic fraction extracted from heated and unheated soil samples was completed. Seven magnetic minerals were observed and counted. The microscopic analysis provided a basis for understanding the mineralogy of typical archaeological soils and the effects of heating on the mineralogical composition of the soils.

Second, thermal step-demagnetization of several of the archaeomagnetic samples recovered from experimental hearths was conducted. The difference between magnetite and hematite as remanent carriers is quite distinct and may become important when considering the primary remanence in an archaeological soil. Although both magnetite and hematite are capable of retaining a magnetic remanence, magnetite exhibits much stronger saturation magnetization (by a factor of 200) than does hematite. It may be feasible, then, for a CRM held by hematite grains to be dominated by a PTRM held in magnetite grains within the fired material. As suggested in studies by Sternberg, Butler, and McGuire (1980), magnetite is the primary carrier of magnetic remanence in archaeological features. Thermal step-demagnetization (Yu, this volume) may allow us to distinguish between a magnetite remanence and a hematite remanence, but because this procedure is very time-consuming, only selected specimens from six samples were chosen for treatment in this manner. The temperatures at which the samples lost their remanence were compared with the firing temperatures of the hearths to determine the possible source or sources of remanence and to identify the ferromagnetic mineral carrying the remanence.

To provide control over firing conditions, the studies entailed the construction of 12 experimental hearths, which were designed to resemble prehistoric features recognized in the Dolores River Valley in southwestern Colorado. The 12 hearths were constructed in four areas in the valley. The four areas represent different soil types with varying textures. Each of the four areas contained three hearths that were fired under controlled conditions. One hearth from each area was fired for three hours at temperatures exceeding the T_c of magnetite (580° C), and the remaining two were fired at lower temperatures (approximately 400° C) for three hours. In addition, hearths 2, 5, 8, and 11 were all heated on three different occasions for a total of approximately 15 hours. A total TRM should occur only in the hearths that exceeded T_c. Soil samples were recovered before and after firing the hearths. Soil samples of the postfiring material were used for hydrometer analysis of textural percentages by the Colorado State University Soils Laboratory to determine the sand, silt, and clay content and the total iron percentage. Although the percentage of iron in a material is a gross value representing the 'free' iron ions as well as the iron caught up in various minerals, including magnetite and hematite, it is indicative of the potential magnetic capabilities of a matrix (Strangway 1970:7). Iron oxide percentages from 2 to 10% (Tarling 1975:186; Michels 1973:137; Tite and Mullins 1971:213) have been associated with archaeological soils. Soils in this study had iron percentages at and below 2%. Total iron percentages determined for prehistoric samples from the Dolores Archaeological Program (Hathaway and Eighmy 1982:48) indicate similar values for total iron content within this area. The firing temperatures, textural percentages, and iron content for each of the 12 hearths are presented in Table 11.1. Note that the hearths with the highest clay content tend to correspond to those with the highest iron content.

The unfired and fired soil samples (a total of 24 samples) were

Table 11.1. The Firing Temperature, Soil Textural Percentages, and Iron Content of Experimental Hearths

Hearth No.	Percent Sand	Percent Silt	Percent Clay	Percent Iron	Firing Temp. (° C)
1	38%	44%	18%	1.95%	630°
2	35	44	21	1.86	365
3	31	45	24	1.92	413
4	59	31	10	1.28	702
5	61	27	12	1.74	390
6	55	21	24	2.08	396
7	43	35	22	1.66	688
8	45	32	23	2.03	375
9	41	33	26	1.67	383
10	28	28	44	2.56	651
11	17	30	53	2.61	385
12	17	29	54	2.50	409

then prepared for the microscopic studies. The magnetic fractions of the samples were extracted with a powerful hand magnet, and polished sections were made. The 24 polished sections were viewed with a reflective microscope at 400× magnification. The modal analysis consisted of a point count of seven opaque magnetic minerals: magnetite, hematite, ilmenite, altered ilmenite, two phases of martite, and a hematite cement. The count was continued until approximately 300 minerals had been tallied or until all the minerals in a polished section had been counted. An additional mineral was counted concurrently with the point count of the above minerals but not included in the final tally due to its profuse occurrence in heated material. This mineral is described by Mason and Berry (1959:179) as botryoidal hematite grains, which are small, rounded nodules of hematite that may occur singly or in clustered bunches. The clustered bunches of botryoidal hematite grains were counted in the modal analysis as hematite cement, but when occurring as a single grain, they were counted separately from the modal analysis.

Thermal step-demagnetization of selected specimens from six samples was conducted. Because these samples were a part of several other studies (see Hathaway 1982b), the samples were all demagnetized by the alternating field (AF) method to 20 mT prior to thermal treatment. Although the intensity of the samples dropped appreciably from the NRM (over 50%), the remanent directions measured were relatively stable through AF demagnetization (Hathaway 1982b:179–182), with the possible exception of sample 12. All mean sample remanent directions, however, were within 10° of the reference direction at the 20 mT level. Samples 4 through 6 and 10 through 12 were selected for this analysis. They represent the extreme cases of sand, clay, and iron percentages. The progressive method of thermal demagnetization (McElhinny 1973:96) was used. A total of 22 specimens was heated to 150° C and 300° C and then, depending on the physical condition of the individual specimens (the plaster encasing the specimens tended to crack and powder after several steps), to 400° C, 475° C, 500° C, and/or 580° C. At least two specimens from each sample were demagnetized at 580° C (the T_c of magnetite). The source of remanence (CRM, PTRM, or TRM) was identified by comparing the results of intensity and direction with the firing temperature of the hearths. If CRM is the major source of remanence in those hearths that did not attain T_c during firing, the remanence should remain after thermal demagnetization above the firing temperature. If, conversely, the remanence was acquired as a PTRM during firing, then the remanence should be removed at temperatures achieved during firing. The two samples for which the hearth firing temperatures reached T_c (samples 4 and 10) should exhibit typical TRM behavior during thermal demagnetization.

RESULTS

The results from the modal analysis are presented in Table 11.2. This analysis indicates the occurrence of several chemical and mineral alterations as a result of heating the parent material. Magnetite grains are more frequent (up to 50%) in the parent material than in the heated material. Some of the magnetite may be oxidizing, because there is a slight increase in the presence of the two phases of martite. The percentages of hematite detrital grains varied over only a small range from the heated to unheated soils. This may be due to the way the magnetic fraction was obtained. Since the hematite grains are less magnetic, they may not be as readily extracted by magnetic methods. However, the abundance of both hematite cement and the individual botryoidal grains in heated soils indicates that hematite was being extracted. The increase in single botryoidal grains in heated soils is very marked and tends to correlate positively

Table 11.2. Results of Modal Analysis

Sample Desig.[b]	N	Hem.	Magn.	Mart. 1	Mart. 2	Ilm.	Alt. Ilm.	Hem. Cem.	No. Botry. Hem.
					Percentage of Grains Counted[a]				
1a	339	18.6	44.3	23.6	4.1	2.1	0.6	6.8	34
1b	300	7.7	22.3	33.3	6.7	1.0	1.3	28.0	191
2a	311	11.9	38.9	29.9	4.8	1.9	1.0	11.9	73
2b	300	8.0	27.7	34.0	7.3	1.0	1.0	21.3	280
3a	301	14.6	48.8	17.9	4.3	1.0	0.7	12.6	78
3b	320	10.6	31.3	31.6	5.9	1.6	2.5	16.9	157
4a	300	9.3	39.0	29.0	3.7	1.7	1.7	16.3	68
4b	300	8.0	14.0	17.7	10.3	0.7	9.0	40.3	415
5a	300	13.3	43.7	23.7	5.3	0.3	0.3	13.3	62
5b	300	9.3	20.7	26.7	11.7	0.7	2.0	29.0	169
6a	300	8.7	38.0	27.0	6.7	0.7	0.7	18.7	80
6b	204	19.6	18.0	17.6	5.4	0.5	4.9	32.8	317
7a	306	10.5	48.7	20.3	2.3	0.7	1.6	16.0	44
7b	300	13.0	23.7	23.7	5.3	0.3	0.3	34.0	192
8a	300	10.0	43.7	21.3	6.7	0.3	1.0	17.7	39
8b	300	10.0	20.0	30.3	8.0	0.0	0.7	30.7	18
9a	301	14.0	48.8	16.0	3.0	1.0	1.0	16.9	73
9b	300	10.3	22.3	29.7	4.7	0.3	0.7	32.0	125
10a	300	9.3	50.3	24.7	5.0	1.3	0.7	9.0	29
10b	300	6.7	12.0	27.7	5.7	0.3	0.7	47.3	388
11a	182	9.3	56.6	13.2	8.8	0.6	2.2	9.9	13
11b	300	7.0	17.0	33.7	6.0	0.0	0.0	35.7	331
12a	300	7.7	54.0	20.3	5.7	2.7	0.3	10.0	36
12b	300	10.0	31.3	34.0	6.3	0.7	0.0	14.3	131

[a]Abbreviations are as follows:

Hem.	Hematite
Magn.	Magnetite
Mart. 1	Primarily magnetite grain
Mart. 2	Primarily hematite grain
Ilm.	Ilmenite
Alt. Ilm.	Altered ilmenite
Hem. Cem.	Hematite cemented botryoidal grains
No. Botry. Hem.	Number of singular botryoidal hematite grains

[b]The number indicates the experimental sample number. An appended *a* designates unheated samples; an appended *b* designates heated samples.

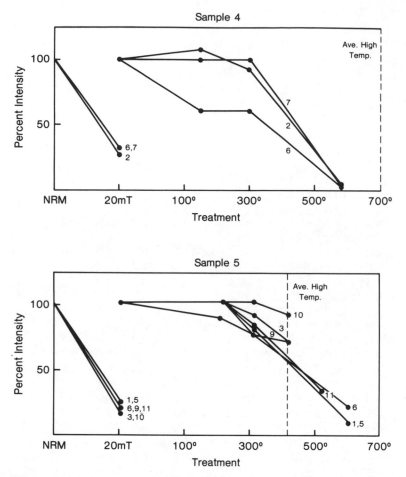

Figure 11.1. Intensity curves for specimens 2, 6, and 7 from sample 4 and for specimens 1, 3, 5, 6, 9, 10, and 11 from sample 5.

with the hearth firing temperature and firing duration. The increase in these grains is also positively correlated with the total iron content of the material (see Table 11.1). When compared with the NRM mean sample intensities, however, the highest increases in the botryoidal grains over the 12 groups are associated with samples exhibiting the lowest NRM mean intensities (note samples 10 and 11). This trend may be due to the predominance of hematite, a much weaker ferromagnetic mineral, in hearths 10 and 11 and a marked reduction in magnetite in the heated material.

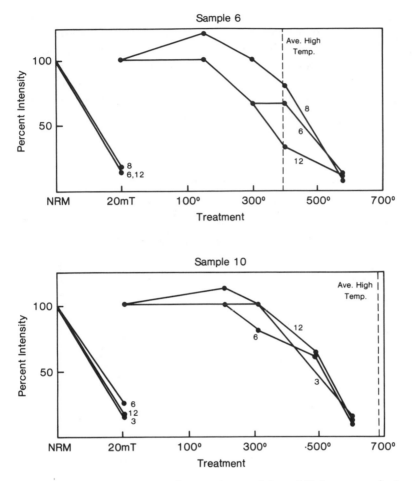

Figure 11.2. Intensity curves for specimens 6, 8, and 12 from sample 6 and for specimens 3, 6, and 12 from sample 10.

The results of the thermal demagnetization of selected specimens from samples 4 through 6 and 10 through 12 are illustrated in Figures 11.1–11.10. For evaluation, the reference location and hearth firing temperatures are indicated on the diagrams. The samples that were heated to T_c (samples 1, 4, 7, and 10) produced different results. At 300° (a temperature lower than the T_c of either magnetite or hematite), the declinations of the specimens from sample 4 are very different from the reference declination (Fig. 11.4). In addition, the intensity is nearly zero at 580° C (Fig. 11.1). This indicates the possibility of chemical change during the demagnetization process. It is also unfortunate that the lack of thermal demagnetization steps from 300 to 580° C inhibits our obtaining a better picture of the TRM curve for this sample. Sample 10, however, portrays a typical TRM curve (Fig. 11.2) with reduced intensities (approximately 10% remaining) at 580° C but with good remanent directions relative to the reference direction in two of three specimens (Fig. 11.8). These facts indicate

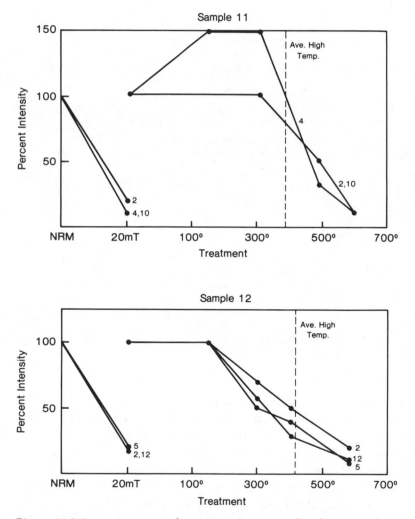

Figure 11.3. Intensity curves for specimens 2, 4, and 10 from sample 11 and for specimens 2, 5, and 12 from sample 12.

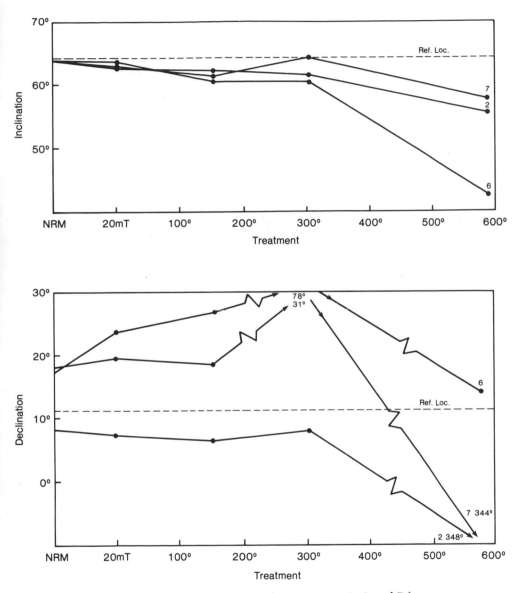

Figure 11.4. Inclination and declination for specimens 2, 6, and 7 from sample 4.

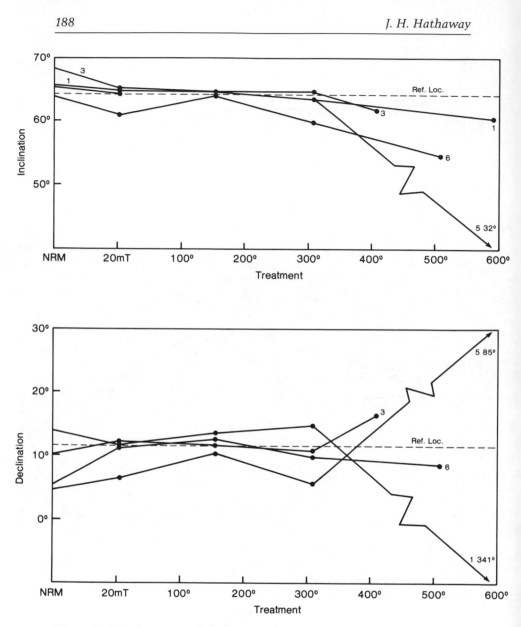

Figure 11.5. Inclination and declination for specimens 1, 3, 5, and 6 from sample 5.

that a TRM (CRM?) carried by hematite was a contributor of the magnetic remanence in this hearth.

Hearths 5, 6, 11, and 12 (Figs. 11.1, 11.2, and 11.3) were all heated to temperatures below the T_c of magnetite and hematite and should, if the remanence was caused primarily by a PTRM, lose their remanence at approximately 400° C. The directional information from sample 12 (Fig. 11.10) indicates that the stable remanence is mostly

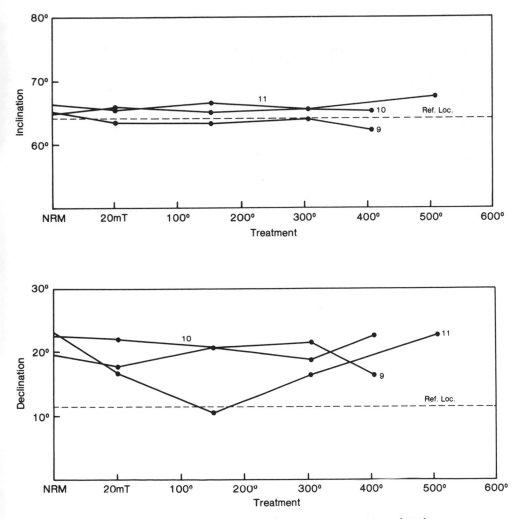

Figure 11.6. Inclination and declination for specimens 9, 10, and 11 from sample 5.

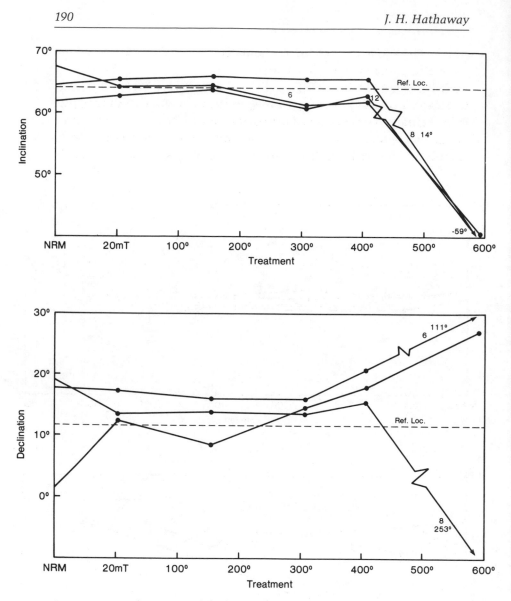

Figure 11.7. Inclination and declination for specimens 6, 8, and 12 from sample 6.

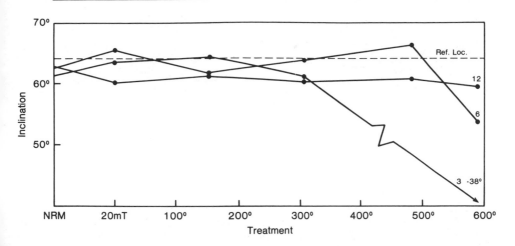

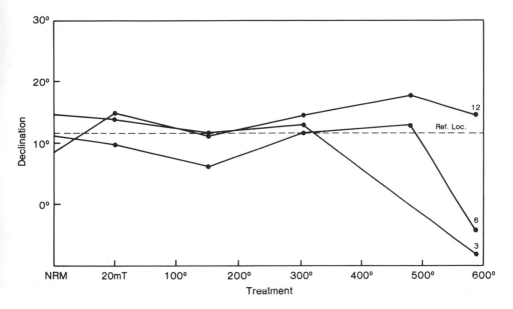

Figure 11.8. Inclination and declination plots for specimens 3, 6, and 12 from sample 10.

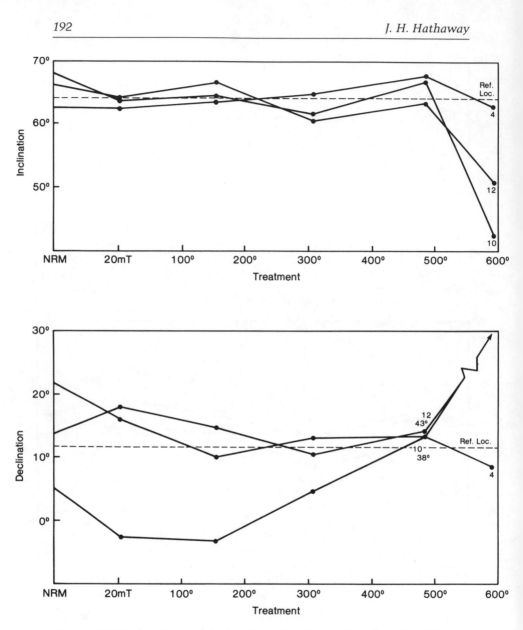

Figure 11.9. Inclination and declination plots for specimens 4, 10, and 12 from sample 11.

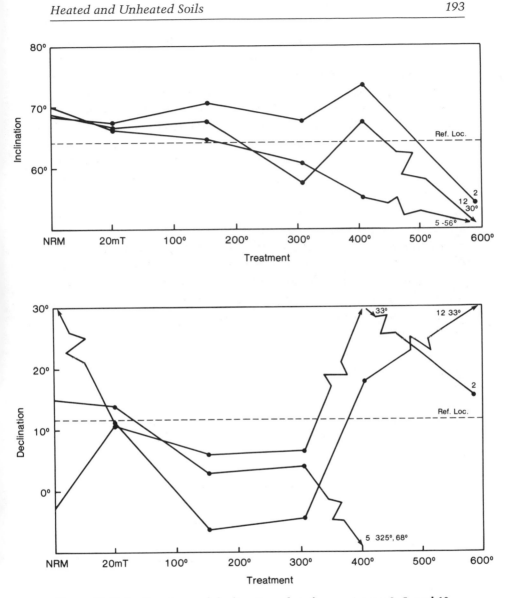

Figure 11.10. Inclination and declination plots for specimens 2, 5, and 12 from sample 12.

gone at the firing temperature of the hearth. Therefore a PTRM is likely to be the primary source of remanence in this hearth. The results from samples 5, 6, and 11, however, indicate the possibility of CRM. All of the specimens from these samples which were demagnetized above the temperature of the hearths indicate intensities of approximately 10% of the NRM at 580° C (Figs. 11.1, 11.2, and 11.3). Results of the remanent directions, however, indicate that about 50% of the specimens no longer hold a normal direction after 580° C as compared with the reference directions (Figs. 11.5, 11.6, 11.7, and 11.9). This observation indicates that the minerals carrying the remanence may be either magnetite or hematite. When the thermal demagnetization results are compared with the modal analysis, the major difference between the sample that still retained normal directions (sample 11) and the sample that did not (sample 6) is a marked decrease in martite in sample 6 and a marked increase in martite in sample 11. Both samples showed decreases in magnetite, although in sample 11 this was more marked (almost 70%).

SUMMARY

Microscopic analysis of ferromagnetic minerals has shown that the firing of archaeological soils results in the genesis of botryoidal hematite grains, a decrease in magnetite grains, and an increase in martite grains. Although these changes undoubtedly result in a CRM, the relative contribution of the ferromagnetic minerals to the CRM is unclear. Numerically, hematite is the most common altered grain in heated soils, but the thermal demagnetization studies could not show that the CRM is carried primarily by hematite as opposed to magnetite grains. Regardless of the magnetic mineralogy, the CRM acquired was present in the majority of test cases (3 out of 4) from hearths heated below 500° C. Although TRM and CRM were indistinguishable by methods of thermal demagnetization, the mineralogical studies indicated that CRM may also be an important part of the remanence acquired at temperatures approaching the T_c of magnetite.

PART 4

Results

Introduction

This section presents the results of archaeomagnetic directional studies from the Americas. Sternberg and McGuire (Chapter 12) derive an archaeomagnetic secular variation curve for the American Southwest for the period A.D. 700–1450. Eighmy, Hathaway, and Kane (Chapter 13) look at a refinement of secular variation in the Southwest during the period A.D. 700–900, utilizing the numerous, well-dated archaeomagnetic samples recovered as part of the Dolores Archaeological Program. Wolfman presents results describing secular variation for the midcontinental region, A.D. 650–1500 (Chapter 14), and for Mesoamerica, A.D. 1–1200 (Chapter 15). In both cases, he discusses the implications of these results for the archaeological chronologies of these regions. The only significant data set from the Americas not described in detail herein is that of DuBois (1975, 1982, 1989; Watanabe and DuBois 1965).

CHAPTER 12

Archaeomagnetic Secular Variation in the American Southwest, A.D. 700-1450

ROBERT S. STERNBERG

AND RANDALL H. MCGUIRE

The ability to infer archaeomagnetic dates requires the existence of data on the secular variation, or temporal change, of the archaeomagnetic field. Archaeomagnetic dates are then inferred by comparing the archaeomagnetic direction of the feature to be dated with the secular variation curve. We have used archaeomagnetic results from 73 dated features to determine the secular variation of archaeomagnetic direction in the American Southwest for the period A.D. 700–1450. The application of quantitative smoothing techniques yielded a secular variation curve that accounts for the uncertainties inherent in the raw data and that quantifies the uncertainty in the resulting curve. This enables statistical methods to be employed in the inference of archaeomagnetic dates. Our results compare favorably with those from other archaeomagnetic studies in the United States. An examination of three sets of archaeomagnetic dates that had previously disagreed with independently determined dates suggests that our secular variation curve is more accurate than the DuBois curve (1975a, 1975b), which has previously been used for archaeomagnetic dating in the American Southwest.

MATERIALS AND METHODS

Sample Collection

Archaeomagnetic samples were collected from 158 features at 33 archaeological sites in eastern Arizona, western New Mexico, and southwestern Colorado. The locations of the sites are shown in Figure 12.1. General information regarding the location, provenience, and dating of the features can be found in Sternberg (1982). The features sampled were primarily hearths or fire pits (117 features). Other types of features sampled less frequently included plastered or un-plastered burned floors (13 features) and walls (23), small roasting pits and hornos (3), and cremation pits (2).

Sample collection during the early work for this study was done by J. L. Eighmy, then in the Department of Anthropology at the University of Arizona in Tucson. Afterward, sampling was supervised by R. H. McGuire. When feasible, samples were collected by Eighmy, McGuire, or R. S. Sternberg. Otherwise, archaeologists present on the site were trained in sampling procedures. This made it easier to collect a larger number of features, albeit sometimes at the expense of experience and procedural uniformity (Lange and Murphy, this volume, chap. 3).

Standard methods of archaeomagnetic sampling (Eighmy 1980b and this vol., chap. 2) were used. The occasional collection of burned floors, walls, or other features required specialized procedures (Eighmy 1980b). Once the baked clay to be collected was cut, it was encased in plaster of paris, which was poured into an aluminum mold. The resulting cubes were 2.67 cm (1.05 in) on a side, with about one-fourth of the cube actually being baked clay. Samples were oriented azimuthally with a magnetic compass. Usually 8 to 12 samples per feature were taken.

Site is the usual paleomagnetic term for the locale of a collection of samples that represents an instantaneous recording of the earth's magnetic field. However, *site* is an awkward term for a collection of archaeomagnetic samples because it conflicts with the term *archaeological site*. Thus the term *archaeomagnetic feature* will be used here as the equivalent of a paleomagnetic site, while the term *site* will refer to an archaeological site. Because most of the features are hearths, these terms will be used interchangeably. An individually oriented plaster cube is herein called a specimen (although usually called a sample in the paleomagnetic literature). Our convention for a typical specimen designation is AB003D, where AB is a two-letter acronym for the archaeological site, 003 is the feature number at the site (third feature from site AB), and D is the specimen from that feature, lettered consecutively from A for the first specimen (thus D is the fourth specimen from feature AB003).

Laboratory Procedure

Standard paleomagnetic laboratory techniques (Collinson 1983) were used. Specimen magnetization was measured on a cryogenic magne-

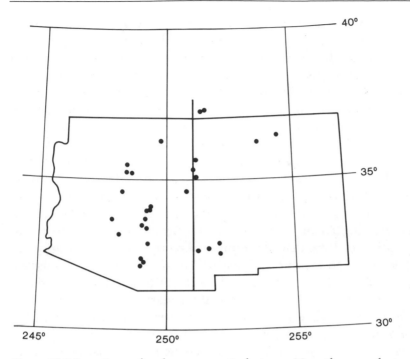

Figure 12.1. Locations of archaeomagnetic features. More than one feature was collected at some locations.

tometer when possible, but a spinner magnetometer was used when the magnetization was too strong or when the cryogenic magnetometer was not filled with liquid helium. The natural remanent magnetizations (NRM) of all specimens from a feature were measured before beginning demagnetization.

Alternating field (AF) demagnetization was used to remove secondary components of magnetization. Such magnetization can be acquired through various mechanisms at some time subsequent to the last intense firing of the feature and may be unrelated (not parallel) to the desired archaeomagnetic direction. AF demagnetization was appropriate because rock magnetic work (Sternberg 1982) showed that the remanence was carried by low-coercivity grains, presumably magnetite or titanomagnetite. Thermal demagnetization was not practical because the repeated heatings caused the plaster of paris to dehydrate and crack, destroying the orientation of the specimen. In the few cases in which all specimens from a feature were thermally demagnetized after AF demagnetization, there was no improvement in results.

For all but 10 features, at least one specimen was subjected to progressive AF demagnetization. Typical peak fields used were 2.5, 5, 10, 15, 20, 30, 40, 60, 80, and 100 mT (25–1000 oersteds). The initial pilot specimens used for progressive demagnetization were chosen because their magnetization and direction were typical for the NRM measurements from the corresponding feature. Additional pilot specimens were also progressively demagnetized if the results from the first specimen were ambiguous, if the NRM directions were poorly clustered, if some specimens had atypical NRMs, or if extra confidence in the results was desired. The optimal demagnetization step at which the remaining specimens were demagnetized was chosen by examining the behavior of the pilot specimen or specimens and selecting a demagnetization step at which the direction of magnetization had stabilized. The mean direction of magnetization for the feature and measures of dispersion (the precision parameter k and the α_{95} angle) were calculated for the NRMs and optimal demagnetization step by applying Fisher (1953) statistics.

Occasionally all specimens from a feature were demagnetized at two or more steps, especially if a stable magnetization could not be isolated in the pilot specimen. The step yielding the least dispersion, as indicated by the highest k value or smallest α_{95}, was then chosen as the optimal step. The undemagnetized NRM results were never used as the optimal demagnetization step, however, even if the α_{95} was lower than for the demagnetized results. If all specimens had acquired a large viscous remanent magnetization (VRM) component parallel to the present field direction, their magnetizations could disperse as this common vector was removed during demagnetization. The NRMs would thus show the best precision or clustering, but the mean NRM direction would not be parallel to the archaeomagnetic field.

Outlier Analysis

Careful consideration was given to the identification and treatment of outliers. These are specimens with magnetization directions seemingly discordant with those from other specimens from the same feature. Grubbs (1969) gives a clear exposition of the general problem of outlier analysis upon which our treatment is based. An outlier is safely identified as being unrepresentative of the desired population if an experimental or physical reason for the discordance can be isolated. We checked our field notes to look for physical reasons that might explain any specimens that had obviously distinct directions of magnetization (Aitken and Hawley 1966). Various comments in the field notes may give clues to anomalous directions: material that came loose from its pedestal during sampling; poorly burned material as judged by color or hardness; or the presence of roots, twigs, or rodent burrows in the specimen. A schematic map of the sample collection is also useful. If one or more specimens were collected from a separate area of the feature, material or firing conditions (e.g., lower temperature) peculiar to that part of the feature could explain disparate directions of magnetization. Other magnetic characteristics of a specimen can also provide the corroborative evidence for classifying it as anomalous. A specimen that is particularly unstable upon demagnetization or that has magnetization more than an order of magnitude lower or higher than the others in the feature is suspect, especially if the specimen was also collected from a distinct area of the feature. Such evidence could suggest an absence of stable thermoremanence or the addition of a large isothermal remanence due to a lightning strike.

Sometimes a direction of magnetization appeared discordant even though there was no obvious physical evidence to suggest why this specimen should have been an outlier. Of course, such a specimen may represent a case of extreme but nonetheless random variability. Such a specimen could still be a "true" outlier, however, due to undetected or undetectable reasons, including variability in the firing temperatures (Chelidze 1966; Krause 1980) and magnetization in the feature without corresponding changes in color and hardness; mechanical disturbance during original use, subsequent burial, or archaeological excavation; and collection errors. When *a priori* physical evidence for identifying outliers was absent, we used numerical outlier tests. These tests were routinely applied for all results. They are described in detail in Sternberg (1982) and are similar to those suggested by Beck (1983, 1985). Because it is difficult to apply a rigorously correct statistical outlier test (Fisher 1985; Fisher et al. 1981; Fisher et al. 1983; Lewis and Fisher 1982; McFadden 1982, 1985; Van Alstine 1980; Van Alstine and de Boer 1978), it is most important to adopt a consistent and conservative approach in treating outliers. These criteria are perhaps more important than the exact form of the test. Archaeomagnetists in the United States (Krause 1980; Nichols 1975; Wolfman 1982) have previously developed outlier tests similar to that used by Harrison and Lindh (1982) for paleomagnetic poles.

When an outlier was identified by either physical characteristics or an outlier test, it was deleted from the data set for that feature. A new average direction and precision indicators were then calculated for the feature.

RESULTS

Feature Directions and Virtual Geomagnetic Poles

The behavior of specimens during alternating field demagnetization varied. Typically, specimen directions would move 5–10° upon demagnetization, stabilizing at a demagnetization peak field of about 15 mT. Thus 15 mT was the optimal demagnetization step most often used. Other specimens, however, showed quite different and sometimes rather complex behavior, such as a much greater change in direction or stabilization at a different demagnetization step. Details of our demagnetization results for several features are presented in Sternberg (1982).

All specimens from the 158 archaeomagnetic features collected were measured, and they provide useful statistical information. Of these 158, we have assigned dates for remanence acquisition to 85 features, which could therefore be used for the analysis of secular variation. The other, undated features were collected from excavations for which the chronological evidence was still incomplete. These features will be used to augment the present data set when their dates are determined. Twelve dated and eleven undated features had α_{95}s > 10°. Sternberg (1982) suggested that the poor precision for these features was due to low-temperature firing. Thus, only the other 73 dated features, with α_{95}s < 10°, were used to construct the secular variation curve. The greatest number of independently dated features from a single site was 12, from Grasshopper (GR). All features were treated as independent results. The paleomagnetic results for these 73 features are summarized in the Appendix, Table A-1. More complete provenience data and the results for the other 85 features are given in Sternberg (1982).

The results for all dated features are shown in Figure 12.2 as separate plots of magnetic declination (D) and inclination (I) vs. time. The age ranges assigned to the features are depicted on the separate D and I plots. Statistical uncertainties in D and I are also shown. For two standard errors of the mean, $\Delta D = \alpha_{95}/\cos(I)$ and $\Delta I = \alpha_{95}$.

The scatter and uncertainties in the data limit the resolution of the inferred magnetic field changes. One way of considering this limitation is to look separately at the distribution of the uncertainties in the independent variable (time) and the dependent variable (direction). To reconstruct the secular variation, the target date of interest for an archaeomagnetic feature is the last intentional intense heating, presumably shortly before room abandonment (Dean 1978; Sternberg and McGuire, this volume, chap. 6). This date might be inferred using a variety of dating techniques (e.g., tree-ring, ^{14}C, and ceramic) to determine various dated events, as well as various archaeological arguments (e.g., superposition and cross-dating) to infer bridging events to the target date in question. In some cases, the estimated firing dates were supplied by project archaeologists; in others, we interpreted the dates based on the chronological data made available to us. All the dates supplied by archaeologists from current excavations were reevaluated as further chronological information from those sites became available. A histogram of the age ranges assigned to the features is shown in Figure 12.3. The ranges vary from a minimum of 4 years for a historic site and 9 years for a prehistoric site to a maximum of 300 years. The median age range is 50 years, with an interquartile range of 30–100 years.

A histogram of the α_{95} values for the 135 demagnetized mean feature directions with $\alpha_{95}s < 10°$ is shown in Figure 12.4. The other 23 features, with $\alpha_{95}s > 10°$, were interpreted as being unacceptable paleomagnetic material; the $\alpha_{95}s$ for this group appeared to represent a different population of samples, perhaps due to poor firing (Sternberg 1982). The median α_{95} for the acceptable group is 3.1°, with an interquartile range of 2.1°–4.3° and a total range of 1.1°–8.0°.

The archaeomagnetic directions and $\alpha_{95}s$ were transformed to virtual geomagnetic poles (VGP) and ovals of confidence, specified by *dm* and *dp* (Appendix, Table A-1). Although the use of VGPs removes the geographic effect of the dipole field on magnetic directions, the nondipole field causes some scatter of VGPs even over a restricted geographic area. Features for this study were collected from a geographic area of about 5° × 5° (Fig. 12.1). Analyses of the present geomagnetic field by Shuey et al. (1970), Champion (1980), and Sternberg (1982) suggest that even contemporaneous VGPs from opposite extremes of the Southwest may differ by as much as 2°. Thus the construction of a VGP curve for the Southwest will incorporate this

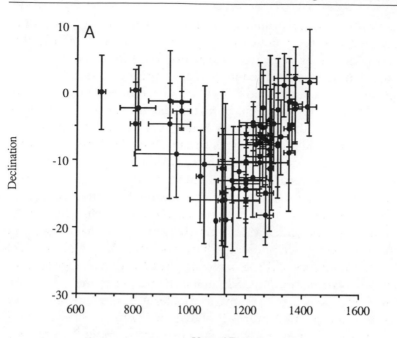

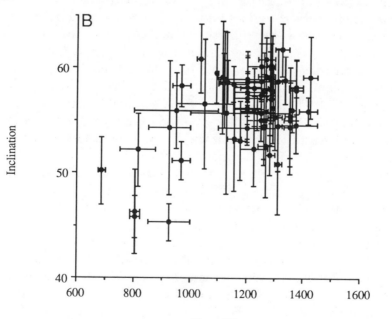

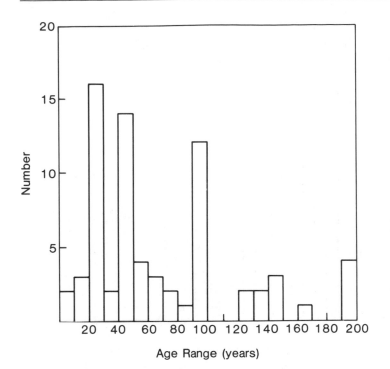

Figure 12.3. Age ranges for dates on archaeomagnetic features. Two features with age ranges greater than 200 years are not plotted.

inherent scatter in the data. The corresponding advantage is that any anomalies in the magnetic field that might be present at a single site will be averaged out.

Smoothing the VGP Data

It is desirable to fit a smooth curve to the data in order to extract a signal while suppressing noise. To do this, the moving-window

Figure 12.2. Archaeomagnetic feature direction. Feature directions of magnetization at the optimal demagnetization step were transformed through the VGP to equivalent directions at the location of Tucson (32.25° N, 110.83° W). (A) Declinations, with error bars showing age ranges of features along the abscissa and two standard errors of the mean *D* (corresponding to the α_{95}) along the ordinate. (B) Inclinations, with error bars showing age ranges of features and two standard errors of the mean *I*.

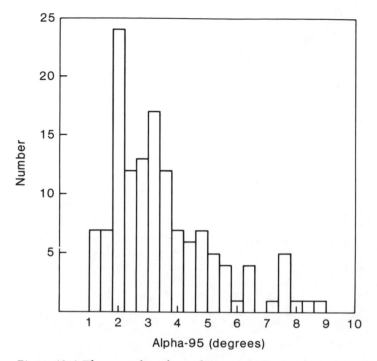

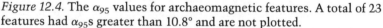

Alpha-95 (degrees)

Figure 12.4. The α_{95} values for archaeomagnetic features. A total of 23 features had α_{95}s greater than 10.8° and are not plotted.

smoothing method incorporating weighted Fisher statistics (Sternberg and McGuire, this volume, chap. 6) was used. This numerical method accounts for uncertainties in both the independent variable (feature ages) and the dependent variable (feature directions) in the raw data and produces a smoothed curve as well as estimates of precision for the curve. This statistical nature of the secular variation curve allows comparisons to be made with similarly constructed secular variation curves, with individual archaeomagnetic results, and with analytical models of secular variation.

First, outlying VGPs were deleted from the data set. The test used was essentially the same as that used to detect specimen outliers within a feature. The six features thus flagged as outliers were MF001, CS001, NR003, CH004, GR007, and FL002. A similar outlier test for feature directions is used by Soviet archaeomagnetists (Burlatskaya et al. 1977; Nachasova 1972).

After deleting these six features, 67 independently dated hearths with α_{95}s $< 10°$ were left in the data set. One of these, SX001, was fired early this century and was therefore not used in the secular variation analysis. The moving window was then applied to the remaining 66 features. Windows of 25, 50, and 100 years were used, corresponding to the peaks in the age range distribution of Figure 12.3. The increment between successive windows was half their length. The trends of the three VGP paths calculated with windows of 25, 50, and 100 years were quite similar. The 25-year window produced a more zigzag curve. Judging by the relatively smooth secular variation curves observed in this century, this zigzag appearance is probably the result of noise in the data and the presence of fewer points per interval rather than real behavior of the archaeomagnetic field. The 50- and 100-year windows yielded very similar, smoother results. For the final window configuration, a 100-year window was chosen for the period A.D. 700–1050, and a 50-year window for the period A.D. 1000–1450, in which the data are denser and more detail is obtainable. (Dashes are used to designate age ranges; otherwise, ages refer to interval midpoints.) This combination was chosen to obtain a VGP path that exhibited both good smoothness and resolution.

The final southwestern VGP curve for this window configuration is shown in Figure 12.5. Figure 12.5a plots only the mean pole positions. Figure 12.5b includes the interval A95s as well (α_{95} refers to paleomagnetic directions; A95 refers to poles). The interval VGPs were transformed back to archaeomagnetic directions at the site location for Tucson, Arizona (32.25° N, 110.83° W). These secular variation curves for D and I, including error bands representing two standard errors of the mean, are shown in Figure 12.6. Table 12.1 lists the VGPs for each window along with corresponding directions and the angular rates of change for both quantities. These rates were calculated using the midpoints of each interval of time. The secular variation of the VGP ranges from 0.004° to 0.358° per year, with a mean of 0.057° ± 0.155° per year and a median of 0.036° per year. The rapid period of motion from A.D. 1000 to 1025 corresponds to the decrease in declination for this time evident in Figure 12.2. A small data gap prevents a more detailed picture of this apparently rapid movement. The secular variation is quite steady for the period A.D. 1125–1425.

The declination shows a 600-year oscillation with a peak-to-peak amplitude of about 15°. The mean declination is westerly over the entire record. The sharp declination minimum at A.D. 1075 corresponds to a distinctly low-latitude VGP. The inclination increases from 47.4° to 60.0° between A.D. 750 and 1025, decreases to 57° at A.D. 1150, and remains essentially constant thereafter. Other geophysical aspects and implications of this study are discussed in Sternberg (1989b).

Previous suggestions that archaeomagnetic secular variation curves should be represented by a band of finite thickness (Eighmy et al. 1978, 1980; Wolfman 1979) rather than simply a line are now supported in a quantified fashion. The width of the band—represented by the A95s for the interval VGPs—is variable, ranging from 1.33° to 5.28°. The value of A95 tends to decrease (i.e., the precision of the curve increases) as N_j, the effective number of points per interval of time increases (see Table 12.1). As N_j continues to increase, A95 reaches a limit rather than continuing to decrease (see further discussion of N_j in Sternberg and McGuire, this volume, chap. 6). This minimum for A95 is comparable to the best α_{95}s obtained for individual features. DuBois (1975c) and Burlatskaya and Nachasova (1978) also indicated that the precision and accuracy of the curve is comparable to that of the individual features.

DISCUSSION

The validity of the archaeomagnetic record depends in part on the ability to replicate the secular variation pattern in nearby areas. The data sets that will be compared here are those North American archaeomagnetic data from the past 2,000 years that are available as tabulated results from individual features. The two such extant data sets come from the Dolores Archaeological Program in southwestern Colorado (Eighmy et al., this volume; Hathaway et al. 1983) and from Arkansas and neighboring states (Wolfman 1979, 1982, this volume, chap. 14). Following these comparisons, three examples of archaeomagnetic dating using our secular variation curve are presented to support the validity of our curve.

Figure 12.5. Southwestern smoothed VGP path. This is the optimal VGP curve, with precision weighting and variable window length. Some points are labeled with their interval midpoint in years A.D. (A) Mean interval VGPs; also shown is the VGP path corresponding to direct measurements of the field in Nogales, Arizona, A.D. 750–1475 (solid circles), and Tucson, A.D. 1855–1970 (open circles). (B) Mean interval VGPs with associated A95s.

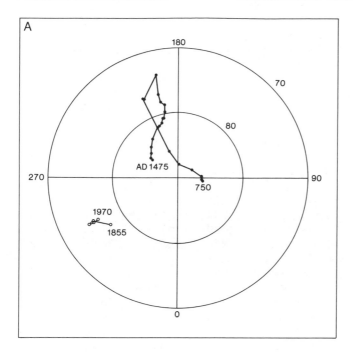

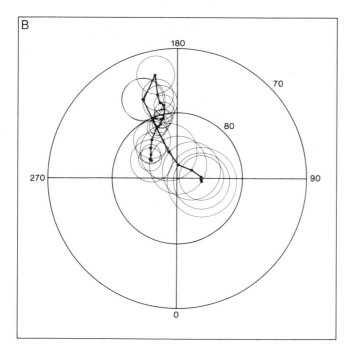

Table 12.1. Interval Averages for Smoothed VGPs, Archaeomagnetic Directions, and Rates of Change

Age Range (Years A.D.)	N	N_j	A_{95}	k	Plat	Plong
700–800	3	1.26	5.28°	546	86.21°	82.50°
750–850	4	2.97	4.31	455	86.29	85.59
800–900	6	2.74	3.44	380	86.32	92.82
850–950	6	2.30	4.38	235	87.45	118.58
900–1000	6	3.92	4.38	235	88.00	176.00
950–1050	8	4.26	4.41	158	85.82	198.09
1000–1050	4	1.62	3.16	847	76.91	204.09
1025–1075	4	1.45	3.34	757	77.03	203.59
1050–1100	5	1.76	2.89	703	73.90	192.20
1075–1125	11	4.92	2.39	365	76.98	193.53
1100–1150	10	5.71	2.58	351	78.20	193.13
1125–1175	18	5.46	1.51	525	78.71	190.38
1150–1200	17	7.00	1.52	554	79.82	191.34
1175–1225	21	7.67	1.40	519	80.66	193.72
1200–1250	21	8.33	1.43	496	80.73	194.73
1225–1275	29	11.77	1.33	404	81.40	197.06
1250–1300	26	17.92	1.43	392	81.73	200.36
1275–1325	26	15.22	1.49	362	81.76	202.49
1300–1350	11	6.91	2.75	276	82.99	213.64
1325–1375	10	6.63	2.28	451	83.93	221.52
1350–1400	9	5.74	1.54	1124	84.57	227.98
1375–1425	5	2.45	1.76	1896	84.96	235.21
1440–1450	3	2.10	3.16	1521	85.31	236.07

NOTE: The column headings are defined as follows:

N   number of data points within or overlapping each window
N_j effective amount of data in each window
A95   size in degrees of the 95% cone of confidence
k   precision parameter for the mean VGP position
Plat   latitude of the mean VGP position
Plong   east longitude of the mean VGP position
VGP   mean rate of change of the VGP between midpoints of successive windows
I   inclination for the field direction in Tucson corresponding to the VGP
D   declination for the field direction in Tucson corresponding to the VGP
Dir   mean rate of change of the direction

VGP (deg./yr.)	I	D	Dir (deg./yr.)
—	47.43°	359.00°	—
.0042	47.58	358.81	.0040
.0093	47.79	358.32	.0079
.0354	49.75	357.75	.0399
.0447	52.20	357.72	.0490
.0489	54.28	356.04	.0462
.3577	60.02	347.75	.2912
.0066	59.88	347.78	.0058
.1690	59.06	342.38	.1146
.1239	58.18	346.18	.0867
.0489	57.61	347.53	.0367
.0300	56.93	347.81	.0276
.0450	56.64	349.17	.0320
.0373	56.61	350.34	.0258
.0071	56.71	350.52	.0057
.0305	56.67	351.47	.0211
.0234	56.87	352.16	.0171
.0123	57.08	352.43	.0102
.0767	57.24	354.85	.0528
.0519	56.98	356.45	.0363
.0364	56.71	357.54	.0262
.0306	56.56	358.48	.0216
.0143	56.25	358.67	.0131

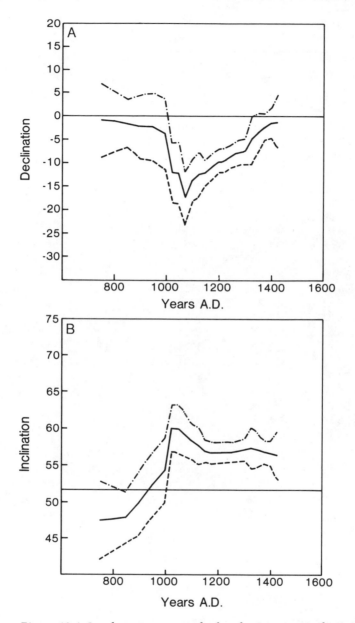

Figure 12.6. Southwestern smoothed archaeomagnetic directions, with the
optimal VGP path transformed to equivalent directions in Tucson. Also
shown are the directions at this location for a geometric axial dipole field
$(D = 0°, I = 51.60°)$. (A) D vs. time. Solid line corresponds to mean D, and
broken lines correspond to A95. (B) I vs. time. Solid line corresponds to
mean I, and dashed lines correspond to A95.

Dolores, Colorado

Hathaway et al. (1983; see also Eighmy et al., this volume) sampled 96 archaeomagnetic features as part of the Dolores Archaeological Program in southwestern Colorado. Their secular variation data base consisted of 36 independently dated features with $\alpha_{95}s < 2.5°$. We took the feature declinations and inclinations tabulated by Hathaway et al. and reduced them through the VGP to a common site location in Tucson. These transformed directions are plotted in Figure 12.7 along with those from this study and from Arkansas (see the following section). For clarity, the error bars are omitted. The declination results from the Dolores project look quite similar to those from this study. The Dolores inclinations, however, show substantial scatter and are generally lower than the few contemporaneous southwestern results. This could be due to a combination of rapid secular variation and small errors in the ages assigned to feature firing (Chelishvili 1971).

We smoothed the available raw data from Dolores with the moving-window technique, using a window length of 50 years and increments of 25 years. No precision weighting was used, because the data set used had no $\alpha_{95}s > 2.5°$. The interval results are given in Table 12.2, and the mean VGPs are plotted in Figure 12.8 along with the southwestern and Arkansas VGP paths. This moving-window VGP curve is quite similar to the curve drawn through the data by Hathaway et al. The major difference is that their final point at A.D. 900 is located at about 82° N, 47° E, whereas the moving window calculates a final point at 87° N, 157° E for the interval A.D. 900–950.

The comparison of the southwestern and Dolores curves in Figure 12.8 shows that the final Dolores VGP for A.D. 900–950 agrees nicely with the southwestern curve for this period. Secular variation is slow on both the Dolores curve from A.D. 850 to 900 and on the southwestern curve from A.D. 750 to 850, possibly representing the same secular variation feature, although the dates and VGP locations are both a bit different. There is a systematic offset between the two curves from A.D. 750 to 900, during which time the directions are different at the 5% significance level for all 50-year intervals except A.D. 875–925 and 900–950. This apparent discrepancy may be due to the sparseness of the southwestern data for the period of overlap. The possibility also exists that the Dolores data, coming from a restricted

Table 12.2. *Colorado and Arkansas VGP Paths*

Age Range (Years A.D.)	N	N_j	Plat	Plong	A95	k
Colorado						
625–675	2	1.67	83.29°	211.41°	18.59°	183
650–700	4	1.92	89.59	167.53	9.77	89
675–725	6	1.83	85.48	40.30	3.94	290
700–750	5	2.33	84.37	52.66	3.01	647
725–775	6	3.54	83.85	55.27	2.57	680
750–800	11	7.75	82.10	57.20	2.55	321
775–825	13	8.67	80.88	57.68	2.76	226
800–850	6	4.17	79.95	54.99	5.52	148
825–875	15	6.69	85.87	30.96	2.17	310
850–900	19	17.32	86.02	25.52	1.61	434
875–925	17	13.43	86.25	31.36	2.07	298
900–950	4	1.52	87.38	156.72	4.95	346
Arkansas						
1100–1200	12	4.12	80.60°	186.15°	2.31°	354
1150–1250	17	6.45	81.45	186.53	1.77	409
1200–1300	17	8.79	81.84	186.73	1.68	450
1250–1350	24	9.91	82.70	195.13	1.65	322
1300–1400	23	9.92	83.83	206.53	1.68	326
1350–1450	17	6.81	84.30	214.80	2.11	286
1400–1500	13	5.22	84.82	223.95	3.23	165
1450–1550	11	3.93	86.58	230.95	3.52	170
1500–1600	5	1.72	88.64	234.95	5.03	233
1550–1650	4	1.22	87.96	216.13	7.10	169

NOTE: The column headings are defined as follows:

Age Range	window interval
N	number of features overlapping the window
N_j	effective number of points per interval
Plat	latitude of the interval average VGP
Plong	longitude of the interval average VGP
A_{95}	size in degrees of the 95% confidence interval
k	precision parameter

Figure 12.7. North American archaeomagnetic directions (feature means only). Circles are results from this study; crosses, from Colorado (Hathaway et al. 1983); and triangles, from Arkansas (Wolfman 1982). (A) *D* vs. time. (B) *I* vs. time.

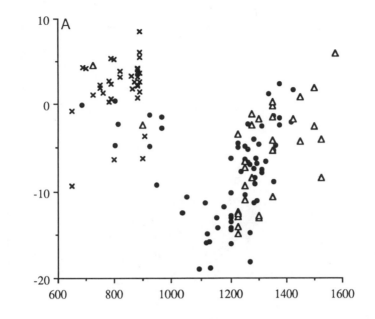

Years AD

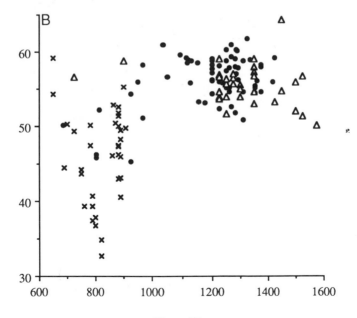

Years AD

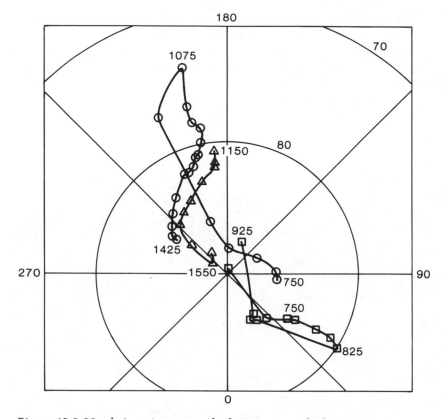

Figure 12.8. North American smoothed VGPs. Smoothed VGPs are given in Table 12.1 for this study and in Table 12.2 for Colorado and Arkansas. Circles are derived from data of this study; squares, from Colorado data; and triangles, from Arkansas data. Some VGPs are labeled with their interval midpoints. All dates are years A.D.

geographic area, may be recording a local anomaly of the magnetic field.

Arkansas and Vicinity

Wolfman (1979, 1982; see also this volume, chap. 14) measured 52 features from Arkansas and adjacent areas in the southeastern United States. Thirty-seven of these are independently dated and satisfy Wolfman's reliability criterion of $\alpha_{95} < 4°$. We also reduced the Arkansas declinations and inclinations to the common site location of Tucson by transformation through the VGP. The resulting mean directions are plotted in Figure 12.7 with the southwestern and Dolores data. The Arkansas results appear to be internally consistent and concordant with contemporaneous southwestern data.

The moving window was also applied to the Arkansas VGPs. A 100-year window was used because the firing dates for the Arkansas features, based on ^{14}C dates, are less precisely known than many of the tree-ring dates from the Southwest and Dolores. No precision weighting was used because Wolfman had already screened out higher α_{95}s from the data set. The resulting Arkansas VGP path is given in Table 12.2 and plotted in Figure 12.8. Wolfman's own VGP curve (see Wolfman 1979, 1982) is significantly different, as discussed in the next section. The Arkansas and Southwest moving window VGP curves are in excellent agreement (Fig. 12.8), tracking parallel to one another for the same period of time. The angular differences between pairs of contemporaneous 100-year window averages were calculated. None of these differences, ranging from 1.15° to 1.69°, was statistically significant at the 5% level. There is, however, a systematic offset between the two curves. The probability that all seven Arkansas points would fall by chance on the same side of the southwestern curve is $(\frac{1}{2})^7 = 0.0078$. The Arkansas area is at the same general latitude of 35° N as the Southwest, but is about 17° of longitude (1,550 km) to the east. For a 17° geographic separation of sites, a 4° discrepancy between VGPs would be expected on the average for the present-day nondipole field (Sternberg 1982:Fig. 16). Thus the small but consistent difference in archaeomagnetic directions for these two areas can easily be explained by the nondipole field. The Arkansas secular variation proceeds at a steady rate from A.D. 1150 to 1600, a pattern that is also evident from A.D. 1100 to 1425 on the southwestern curve.

The Southwestern Results of R. L. DuBois

The criterion of tabulated data for comparing archaeomagnetic results unfortunately precludes proper evaluation of the southwestern data base accumulated by R. L. DuBois. Over the past 15 years, DuBois has sampled about 1,400 archaeomagnetic features (see DuBois 1982). Some preliminary results, mostly not demagnetized, were graphed as declinations and inclinations with error bars (Watanabe and DuBois 1965); otherwise, only the final VGP curves have been presented (DuBois 1975a, 1975c). Final analysis of DuBois's results must await an opportunity to evaluate these data more fully.

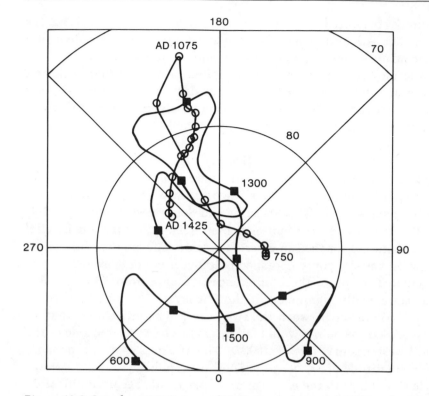

Figure 12.9. Sternberg-McGuire and DuBois southwestern VGP paths. The Sternberg-McGuire curve (circles) is from this study (Table 12.1). The DuBois (1975a, 1975c) curve is indicated by squares. Some VGPs are labeled with their associated ages.

Many archaeomagnetic dates and some secular variation arguments, however, have been based on the DuBois VGP curve, so it is worthwhile to compare that curve with the one that has been derived in this study for the same region.

The southwestern VGP curves from this study (the Sternberg-McGuire curve) and from DuBois (1975a, 1975b) are shown together in Figure 12.9. DuBois's curve has been digitized from original figures. Time is indicated on DuBois's curve with century marks. The two curves do show a general similarity. This is comforting, because both ostensibly represent the same phenomenon. There are, however, two significant differences between the curves. First, the Sternberg-McGuire curve does not show the large loop found in the DuBois curve at about A.D. 1300. Second, the Sternberg-McGuire curve runs about 100 years ahead of the DuBois curve for the period A.D. 1000–1250 (Sternberg-McGuire dates). Thus the VGPs are similar, but their timing is different.

In a more recent summary of his southwestern archaeomagnetic results, DuBois (1982) reported important periodicities of 320 and possibly 1,600 years for declination and 325 and 600 years for inclination. The declination is easterly at A.D. 600, 900, and 1575 and westerly at A.D. 850 and 1200. The inclination ranges from about 40 to 60°, with minimums at A.D. 875, 1300, and 1575. These trends are not in good agreement with those shown in Figure 12.6. On the other hand, DuBois's (1982) VGPs are scarce between longitudes 90° E and 170° E, and VGP latitudes are greater than 70°; both these patterns are in agreement with other southwestern results (Fig. 12.8).

The source of these discrepancies is problematical because of the unavailability of DuBois's data. Magnetic anomalies seem an unlikely problem since both curves are based on features from throughout the Southwest. Many of DuBois's results are from Chaco Canyon, New Mexico. The sedimentary terrane there makes it an unlikely area for an anomalous field. Neither are laboratory procedures suspect. A possible explanation for at least part of the discrepancy is the different ways in which the secular variation curves are determined from the data, since DuBois draws his curves freehand. For further comments on these two curve construction methods, see chapter 6. A recent reassessment of the independent age control from Chaco Canyon has apparently accounted for much of the timing discrepancy mentioned above (DuBois 1989).

Archaeomagnetic Dating

Three cases in which archaeomagnetic dating has been used in the Southwest suggest that the earlier calibration of the Sternberg-McGuire VGP path (relative to DuBois's 1975 curve) is correct. Six paleomagnetic sites from Champion's (1980) study of Holocene volcanic rocks from the western United States fall within the range of time covered by the southwestern archaeomagnetic curve. Five of these six are from the San Francisco volcanic field near Flagstaff, Arizona. Anomalous tree-ring growth in this area suggests an episode of volcanism between A.D. 1065 and 1067 (Breternitz 1967; Smiley 1958). The sixth result from the Ice Spring flow in Utah is associated with a radiocarbon date. We recalibrated this date using the new ^{14}C calibration tables of Klein et al. (1982) to give a date of

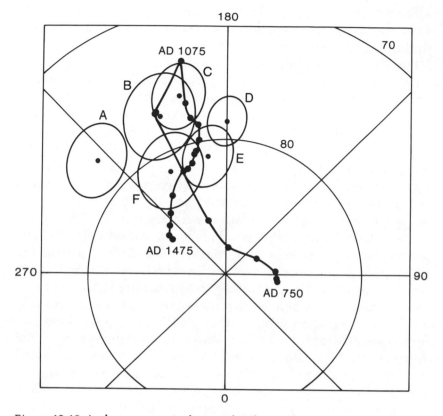

Figure 12.10. Archaeomagnetic dating of Holocene lavas. VGPs for some
Holocene volcanic rocks in the western United States (Champion 1980)
are compared with the smooth VGP curve from this study. Flows are
(A) Kana-a, (B) Vent 512, (C) Gyp Crater, (D) Bonito, (E) Sunset Crater,
and (F) Ice Spring.

A.D. 1230–1405. Champion (1980) also assigned archaeomagnetic
dates to these results based on DuBois's VGP curve.

The VGPs for these six results are shown with the Sternberg-
McGuire VGP curve in Figure 12.10. The archaeomagnetic directions
track around the VGP curve in accordance with their stratigraphic
order: Kana-a (lowest), Gyp and Vent 512, Bonito, and Sunset Crater
(highest). Archaeomagnetic dates were calculated using our curve
and the methods described in Sternberg and McGuire (this volume,
chap. 6). Table 12.3 compares the dates Champion assigned to these
units with those derived here. The Kana-a flow has a direction significantly different from all points on our curve, so it was not datable.

Otherwise, Champion's dates based on DuBois's curve are consistently later than interpretations based on our curve. This is a result of the temporal offset between the Sternberg-McGuire and DuBois curves. The revised archaeomagnetic dates from Gyp Crater and Vent 512 are consistent with the tree-ring evidence for volcanic activity at A.D. 1066. On the other hand, the oldest date based on DuBois's curve is about a hundred years later than expected from the tree-ring dates.

Table 12.3 also gives Champion's archaeomagnetic date for the Ice Spring flow and the recalibration of the original ^{14}C date. There are two possible archaeomagnetic age ranges for this flow based on the Sternberg-McGuire curve. The later option is consistent with the ^{14}C age (as is Champion's archaeomagnetic date).

The second example involves the dating of archaeological sites from Chaco Canyon, New Mexico. More than 1,000 tree-ring dates and 100 archaeomagnetic dates are available from Chaco Canyon (Windes 1980), making this one of the most densely sampled areas in the world for both these techniques. Only two tree-ring dates (A.D. 1171 and 1178) from the canyon postdate A.D. 1130. Thus the conventional archaeological interpretation is that Chaco Canyon was abandoned in the middle of the twelfth century. There are hundreds of

Table 12.3. Archaeomagnetic Dates for Holocene Lavas

Flow	Champion[a] (Years A.D.)	This Study[b] (Years A.D.)
Kana-a	1150	None
Vent 512	1190	1000–1175
Gyp Crater	1190	1000–1175
Bonito Flow	1230	1100–1175
Sunset Crater	1250	1100–1325
Ice Spring	1290	950–1050
		1175–1375
(^{14}C)	1230–1405	

[a]Dates from Champion (1980) are archaeomagnetic dates based on secular variation curves of DuBois (1975c). Ice Spring is also dated by ^{14}C.

[b]Dates from this study are 5% significance level archaeomagnetic age ranges based on the Sternberg-McGuire secular variation curve. There are two options for the new Ice Spring date.

tree-ring dates from the terminal Bonito Phase, so it is unlikely that the lack of tree-ring dates postdating A.D. 1180 could be due to insufficient sampling. The archaeomagnetic dates, from R. L. DuBois, cluster into three groups: A.D. 1065–1100, 1125–1260, and 1365–1400 (Windes 1980). Many of these dates fall long after the conventional tree-ring-based abandonment date. Some archaeomagnetic dates fall about 50 years later than directly associated tree-ring and ^{14}C dates. Toll et al. (1980) have suggested revisions in the tree-ring-based chronology to accommodate these younger archaeomagnetic dates, moving the end of the Bonito Phase from A.D. 1150 to 1220. Unfortunately, the paleomagnetic data upon which these archaeomagnetic dates are based are not available. This prohibits a proper reevaluation of the dates based on the Sternberg-McGuire curve. Figure 12.9, however, indicates that because of the doubling back of both curves and the time shift between the two VGP curves, all Chaco archaeomagnetic results may be consistent with revised dates earlier than A.D. 1150. Earlier archaeomagnetic dates based on the Sternberg-McGuire curve would be consistent with the abundant tree-ring evidence.

The third example involves a number of archaeomagnetic dates reported from Sedentary-period Hohokam sites (Schiffer 1982). The traditional age range for the Sedentary period is A.D. 900–1100. The oldest Sedentary archaeomagnetic date is A.D. 957–1012, and the youngest is A.D. 1180–1230. The dates, from DuBois and Wolfman, are based on DuBois's VGP curve. Schiffer (1982) revised the age range of the Sedentary period to be consistent with these archaeomagnetic dates. Again, use of the Sternberg-McGuire curve would probably make the Sedentary archaeomagnetic dates older and hence consistent with the traditional age range given for this period. Although most of these data are unavailable for further analysis and redating, Wolfman (1977) did give the paleomagnetic data for two VGPs; he interpreted archaeomagnetic dates of A.D. 1155–1205 and A.D. 1153–1215 based on DuBois's curve. We reevaluated these dates using the Sternberg-McGuire curve to obtain archaeomagnetic dates of A.D. 1000–1175 for both features. These dates are consistent with the traditional earlier age range for the Sedentary period.

Although an examination of DuBois's data is necessary before the discrepancies between the two southwestern VGP curves can be fully explained, the evidence from these applications of archaeomagnetic dating appears to favor the validity of the Sternberg-McGuire curve. The sedimentary record of secular variation from Fish Lake, Oregon, also shows excellent agreement with the Sternberg-McGuire curve (Verosub and Mehringer 1984; Verosub et al. 1986).

CONCLUSION

All the archaeomagnetic data sets from North America show a reasonable resemblance to one another. The results of this study and those of Wolfman (1982), when analyzed with the same curve-fitting technique, show particularly good agreement. This speaks well for the ability of archaeomagnetism to recover the basic patterns of secular variation of the earth's magnetic field and to be used in turn for archaeomagnetic dating. Discrepancies between our results and those of Hathaway et al. (1983) for the period A.D. 700–950 may be resolved when more data become available for this period. There are also significant differences between the secular variation curve for the American Southwest derived here and that previously presented by DuBois (1975a, 1975c) for the same region and period of time. A comparison of archaeomagnetic dates based on these two curves with independent chronological information for recent volcanic rocks and for archaeomagnetic features from Chaco Canyon and from Hohokam sites suggests that our new curve is more accurate than DuBois's. We expect that our curve will be modified in detail and extended backward and forward in time as more results are added to the data base. The precision of the curve should also be improved for intervals of time in which the data are currently sparse.

ACKNOWLEDGMENTS

This research was carried out as part of Sternberg's Ph.D. dissertation in the Department of Geosciences at the University of Arizona and while McGuire was obtaining his Ph.D. from the Department of Anthropology in the same institution. We greatly appreciate the cooperation of the many archaeologists who shared material and information with us. We wish to thank R. F. Butler for his advice and support during the course of this study. J. L. Eighmy first interested us in this problem and collected samples in the early stages of the study. Laboratory assistance was provided by J. Hart, C. Shelden, and P. Debroux. Preprints of articles were kindly supplied by D. Wolfman, J. L. Eighmy, and J. H. Hathaway. Financial support was provided by NSF grants EAR79-19726, EAR77-22340, and EAR81-16196.

CHAPTER 13

Archaeomagnetic Secular Variation in the American Southwest, A.D. 700-900: Final Results from the Dolores Archaeological Program

JEFFREY L. EIGHMY, J. HOLLY HATHAWAY,
AND ALLEN E. KANE

DATED POLE POSITIONS FROM DOLORES

Efforts to mitigate the impact of damming the Dolores River by the McPhee Dam in order to store irrigation water have resulted in the excavation of several prehistoric villages, most of which were inhabited during the seventh through ninth centuries A.D. Thirty-six of the many burned features archaeomagnetically sampled from these sites by 1980 served as the basis for a preliminary modification of the Southwest virtual geomagnetic pole (VGP) curve between A.D. 700 and 900 (Hathaway et al. 1983). Subsequently, program archaeologists were able to date independently other pole positions determined prior to 1980, and after 1980, 23 additional tree-ring-associated archaeomagnetic pole positions were added to the set. A total of 82 independently dated pole positions has been collected from the Dolores Archaeological Program (DAP) (Appendix, Table A-2). This set includes 61 tree-ring-dated pole positions and 21 ceramic-dated pole positions. Of the 61 tree-ring-dated pole positions, 9 are dated by the association of the sampled feature with tree-ring-dated occupations at the same site, 11 are dated by a combination of incomplete tree-ring specimens and good ceramic dating, and 41 are solidly dated by the direct association of the sampled feature with tree-ring dates. Fifty-six of the ancient directions were determined with precisions (α_{95} values) of less than 2.5°, while 26 of the sample directions had precisions of 2.5° to 3.5°. Slight differences between results reported here and in our earlier paper (Hathaway et al. 1983) are the result of additional demagnetization treatment and/or a more conservative specimen outlier evaluation. Data reported in this paper should be considered final results for those samples. Detailed information on the dating is on file at the Colorado State University Archaeometric Laboratory.

Age estimates for pole positions without directly associated tree-ring dates are naturally less precise than those with associated tree-ring dates. Therefore, the date range assigned to these samples is greater than that for the more tightly dated samples. Of even greater concern is the question of the accuracy of the independent dating of those pole positions without associated absolute dates. During the collection of this data base, we noted that as more information became available to the DAP archaeologists, the estimated age of a pole position might be modified by as much as 50 years. The degree of change in independent dating can be illustrated with data from five sites in the DAP at which multiple samples were collected and for which independent age assessments were determined for inclusion in an earlier paper (Eighmy et al. 1982) (Table 13.1). The average change in the estimation of the dating range from the earlier paper to the most recent assessment developed by project personnel for this paper was 28 years. In some North American culture areas, a change of 30 to 60 years might not be significant, but in the Dolores area the cultural-historical reconstruction is thought to be relatively accurate, with phase and subphase lengths of only 50 to 200 years (Kane 1984:25–32). A change of only 30 years, for example, represents, on average, about 17% of the estimated occupation span of the villages from which the samples were collected (Table 13.1). For this reason, particular care was taken in the independent dating of samples when other associated dating was absent.

To insure the accuracy of age assignments for samples that lack associated tree-ring dates but that have been included in this analysis, we used only samples collected from sites excavated prior to 1980 and for which final analysis and interpretive reports have been prepared. Much of the ceramic analysis conducted on the DAP by task specialists has been calibrated by tree-ring association, and the dates provided are believed to be more accurate than those previously available in the Southwest culture area (Blinman 1984). We believe that the estimates given are accurate, are the best available, and will not be further refined until much more archaeological work is done in southwestern Colorado. All 82 DAP pole positions are believed to date from A.D. 620 to 920, but the ages of the pole positions are not distributed evenly throughout the 300-year period. A majority (54) are believed to fall within the short 50-year span

Table 13.1. Change in the Estimation of the Age in Years of Archaeo-magnetic Pole Positions During the Course of Several Years of Analysis

Site	No. of Samples	Average Change in Initial Date	Average Change in Terminal Date	Site Age Range	Reference for Site Age Range
5MT0023	7	37	29	150	Hathaway et al. 1983:52
5MT2182	2	5	5	100	Hathaway et al. 1983:52
5MT4475	2	5	15	175	Hathaway et al. 1983:52
5MT4671	5	41	43	175	Yarnell 1983; Wilshusen 1984
5MT4725	2	15	30	75	Hathaway et al. 1983:53

between A.D. 850 and 900. The A.D. 880 to 900 decades in particular contain many of the dated pole positions.

SECULAR VARIATION AS SEEN
FROM THE DOLORES ARCHAEOLOGICAL PROGRAM

Previously, the secular variation curve based on DAP data was constructed by visual inspection and limited pole position averaging (Hathaway et al. 1983), but recently Sternberg (Sternberg 1982; Sternberg and McGuire, this volume, chap. 6) has developed a technique for numerically analyzing temporal change in the geomagnetic field as reflected in changes in the averaged VGP positions over successive time periods. The collation of the 82 samples from the DAP gives us the opportunity to use this technique for mathematically depicting secular variation for the Dolores area as reflected in the data between A.D. 700 and 900. The technique is an averaging routine. All pole positions within a specific "window" of time are considered in deriving an estimate of the pole during that period. Samples that independently date totally within the window are weighted more heavily than those that fall partially outside the window. The total percentage overlap gives an idea of the effective amount of pole position information available in calculating the averaged location. In the present analysis, samples were also weighted according to their precisions, with tight-clustered samples being given more weight. Sternberg also adapted Fisher statistics to indicate the precision with which the average pole position of a given window can be estimated. The precision in estimating a given averaged pole position is a function of the number and clustering of dated pole positions within the time frame. A virtual geomagnetic pole curve is then built from a series of sequential, overlapping windows. Different window lengths can be used, and this affects the detail and/or noise included in the VGP curve description. For this paper a window length of 20 years, similar to the median independent age range for the data set, was selected (Tarkhov 1964).

Several of the samples included in the data set are suspected outliers. For example, samples 5MT4644-2 and 5MT4644-6, collected from the rim and base of the hearth of Pithouse 2 at site 5MT4644, produced very different directions. The wall of Pithouse 2 was also sampled (5MT4644-3). The pole positions of the 5MT4644-3 wall sample and the 5MT4644-2 rim sample are much closer to each other than they are to the pole position of the hearth base sample. Therefore 5MT4644-6 was judged an inconsistent outlier. Other samples were judged to be outlying pole positions when the position had less than a .005 probability of coming from the same population of samples at all time windows within which that sample's age range was included (Sternberg 1982; Sternberg and McGuire, this volume, chap. 6). Thus samples 5MT2182-3, 5MT2192-4, 5MT4512-3, 5MT4644-6, 5MT4644-7, and 5MT4644-9 were considered unlikely to be part of the populations of samples from any of the time windows relevant for the age range of these samples. It should be noted that, as described above, the DAP data set was preselected to include only tightly clustered (i.e., $\alpha_{95} \leq 3.5°$) and well-dated ($\leq \pm 50$ years) samples. By these criteria, the Sternberg-McGuire data set (Sternberg 1982; Sternberg and McGuire 1982 and this volume, chap. 12) would contain 38 samples.

The resulting smoothed VGP curve based on Dolores data (Table 13.2, Fig. 13.1) suggests a slower rate of change than that depicted in our 1983 article, but the overall agreement between the two curves is good. Significant differences exist between this curve and the pre–A.D. 900 period of the smoothed Southwest VGP curve of Sternberg and McGuire (1981a; this volume, chap. 12). Sternberg and McGuire show essentially no movement in the geomagnetic field between

A.D. 700 and 900 (a mean of about 0.02°/year). We believe that this apparent slow rate of change is due to the paucity of data on which the Sternberg-McGuire version is built during this period. Further, only one of the Sternberg-McGuire samples dated prior to A.D. 900 produced a good, well-dated (as defined in this paper) virtual geomagnetic pole.

The pre–A.D. 850 portion of the smoothed VGP curve is known with much less precision than the post–A.D. 870 portion because of the much lesser density of data points compared to the latter portion. For this reason, we believe the A.D. 830–850 smoothed VGP is being "pulled" closer to the A.D. 870–890 smoothed VGP by the greater number of points from the latter era, which overlap and influence the calculation of the A.D. 830–850 smoother VGP. Therefore, we are not convinced that the rapid polar movement depicted between mid-point 825 and mid-point 850 is real. It could be an artifact of the averaging routine and the paucity of data between A.D. 825 and 850. As more data are gathered for this period, we believe that this problem will be alleviated and that changes in the curve will appear more uniform.

Table 13.2. Smoothed Virtual Geomagnetic Pole Locations as Seen from Dolores, Colorado, A.D. 700–900

Window (Years A.D.)	Plat	Plong	Arc Dist.	A95	Precision	N	N$_j$
690–710	85.47	27.78		4.76	671.04	3	1.08
715–735	84.71	49.97	2.03	2.68	507.11	7	1.37
740–760	82.80	58.55	2.12	2.19	762.06	7	1.75
765–785	82.89	87.88	0.12	1.42	929.90	12	2.89
790–810	79.65	50.45	3.42	1.49	709.74	14	4.88
815–835	79.34	51.19	0.34	1.55	658.85	14	3.97
840–860	85.78	37.85	6.63	2.41	456.05	9	2.01
865–885	85.23	23.67	1.24	0.92	497.54	48	23.86
890–910	84.97	26.70	0.37	1.05	431.54	43	20.32

NOTE: Smoothed virtual geomagnetic pole locations are defined in terms of the window, latitude of the virtual geomagnetic pole (Plat), longitude of the virtual geomagnetic pole (Plong), change in geomagnetic pole location between successive windows (arc distance), size in degrees of the 95% confidence interval (A95) (Sternberg and McGuire, this volume, chap. 6), Fisherian estimate of precision (k), number of pole positions occurring in the window (N), and the total amount of actual temporal overlap of pole position ages of the window range expressed as the number of pole position equivalents (N$_j$).

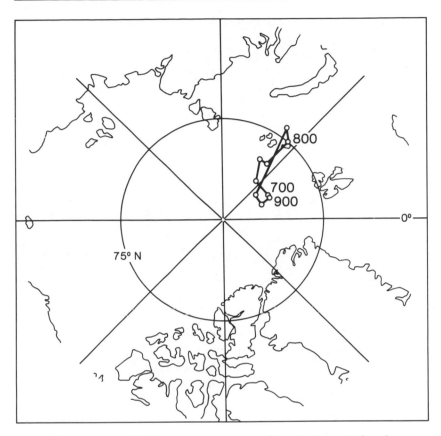

Figure 13.1. The smoothed VGP curve as seen from Dolores, Colorado, A.D. 700 to 900.

A LIMITED TEST OF THE A.D. 700–900 SEGMENT

A very limited test of the proposed modification of the A.D. 700–900 segment of the Southwest VGP curve is available. Concurrently with work at Dolores, we were actively looking for other dated pole positions from this era. Only three good, well-dated pole positions were recovered. These came from Southern Illinois University's Black Mesa Project. The Black Mesa project area was at approximately 36° N, 250° E. All these pole positions had suites of associated tree-ring dates which served as the basis (but not the sole criterion) for independently dating the pole positions. The samples were collected by Kim Smiley, and we are grateful to Dr. Smiley and the Black Mesa Project for making this portion of the analysis possible. Detailed

Table 13.3. Three Archaeomagnetic Pole Positions from Black
Mesa, Arizona, Dated by Independent Means and by the A.D. 700–
900 Segment of the Southwest VGP Curve

		VGP		Age Assessment (Years A.D.)	Archaeomagnetic Dating at the 5% Significance Level
Sample	α_{95}	Plat	Plong		
AZ:D:11-2023-1	1.28	85.36	54.99	852–870	680–750 760–780 840–860
AZ:D:11-2025-1	1.21	83.46	38.62	860–880	680–750 760–780 840–860
AZ:D:11:2068-1	2.70	84.31	58.77	873–880	680–790 830–860

information on associated dates is on file at the CSU archaeometric
lab. The independent age ranges for the samples are given in Table
13.3 along with archaeomagnetically determined dates based on the
curve development from the Dolores Archaeological Program results. The archaeomagnetic dating was established by the statistical
method developed by Sternberg (1982) as described by Sternberg and
McGuire (this volume, chap. 6). This method is essentially a modification of traditional paleomagnetic statistical tests, as it tests the
hypothesis that a given archaeomagnetic sample has a direction the
same as each of a series of samples of a known age range. Operating
at the 5% significance level, we could conclude that a sample being
dated is probably not different from the mean pole positions of other
samples known to date within a specific time range if there is only a
5% chance that the unknown sample location is different from dated
samples in that time range, or window. For example, we cannot reject the hypothesis that sample AZ:D:11-2023-1 is different from the
location of samples known to date within the A.D. 680–750, 760–
780, and 840–860 time periods.

Of the archaeomagnetic interpretations possible for these three
samples, the mid-ninth-century interpretations are most likely
based on independent evidence. In all three cases, these mid-ninth-
century dates are acceptable even if slightly earlier than expected
(Smiley, personal communication 1984).

A SMOOTHED SOUTHWEST MASTER VGP CURVE

The A.D. 700 to 900 segment can be combined with other tightly clustered, well-dated samples to reconstruct a smoothed Southwest master VGP curve. Data used for this construction come from the Dolores data and from those published by Sternberg and McGuire (this volume, chap. 12; Sternberg 1982). The Sternberg-McGuire set, however, was subject to the same criteria as those used in the Dolores set—that is, only samples with α_{95}s ≤ 3.5° and independent dating ≤ ± 50 years were included. This criterion allowed 38 of the Sternberg-McGuire pole positions to be added to the expanded Dolores set, for a total of 114 tightly clustered, well-dated pole positions. Most of the Sternberg-McGuire set postdate A.D. 900, and most of the Dolores set predate A.D. 900. As can be seen in Table 13.4, few VGPs exist between A.D. 925 and 1100, but as would be expected, the resultant curve is similar in form to previously published versions (Hathaway et al. 1983; Sternberg 1982; Sternberg and McGuire, this volume, chap. 12).

ARCHAEOMAGNETIC RECORDS OF ANCIENT POLE POSITIONS

The large number of data points for the 880–900 window gives us an opportunity to look at the apparent limits to the precision of archaeomagnetically determined estimates of smoothed VGP positions (Fig. 13.2). Looking only at the 14 pole positions that are expected to date entirely within the A.D. 880–900 window, one notices considerable scatter among the locations (about 10°, measured in angular distance). The important question in archaeomagnetic dating concerns the origin of the scatter and the means of reducing it to produce better dating results.

In general, scatter in archaeomagnetically estimating the VGP of a given time range can be induced by at least four factors: (1) the use of pole positions determined from a wide geographic region, (2) the use of imprecisely dated pole positions, (3) the presence of undetected feature movement and sample collection error, and (4) the accuracy with which the fired material records the magnetic direction of the geomagnetic field. We know that, for the Southwest, regional variation would add only about 1° to this scatter (Eighmy et al. 1980:510) (Fig. 13.2). In Figure 13.2 the relative magnitude of this contribution is illustrated with the plots of four 1961 VGPs from widely separated Southwest locations. In the case of the 14 pole posi-

Table 13.4. A Smoothed Southwest VGP Curve Based on a Combined Set of Good, Well-Dated Dolores and Sternberg-McGuire Data

Window (Years A.D.)	Plat	Plong	Arc Dist.	A95	k	N[a]	N$_j$[b]
690–710	35.95	28.61	—	3.53	679.56	4	1.47
715–735	84.71	49.97	49.15	2.66	507.11	7	1.37
740–760	82.80	58.55	2.12	2.19	762.06	7	1.75
765–785	82.98	52.91	0.72	1.58	588.39	15	5.35
790–810	80.26	51.32	2.73	1.61	566.55	15	5.45
815–835	79.10	55.22	1.35	2.40	404.45	10	2.30
840–860	85.78	37.85	6.99	2.41	456.05	9	2.01
865–885	85.56	22.22	1.20	0.92	498.46	48	18.91
890–910	84.97	26.70	0.69	1.05	431.54	43	20.32
900–950	87.35	28.22	2.38	1.75	264.36	26	7.93
925–975	86.79	214.22	5.85	15.69	255.47	2	1.22
950–1000	86.79	214.22	0.00	15.69	255.47	2	1.56
975–1025	86.02	212.44	0.78	8.27	223.11	3	0.95
1000–1050	—	—	—	—	—	—	—
1025–1075	73.98	207.86	—	21.14	141.67	2	1.00
1050–1100	70.65	198.08	4.45	21.45	137.69	2	1.44
1075–1125	73.40	196.27	2.81	4.94	240.61	5	3.05
1100–1150	74.28	195.88	0.89	6.05	231.37	4	3.06
1125–1175	76.34	192.69	2.21	2.26	521.92	9	2.78
1150–1200	78.95	192.90	2.61	2.16	570.23	9	3.75
1175–1225	80.19	194.65	1.28	2.15	451.02	11	4.75
1200–1250	79.94	197.23	0.51	2.43	293.02	13	5.50
1225–1275	79.67	204.45	1.31	2.88	153.87	17	6.91
1250–1300	79.91	208.77	0.80	3.10	142.98	16	11.75
1275–1325	80.24	209.85	0.38	2.88	176.98	15	10.17
1300–1350	81.18	228.09	3.08	4.74	376.96	4	3.17
1325–1375	83.06	229.91	1.90	3.11	604.39	5	3.17
1350–1400	84.13	229.23	1.07	1.90	1623.61	5	3.56
1375–1425	84.87	230.79	0.75	1.90	4201.07	3	1.62

[a]Number of pole positions occurring in the window.

[b]Total amount of actual temporal overlap of pole position ages of the window range expressed as number of pole position equivalents.

Observed Southwest VPGs   Experimental Hearth VGPs

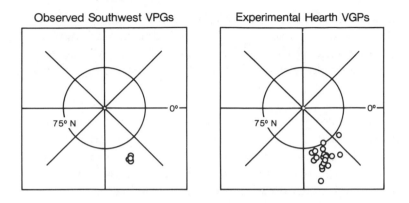

880 to 900 VGPs

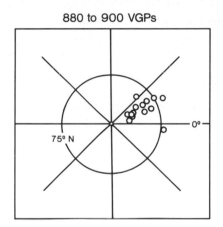

Figure 13.2. Comparison of sets of VGPs calculated from various data sources.

tions from Dolores dating from A.D. 880 to 900, we can be confident that regional variation is not the source of the scatter noted, because the samples were all collected within 35 km of each other in southwest Colorado. Some of the scatter is undoubtedly due to inaccuracies in independently dated samples, but when the results of experimental hearths are considered, dating error may not be as important a source of error as are the remaining two sources: collection error and thermoremanent magnetization acquisition and maintenance. Under relatively controlled conditions, the archaeomagnetic collection and analysis of modern hearths (Hathaway 1982b; Krause 1980; Smith 1981) produced a set of 19 VGPs (see Smith, Hathaway, and Krause, this volume) with a scatter of about 10°. This 10° figure is of the same magnitude as that noted for the A.D. 880–900 prehistoric set.

The most serious implication of these observations is that although large sets of pole positions allow us to estimate an averaged VGP location relatively accurately to less than 2° (Sternberg 1982; Sternberg and McGuire, this volume, chap. 6), any one sample could easily fall 5° away from this smoothed VGP position. Therefore, some unknown but significant amount of the archaeomagnetic dating imprecision (i.e., in the range of 100 to 200 years) suggested by Sternberg and McGuire (this volume, chap. 6) may be irreducible because it is inherent in the acquisition and maintenance of thermoremanent magnetism and in the limitations of archaeomagnetic collection and analysis.

ACKNOWLEDGMENTS

This research was made possible by the cooperation and support of the Dolores Archaeological Program and the U.S. Bureau of Reclamation. Substantial support was also received from the National Science Foundation under grant BNS82-01386.

CHAPTER 14

Archaeomagnetic Dating in Arkansas and the Border Areas of Adjacent States—II

DANIEL WOLFMAN

In a previous article, "Archaeomagnetic Dating in Arkansas and the Border Areas of Adjacent States" (Wolfman 1982), the basic data supporting the development of a curve for the A.D. 1200–1500 time period for this area were reported and the archaeological implications of some of the results were discussed. The results from the 52 samples reported in that article (Wolfman 1982) are reproduced in Table 14.1 and in the Appendix in Table A-3. Those obtained from 27 samples measured since then are reported in Tables 14.2 and A-3. The broad implications of all of the archaeomagnetic data thus far obtained from this area are discussed below.

There have been numerous recent advances in both archaeomagnetism and our understanding of the archaeology of Arkansas. Fortunately, summaries of these topics have been presented in several publications in the past few years, obviating the need to review them in this paper. Archaeomagnetism and related topics in secular variation have been discussed in review articles (Wolfman 1984; Barton and Merrill 1983) and an edited volume (Creer et al. 1983), as well as the other papers included in this volume. My earlier article on archaeomagnetic dating in Arkansas and the border areas of adjacent states (Wolfman 1982) contains a concise discussion of archaeomagnetic dating. A more thorough treatment of the history and theory of this method, including a discussion of laboratory and collecting procedures, can be found in a more recent publication (Wolfman 1984). Collecting procedures are discussed in considerably more detail in other publications (Wolfman 1978; Eighmy 1980b). Important syntheses of a wide range of regional problems in Arkansas archaeology can be found in two recent edited volumes (Trubowitz and Jeter 1982; Davis 1982). The former volume, titled *Arkansas Archeology in Review*, contained the earlier article on archaeomagnetic dating in this area (Wolfman 1982). The latter volume, the so-called State Plan, provides not only regional syntheses but also statements of regional research problems. Additional recent discussions of the archaeology of specific portions of the state can be found in works on the Mississippi Valley (Morse and Morse 1983), the Great Bend of the Red River (Schambach 1982), and the Ozarks (Sabo et al. 1982; Brown 1984; Sabo 1986a). Recent syntheses of the archaeology of Oklahoma (Bell 1984) and Missouri (Chapman 1975, 1980) should also be noted.

Archaeomagnetic direction studies in Arkansas and the border areas of adjacent states are of considerable interest for a variety of reasons. Among these are (1) the potential they offer for the development of a long sequence of secular variation data; (2) the potential application of tree-ring dating in late prehistoric time periods (and perhaps some earlier periods as well), which could lead to the extremely accurate calibration of at least a portion of the archaeomagnetic polar curve; and (3) their potential for solving both general and specific archaeological and geophysical problems.

The first step in developing archaeomagnetic dating in an area is the construction of a polar curve. Currently, the longest curves are those for western Europe (Thellier 1981) and Japan (Hirooka 1971), which are on the order of 2,000 years in length. Prior to this study, a well-defined but rather short curve for the time period A.D. 1200–1500 was available for Arkansas and the border areas of adjacent states (Wolfman 1982). There are now some additional data for the A.D. 1050–1200 and ca. A.D. 600–1000 time periods, and preliminary versions of the sections of curve for these time periods are suggested below. The earliest sample yet collected in this area came from a late Middle Archaic period (ca. 3000 B.C.) feature. Based on the existence of settled life in Arkansas and the border areas of adjacent states in habitation sites of significant size and reported finds of suitable baked features at Poverty Point and related sites of Late Archaic–Early Woodland times (as early as ca. 1500 B.C.), there is a good possibility that a 3,500-year-long polar curve will be developed for this area in the not-too-distant future. The recent development of a polar curve for most of the approximate time period 9000–7000 B.P. from samples collected at Modoc Rock Shelter in southern Illinois (Wolfman et al. 1982) suggests that a polar curve covering most of the Holocene for one or more regions in the central United States can be developed.

In many situations, archaeomagnetic dating can resolve chronometric problems where great precision is needed. The accuracy of
the results obtained, however, depends on the manner in which the
curve is calibrated. (See Wolfman 1982:279 and Wolfman 1984:395
for discussions of the crucial distinction between precision and accuracy.) The successful application of dendrochronology to historic
sites in Arkansas and the recent development in Arkansas of a bald
cypress chronology covering more than 800 years (Stahle and Wolfman 1985; Stahle et al. 1986) strongly suggests that very accurate
calibration of the archaeomagnetic polar curve can be obtained, at
least in the late prehistoric period. The potential for a very long bald
cypress tree-ring chronology for most or all of the Holocene has been
noted (Stahle et al. 1986). Consequently, some earlier sections of the
curve may also be very accurately calibrated, and this will, of course,
greatly enhance all archaeological dating studies. But perhaps the
greatest importance of accurately calibrated archaeomagnetic results will be in geophysics. Due to the presence of a tree-ring-cali-
brated curve in the American Southwest (about 1,000 miles due west
of Arkansas) (DuBois and Wolfman 1970; DuBois 1975c; Sternberg
1982; Wolfman 1984; Sternberg and McGuire, this volume, chap. 12),
a dendrochronologically calibrated curve for Arkansas would allow a
tightly controlled comparison of secular variation in the two areas
and provide important information about the nature and rate of westward or eastward drift of the geomagnetic field. (See Yukutake 1967
and Merrill and McElhinny 1983:41–45, 95–98, 114–118, for general
discussions of westward drift, and Wolfman 1979 and Sternberg and
McGuire, this volume, chap. 12, for discussions of the importance of
the Southwest and Arkansas data in this regard.) In addition, recent
studies in geomagnetism have utilized archaeomagnetic data from
around the world to try to isolate dipole and nondipole contributions
to secular variation (Champion 1980:123–158; Merrill and McElhinny 1983:98–106). The success of this type of analysis ultimately
depends on accurate absolute dating of the archaeomagnetic results.

I have discussed the importance of high-precision archaeomagnetic results in archaeology in a general way elsewhere (Wolfman
1984 and this volume, chap. 16). Within Arkansas there are numerous situations in which such results can make a significant contribution to the resolution of important regional and statewide archaeological problems. Many of the regional problems are discussed in the

Table 14.1. Archaeomagnetic Data Reported in Wolfman
(1982:286–287)

Lab No.	Field No.	Site Name	Site No.	Feature
FE02	6-18-74FE	Ferguson	3HE63	Feat. 49 (hearth); Md. A north
FE03	6-19-74FE	Ferguson	3HE63	Baked earth in Feat. 222 (ext.); sub-Md. A
AR05	7-18-74ARM	Armorel	3MS23	Feat. 28; hearth
AR06	7-19-74ARM	Armorel	3MS23	Feat. 27; posthole
NA07	7-20-74NAP	Knappenberger	3MS53	Feat. 7; floor
CH09	8-6-74CHU	Chucalissa	40SY1	Unit 5, Str. 1; upper baked floor
KI14	8-11-74K	Davis	3PI13	Lower baked floor, temple md.
GL20	10-6-74GL	Gee's Landing	3DR17	Floor 74 cm below top of md.
BM21	10-7-74BM	Boone's Mds.	3CA9	Md. 6; baked floor
HE25	11-30-74HE	Hedges	3HS60	Unit 62:40-Feat. 5 baked floor
BS27	12-5-74BS	Bayou Sel	3CL27	Baked earth in Feat. 1
BS28	12-6-74BS	Bayou Sel	3CL27	Baked earth in Feat. 7
BS29	12-7-74BS	Bayou Sel	3CL27	Baked earth in Feat. 3
BS30	12-8-74BS	Bayou Sel	3CL27	Baked earth at Strat. 4/ Feat. 3 contact
BS31	12-9-74BS	Bayou Sel	3CL27	Baked earth in Feat. 3
BS32	12-10-74BS	Bayou Sel	3CL27	Baked earth in Strat. 5 (below Feat. 3)
BS33	12-11-74BS	Bayou Sel	3CL27	Baked earth in Strat. 5 (below BS32)
WF36	12-12-74WF	Watts Field	3UN18	Md. D, Floor 1
BS37	2-14-75BS	Bayou Sel	3CL27	Baked earth; S side of site
SL38	5-31-75SL	Shallow Lake	3UN52	Feat. 6; hearth
SL39	5-30-75SL	Shallow Lake	3UN52	Feat. 7; baked earth
SL40	6-1-75SL	Shallow Lake	3UN52	Feat. 9; floor of Str. 1
ST41	7-2-75ST	Standridge	3MN53	Wall fdn. of Feat. 1
SL42	8-8-75SL	Shallow Lake	3UN52	Feat. 12; hearth
ST43	8-8-75ST	Standridge	3MN53	Feat. 8; upper floor
ST45	8-9-75ST	Standridge	3MN53	Feat. 12; floor

[a]The estimated date is the date range suggested by all chronological evidence aside from archaeomagnetic data.

[b]NYN = not yet named

[c](p) = probable

Phase or Period	Estimated Date A.D.[a]	Archaeo-magnetic Date
Haley	1200–1300	1265 ± 20
Haley	1200–1300	1285 ± 20
Nodena	1350–1700	1335–1405
Nodena	1350–1700	
Nodena(?)	1350–1700	1290–1335
Walls	1450–1550	1410–1485
?	?	1080–1400
Gran Marais	1200–1300	1235–1280
Historic	1500+	1270–1355
Late Caddo	1450–1700	1450–1535+
Historic(?)	1500+?	
Mid-Ouachita	1300–1400	
Historic(?)	1500+?	
Historic(?)	1500+?	
Historic(?)	1500+?	
Historic(?)	1500+?	1335–1405; 1245–1300
Historic(?)	1500+?	
Gran Marais	1200–1350	
?	?	
Gran Marais	1200–1300	
Gran Marais	1200–1300	
Gran Marais	1200–1300	
NYN[b]	ca. 1450	
Gran Marais	1280–1330	1280–1330
NYN	1300–1400	1420 ± 30
NYN	1300–1400	1345–1415

Table 14.1. (Continued)

Lab No.	Field No.	Site Name	Site No.	Feature
ZB48	8-28-75ZB	Zebree	3MS20	Feat. 280; baked earth
ZB49	8-29-75ZB	Zebree	3MS20	Feat. 282; hearth
HZ50	10-27-75HZ	Hazel	3PO6	Stat. C; upper baked floor
HZ51	10-28-75HZ	Hazel	3PO6	Stat. C; lower baked floor
HZ52	10-29-75HZ	Hazel	3PO6	Stat. G; upper baked floor (below HZ60)
HZ53	10-30-75HZ	Hazel	3PO6	Stat. G; lower baked floor (below HZ55)
HZ54	10-31-75HZ	Hazel	3PO6	Stat. D; upper baked floor
HZ55	11-1-75HZ	Hazel	3PO6	Stat. G; lower hearth (below HZ52)
HZ56	11-2-75HZ	Hazel	3PO6	Stat. D; mid baked floor
HZ57	11-3-75HZ	Hazel	3PO6	Stat. B; baked floor
HZ58	11-4-75HZ	Hazel	3PO6	Stat. D; lowest baked floor
HZ59	11-5-75HZ	Hazel	3PO6	Stat. E; baked floor
HZ60	11-6-75HZ	Hazel	3PO6	Stat. G; upper hearth
BM61	11-12-75BM	Boone's Mds.	3CA9	Md. 3; Hearth 1
LI64	11-18-75LIL	Lilborn	23MN38	Area B; Str. B; floor
ST67	6-16-76ST	Standridge	3MN53	Feat. 17; floor
ST68	6-24-76ST	Standridge	3MN53	Feat. 12; floor
AM69	6-27-76AM	Amos	3MN62	Feat. 3; floor
ST70	6-30-76ST	Standridge	3MN53	Feat. 17; floor
ST72	7-16-76ST	Standridge	3MN53	Feat. 1; floor
EA89	6-22-77EA	East	3CL21	Md. D, Feat. 1; floor
EA90	6-23-77EA	East	3CL21	Md. B, Feat. 2; floor
MM91	6-23-77MM	Moore Md.	3CL56	Feat. 1; baked floor
BE92	6-23-77BE	Bell Md.	3CL51	Feat. 1; baked earth
AN93	6-24-77AN	Antoine Md.	3CL60	Feat. 1; baked floor
BO94	9-7-77BOY	Boydell	3AS58	Feat. 2; baked clay over burial 5

Phase or Period	Estimated Date A.D.[a]	Archaeo-magnetic Date
Big Lake	800–1000	1070–1135
Lawhorn(p)[c]	1100–1350(p)	1170–1280
Lawhorn(p)	1100–1350(p)	1200 ± 20; 1255 ± 20
Lawhorn(p)	1100–1350(p)	1180 ± 20
Parkin(p)	1350–1500(p)	1265–1495
Lawhorn(p)	1100–1350(p)	1335 ± 20
Lawhorn(p)	1100–1350	1195–1260
Lawhorn or Parkin	1100–1500	1325–1420
Lawhorn(p)	1100–1350(p)	1215–1240
Lawhorn or Parkin	1100–1500	1230 ± 20
Lawhorn(p)	1100–1350	1225 ± 25
Lawhorn or Parkin	1100–1500	1185–1275
Parkin(?)	1350–1500(?)	
Coles Creek	650–800	635–700(?)
Cairo Lowland	1200–1400, 1250–1350(p)	1335–1425
NYN	1300–1400(?)	1330–1440
NYN	1300–1400(?)	off curve
NYN	ca. 1450	1385–1475
NYN	1300–1400(?)	1375 ± 20
NYN	ca. 1450	off curve
Early or Middle Caddo	1100–1450	1270 ± 20
Early or Middle Caddo	1100–1450	1400 ± 25
Middle or Late Caddo	1300–1700	1400 ± 20
?	?	1075–1130(?), 1340–1410
Middle Caddo(?)	ca. 1350	1325–1440
Bartholomew	1200–1300	

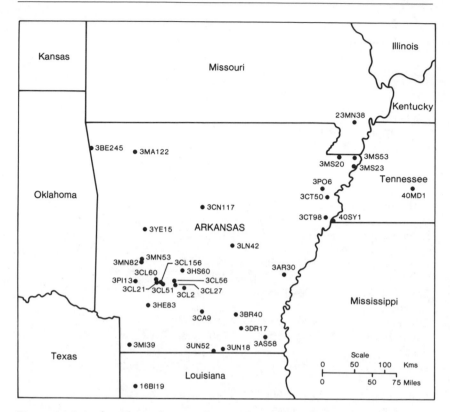

Figure 14.1. Archaeological sites where archaeomagnetic samples have been collected in Arkansas and the border areas of adjacent states.

two recent edited volumes mentioned above (Trubowitz and Jeter 1982; Davis 1982). As discussed below, archaeomagnetic dating is beginning to help resolve some of these problems.

Problems of a broader than regional nature are in some cases particularly amenable to solution using archaeomagnetic dating. Because they were not specifically addressed in the State Plan (Davis 1982), a few key problems are touched on here in a very general way.

Arkansas is a particularly interesting state archaeologically because of its varied environmental zones. Areas with such variation have figured significantly in recent theoretical discussions of cultural evolution in which environmental diversity has been used to "explain" the development of agriculture, stratified societies, and civilization (e.g., Flannery 1965; Adams 1966). Where developments are rapid and the material culture sequences are distinct in each region, neither radiocarbon dating nor stylistic cross-dating provides the sufficiently fine-scaled chronometric results needed to attack these evolutionary problems. In an area the size of Arkansas, where a single polar curve suffices, archaeomagnetic dating is ideally suited to handling questions related to such changes. Where these questions are addressed on a statewide basis, particularly for the Middle Woodland to Protohistoric periods, when culture change was the most rapid, archaeomagnetic dating should be of considerable assistance in resolving major chronological problems and allowing for direct comparison of temporally equivalent events.

In the following pages several significant topics are addressed: (1) further support for the ca. A.D. 1220–1500 section of the Arkansas polar curve; (2) extension of the Arkansas polar curve to time periods earlier than A.D. 1220; (3) individual archaeomagnetic dates and their significance; and (4) the age of the appearance of platform mounds in western Arkansas and possible explanations for their appearance in northwest Arkansas and adjacent parts of the Ozarks in neighboring states beginning about A.D. 900. The data for the samples measured since the previous article (Wolfman 1982) was published are listed in Tables 14.2 and A-3, and are shown in Figures 14.2 and 14.3. (See Fig. 14.1 for a map of Arkansas and the border areas of surrounding states showing the locations of archaeological sites where archaeomagnetic samples have been collected.)

ARCHAEOMAGNETIC RESULTS
FOR THE A.D. 1200–1450 TIME PERIOD

The results from fourteen additional archaeomagnetic samples in the age range A.D. 1200–1450 are reported here (Tables 14.2 and A-3). Twelve of the fourteen results have α_{95} values less than 4°. These agree very closely with the curve presented in the earlier article (Wolfman 1982:290; also, see Fig. 14.2), and their archaeomagnetic dates (see Table 14.2) are all within the age range estimated by the archaeologists in charge of the excavation at the sites where the samples were collected. (Because of their large α_{95} values, the two other results in this age range shown in Table 14.2 are not discussed further.) As noted above, the accuracy of the archaeomagnetic dates (see Table 14.2, col. 8) is subject to the veracity of the calibration and configuration of the curve. I do not believe that the "true" configura-

Table 14.2. Archaeomagnetic Data for Samples Collected Since
Wolfman (1982)

Lab No.	Field No.	Site Name	Site No.	Feature
FE13	8-10-74FE	Ferguson	3HE63	Md. A; hearth in Feat. 345
TN17	10-2-74TN	Bell Burial Md.	3CL2	Floor 81 cm below surface
CA19	10-4-74CAL	Calloway Md.	3CL156	Floor 71 cm below surface
BM22	10-8-74BM	Boone's Mds.	3CA9	Md. 1; Floor 1
BS34	12-12-74BS	Bayou Sel	3CL27	Baked earth in Stratum 6A
SL39	5-30-75SL	Shallow Lake	3UN52	Sq. 27; Feat. 7
ST44	8-7-75ST	Standridge	3MN53	Wall and floor of Feat. 1
ST47	8-19-75ST	Standridge	3NM53	Feat. 18; hearth
LI62	11-16-75LIL	Lilborn	23NM38	Area A; Struct. 1; floor (1975 excav.)
LI63	11-17-75LIL	Lilborn	23NM38	Area B; Struct. 3; flr.
BL66	4-26-76BLUF	Bluffton Mds.	3YE15	N. md.; baked floor in House 1
AM71	7-5-76AMOS	Amos	3MN62	N19W46; Feat. 6; floor
SS95	8-27-78SSG	Saline Sand and Gravel	3BR4	Feat. 1; hearth
TO106	8-2-79TOL	Toltec	3LN42	Md. D; N43E1443 E. Trench; Feat. D-7
MY110	3-11-80MY	Myers (Sulphur River Md.)	3MI19	Feat. 3A; hearth
RM124	8-14-80RM	Roland Mound	3AR30	Feat. 7; hearth
CO125	8-16-80CON	Conley	16BI16	N20W110; Feat. 4; hearth
BL129	12-14-80BL	Brougham Lake	3CT98	Feat. 83; hearth
WA130	2-20-81WSA	W. S. Alexander	3CN117	Test Unit 9; Feat. 2; hearth
HM131	7-14-81HM	Huntsville Mds.	3MA122	N42W0; Feat. 4; hearth
PM143	8-25-81PM	Pinson Mounds	40MD1	N1000E998; Feat. 6; cremation
HM151	10-11-81HM(A)	Huntsville Mds.	3MA22	N42E0 and N44E0; Feat. 57; hearth

Phase or Period	Estimated Date A.D.	Archaeo-magnetic Date A.D.
Haley	1200–1300	1245–1295
	1200–1500	1220–1245
Early-middle Caddo	1200–1450	1290–1325
Gran Marais	ca. 1150	1165–1205
	1400–1600	1325–1345 or 1385–1435
Gran Marais	1200–1300	1275–1335
Late Buckville	1450–1500	
Early Buckville	1300–1350	1330–1415
Cairo Lowlands	1100–1250	1225–1250
Cairo Lowlands	1200–1300 ?	1215–1245
Late Buckville	ca. 1450	
Late Caddo	1400–1500	
Early-middle Coles Creek	700–900	
Haley	ca. 3000	1275–1340
Coles Creek	700–1000	1175–1205
Late Middle Archaic	ca. 3000 B.C.?	
Late Baytown; could be Miss.	700–900 or later	1120–1150
Early-middle Coles Creek	700–900	
Mid Loftin	ca. 1100	1065–1105
Middle Woodland	100 B.C.– A.D. 400	
Late Loftin	ca. 1150–1250	1125–1195

Table 14.2. (Continued)

Lab No.	Field No.	Site Name	Site No.	Feature
HM152	10-11-81HM(B)	Huntsville Mds.	3MA22	N46W2 and N48W2; Feat. 54; flr.
CH154	8-18-81CHUC	Chucalissa	40SY1	Unit 6; House 3; baked floor
AL157	12-9-81ALEX	W. S. Alexander	3CN117	Trench E; Feat. 20; earth oven
GS189	7-26-82	Goforth-Saindon	3BE245	Baked floor in Stratum VB
CT201	4-1-83CT(A)	Little Cypress Bayou	3CT50	Feat. 376; hearth
CT202	4-1-83CT(B)	Little Cypress Bayou	3CT50	Feat. 28 (Seg. B); hearth
CT203	4-2-83CT(A)	Little Cypress Bayou	3CT50	Feat. 295; hearth
CT204	4-2-83CT(A')	Little Cypress Bayou	3CT50	Feat. 294; hearth
CT205	4-2-83(B)	Little Cypress Bayou	3CT50	Feat. 316; hearth
CT206	4-2-83(B')	Little Cypress Bayou	3CT50	Feat. 317; hearth
CT207	4-3-83(CT)	Little Cypress Bayou	3CT50	Feat. 300; hearth

tion of the curve is significantly different between A.D. 1200 and 1500 nor that the calibration error exceeds 50 years (and may not be that large) anywhere in this time period.

In a general way, the results are in good agreement with previously obtained archaeomagnetic results. The VGP for FE13 from the Ferguson site is in very close agreement with the results obtained from two other samples collected at this site (FE02 and FE03), as reported previously (Wolfman 1982). These results and that obtained from the Myers site (MY110) continue to support the dating of the Haley phase in the ca. A.D. 1200–1300 time period.

The dates for several sites with platform mounds in the Ouachita drainage (samples TN17, CA19, SL39, and SL42) and the western Ozarks (GS189 and HM152), discussed below, are in good agreement with previous results. Although the VGP obtained for a sample

Phase or Period	Estimated Date A.D.	Archaeo-magnetic Date A.D.
War Eagle	1250–1350	1320–1355
Walls	1300–1600	1420–1470
Early-middle Coles Creek	700–900	
Lake Harlan– Early Spiro	1000–?	1205–1265
Baytown	400–700	
Baytown	400–700	
Baytown	400–700	
Baytown	400–700	
Baytown	400–700	
Baytown	400–700	
Baytown	400–700	

(ST47) collected at the Standridge site, which is in the upper Ouachita drainage, is 2.5° off the curve, its oval of confidence intersects the curve in an acceptable time range.

The Ferguson site results (FE02, FE03, and FE13), those from Chucalissa (CH09 and CH154), and the two most recent results obtained from samples collected at the Lilborn site in southeastern Missouri (LI62 and LI63) provide evidence of intrasite contemporaneity on a much finer scale than could be obtained with other methods.

EXTENSION OF THE ARKANSAS CURVE

Extension of the Arkansas polar curve to time periods earlier than A.D. 1200 is one of the most crucial problems in archaeomagnetic dating in this area today. While some similarity between the South-

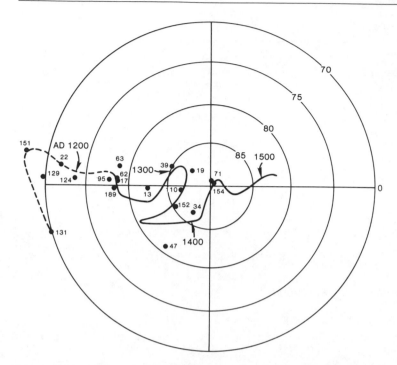

Figure 14.2. Arkansas archaeomagnetic curve, ca. A.D. 1220–1500 (from Wolfman 1982:290), a tentative curve from ca. A.D. 1050–1220, and VGPs of previously unreported samples. (As discussed in the text, RM124 and BL129 may be somewhat older than A.D. 1050.) Point numbers are the lab numbers of Table 14.2 without their prefixes.

west and Arkansas curves is likely in all time periods, it is by no means certain that the strong similarity observed between A.D. 1200 and 1500 (Wolfman 1982:292) will extend to other time periods.

A.D. 1050–1200

At the time I wrote the earlier article on archaeomagnetic results from Arkansas (Wolfman 1982), the curve from ca. A.D. 1180 to 1500 appeared to conform to the then accepted Southwest configuration (DuBois and Wolfman 1970; DuBois 1975c), with only a few minor deviations. However, the earliest portion of the curve was only weakly supported by one or possibly two data points. Several samples measured since that article was written suggest that the Arkansas curve swings considerably farther south in the A.D. 1050–1200 time period than was thought previously. Interestingly, these new data are in agreement with recent results from the Southwest, which also suggest a similar southward swing at about the same time (Sternberg 1982; Sternberg and McGuire, this volume, chap. 12).

Most important among the Arkansas results during this time period are three from structures on mounds in the western Ozarks (HM131, HM151, and GS189). On the basis of radiocarbon dates and some stylistic traits, it seems that these samples, as well as almost all of the mounds in this region in Oklahoma and Missouri, date to the time of the nearby Arkansas River valley Harlan phase and the

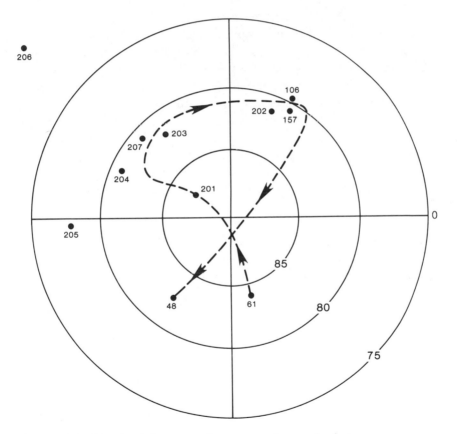

Figure 14.3. VGPs for Arkansas archaeomagnetic samples between approximately A.D. 650 and 950 and a very tentative polar curve for this time period. Point numbers are the lab numbers of Table 14.2 without their prefixes.

early part of the Spiro phase (A.D. 900–1350). Limited mound use in later time periods is possible, but by no means proven. Another sample (BM22) from a baked floor in Mound 1 at the site of Boone's Mounds also strongly suggests a southerly swing in this time period. In addition, the result Richard Dodson and I (Hargrave et al. 1983:43–45) recently obtained from a sample collected at the Bridges site (VGP: N 73.4; long.: W 172.5) in central Illinois (ca. 100 miles north of the area where the Arkansas curve was developed) also supports the southerly swing during the A.D. 1050–1200 time period.

Two additional samples, BL129 (from Brougham Lake) and RM124 (from Roland Mound), produced similar VGPs, but there is some doubt as to their temporal placement in the A.D. 1050–1200 period. Brougham Lake had both Mississippian and Baytown components. When I collected BL129 I was told that because the feature (a baked rectangular pit) from which the sample was obtained was truncated, it was not possible to place it confidently in either component. However, analysis of the material in the feature suggests it belonged to the earlier component, due to the presence of Baytown and the absence of Mississippian sherds in it and a radiocarbon date of A.D. 780 ± 80 (Klinger et al. 1983).

Although there were some Mississippian sherds on the Roland Mound site, they were not present in great numbers. John House (personal communication), who worked on the excavation in 1967 and reexcavated the sample with me in 1980, believes there is little doubt that the sample was collected from a feature dating to the Coles Creek period (ca. A.D. 700–1000).

There are three possible explanations for the results obtained from the Brougham Lake and Roland Mound samples (one explanation, of course, might be true for one sample while another might explain the second result): (1) The remanent magnetic direction is not closely parallel to the direction of the geomagnetic field at the time the features were baked. Although rare, this seems to be the case for two results previously obtained at the Standridge site (Wolfman 1982:295). (2) The dates suggested for the baked features on the basis of other evidence may be incorrect and the baked features may actually date shortly before A.D. 1200. (3) The curve might include the VGPs obtained for BL129 and RM124 between A.D. 600 and 750. But because of the results from the 3CT50 samples discussed below (see also Table 14.2 and Fig. 14.3), the configuration of the Southwest curve in this time period, and the result obtained from BM61, I think this is unlikely.

Pre–A.D. 1050 Results

In the earlier article (Wolfman 1982) the results from two samples thought to date from earlier than A.D. 1050 were reported (ZB48 and BM61, see Table 14.1). Although the number of results reported has increased to 16, much more work must be done before sections of the curve earlier than A.D. 1050 can be constructed with confidence. In addition, some of the results are ambiguous, and others have disappointingly poor precision. Of these 16, two are quite early (CO125, late Middle Archaic, and PM143, Middle Woodland) and two (BL129 and RM124) were discussed above. No further comments will be made about these four results except to note that the collection of CO125 and PM143 and the reasonably good precision obtained from them suggest that considerable extension of the polar curve will be possible. With respect to the remaining 12 (see Fig. 14.3), the following can be said.

ZB48. An archaeomagnetic date of A.D. 1070–1135 was suggested in Wolfman (1982) on the basis of a comparison with an early version of the Southwest polar curve (DuBois and Wolfman 1970b; DuBois 1975c). However, recent research (e.g., this volume, chap. 13; Sternberg 1982) suggests that the calibration of the Southwest curve used when Wolfman (1982) was written in 1981 is in need of considerable adjustment. A date of ca. A.D. 950 seems more in accord with current evidence.

TO106, WA130, and AL157. These three samples were collected from early or middle Coles Creek period contexts at the Toltec and W. S. Alexander sites. The results obtained for one of them, WA130, had very poor precision (α_{95} = 22.5°). The VGPs for the other two samples (both with α_{95} values of less than 4°) are nearly identical (Fig. 14.3). Comparison with the Southwest polar curves for this time period (DuBois and Wolfman 1970b; Wolfman 1984:406; Eighmy et al., this volume) suggests a date of ca. A.D. 830, which is in accord with estimates of the age of the early Coles Creek period (ca. A.D. 700–900) (Rolingson 1982:62; personal communication) and with radiocarbon dates at Toltec and Alexander (House 1985:105).

CT201–CT207. Salvage excavations undertaken in early 1983 at 3CT50 uncovered a large number of shallowly buried baked features in association with Baytown period ceramics (A.D. 400–700). This was the first opportunity to collect samples from this time period since I began archaeomagnetic work in the state nearly nine years earlier. Recently obtained radiocarbon dates (Dicks and Weed 1986) suggest that the baked features sampled for archaeomagnetic dating are of late Baytown age.

Although the site had been plowed many times to a depth near or at the top of the baked features and was thoroughly saturated with water at the time of the excavation, seven of the features, including two overlapping pairs, seemed, on the basis of visual inspection, to be worth sampling. The results, however, were disappointing. Five of the seven had α_{95} values greater than 4.0°, with the two best values only 3.5° and 3.7°. Despite their poor precision, these data suggest a configuration for the Arkansas curve during at least a portion of the time of occupation of 3CT50 (see Fig. 14.3). Five of the VGPs (201–204 and 207), including the two with the lowest α_{95} values, together with the Toltec (TO106), W. S. Alexander (AL157), and Zebree (ZB48) results, suggest a loop similar (but displaced to the west when looking north from Arkansas) to that proposed for the Southwest for the A.D. 750–950 time period more than 15 years ago (DuBois and Wolfman 1970b; see Wolfman 1984:406). However, the Dolores modification of the Southwest curve (this volume, chap. 13), which is based on considerably more data, suggests a considerably narrower curve about 50 to 75 years later in time. Given the poor precision of the results from 3CT50, the loop shown in Figure 14.3 may indeed be considerably narrower and a bit later in time, thus making it much more similar to the Dolores modification. Interestingly, a portion of the loop shown in Figure 14.3 is very similar to the A.D. 580–750 section of the Mesoamerican polar curve (Wolfman, this volume, chap. 15). The two results that were far from this path (CT205 and CT206, see Fig. 14.3) were obtained from samples collected from overlapping baked features.

Although the precision is poor, it should be noted that while accurate results are usually precise, it is conceivable that a baked feature could be disturbed in a manner such that the average direction is quite accurate but has an α_{95} value greater than 4°. Conversely, it is also possible for a baked feature to move as a unit. In this case, the precision might be very good but the average result inaccurate.

While these two possibilities are not normal, they should be kept in mind when evaluating archaeomagnetic results, especially those obtained from 3CT50.

The poor precision obtained from 3CT50 requires an explanation. At the time the field work was undertaken, the features from which the samples were collected appeared to be undisturbed and very well baked. However, only two of the seven results had α_{95} values of less than 4° (see Table 14.2). Samples collected from similar baked features usually (about 70–75% of the time) have α_{95} values of less than 4°. Due to the shallow depth of the baked features, three explanations for the poor results seem possible: (1) While the well-baked features appeared to be intact, it is conceivable that these shallowly buried features were slightly disturbed during plowing. (2) Alternatively, or perhaps in addition, expansion and contraction of the soil due to natural processes may have had a significant effect. When I visited the site, the ground was thoroughly saturated. It was reported that after the baked features had been excavated the ground had been soaked and had dried out several times, and large cracks had appeared in the soil following drying. All soil in Arkansas is subject to some expansion and contraction, however, and reliable archaeomagnetic results have been obtained throughout the state. Consequently, prior to the work at 3CT50 it was assumed that errors due to this source would be small or nonexistent. An unusually large amount of soil expansion and contraction at 3CT50, however, particularly after excavation but prior to sample collection, may have disturbed the soil sufficiently to cause, or at least contribute to, the poor results. (3) While the possibility that the New Madrid earthquakes (1812–1814) may have had some effect cannot be entirely eliminated, the absence of visible damage to or tilting of the features suggests that errors due to this source are unlikely (Wolfman 1982:297). Other explanations, such as collecting or laboratory error, seem extremely unlikely.

BM61. The final pre–A.D. 1050 sample (BM61) was collected from a hearth in a midden at the site of Boone's Mounds on the Ouachita River. On the basis of a single sherd and cross-dating to the radiocarbon-dated Yazoo Basin sequence developed by Phillips (1970:7, 71) more than 15 years ago, a date in the range of A.D. 700–850 for the hearth has been suggested (Wolfman 1982:297). Assuming that something resembling the curve which was fitted to the data from 3CT50 is correct and using a calibration similar to that recently proposed for the Southwest at ca. A.D. 700–900 (this volume, chap. 13), a date not too much before A.D. 700 might be suggested for BM61.

As more archaeomagnetic data become available from Arkansas, the Southwest, and Mesoamerica, some very interesting geomagnetic and archaeological patterns may emerge in the ca. A.D. 600–900 time period. However, speculation on what they might be is best left until better data are obtained on all three areas. In the meantime, it should be emphasized that due to the poor precision of the 3CT50 results and the limited number of archaeomagnetic samples from Arkansas and adjacent states for the A.D. 600–1000 time period, the configuration shown in Figure 14.3 must be used very cautiously.

THE AGE OF PLATFORM MOUNDS IN WESTERN ARKANSAS

The nature of the evolution from Woodland to Mississippian patterns and the transition from burial to temple and/or platform mounds in the Coles Creek period have been central problems for many years. This transition, in at least some parts of the Mississippi Valley and the Trans-Mississippi South, is probably indicative of major changes in social organization and is therefore a problem of considerable importance. Precise and accurate dating of such structures is crucial to any sort of resolution of this problem. The presence of hearths, cremation pits, and baked floors in many of these mounds provides abundant opportunities for archaeomagnetic dating. No more than a brief discussion of the problem is possible in a paper of this nature. While recognizing the haphazard nature of the sampling (and thus potentially skewed results), some patterns are beginning to emerge from the chronometric data obtained in western Arkansas and bordering states in recent years.

The origin of platform mounds in the Mississippi Valley is still not entirely clear. The great majority of the mounds have not been excavated, and great caution should be exercised in classifying mounds on the basis of superficial examination (see, e.g., Phillips 1970:8). Nonetheless, it seems safe to say that platform mounds appeared in the Mississippi Valley south of Arkansas prior to the beginning of the Coles Creek period (Belmont 1982). The earliest such mounds in Arkansas may be those found at Toltec and related early Coles Creek period sites from ca. A.D. 800. Based on recent radiocarbon and archaeomagnetic dates, platform mounds seem to appear in western Arkansas at a somewhat later date.

The Caddoan Area of Southwest Arkansas

One of the more interesting results obtained by archaeomagnetic dating in Arkansas thus far is that the mounds at the East site do not, as had been suggested previously, predate A.D. 1200 (Wolfman 1982:295). In fact, all of the archaeomagnetically dated mounds of the Caddoan area of southwest Arkansas, including those in the drainages of the upper and middle Ouachita River, date later than A.D. 1200. While the ages of the great majority of the mound sites in southwest Arkansas remain to be determined, this emerging pattern is reinforced by radiocarbon dating and ceramic studies. This suggests that other claims for pre–A.D. 1200 mounds in southwest Arkansas and the adjacent parts of Texas, Louisiana, and Oklahoma need to be reexamined carefully. An archaeomagnetic date for a mound floor at Boone's Mounds in the Felsenthal region of the lower Ouachita Valley (sample BM22) is slightly earlier than A.D. 1200. Mounds in this intermediate region may provide a link between those earlier mounds in the lower Mississippi Valley and their later appearance in southwest Arkansas.

The Ozarks

For many years the Ozarks have been viewed as occupying a marginal position outside the mainstream of developments during the Mississippian period. Recently, however, several scholars have argued that this was not the case (Fritz 1979, 1986; Sabo et al. 1982; Brown 1984). One of the key features in this argument is the presence of previously unknown (or at least ignored) mounds in the western Ozarks.

Platform mounds first appear in extreme eastern Oklahoma in the Arkansas Valley and the adjacent western Ozarks region in Oklahoma, Missouri, and Arkansas in the Harlan phase (A.D. 900–1200). Such mounds at the two major sites in Oklahoma, Harlan and Spiro, appear to occur as early as the beginning of this phase. The radiocarbon dates from mounds in the western Ozarks that have recently been summarized and discussed by Sabo (1986b) and the archaeomagnetic dates reported here (HM131, HM151, and GS189) strongly suggest that platform mound building with structures on top (i.e., "temple mounds") was strong in the A.D. 900–1350 period but weaker or perhaps absent after that in the western Ozarks. An archaeomagnetic date of A.D. 1025 ± 45 processed by the University of Oklahoma lab from the Parris Mound in the Oklahoma Ozarks just west of the Arkansas line has been reported (Muto 1978). This date is apparently in good agreement with the radiocarbon dates and the earliest archaeomagnetic result from Huntsville. Unfortunately, it is not possible to rigorously compare this result with the archaeomagnetic data in this article. As is standard practice at the University of Oklahoma lab, neither the VGP nor geomagnetic direction data were reported. In addition, the configuration and calibration of the curve used to obtain the date have never been published.

An hypothesis for the appearance of at least some of these mounds at this time suggested by George Sabo (personal communication 1984) is that these sites functioned primarily as nodes along a trade route between Spiro and Cahokia. With the decline of Cahokia at about 1250, one of the primary reasons for mounds in the western Ozarks was removed. This hypothesis also provides a possible explanation for the absence of mounds in the central and eastern Ozarks and suggests that recent attempts (Sabo et al. 1982; Brown 1984; Fritz 1986) to elevate the Ozark Bluff dwellers to higher levels of sociocultural integration may in fact have been premature. The period of mound construction in the western Ozarks during the first half of the Mississippi period then can be seen as due to, or promoted by, outsiders because an important trade route passed through the region.

An alternative, but not necessarily conflicting, hypothesis is more environmentally based. It should be recalled that the time of the Harlan phase (A.D. 900–1200) coincides with the Neo-Atlantic climatic episode (Bryson and Wendland 1967). Further, the Ozarks do not form a unified region but rather consist of at least four environmentally distinct regions (Raab et al. 1982), with the extreme western Ozarks very similar to adjacent portions of the Arkansas River valley. Consequently, the climatic changes of the Neo-Atlantic may have brought about the cultural changes that led to the Harlan phase way of life in both the Arkansas River valley and the western Ozarks. In this regard, it should be noted that the Harlan site itself is within the southernmost portion of the western Ozarks. As more data become available it will be interesting to see what combination of historical and environmental factors (including those mentioned here) was responsible for the appearance of mounds in the western Ozarks during the Harlan and first half of the succeeding Spiro phase.

SUMMARY

Archaeomagnetic samples collected in Arkansas and the border areas of adjacent states have provided the basis for a section of polar curve from about A.D. 1220 to 1500. This section is very similar to the curve for the American Southwest for approximately the same period. Sparse data, some of which are not of high precision, suggest that the curve for the A.D. 650–1220 time period is also similar to the Southwest curve. It is not unlikely that the configuration of this earlier section will soon become much clearer. Ultimately, a continuous curve back as far as 1500 B.C. will probably be developed. The development of earlier sections of curve in Arkansas will depend on the discovery of deposits with abundant baked features from the Archaic period, which have yet to be found.

Calibration of the Arkansas curve, which is dependent on radiocarbon dating, is probably not as accurate as that obtained for the Southwest curve. The latest section may eventually be calibrated using tree-ring dating, as may earlier sections. If this is accomplished, even in part, important information about lateral (westward or eastward) drift of the geomagnetic field can be determined.

Extension and refinement of the existing sections of the curve, their more accurate calibration, and increased numbers of samples collected in all time periods will greatly aid in the solution of processual and culture-historical problems. In the future, the greatest contribution of archaeomagnetic dating in archaeology in Arkansas and in other areas will be in those situations that require the high precision offered by this method.

ACKNOWLEDGMENTS

The work discussed in this chapter is the product of my collaboration and interaction with many scholars. First, I would like to thank those archaeologists whose excavations produced the samples reported here: Ann Early, E. Thomas Hemmings, John House, Dan Morse, Martha Rolingson, George Sabo, Frank Schambach, and V. K. Pheriba Stacey—all of the Arkansas Archeological Survey—and Jeffrey

Altschul of New World Research, John Cottier of Auburn University, Marvin Kay of the University of Arkansas, Timothy Klinger of Historic Preservation Associates, "Gib" Reeves of the Arkansas Archeological Society, and Gerald Smith of Memphis State University. In addition to providing the samples, most of these individuals provided valuable information about chronology and other aspects of the archaeology in the regions in which they were working. I would particularly like to thank John House, Marvin Jeter, and George Sabo for lengthy discussions about regional chronologies in Arkansas. I measured the samples in the Rock Magnetism Laboratories at the University of Pittsburgh (Victor Schmidt, Director) and the University of California at Santa Barbara (Michael Fuller, Director, with J. Robert Dunn in charge of day-to-day operation). I would like to thank the directors and others working in these laboratories for assistance and helpful discussions. Particular thanks are due to J. Robert Dunn, who wrote the program and entered the data that led to the determination of the archaeomagnetic dates reported in column 8 in Table 14.2. Most of the work was supported by the Arkansas Archeological Survey, with additional funds coming from contracts with the U.S. Army Corps of Engineers for collecting and measuring samples from Little Cypress Bayou (3CT50), Brougham Lake (3CT98), and the Alexander site (3CN117). Earlier drafts of the manuscript were read by Marvin Jeter and the editors of this volume. Their suggestions and editorial comments contributed significantly. While I greatly appreciate the contributions of the above-named individuals, I alone take responsibility for the content of the chapter and any errors it may contain. Finally, I would like to thank David Coffman for initial drafting of the figures and Mrs. G. G. Williams and Mrs. Mary Ann Long for typing several drafts of the manuscript.

CHAPTER 15

Mesoamerican Chronology and Archaeomagnetic Dating, A.D. 1-1200

DANIEL WOLFMAN

Mesoamerica is defined as an area co-tradition in central and southern Mexico, Guatemala, Belize, El Salvador, and western Honduras where civilization developed between 2000 B.C. and A.D. 1521. Variant interpretations of the term *Mesoamerica* have led to some differences of opinion about its areal extent (Kirchoff 1943; Parsons 1969; Willey 1966; see Fig. 15.1). However, most of the important developments took place within the restricted area suggested by Parsons (1969:153–154), with the northern boundary formed by the northern borders of the Mexican states of Michoacán, Hidalgo, México, and Veracruz, and the southeastern boundary formed by including the western third of Honduras and all of El Salvador.

Control of the temporal dimension is one of the most basic problems in archaeology. Interest in chronometric problems in Mesoamerica has been, and continues to be, greatly enhanced by the presence of native calendars. The Maya Long Count calendar, most commonly recorded on stone monuments in eastern Mesoamerica, was the only pre-Columbian calendar in the Western Hemisphere capable of uniquely recording individual days over many centuries (Thompson 1960:141–156). In addition, there is a rich tradition of native histories throughout the area, many of which contain calendrical information (e.g., Caso 1949; Jiménez-Moreno 1941, 1954–55; Kelley 1950; Kirchoff 1950, 1954–55, 1955). Archaeological work during the current century has led to the development of regional sequences that have been aligned by ceramic and architectural cross-dating. During the past 30 years the radiocarbon method has provided a framework of absolute dating for the area. Following a long period of disagreement, much of it revolving around divergent views about the correct correlation of the Maya and Christian calendars and some anomalous radiocarbon results, for about a decade (1972–

1983) there was general agreement about the broad outlines of Meso-american chronology. However, dissenting views suggesting that the generally accepted absolute scale for a considerable portion of time is too early have recently emerged (Kelley 1983; Chase 1985; Lincoln 1985). Current disagreements revolve around the correlation of the Maya and Christian calendars, ethnohistorical documents, and the regional sequence in the Northern Maya Lowlands. Recent research (Klein et al. 1982; Stuiver 1982; see also Stuiver and Kra 1986) that indicates that conventional radiocarbon dates for the time period A.D. 1–1200 are approximately 50 to 100 years too old also suggests that previously developed chronometric schemes may need to be moved forward in time. In addition, recent improvements in the quality of radiocarbon methodology suggests that current views about chronology in most areas will soon need to be reviewed. These improvements have led some to say that no ^{14}C results reported prior to about 1980 should be used. While I believe this statement is too stringent, there is *at least* a grain of truth in it. As discussed below, at some time in the future we are going to have to evaluate the chron-ometric picture in Mesoamerica, using only carefully collected and selected ^{14}C samples processed using very high quality laboratory procedures. Current arguments and the need to resolve numerous fine-scale chronological problems clearly indicate the need for addi-tional chronometric information for Mesoamerica.

The archaeomagnetic dating method is beginning to provide chronometric results throughout Mesoamerica with a previously un-obtainable precision (for discussions of precision and accuracy in ar-chaeomagnetic dating, see Wolfman 1984:395–399; Sternberg and McGuire, this volume, chap. 6; Wolfman, this volume, chap. 16). These results, which have led to the development of a polar curve for the ca. A.D. 1–1170 time period, are presented and discussed below. Of particular importance is the fact that, in addition to resolving traditional culture-historical problems, archaeomagnetic dating can provide the temporal control needed for processual studies.

CHRONOMETRIC STUDIES IN MESOAMERICA

A complete understanding of the nature of modern chronometric problems in an area depends on the manner in which regional chronologies were developed. In addition, archaeomagnetic dating depends on independent chronometric information for its calibra-

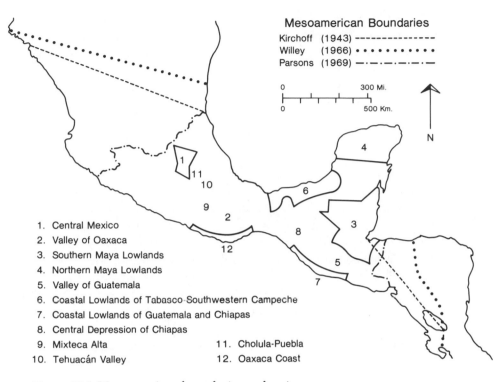

Figure 15.1. Mesoamerican boundaries and regions.

tion. Consequently, the development of chronometric studies in Mesoamerica is reviewed briefly below. A more detailed discussion of this topic, including the independent dating of regional sequences based on radiocarbon dating, stratigraphy, seriation, ceramic cross-dating, and native calendars, can be found in my dissertation (Wolfman 1973). Although considerable data have been obtained in the past 15 years, with a few notable exceptions discussed below my view of the overall relative chronological picture has not changed greatly.

Among the most important new data and interpretations are radiocarbon dates relating to the end of Tula (Diehl 1981), cross-dating that suggests that the Monte Albán IV–V transition (Blanton 1978:27–29) is earlier than was previously thought, and perhaps most important, Lincoln's arguments that the Puuc and Mexican periods in Yucatan are totally contemporaneous rather than sequential. While the sequential view was widely accepted by most archaeologists (including me), there were those who, more than a quarter of a century ago, argued that these two phases partially (Lothrop 1952; Rands 1954) or totally (Thompson 1959) overlapped. Of more general concern, as noted above, are the new calibrations of the radiocarbon time scales which suggest that conventional ^{14}C dates in the A.D. 200–1250 period are 50 to 100 years too early (Klein et al. 1982; Stuiver 1982). Also, two sources of error in radiocarbon dating that are particularly likely to be present in the Maya Lowlands, post-sample growth error and calcium carbonate contamination, provide results that are too early.

The temporal sequence across all of Mesoamerica is divided into three broad periods: the Preclassic, the Classic, and the Postclassic. Since the Long Count calendar in the Maya Lowlands spans the approximate A.D. 300–900 time period (using the most widely accepted Goodman-Martinez-Thompson [G-M-T] correlation), these dates have been widely used as the beginning and end of the Classic period. As I have discussed elsewhere (Wolfman 1973), the dates A.D. 100 and 700 (within the G-M-T framework) more nearly correspond to major cultural shifts throughout the area. Therefore, I would prefer to use these dates for the beginning and end of the Classic period. However, since the A.D. 300 and 900 dates are so widely used, they are retained here. The Preclassic began at about 2000 B.C., and the Postclassic ended in A.D. 1521. The regional sequences are divided into series of named and numbered phases.

Stratigraphy and Cross-Dating

Early studies including stratigraphic excavations beginning with the work of Boas (1913), Gamio (1913), and Tozzer (1921), stylistic cross-dating (particularly between Teotihuacán and Kaminaljuyu [Kidder et al. 1946], the Maya Lowlands and Teotihuacán [Linne 1942:178], and Kaminaljuyu and the Maya Lowlands [Kidder et al. 1946:178–180, 236–237]), compilations of ^{14}C data (e.g., Wauchope 1954), and syntheses (Peterson 1959; Wolf 1959) were helpful in developing a chronometric framework for Mesoamerica. However, it was not until the extensive excavations in habitation sites in the Tehuacán Valley were undertaken beginning about 1960 that a convincing area-wide chronology appeared. Deeply stratified deposits were found in many of the open and cave sites excavated during the course of this project. The analysis of the materials from these excavations and the comparison of them with materials from elsewhere in the Meso-

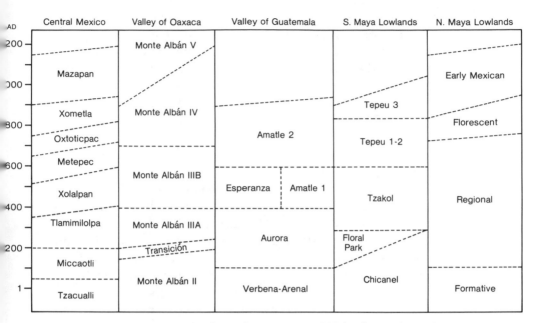

Figure 15.2. Mesoamerican chronology, A.D. 1–1200 for five major regions as suggested by uncorrected radiocarbon results and cross-dating (Wolfman 1973:138).

american area led to a chronometric synthesis for the entire area from about 12,000 B.P. to the conquest which, with minor modification, is apparently valid today (MacNeish et al. 1970). The very consistent series of radiocarbon results from these excavations provided the time scale on the chronological charts that were developed (Johnson and MacNeish 1972). My analysis of the major regional sequences in the A.D. 1–1200 time period from a somewhat different perspective several years later (Wolfman 1973; see Fig. 15.2) was in essential, but not complete, agreement with the conclusions reached by MacNeish et al. (1970) and Johnson and MacNeish (1972).

Radiocarbon Dating

As in other parts of the world, radiocarbon dating has revolutionized our understanding of prehistoric chronology in Mesoamerica. Prior to the application of radiocarbon dating in this area, there was considerable difference of opinion about the age of the phases in the various regional sequences. At that time, the only clues to absolute

age came from native histories and calendars. Some interpretations
of these data were seriously in error. Proposed correlations of the
Maya and Christian calendars differed by more than 750 years (for
discussions of the correlation problem, see Thompson 1935; Wolfman 1973:80–97; Kelley 1976:27–52; and Kelley 1983). Fifty years
ago, interpretations of Aztec legends based on the mistaken assumption that Teotihuacán was Tollan of the traditions led to errors of up
to about 500 years in estimates of the ages in the Valley of Mexico
sequence (Vaillant 1941:26–37).

Although the basic Mesoamerican temporal sequences in the A.D.
1–1200 time period were calibrated using radiocarbon dating more
than 15 years ago (MacNeish 1964; MacNeish et al. 1970; Johnson
and MacNeish 1972; Wolfman 1973; also, see Fig. 15.2), some problems still remain. The earliest reports on the work in the Tehuacán
Valley used conventional (i.e., uncorrected) ^{14}C dates (e.g., MacNeish
1964). Later, Johnson and Willis (1970) and Johnson and MacNeish
(1972) corrected these ^{14}C dates, using the results obtained from
known age samples published by Suess (1968), Damon (1968), and
others. Because of the rather limited radiocarbon data on known age
samples and the fact that some of the early published curves showed
little or no difference between tree-ring ages and radiocarbon years
between A.D. 1 and 1200 (e.g., Ralph and Michael 1967), especially
when statistical variation in the results was taken into consideration, along with other reasons, some scholars (including me, see
Wolfman 1973) chose to work with conventional dates. Due to the
use of different time scales and perhaps some differences in phase
definition and identification, the temporal charts prepared by the
Tehuacán Valley project personnel and those contained in my dissertation (Wolfman 1973) are offset by as much as 100 years.

The correct calibration of the radiocarbon time scale continues to
be a crucial issue. Until very recently, archaeologists used the calibration tables published by Ralph et al. (1973), Damon et al. (1974),
and Clark (1975) to correct their dates. Dates corrected with the
Damon et al. calibration, which was widely used by archaeologists
in the United States, run about 50 years later than conventional ^{14}C
results during the A.D. 1–900 time period and not quite that much
later for A.D. 900–1200. Two new calibrations of the radiocarbon
time scale (Klein et al. 1982; Stuiver 1982; also see updates in Stuiver
and Kra 1986 [particularly the correction program by Stuiver and
Reimer (1986)], which were published after the initial drafts of this

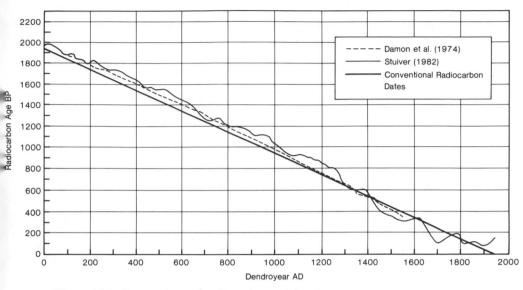

Figure 15.3. Comparison of radiocarbon calibration curves.

chapter were written) suggest that conventional dates are about 50 to 100 years earlier than calendar dates during the A.D. 1–1200 time period (Fig. 15.3).

While the two new calibrations suggest very similar results, they differ considerably in the way in which they are presented and the time periods covered. The Klein et al. (1982) calibration, which covers the past 8,000 years, is based on radiocarbon measurements on 1,154 tree-ring-dated samples. Most of these samples were taken from bristlecone pine (*Pinus longaeva*) and giant sequoia (*Sequoia gigantea*). The measurements were made at five laboratories (Arizona, Groningen, La Jolla, Pennsylvania, and Yale). The results are presented in tables that translate conventional radiocarbon dates with six different sigma values (20, 50, 100, 150, 200, and 300 years) to 95% confidence intervals of calendar years. Stuiver's (1982) calibration is based on 195 high-precision measurements (with sigma values of about 15 years) made on tree-ring-dated samples of Douglas fir (*Pseudotsuga menziesii*) and sequoia (*Sequoiadendron giganteum*). All of the measurements, which cover the A.D. 1–1950 period, were made in Stuiver's lab at the University of Washington. These data are presented in the form of a plot of radiocarbon age vs. tree-ring years in Figure 15.3. Errors associated with calibration and/or errors in the determination of archaeological radiocarbon dates may be significant. Consequently, a simple shifting of dates forward, using calibration procedures, in the A.D. 1–1200 time period will not necessarily provide accurate results.

A complete reevaluation of all the radiocarbon dates thus far reported in Mesoamerica is beyond the scope of this paper. If such a review is ever undertaken, it should include not only the correction of all the conventional dates using the Stuiver and Reimer (1986) calibration program—including the latest revision, which is obtainable from the authors—but also an evaluation of the results in light of what is currently known about such problems as contamination and isotopic fractionation (see Browman 1981; Polach 1976; Wolfman n.d.). Unfortunately, it is not always clear how the samples were handled in the laboratory and what corrections have or have not been made. Therefore, given the nature of the problems that need to be resolved, such a review would probably not be very successful. Rather than agonizing over all the possible sources of error that *might* be present in samples already processed, I would prefer, at some future time when a sufficient number of high-quality results are available, to synthesize only those results obtained from samples that have been collected and processed according to very strict standards. Such samples must come from deposits in which the cultural association is very clear, and they should receive complete pretreatment in the laboratory rather than so-called routine procedures (see Polach 1976:284, 286). Unfortunately, we must wait an unknown number of years before enough high-quality results are available.

Surprisingly few radiocarbon results from samples from crucial contexts have been published in the past 15 years. For the reasons discussed above, the results published since my dissertation was completed have not clarified the overall chronometric picture. The chronological chart I developed just over 15 years ago, based on all sources then available, prior to analyzing the archaeomagnetic results (Wolfman 1973:138), is reproduced and used here (Fig. 15.2). The slanted lines in this figure indicate possible temporal overlap of the phases. Since conventional radiocarbon dates were used in developing this chart, the possibility of shifting the absolute scale from 50 to 100 years later must be considered.

Finally, while some chronometric advances will undoubtedly be made using more carefully processed radiocarbon samples, I believe we are approaching the time when we will have learned as much as we can about developing an overall chronology from traditional approaches to this dating method. This is particularly true because the configuration of the recent calibration curves often leads to large 95% confidence intervals for calendar ages. Consequently, traditional approaches cannot provide dates with the precision and accuracy needed to resolve the fine-scale temporal problems with which we are currently dealing. Significant new advances, however, may be made by using an approach referred to as "curve fitting" or "wiggle matching" in areas where occasional pieces of wood with many rings have been recovered (see Pearson 1986). Under the proper circumstances, multiple radiocarbon measurements on samples collected from sequential rings should show the flat spots and other diagnostic features of a section of the calibration curve. By comparing the "radiocarbon signature" of a multiringed piece of wood with the calibration curve, a date might be obtained with an accuracy of about ±20 years. The appearance only recently of the new high-precision calibrations has made this approach feasible. Dating large pieces of wood in this manner will, of course, be accompanied by all the problems associated with dendrochronology (e.g., the absence of outside rings and the re-use of construction beams). But even a few accurate dates obtained in Mesoamerica in this manner may serve to answer crucial questions. This would be particularly important in situations in which associated archaeomagnetic samples were collected. In this case, a few very accurately dated points on the archaeomagnetic polar curve could assist in providing tightly calibrated archaeomagnetic dating throughout the area.

The Correlation Problem

The problem of trying to correlate the Maya Long Count calendar with the Christian calendar has intrigued scholars for more than a century (for discussions of the history of work on this problem and many of the proposed correlations, see Kelley 1976:27–52 and Kelley 1983). A variety of correlations at intervals of about 260 years is based on calendrical information recorded shortly after the Spanish arrived in Yucatan and the assumption of an unbroken calendar from the beginning of the Classic period until the conquest. Most Mesoamericanists currently prefer the Goodman-Martinez-Thompson (G-M-T) correlation, which places the beginning of the Classic at ca. A.D. 300, but the Spinden correlation (about 260 years earlier) and the Vaillant correlation (about 260 years later) both have had adherents in the past quarter century.

Following the development of radiocarbon dating, many chronometric arguments were reduced to trying to decide between the Spinden and the G-M-T correlations. While some of the original ^{14}C dates seemed to favor the Spinden correlation (Kulp et al. 1951; Libby 1955), most of the conventional radiocarbon dates since then seem to favor the G-M-T. However, corrected dates, particularly those using the recent Klein et al. (1982) and Stuiver (1982) calibrations, suggest the possibility of a correlation from 50 to 100 years later than the G-M-T.

Twenty years ago, some data from Yucatan (Andrews 1965) and Oaxaca (Paddock et al. 1968) were interpreted in such a way as to suggest that at least some radiocarbon results supported the Spinden correlation. Most of their arguments seem to have been based on a lack of appreciation of the role of the Putun Maya throughout Mesoamerica as early as A.D. 700 (Thompson 1970; Wolfman 1973:126–137). In addition, I believe too much reliance was placed on the results from some radiocarbon samples from the Northern Maya Lowlands that may have had calcium carbonate contamination. However, a decade later at least one Mayanist (Andrews 1978) argued that there was still some evidence in favor of the Spinden correlation or one close to it.

One of the reasons the G-M-T correlation is particularly attractive is that some very important astronomical information recorded in the Maya glyphs which was not understood at the time the G-M-T correlation was first proposed is consistent with it (Teeple 1930). In addition, Lounsbury (1983) has recently discovered further astronomical support for the G-M-T correlation. On the other hand, the interpretation of certain astronomical information in the glyphic texts associated with Long Count dates cannot be reconciled with this correlation, which suggests the possibility of a break in the Maya calendar prior to the conquest (Kelley 1983). This is a very complex problem, in part because not all of the apparent astronomical data recorded on stelae and in the codices are consistent, and there is some doubt about many of the astronomical interpretations. David Kelley has worked on this problem for many years and has proposed several possible correlations that take into account different portions of the astronomical data (e.g., Kelley and Kerr 1973; Kelley 1976:27–52; Kelley 1983). Others have also used this approach. Schove (1977), for instance, has proposed a correlation that is about 87 years later than the G-M-T, and Kaucher (n.d.) has suggested one about 30 years later than that. Recently, Kelley (1983) proposed a correlation about 216 years later than the G-M-T which is in accord with more of the (probable?) astronomical information recorded in the glyphs than any of the others. The Kelley correlation is not, of course, in accord with the calendar in use in Yucatan in the 16th century. Kelley argues rather convincingly, however, for a break in the Maya calendar between the end of the Classic period (A.D. 900, using the G-M-T correlation) and the conquest (1983:194–200). The Kelley correlation also receives support from some of the recent discussions that favor the Vaillant correlation or one near it (Chase 1985; Lincoln 1985).

Other Dating Methods

It is unfortunate that the only absolute dating method widely used in Mesoamerica is carbon 14. Consequently, the chronological charts and the calibration of the archaeomagnetic polar curve ultimately depend on this dating method. Secular variation of carbon 14 in the atmosphere and other problems inherent in the radiocarbon method, ranging from the lack of association of the sample with the cultural feature to be dated to sample contamination, which were briefly mentioned above, are well known to archaeologists (see Browman 1981; Polach 1976; Wolfman n.d.). In addition, some very strange individual results and occasionally apparently inaccurate results on whole series of samples (e.g., Bernal 1965; see also Millon 1973:60–61 and Wolfman 1973:35–38) have been reported in the literature. Due to these questions and the remaining disagreements about the correlation of the Maya and Christian calendars, additional independent chronometric information is clearly needed.

Occasional obsidian hydration and thermoluminescence dates have been reported, and eventually these methods may make significant contributions to chronometric studies in this area. It has been demonstrated that tree-ring dating can be applied in northern Mexico (Scott 1966; Wolfman 1968), and someday it may be applied in Mesoamerica. Preliminary dendrochronological studies on tropical trees, including some in Guatemala (Jacoby 1981) have been undertaken recently (Eckstein et al. 1981). Much more research is needed, however, before this dating method can be used to date prehistoric deposits in Mesoamerica—if, indeed, it can ever be used there.

Recent work on ice cores (Hammer et al. 1980; Johnsen et al. 1972; Thompson et al. 1979, 1985) and frost-damaged tree rings (LaMarche and Hirschboeck 1984) offer considerable hope of ascertaining the age of extremely large volcanic events in Mesoamerica with a precision and accuracy approaching that of traditional tree-ring dating. On the basis of their work with frost-damaged tree rings, LaMarche and Hirschboeck (1984) have suggested that the eruption of Ilopango occurred in A.D. 119. Future studies of the particulate matter in ice cores may eventually provide a more rigorous test of this suggestion. The chronometric placement of this event is very important because it may have significantly affected cultural development in the Southern Maya Lowlands during the Protoclassic and early Classic. The suggestion has been made that the people fleeing what is now western El Salvador following the Ilopango eruption may have had a significant role in initiating far-reaching culture change, first apparent in the Protoclassic Matzanel phase (ca. A.D. 100–300, using the G-M-T correlation), which brought on the Maya Classic (see Sheets 1979 for a review of this problem). If the G-M-T correlation is correct, the ^{14}C dates (averaging ca. A.D. 200) for this eruption are probably a little too late for the hypothesized migration to have brought about the start of the Matzanel phase. Even the probable frost-ring date of A.D. 119 seems a bit late within the G-M-T framework. Is this further evidence of a correlation later than the G-M-T, an argument against the importance of the Ilopango eruption in Lowland Maya cultural development, or merely an indication that the Matzanel phase started a bit later and was more compressed in time than was previously thought? The importance of dating this volcanic eruption is enhanced because flooding and mud slides may have been caused by this volcanic event, and evidence of such floods and slides have apparently been found in archaeological sites in El Salvador and Honduras (Sheets 1979:552–555).

Clearly, a more detailed analysis of the Protoclassic is needed. Archaeomagnetic samples collected immediately above and/or below the ash deposits from the Ilopango major eruption may eventually provide accurate dating for one point on the Mesoamerican archaeomagnetic curve and allow very precise cross-dating of this event with deposits in the Southern Maya Lowlands and elsewhere in Mesoamerica. Archaeomagnetic sample AL85 (see below) apparently comes from immediately below the Ilopango ash in San Salvador.

Ethnohistorical Research and the Abandonment of Tula by the Toltecs

The analysis of the native historical sources, many of which contain some calendrical data, is another source of chronometric information, particularly for the Postclassic period. One of the most interesting problems in Mesoamerican ethnohistory is the date of the abandonment of Tula by the Toltecs. Unfortunately, analysis of the central Mexican documents is quite difficult due to the use of different calendars in different parts of the area and apparent inconsistencies among sources. In addition, temporal control of the archaeological sequences in the Postclassic is not very good. However, most archaeologists and ethnohistorians seem to have accepted a date of about A.D. 1150–1200 for the Toltec abandonment of Tula. Based on analyses of different documents, Jiménez-Moreno (1954–55:24–25) has argued for a date of ca. 1168–1184 for this event, while Kirchoff (1955:195) has suggested a date near the end of the 12th century. Berlin (1947), by literally interpreting the *Historia Tolteca-Chichimeca* and strictly counting the years back from late pre-Hispanic times, reached a date of 1117 for the abandonment of Tula by the Toltecs, with the Chichimecs leaving 13 years later. A fairly recent evaluation of the documents by Davies (1977:413) produced a date of ca. 1179. A date of 1168 for this event is often used by Mesoamericanists (e.g., Peterson 1959; Wolf 1959) and will be used here as a working hypothesis.

There are, however, dissenting opinions from both ethnohistorians and archaeologists. On the basis of documentary analysis, Molloy and Kelley (n.d.; as discussed in Kelley 1983:168–172) and Molloy (1983) suggest a date of ca. A.D. 1300. This later date is consistent with Kelley's new correlation of the Maya and Christian calendars.

Even more recently, David Kelley (personal communication, 1987) has stated that, based on an ongoing reconstruction of Mesoamerican history from documentary sources that John Molloy and he are undertaking, a correlation about 150 years later than the G-M-T seems about right. Unfortunately, thus far he has not found a satisfactory correlation based on astronomical considerations that would fit this criterion. At the same time, he now feels that there is at least one serious objection to his recently proposed correlation, which is about 216 years later than the G-M-T.

On the basis of some recent radiocarbon dates, Diehl (1981:281) believes that Tula was abandoned by about A.D. 1100 at the latest. The ^{14}C results can be interpreted to suggest a date of A.D. 1000 or even a little earlier, but these radiocarbon results seem to me to be unreasonably early. Ultimately these discrepancies should and probably will be resolved by additional archaeological and archaeometric research at Tula and other central Mexican Postclassic sites.

MESOAMERICAN ARCHAEOMAGNETIC RESULTS

More than 200 archaeomagnetic samples from Mesoamerica, ranging in age from 5000 B.C. to the mid 20th century, have been collected and measured since 1968. Those collected prior to 1973, which dated from about A.D. 1 to about A.D. 1200, were part of my dissertation research (Wolfman 1973). These samples were measured in the University of Oklahoma's archaeomagnetism laboratory. Between 1973 and March 1984 (when I completed the first draft of this chapter), I measured 17 additional Mesoamerican samples dating in the A.D. 1–1200 time range in the rock magnetism laboratories at the University of Pittsburgh and the University of California at Santa Barbara (UCSB).

In the Oklahoma laboratory, the samples were measured on a Princeton Applied Research (PAR) spinner magnetometer. At the University of Pittsburgh, most of the measurements were made using a Superconducting Technology (SCT) cryogenic magnetometer. A few, however, were made using a PAR spinner. At UCSB, measurements were made using an SCT cryogenic magnetometer and a Schonstedt spinner magnetometer (Model SSM-1A, with a custom-built digital analyzer). AF demagnetization was undertaken in both the Oklahoma and Pittsburgh laboratories using custom-built instruments with tumblers. Static AF demagnetizers (both a custom-built and a Schonstedt GSD-1) were used in the Santa Barbara lab. (See Collinson 1975 and Wolfman 1984 for discussions of the various instruments.)

Thus far it has been possible to develop a curve for the approximate A.D. 1–1170 time period. In addition, short sections of curve for the middle and early part of the late Preclassic can be constructed. If additional key samples are collected, a continuous curve from ca. 900 B.C. to A.D. 1170 may be available before too long. Unfortunately, very few samples dating later than ca. A.D. 1200 have been collected.

Such data would be particularly interesting because of our poor time control for the archaeology of the late Postclassic. In addition, the data would allow more extensive comparison with data in the A.D. 1100–1500 range, which are available from elsewhere in the Western Hemisphere, including Peru (Dodson and Wolfman 1983b; Wolfman and Dodson 1986) and, within the United States, the Southwest (DuBois and Wolfman 1970b; DuBois 1975c; Sternberg 1982; Sternberg and McGuire, this volume, chap. 6) and the Southeast (Wolfman 1982 and this volume, chap. 14). In the following discussion, only data from the ca. A.D. 1–1170 period are discussed.

Results from Samples Collected Prior to 1973

Between 1969 and 1972, 96 archaeomagnetic samples dating from approximately A.D. 1–1200 were collected in Mesoamerica. The NRM measurements of 64 of these had α_{95} values less than 4°. (Experience has shown that samples with greater dispersion are often unreliable.) Abbreviated provenience and NRM data for these 64 samples are presented in the Appendix, Table A-4. More complete provenience data, phase assignments, estimated dates, archaeomagnetic dates, and site locations are presented in Tables 15.1 and 15.1a, and most of the data are discussed in greater detail in my dissertation (Wolfman 1973). Only minimal demagnetization was undertaken at the time the dissertation was completed. (Two specimens from many of the samples were cleaned using alternating field demagnetization. Complete demagnetization of these samples was undertaken at the Oklahoma laboratory between 1973 and 1975, but despite several requests, these data have not been provided.)

Almost all of the NRM results with α_{95} values less than 4° are internally consistent and in very good agreement with all other chronometric evidence. These results suggest that, with the exception of several samples from one mound (C-II-14 at Kaminaljuyu), which presumably was struck by lightning, and two samples collected from one posthole at Tula, very little secondary magnetism was present in them. Since viscous remanent magnetism (VRM) is directly proportional to the length of time since the primary remanence was acquired, archaeomagnetic samples generally have much less, and a softer, secondary magnetism of this type than the very ancient rocks customarily used in paleomagnetic studies. In addition, due to the relatively young age of archaeomagnetic samples and their protected location below the ground, any secondary chemical

Table 15.1. Mesoamerican Archaeomagnetic Results, 1969–1972

Lab. No.	Field No.	Site	Feature Description	Provenience
317	2-24-69	Teotihuacán	Baked floor	Teopancaxco Excav. No. TE-20
318	2-25-69	Lambityeco	Fired banquette	Feat. 68-24 in Bldg. 195 sub
319	2-26-69	Lambityeco	Hearth	Feat. 69-2 on Md. 190
321	2-28-69	Lambityeco	Hearth	On Md. 190 No feat. no.
407	7-15-69LAM	Lambityeco	Hearth	On Md. 190 No feat. no.
408	7-19-69BB	Brawbehl	Baked mud under concrete floor	Feat. 69-27
415	8-20-69TULA	Tula	Baked posthole	39 m N of S end of E wall of Palacio Quemado
440	6-13-70TULA	Tula	Baked posthole	24 m N of S end of E wall of Palacio Quemado
458	7-30-70KJ	Kaminaljuyu	Baked floor	46-12-189; Lot 01
469	6-30-70KJ	Kaminaljuyu	Baked floor	46-32-133; top of Md. B-V-11
470	7-1-70KJ	Kaminaljuyu	Baked posthole	46-23-103; Monument Plaza; Feat. 238; NW posthole of set of 4
471	7-2-70KJ	Kaminaljuyu	Baked clay sill	46-23-103; top of Md. C-II-14; Feat. 255
472	7-3-70KJ	Kaminaljuyu	Baked floor	46-23-103; Sq. 24N-41E; 30 cm deep; near top of Md. C-II-14
473	7-4-70KJ	Kaminaljuyu	Baked clay floor	46-23-103; Sq. 24N-41E; 75 cm deep; near top of Md. C-II-14
474	7-5-70KJ	Kaminaljuyu	Baked piedrin floor	46-23-103; Monument Plaza; Feat. 30
476	7-7-70KJ	Kaminaljuyu	Baked clay floor	46-23-103; near top of Md. C-II-14; Feat. 246B
477	7-8-70KJ	Kaminaljuyu	Baked piedrin wall	46-23-103; Monument Plaza; Feat. 68

Period or Phase	Est. Date	Archaeomag. Date (A.D.)
Late Xolalpan	A.D. 425–600	360–455
Early M.A. IV	A.D. 700–800	700–730
Early M.A. V	A.D. 900–1200	1045–1090 or ca. 1200 (?)
Early M.A. V	A.D. 900–1200	1055–1100 or ca. 1200 (?)
Early M.A. V	A. D. 900–1200	1070–1155 or ca. 1200 (?)
M.A. II	250 B.C.– A.D. 200	60–120
Tollan/Fuego	A.D. 1150–1200	—
Tollan/Fuego	A.D. 1150–1200	—
Verbena- Arenal or Aurora	200 B.C.– A.D. 400	25–55
Amatle 2	A.D. 600–900	670–695 or 880–900
Late Esperanza	A.D. 500–600	535–555
Early Esperanza	A.D. 400–500	—
Amatle 2	A.D. 600–900	—
Amatle 2	A.D 600–900	—
Late Esperanza	A.D 500–600	525–545
Early Esperanza	A.D. 400–500	—
Late Esperanza	A.D. 500–600	515–530 or 550–565

Table 15.1. (Continued)

Lab. No.	Field No.	Site	Feature Description	Provenience
478	7-9-70KJ	Kaminaljuyu	Baked clay floor	46-23-103; near top of Md. C-II-14; Feat. 247
479	7-10-70KJ	Kaminaljuyu	Baked clay wall	46-23-103; Monument Plaza; Feat. 36
480	7-11-70KJ	Kaminaljuyu	Baked clay floor	46-23-103; near top of Md. C-II-14; Feat. 261A
481	7-12-70KJ	Kaminaljuyu	Baked piedrin step	46-23-103; 2nd or 3rd step from bottom on S side of Md. C-II-14; Feat. 279
482	7-13-70KJ	Kaminaljuyu	Well baked clay step	46-23-103; step on NW side of Md. C-II-14; Feat. 278
483	7-14-70KJ	Kaminaljuyu	Baked clay floor	46-23-104; in plaza between Mds. C-II-14 and C-II-13; Feat. 280
488	7-18-70TULA	Tula	Baked floor	Tula 70; Test Pit 1; Ext. 26; Lev. 3; Dot 11
527	2-1-71TL	Tierras Largas	Hearth	Area A; Feat. 11
529	2-11-71TL	Tierras Largas	Hearth	Feat. 2, Hearth 1
539	6-14-71HUAP	Huapalcalco	Baked floor	Feat. 30; Rm. 2
540	6-17-81TEOT	Teotihuacán	Baked posthole	Uppermost structure in the Viking Group
541	6-20-71MA	Monte Albán	Baked mud under concrete floor	Baked area No. 11 in Md. 88 on S platform
563	6-15-71HUAP	Huapalcalco	Baked mud on stone wall	Feat. 30; Wall 1
564	6-16-71TEOT	Teotihuacán	Baked posthole	Rm. 7 of Palace 3; Rm. 7 is immediately S of the Palacio de los Jaguares
569	7-2-71PANT	Panteon	Baked clay floor	45 cm below top of Md. in NW face of trench
570	7-2-71CHA	Chachi	Well baked adobe brick wall	Wall in small md. in central part of site

Period or Phase	Est. Date	Archaeomag. Date (A.D.)
Aurora	A.D. 100–400	—
Amatle 2	A.D. 600–900	820–840
Aurora	A.D. 100–400	—
Late Esperanza	A.D. 500–600	—
Aurora or Esperanza	A.D. 100–600	—
Late Esperanza?	A.D. 500–600?	525–545 or 550–570
Tollan	A.D. 950–1200	1095–1140
M.A. IV	A.D. 700–1200	645–680 or 895–940
M.A. IV	A.D. 700–1200	635–670 or 900–945
Xometla	A.D. 750–950	850–880
Late Xolalpan or Metepec	A.D. 425–600 or 525–725	455–510 or 270–350
M.A. IIIB?	A.D. 400–700?	565–600
Xometla	A.D. 750–950	745–785
Late Xolalpan or Metepec	A.D. 425–600 525–725	435–495 or 250–345
Horcones, possibly Francesca or Guanacaste	125 B.C.–A.D. 1 possibly 400–125 B.C.	25 B.C.–A.D. 1
Late Maravillas– Early Ruiz	A.D. 800–1000	885–930

Table 15.1. _(Continued)_

Lab. No.	Field No.	Site	Feature Description	Provenience
580	7-13-71KJ	Kaminaljuyu	Baked clay floor	46-23-103; near top of Md. C-II-14; Feat. 246B
583	7-16-71KJ	Kaminaljuyu	Baked clay wall	46-23-102; Md. C-II-12; Feat. 273
584	7-17-71KJ	Kaminaljuyu	Baked posthole	46-23-000; Md. C-II-4 Str. A
585	7-18-71KJ	Kaminaljuyu	Baked piedrin floor	46-23-020; Md. C-II-4 Str. D
586	7-19-71KJ	Kaminaljuyu	Baked clay floor	46-23-020; Md. C-II-4 Str. L Feat. 1
587	7-20-71KJ	Kaminaljuyu	Hearth	46-33-358; 90 cm deep in test pit extension
596	8-11-71CZ	Cerro Zapotecas	Baked clay floor	Md. 2; Excav. A; bottom of Lev. 6 61 cm below surface
598	8-13-71TULA	Tula	Oven	Tula 70; Unit 3; Feat. 3; Sq. 213
611	10-2-71TULA	Tula	Baked posthole	30 m N of S end of E wall of Palacio Quemado
612	10-3-71TULA	Tula	Baked posthole	5.5 m N of S end of E wall of Palacio Quemado
613	10-4-71TULA	Tula	Baked posthole	24 m N of S end of E wall of Palacio Quemado
744	6-9-72ATZ	Monte Albán	Baked adobe wall	Cerro Atzompa N rm. on W side of main excav. Patio E of ball court
749	6-12-72TOM	Tomaltepec	Oven floor	Feat. 3
754	6-15-72TOM	Tomaltepec	Baked mud floor	Floor A5
766	7-2-72SA	San Andrés	Well baked clay (?) floor	Top of low md. on N side of S plaza
767	7-3-72SA	San Andrés	Baked clay floor	East platform of Str. 1
768	7-4-72VSJ	Tronconera 3	Well baked oven	4–5 m below surface in E face of large quebrada

Period or Phase	Est. Date	Archaeomag. Date (A.D.)
Early Esperanza	A.D. 400–500	—
Amatle 2	A.D. 600–900	700–735
Middle Esperanza	A.D. 500–550	490–525
Late Esperanza	A.D. 500–600	585–610
Amatle 2	A.D. 600–900	825–875 or 745–795
Verbena-Arenal	200 B.C.–A.D. 100	35–95
"Late Classic"	A.D. 500–900	785–820
Tollan	A.D. 950–1200	1140–1190
Tollan/Fuego	A.D. 1150–1200	—
Tollan/Fuego	A.D. 1150–1200	—
Tollan/Fuego	A.D. 1150–1200	—
M.A. IIIB	A.D. 400–700	510–575
M.A. II	250 B.C.–A.D. 200	245–305
M.A. II	250 B.C.–A.D. 200	55–85
Late Classic	A.D. 600–800	715–745
Late Classic	A.D. 600–800	705–755
Late Preclassic	100 B.C.–A.D. 100	65–95

Table 15.1. (Continued)

Lab. No.	Field No.	Site	Feature Description	Provenience
770	7-5-72VSJ	Tronconera 1	Well baked oven	4–5 m below surface in E face of large quebrada
771	7-6-72VSJ	Mango	Well baked oven	Several hundred m E of main bldgs. of Hacienda Valle San Juan
772	7-12-72KJ	Kaminaljuyu	Baked piedrin step	46-23-000; Md. C-II-4 E side of Struct. A, 2nd step from bottom
773	7-13-72KJ	Kaminaljuyu	Baked clay floor	46-23-103; Md. C-II-14
774	7-14-72KJ	Kaminaljuyu	Baked clay floor	46-23-103; Md. C-II-14
775	7-15-72KJ	Kaminaljuyu	Baked clay floor	46-23-020; Md. C-II-4 Str. L, Feat. 2
776	7-20-72EP	El Portón	Baked mud floor	EP-1-1-4/4
777	7-24-72KJ	Kaminaljuyu	Baked clay floor	46-23-210; Md. D-III-6 SW side of top of md.
778	7-25-72KJ	Kaminaljuyu	Baked clay floor	46-23-210; Md. D-III-6 2nd floor from top SW portion of md.
783	8-11-72MAN	Manzanillo (UA-72 Beta)	Baked floor	N Milpa; Sec. 2; Sq. 56AA; Lev. 3
784	8-12-72MAN	Manzanillo (UA-72)	Baked floor	Sq. 55AA; floor that divides Levels 1 and 2
785	8-15-72TULA	Tula	Baked posthole	39 m N of S end of E wall of Palacio Quemado
786	8-15-72TEOT	Teotihuacán	Baked mud-lined postholes in stone wall	Uppermost struct. in Viking Group
787	7-9-72TAZ	Tazumal	Baked floor	N rm. of Struct. I-D

Period or Phase	Est. Date	Archaeomag. Date (A.D.)
Late Preclassic	100 B.C.– A.D. 100	50–90
Late Preclassic	100 B.C.– A.D. 100	45–85
Middle Esperanza	A.D. 500–550	500–520
Esperanza or Amatle 2	A.D. 400–900	—
Amatle 2	A.D. 600–900	—
Amatle 2	A.D. 600–900	595–615
Miraflores	200 B.C.– A.D. 200	15–40
Verbena-Arenal, Aurora, or Amatle 2	200 B.C.– A.D. 400 or 600–900	370–420
Verbena-Arenal, Aurora, or Amatle 2	200 B.C.– A.D. 400 or 600–900	335–355
Teotihuacán III (Early Xolalpan)	A.D. 350–500	470–530 or 245–315
Teotihuacán III (Early Xolalpan)	A.D. 350–500	475–495 or 295–325
Tollan/Fuego	A.D. 1150–1200	—
Late Xolalpan or Metepec	A.D. 425–600 or 525–725	450–520 or 260–340
Early Classic	A.D. 300–600	565–580

Table 15.1a. Locations of Sites Where Archaeomagnetic Samples Were Collected in Mesoamerica

Site	Latitude	Longitude
Central Mexico		
Cerro Zapotecas	19.0	261.7
Huapalcalco	20.1	261.6
Manzanillo	19.0	261.8
Teotihuacán	19.7	261.2
Tula	20.0	260.7
Oaxaca		
Brawbehl	16.9	263.7
Lambityeco	16.9	263.7
Monte Albán	17.0	263.3
Tierras Largas	17.1	263.2
Tomaltepec	17.0	263.3
Chiapas		
Chachi	16.4	267.3
Panteon	16.4	267.3
Guatemala		
El Portón	15.1	269.8
Kaminaljuyu	14.7	269.5
Honduras		
Copán	14.8	270.8
El Salvador		
Altamira	13.7	270.8
Mango	13.3	271.4
San Andrés	13.8	270.6
Tazumal	14.0	270.3
Tronconera 1	13.3	271.4
Tronconera 3	13.3	271.4

remanent magnetism (CRM), if acquired, would ordinarily be small
compared to the total NRM. In particular, the NRM results obtained
in Mesoamerica since 1973 (see below), for which thorough demagnetization studies were undertaken, exhibited only minor secondary
magnetism. Although careful comparative studies have not yet been
undertaken, it seems that samples collected in Mesoamerica exhibit

less secondary magnetism due to VRM than those collected in some other areas.

A review of the NRM results in Table A-4 reveals that only 10 samples (415, 473, 476, 478, 480, 481, 580, 598, 773, and 785) with α_{95} values less than 4° have VGP positions with latitudes less than 75°. Four of these have extremely low latitudes. Seven of them, including three with extremely low latitudes, were collected on Mound C-II-14 at Kaminaljuyu. Comparison of the VGP positions of the remaining samples from this mound (472, 482, and 774) with the curve (Fig. 15.4) reveals that at least two of the three are definitely in aberrant positions as well. These results, especially the extremely low pole positions, suggest that the mound was struck by lightning, which imparted a secondary magnetic component to these samples. Consequently, none of the NRM results from the samples collected on Mound C-II-14 was accepted, and they were not included in the construction and calibration of the Mesoamerican polar curve (Fig. 15.4).

Two specimens from each of the Mound C-II-14 samples collected in 1970 and 1971 were cleaned using progressive alternating field demagnetization. Generally, demagnetization changed the magnetic direction in those specimens that had unacceptably low VGP positions to one that was within 15° of the geographic pole. Such data must be regarded as tentative and except for two samples (478 and 480) will not be considered at this time. The two specimen demagnetized results from samples 478 and 480 are presented in Table 15.2 because they provide what appear to be very consistent results for the early part of the Aurora phase and are the only results from samples dating to the first half of this phase. Most important, they are the two youngest samples in stratigraphic series B (Table 15.3), and their VGPs are in the correct stratigraphic order. Because they are the only results that define the curve between about A.D. 80 and 280, this section is drawn with a broken line. Their VGPs are plotted on Figure 15.4a. The demagnetization of other two-specimen subsamples from other proveniences at Kaminaljuyu and elsewhere with NRM α_{95} values less than 4° produced, at most, minor changes in magnetic direction.

The three remaining samples with VGPs lower than 75° N were collected at Tula. One, from the Canal Locality excavations (see Diehl 1974), has a VGP latitude of 74.9°. Its pole position seems consistent with other data. The other two were collected from the same posthole at the Palacio Quemado (see below). One (415) had a pole position of 54.5° N, 163.2° W, which is very low. Stepwise AF demagnetization of two specimens from this sample changed the latitude from 54.5° to 68.0°, suggesting a secondary IRM component due to lightning or an extremely large VRM. Apparently, AF demagnetization was unable to remove the secondary magnetism completely, which suggests the presence of some secondary CRM. The other sample (785) also had a rather low pole position (72.9° N). Consequently, neither was used in constructing the curve.

The Curve

The curve shown in Figure 15.4, spanning the A.D. 1–1170 time period, was drawn on the basis of the data in the Appendix, Table A-4, and Tables 15.1 and 15.2. These are the data obtained prior to 1973. The curve was drawn based on the distribution of the VGP positions and the chronological order of the VGPs as indicated by stratigraphic superposition and associated ceramics and architecture. Further work will undoubtedly lead to some modification of the configuration of the curve. However, with the exception of the sections between about A.D. 100 and 300 (see Fig. 15.4a) and about A.D. 915 and 1060 (see Fig. 15.4b), both indicated by dashed lines, I expect that such modifications will not be very great. It is certainly possible that the curve for the earlier time interval, which is defined by only one tentative result (sample 478), could be a closed clockwise loop. The calibration was arrived at by a more complex process of considering all of the chronological information available simultaneously to make the best possible estimates. Most of the details of this procedure are discussed below. The time scale based on conventional ^{14}C dates is indicated along the curve at 100-year intervals.

The results presented in Tables 15.1 and 15.2 and shown on Figure 15.4 are remarkable. With very few minor exceptions (749, 440, and 612), all VGPs are within their expected time ranges, based on phase assignments and other nonarchaeomagnetic chronological information. It is possible that a few VGPs may be erroneous, since some of the phases are quite long (i.e., up to 300 years). However, in those cases where stratigraphic superposition of samples occurred, the

Figure 15.4. Mesoamerican polar curve for A.D. 1–1170 with VGPs for samples collected between 1969 and 1972. (A) A.D. 1–300. (B) A.D. 300–1170.

A

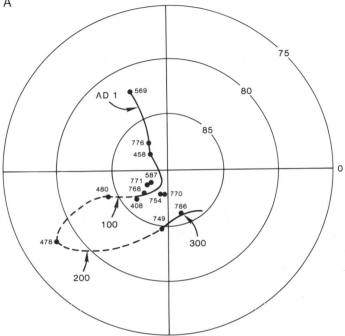

B

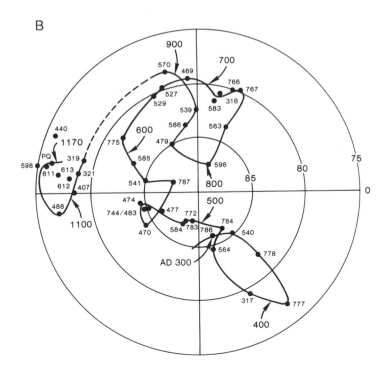

Table 15.2. NRM and Demagnetized (Two-Specimen Subsample) Aurora Phase Results from Kaminaljuyu Mound C-II-14 Stratigraphic Sequence B (See Table 15.3)

Lab. No.	Field No.	NRM			Demag			Level
		Lat.	Long.	α_{95}	Lat.	Long.	α_{95}	
478	7-9-70KJ	8.9	192.2	2.9	77.8	212.7	5.8	10.0
480	7-11-70KJ	38.4	196.0	3.5	84.2	201.8	2.2	20.0

Table 15.3. Stratigraphic Sequences of Archaeomagnetic Samples Collected at Kaminaljuyu. (The samples in each sequence are listed starting with the oldest and ending with the youngest.)

Stratigraphic Sequence A (Monument Plaza, 46-23-103)
  Samples 477, 474, 470, 479

Stratigraphic Sequence B (Mound C-II-14, 46-23-103)
  Samples 480 (same as 582), 478, 476 (same as 580), 471 (same as 579)

Stratigraphic Sequence C (Mound C-II-4, Structure A, 46-23-000)
  Samples 772, 584

Stratigraphic Sequence D (Mound C-II-4, Structures D and L, 46-23-020)
  Samples 585, 775, 586

Stratigraphic Sequence E (Mound D-III-6, 46-23-210)
  Samples 778, 777

VGPs are in the correct order along the curve. Particularly important were the data from the 31 samples collected at Kaminaljuyu, including two collected from each of three features. The importance of this group of samples is greatly enhanced by the fact that 18 of them, including the three repeat samples, were collected from five stratigraphic sequences (Table 15.3). Each sequence is consistent with available information, but note the small loop in the curve described by the three youngest samples in stratigraphic sequence A at ca. A.D. 525–560 (Fig. 15.4b). While there is no question about its temporal location, the configuration of the loop is based solely on the stratigraphic sequence and the VGP positions. Even though the α_{95} values of the three samples are quite small (between 0.3° and 1.1°), the very small size of the loop (about 2.5° for its major axis) clearly indicates that variation in this configuration is possible (i.e., possibly a small "jog" rather than a loop).

Consideration of the VGP positions and all of the chronological data relating to them suggests that the average rate of change of VGP position along the curve between A.D. 1 and 1170 (excluding the small loop between about A.D. 525 and 560) is approximately 1°/9 yr. This rate of change is about the same as that found in the southwestern United States during the time period A.D. 700–1500 when the same curve-fitting procedures are used (DuBois 1975c; DuBois and Wolfman 1970; Wolfman 1984:405–408; see Wolfman, this volume, chap. 16, for a discussion of different curve-fitting procedures and their implications). It should be emphasized that this is an estimated average rate of change. As the ages of the individual VGPs are known within ranges of about 100 to more than 300 years and the magnetic directions are estimated with up to 4° variation at the 95% confidence level, there may be some short-term variation from this average figure. For several sections of the curve, where independent dating information was lacking, the calibration depends on interpolation and extrapolation using this figure. Consequently the exact placement of some of the 100-year calibration points may be somewhat in error. I estimate this error to be no more than 50 and perhaps as little as 25 years, in the A.D. 300–900 period, assuming that the G-M-T correlation or one close to it is correct.

As I have discussed in detail elsewhere (Wolfman, this volume, chap. 16), calibrating an archaeomagnetic polar curve involves a great deal of archaeological inference, particularly in areas outside the southwestern United States where dendrochronology is not available. It is important that the details of this procedure be made available so that others can verify them. Among the most important considerations in developing the calibration of the Mesoamerican curve were the following:

(1) Three samples (768, 770, 771) were collected from ovens at the Hacienda Valle San Juan in El Salvador. Three carbon samples from cultural deposits approximately contemporaneous with the ovens dated from 79 B.C. ± 53, A.D. 32 ± 73, and A.D. 44 ± 65 (Boggs 1972), suggesting that the ovens date from within 100 years of A.D. 1. The VGP positions of the three archaeomagnetic samples are extremely close together (within about 3°). The only ^{14}C date from an oven in the same arroyo where samples 768 and 770 were collected was the

latest. (Unfortunately this oven had eroded away before the archaeomagnetic samples were collected.) This suggests that the three oven
samples date between A.D. 1 and 100.

(2) Sample 480 was collected from an Aurora phase floor. It should
date no earlier than A.D. 100 (see Fig. 15.4a), and it follows the latest
of the Valle San Juan samples by only 3.5° along the curve. This
suggests that sample 480 cannot be much later than A.D. 100 and
that the Valle San Juan samples date in the latter half of the first
century A.D., which is consistent with the radiocarbon evidence.

(3) The VGP position for A.D. 1 was obtained by extrapolating backward along the curve from A.D. 100, 1°/9 yr. This position is consistent with the estimated ages for samples 569, 776, and 458.

(4) The Aurora phase lasted from ca. A.D. 100 to 400. As discussed
above, a beginning date of A.D. 100 is consistent with ^{14}C dated samples from Valle San Juan in El Salvador. Based on all the other archaeomagnetic evidence, the latest Aurora phase sample (777) seems to
fit very nicely just before A.D. 400.

(5) The exact pole positions for A.D. 200 and 300, which lie within
and just outside the poorly defined section of curve from ca. A.D. 80
to ca. 280 respectively (see above), were interpolated from earlier and
later parts of the curve. Sample CO186, collected at Copán in 1982
(see Table 15.4), is thought, on the basis of associated ceramics, to be
of terminal Preclassic—early Classic age (i.e., ca. A.D. 300). It is very
encouraging to note that the VGP for this sample is within 1° of the
interpolated pole position for A.D. 300 (Fig. 15.5).

(6) The middle Esperanza subphase is thought to span the short
period between A.D. 500 and 550. A date of A.D. 525 for the two
middle Esperanza subphase samples collected at Kaminaljuyu (584
and 772), which have almost identical pole positions, seems to be a
reasonable estimate and is consistent with all other data.

(7) The Esperanza phase at Kaminaljuyu ended at about A.D. 600.
Sample 585 was collected from a baked piedrin floor on a structure
with talud and tablero architecture, hallmarks of the Esperanza
phase. Less than half a meter above it, sample 775 was collected
from a baked-clay floor that dates from the Amatle 2 phase (see Stratigraphic Sequence D, Table 15.3). Sample 775 follows sample 585 by
about 3° along the polar curve. The four Kaminaljuyu samples with
VGPs later than sample 775 along the curve (469, 583, 479, and 586)
are, according to the archaeologists who worked at that site, all of

Amatle 2 age. The seven additional Esperanza phase samples from this site all have VGP positions that precede sample 585 along the curve. This strongly suggests that A.D. 600 on the curve is between the VGP positions obtained from samples 585 and 775.

(8) Seven radiocarbon dates have been reported for the early Monte Albán IV cultural level from which sample 318 at Lambityeco was collected (Rabin 1970). One sample gave an aberrant result of A.D. 1055 ± 95. The other six dates ranged from A.D. 640 ± 100 to A.D. 755 ± 90, with an average age of A.D. 708 ± 40 (see Long and Rippeteau 1974 for the averaging procedure used). The beginning of Monte Albán IV is about A.D. 700; therefore a date of about A.D. 730 (obtained from the 14.0° distance along the curve of its VGP from the VGP for A.D. 600) does not seem unreasonable for sample 318, which was directly associated with the ^{14}C sample that dated from A.D. 755 ± 90. It is interesting that there is some similarity between the loop between ca. 700 and 880 on the Mesoamerican curve and loops at about the same time in the Southwest (this volume, chap. 13; see also Wolfman 1984:411) and Arkansas (Wolfman, this volume, chap. 14). While it would be premature to make too much of it, it seems that the curves for the United States are running about 75 years later than the curve for Mesoamerica at this time. As time goes on, such comparisons may assist in the development of more detailed models of the geomagnetic field. Such models may, in turn, eventually assist in archaeomagnetic dating.

(9) Samples 527 and 529 are of Monte Albán IV age. In my original analysis of the nonarchaeomagnetic data, I concluded that Monte Albán IV lasted from about A.D. 700 to 1200, with Monte Albán V gradually replacing period IV from ca. A.D. 900 to 1200 (Wolfman 1973:138). Recently, Blanton (1978:27–29), on the basis of his interpretation of Drennan's (1983) compilation of Oaxacan radiocarbon results and surface survey data, suggested that Monte Albán IV began about A.D. 650 or 700 and was abruptly replaced at about A.D. 950. His position is counter to long-standing "conventional wisdom" about the Valley of Oaxaca sequence. This controversy will not be resolved without further excavating and processing of appropriate chronometric samples. In either case, samples 527 and 529 could date from about either A.D. 670 or 925. Consequently, there may be an 8° section of curve from ca. A.D. 610 (sample 775) to ca. A.D. 685 (sample 469) containing no data points. However, three results

obtained since the first draft of this chapter was written, in March 1984 and therefore not included here, strongly support the configuration shown for this interval.

(10) Following sample 318 from Lambityeco in Oaxaca there are no tight constraints on any dates. The eight VGPs from there through the VGP for sample 570 (ca. A.D. 915) all have reasonable positions, given the independent information about their ages. The last in this series, sample 570 from Chachi, was associated with a large Tepeu 3 sherd. The archaeomagnetic date for this sample, A.D. 885–930, which was obtained by extrapolation forward from the VGP for sample 318, is consistent with the A.D. 800–1000 span usually assigned to the Tepeu 3 phase in the central Petén.

(11) Following sample 570 (at ca. A.D. 915) there is a 12° section of curve without any definite data points. Then there are VGPs for three early Monte Albán V samples (319, 321, and 407). Extrapolation forward from A.D. 915 along an unwavering curve provides ages of 1020 to 1050. There is room for considerable error here, however. The section from samples 570 to 319 could include samples 527 and 529 and perhaps several additional zigs and zags. The archaeomagnetic results from Tula (see item 12 below) suggest that samples 319, 321, and 407 are a little later in time, perhaps from about A.D. 1060 to 1090, and this dating is used on Figure 15.4b and in Table 15.1. However, depending on the configuration of the post–A.D. 1170 curve, these three samples might date to ca. A.D 1200.

(12) The six samples (415, 440, 611, 612, 613, and 785) collected from four postholes baked at the time the Palacio Quemado burned make the burning of this structure the best-sampled event in Mesoamerica. Of the six samples collected there, two from the same posthole (415 and 785) have VGP positions below 75° N and were therefore rejected. The remaining four (samples 440, 611, 612, and 613) have an average pole position of 76.7° N, 168.4° E (which has the designation PQ on Fig. 15.4b). I am tentatively using this value for the VGP at the time this structure burned. While clustered fairly close together, the VGPs from the four samples were more dispersed than expected. Therefore, individual dates were not assigned to these samples on Table 15.1. Exposure to the elements during the 25 years between excavation of the structure and sample collection provided ample time for weathering and the development of some secondary chemical remanent magnetism, which sometimes cannot be removed with

standard demagnetization techniques. Clearly, further sampling of this structure is required. Samples collected deep inside the post-holes, where weathering is likely to be minimal, might provide more consistent results. Laboratory work on such samples should include complete AF demagnetization and perhaps chemical demagnetization experiments (Collinson 1967; Kirshvink 1981) as well.

Extrapolating forward from the VGP for sample 570 (ca. A.D. 915) along an unwavering curve at a rate of change of 1°/9 yr, the date obtained for the burning of the Palacio Quemado is ca. A.D. 1140. As noted above, more variation in the section between the VGPs for samples 570 and 319 than is shown on Figure 15.4b is possible. It is also quite possible that the loop between the points labeled 1100 and 1170 is somewhat larger than that shown in Figure 15.4b. A rate somewhat slower than 1°/9 yr is another possibility. Therefore, this extrapolated date may be a little early.

As discussed above, despite some contradictory evidence, a mid to late 12th-century date derived from ethnohistoric sources for the fall of Tula (and the assumed contemporaneous burning of the Palacio Quemado) seems to be a useful working hypothesis, based on nonar-chaeomagnetic evidence accepted by many Mesoamericanists. A consideration of archaeomagnetic results from other parts of the world provides some additional support for a mid to late 12th-century date for the burning of the Palacio Quemado. (See Barbetti 1977 and Champion 1980 for analyses of large data sets that show the general dipole character of the geomagnetic field during the past 2,000 years.) The apparent loop in the Mesoamerican curve between about A.D. 1050 and 1200 is very similar to the configuration of the curves for the southwestern and southeastern United States at about this time. To some extent it is also similar to the Peruvian curve (Wolfman and Dodson 1984, 1986). There are even some less-pronounced similarities in the west European (Thellier 1981) and Japanese (Hirooka 1971) curves about 100 years later. This suggests that the entire dipole component of the geomagnetic field was oriented in the direction of the Palacio Quemado VGPs from about A.D. 1100 to 1300.

The three lines of evidence (extrapolation, ethnohistory, and geo-magnetism) are, of course, mutually reinforcing. Consequently, a tentative estimated date of A.D. 1168 is used here for the average VGP of the four Palacio Quemado samples. Clearly, additional evidence is needed. Archaeomagnetic data leading to the construction of the curve through the end of the Postclassic and independent dating of samples throughout the Postclassic will help place these results in their correct chronometric positions.

It is of interest that the two VGPs obtained from samples collected from the Canal Locality excavations in another part of Tula (488 and 598) are very close to the average VGP for the Palacio Quemado samples. This confirms Diehl's (1981) impression that the Canal Locality structures were in use near the end of Tula. However, as noted above, the radiocarbon dates obtained from associated features were more than 150 years earlier than the range of dates suggested by most of the ethnohistorical evidence (i.e., 1150–1200) and by the provisional archaeomagnetic results.

Archaeomagnetic Dates

The construction and calibration of the curve provide archaeomagnetic dates for the time period ca. A.D. 1–1170. Along with the additional 14 results discussed below, they provide considerable new data for interpreting Mesoamerican chronology. The results are essentially consistent with the chronologies proposed by MacNeish and his co-workers (e.g., MacNeish et al. 1970:Fig. 153) and me (Wolfman 1973; see also Fig. 15.2, which was developed before archaeomagnetic dating was applied in Mesoamerica).

The range of error for each date (Table 15.1, col. 8; Table 15.4, col. 8) was determined by comparison of the 95% oval of confidence about the VGP with the curve. If the VGP did not fall on the curve for the purposes of obtaining a date with 95% confidence limits, the nearest point on the curve with the oval around it was used. In addition, five years were added to each end of the confidence interval to allow for nondipole variation across Mesoamerica. I have discussed this procedure in more detail elsewhere (Wolfman 1982:284; Wolfman 1984:391, 395–399). This error range is an estimate of the *precision* of the date at about the 95% confidence level but says nothing about its *accuracy*. And, as noted above, due to recent recalibration of the radiocarbon time scale, there is a reasonable chance that the archaeomagnetic dates are a bit early. The dates assigned to samples on the basis of their VGP positions (col. 8 on Tables 15.1 and 15.4) are here referred to as archaeomagnetic dates (or ages) to distinguish them from calendar dates.

None of the archaeomagnetic dates is surprising, but several are worthy of special note. The two results from Huapalcalco (samples

563 and 539) with archaeomagnetic dates of A.D. 745–785 and A.D. 850–880 provide the first direct dating of the Xometla phase in central Mexico. That these dates are well within the estimated time range based on other evidence (see Fig. 15.2) is encouraging. The data obtained from samples collected at Teotihuacán and on the fringes of the Maya area (317, 540, 564, 786, 766, 767, and 787) are also, of course, of considerable interest. Since additional samples from these areas were collected after 1973, a discussion of these results is deferred until the end of the following section.

Samples Collected Since 1973

Since 1973, additional samples have been collected in Mesoamerica. At the time the first draft of this chapter was completed (March 1984), I had measured 17 of them, with estimated ages in the A.D. 1–1200 range. These samples have all been subjected to thorough AF demagnetization procedures. The results obtained from three samples collected at Copán in 1978 have been published previously (Wolfman 1983). Fourteen of them have α_{95} values less than 4°. More than half of the samples have α_{95} values of 2° or less (Appendix, Table A-4, and Table 15.4). The pole positions of these samples are in excellent agreement with the results obtained previously (Fig. 15.5). The excellent agreement of the more recent results with the curve and the fact that the NRM directions of these samples show little difference from their demagnetized directions strongly suggest that the NRM results obtained in the Oklahoma lab prior to 1973 are reasonably reliable. Nonetheless, I expect that minor changes in the configuration of the curve will be necessary as archaeomagnetic research in Mesoamerica continues.

The samples collected since 1973 are particularly important because they include five results from Teotihuacán and nine from Copán and sites on the fringes of the Maya area in El Salvador. The results from these samples provide new data about important Mesoamerican chronometric problems. In the following subsections, they are discussed and compared with archaeomagnetic results obtained from Teotihuacán and the Maya area prior to 1973.

Teotihuacán. There have been some long-standing disagreements about the dating of the late Preclassic and Classic period phases at Teotihuacán. Archaeomagnetic results from this site indicate that a thorough review of the problem is needed. Particularly important is

Table 15.4. Mesoamerican Archaeomagnetic Results for Samples
Collected Since 1973

Lab. No.	Field No.	Site	Feature Description	Provenience
AL85	18-VIII-76 ALTA	Altamira	Baked clay basin	Probably immediately below the Ilopango ash
CO100	6-16-79 COP	Copán	Oven	PAC 78; OP IV; Str. 99; Oven No. 1
CO102	6-18-79 COP	Copán	Baked posthole	PAC 78; OP IV; Str. 71
SA158	8-20-77 SAND	San Andrés	Baked floor	Floor near center of Str. 7
SA159	20-IX-77 SAND	San Andrés	Baked floor	Uppermost floor at SW corner of Str. 7
TE170	4-5-82(A) TEOT	Teotihuacán	Baked posthole	Ciudadela; Conjunto 1D; Grupo E; Portico
TE171	4-5-82(A) TEOT	Teotihuacán	Baked column mold and wall plaster	Ciudadela; Conjunto 1D; Grupo A; Cuarto 5; lado sur de la entrada
TE172	4-6-82(A) TEOT	Teotihuacán	Baked column mold	Ciudadela; Conjunto 1D; Grupo B; Cuarto 7; Columna oeste del portico
TE173	4-7-82 TEOT	Teotihuacán	Baked doorjamb mold	Map Grid N 2 W 1 Unidad 11, Cuadro 85 muro norte de la habitación este de la plaza uno oeste de la estructura 57B
TE176	4-15-82 TEOT	Teotihuacán	Baked doorjamb mold	Map Grid N 2 W 1 Unidad Punto 36; Pasillo entre cuartos C8 y C10, acceso sur
CO183	4-29-82(A) COP	Copán	Baked clay floor	CV36; Op. XV; Str. 95; Feat. 7; Sq. S22W52; Lev. 1
CO185	4-30-82(A) COP	Copán	Baked clay floor	CV36; Op. XV; Feat. 1 Sq. S38W46; bottom of Lev. 2
CO186	5-2-82 COP	Copán	Oven	CV30; Op. IX; Str. 191; Feat. 10
CO188	5-4-82 COP	Copán	Large hearth	CV30; Op. IX; Str. 191; Feat. 11

ᵃ(p) = probable

Period or Phase	Est. Date	Archaeomag. Date (A.D.)
Probably Late Preclassic	ca. A.D. 119?	75–135(p)[a]
Late Classic	A.D. 600–740	510–570
Early Classic	A.D. 300–600	560–585
Middle Classic	ca. A.D. 600	560–590
Late Classic	A.D. 600–800	740–765 or 850–875
Late Xolalpan or Metepec	A.D. 425–600 or 525–725	465–505 or 285–330
Late Xolalpan or Metepec	A.D. 425–600 or 525–725	475–495 or 295–325
Late Xolalpan or Metepec	A.D. 425–600 or 525–725	480–510 or 285–310
Late Xolalpan or Metepec	A.D. 425–600 or 525–725	465–495 or 290–315
Late Xolalpan or Metepec	A.D. 425–600 or 525–725	410–480 or 300–375
Late Classic	A.D. 600–800	835–865
Late Classic	A.D. 600–800	495–570
Early Classic	ca. A.D. 300	275–325
End of Middle Classic	ca. A.D. 600	575–600

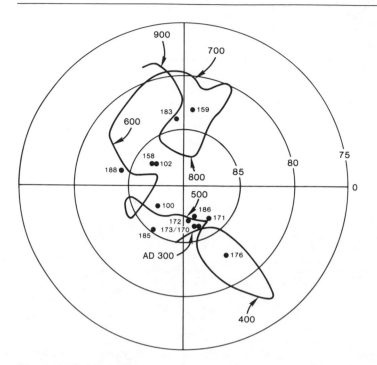

Figure 15.5. Mesoamerican polar curve for A.D. 300–900, with VGPs for samples collected since 1973.

the dating of the Xolalpan phase. Most Mesoamericanists who have examined this problem place this phase sometime between ca. A.D. 350 and 650 (MacNeish et al. [1970:Fig. 153] and Johnson and Mac-Neish [1972:Fig. 4]: A.D. 425–600; Wolfman [1973:29–38, 115–126, 138, Table 10]: A.D. 350–600; Millon [1973:60–61 and Fig. 12]: A.D. 450–650; Sanders et al. [1979:93]: A.D. 500–650). These dates were based on a few radiocarbon results from central Mexico and radiocarbon dates from, and cross-dating with, other parts of Mesoamerica (most importantly, the Maya Highlands and Southern Lowlands).

It is very encouraging to note that recent accelerator mass spectrometer (AMS) measurements on five ^{14}C samples from Teotihuacán seem to support in a general way these estimates of the age of the Xolalpan phase (Gowlett et al. 1987). However, these new results are neither sufficiently large in number nor precise and accurate enough to provide more support for any of the four alternative datings of the Xolalpan phase offered above.

That my estimate of the time span of the Xolalpan phase (Wolfman 1973) was earlier than those suggested by others is presumably due in part to their use of corrected ^{14}C dates. However, it should be recalled that these scholars base absolute dating in the Southern Maya Lowlands and to a lesser extent (by cross-dating) the Southern Maya Highlands and Teotihuacán, on the G-M-T correlation. Since the G-M-T is apparently in better agreement with conventional rather than corrected radiocarbon dates, all their implicit arguments may not be consistent, or more likely, there may be enough leeway in the available data to accommodate several alternatives.

That there was a great fire, or a series of contemporaneous fires, in the central part of Teotihuacán that was in some way related to the decline of this great city has been recognized for many years (Armillas 1944, 1950; Bernal 1965; Millon 1981, 1988). The dating of this event should help clarify Teotihuacán chronology. But unfortunately there is disagreement as to whether this event took place in the Xolalpan phase (Acosta 1972; Armillas 1944; Bernal 1965) or the Metepec phase (Millon 1981).

In addition, despite the general agreement among the scholars cited above about the age of the Xolalpan phase, there is some evidence for an earlier chronology at Teotihuacán. Bernal (1965) summarized 14 conventional radiocarbon dates that he suggested supported the idea that the Xolalpan phase (which he saw ending by fire at Teotihuacán) may have dated from as early as ca. A.D. 150–300. But, based on cross-dating with the Maya area, this is consistent with the improbable Spinden correlation and not the G-M-T. Bernal did, however, allow the possibility that the Xolalpan phase dated from as late as A.D. 300–450. He further suggested that the city continued to exist with a nearly abandoned center throughout the Metepec phase. (The 14 conventional radiocarbon dates ran from A.D. 50 ± 80 to 370 ± 80, with the second youngest date A.D. 150 ± 80.

Based on the association of Teotihuacán and Oaxaca-style ceramics found in the so-called Oaxaca Barrio at Teotihuacán, Paddock (1967, but see also Paddock 1983) has also argued for an early Teotihuacán chronology. While Millon (1973:60–61) allows that an early chronology is *possible*, he and others have argued that the beams from which most of the ^{14}C samples discussed by Bernal came were cut for use in earlier structures and were later reused in the buildings in which they were found. Also, some or all of the samples from the beams may have been subject to post-sample growth error if the outer rings of the logs from which the vigas were cut were not sampled. This could easily have been the case if all or some of the sapwood was missing due to rot or intentional shaping of the beams. The dates at the late end of the A.D. 50–370 time span, including two obtained on small pieces of charcoal (i.e., not from construction timbers), might be interpreted to support the late chronology due to secular variation of atmospheric ^{14}C (Fig. 15.3; see also Klein et al. 1982 and Stuiver 1982). Similarly, corrected ^{14}C dates would add about 100 years to Bernal's estimates for the end of the Xolalpan phase.

Archaeomagnetic results were obtained on four Teotihuacán samples collected prior to 1973 (samples 317, 564, 540, and 786, the last two of which were collected from the same structure in the Viking Group). Five additional samples—three from Conjunto 1D in the Ciudadela (TE170, TE171, and TE172) and two from baked features close together on the west side of the Street of the Dead (TE173 and TE176)—were collected in 1982 from the latest construction levels at these locations. Of these nine samples, only one (317, which is thought to be late Xolalpan in age) was collected away from the center of the city. The other eight came from features that were apparently baked in the great fire that occurred in the Xolalpan or Metepec phase. The archaeomagnetic results indicate (see Tables 15.1 and 15.4 and Figs. 15.4b and 15.5) that all seven of these features could have baked simultaneously at either about A.D. 310 or 475 due to the crossover point at 85.5° N, 59.0° W (see Figs. 15.4b and 15.5). Due to the rather narrow loop between A.D. 310 and 475, alternative dates are also possible for sample 317 (see Fig. 15.4b and Table 15.1).

The two possibilities for the archaeomagnetic dates for these nine samples, coupled with the disagreement about the phase in which the great fire occurred, suggest several alternative scenarios: (1) The early alternatives for these archaeomagnetic results, which seem unlikely, support an early chronology, with the great fire at the end of the Xolalpan phase, long before the city was abandoned, as was suggested by Bernal (1965). (2) The later alternatives for the archaeomagnetic dates, with the fire occurring at the end of the Metepec phase, would also support an early chronology but without requiring Teotihuacán to have existed for many years after the destruction of its center. This, however, does not seem to be consistent with cross-dating to other parts of Mesoamerica, particularly the Maya area. (3) The later alternatives, with the fire at the end of the Xolalpan or early in the Metepec phase, seem to support a chronology somewhere between that suggested by Bernal and those suggested by the other scholars cited above. (4) Another possibility, which would require only minimal adjustment of the phase dates favored by most scholars and which is in accord with the late alternatives for the archaeomagnetic results, is that the great fire occurred in the middle, rather than at the end, of the Xolalpan phase. While this final possibility has not been suggested previously, it may ultimately be the most viable hypothesis.

In any event, these archaeomagnetic results indicate that a thorough review of this whole problem is clearly needed, and strong consideration should be given to Bernal's suggestion that the central part of Teotihuacán was burned many years before the rest of the city was abandoned.

Teotihuacán and Kaminaljuyu. The recent archaeomagnetic results from samples collected in the Ciudadela and along the Street of the Dead present an opportunity for precise relative dating of the extensive burning at Teotihuacán (apparently ca. A.D. 475–500) and Teotihuacán influence at Kaminaljuyu during the Esperanza phase (see Kidder et al. 1946; Cheek 1977a, 1977b; Sanders 1977). Interestingly, the archaeomagnetic results for the massive burning at Teotihuacán are all earlier than the archaeomagnetic dates for the middle and late Esperanza samples collected at Kaminaljuyu, which run from A.D. 525 through 585. Unfortunately, the early Esperanza phase samples collected at Kaminaljuyu (471, 476, and 580)—all from baked features in Mound C-II-14—had aberrant magnetic directions, apparently due to the mound's being struck by lightning. The archaeomagnetic results strongly suggest that Teotihuacán influence at Kaminaljuyu, which began in the early Esperanza phase prior to the major burning at Teotihuacán, lasted for nearly one hundred years after this event. While a review of the various theories about the nature of the relationship between Teotihuacán and Kaminaljuyu is beyond the scope of this chapter, any viable theory must account for the continuance of this outside influence during the middle and late Esperanza phases following the major burning (and presumed decline) at Teotihuacán. The collection and measurement of early Esperanza phase samples, as well as samples from contexts earlier than the extensive burning at Teotihuacán (apparently ca. A.D. 475–500), should go a long way toward refining our understanding of the relative chronologies of these two sites and the nature of the relationship between them.

The Correlation Problem. Most Mesoamericanists use a chronology consistent with the G-M-T correlation, but other interpretations are possible. As discussed above, 15 to 20 years ago several archaeologists working in Mesoamerica argued that some data supported the Spinden correlation or one close to it (Andrews 1965; Paddock et al. 1968). Based on cross-dating, the Teotihuacán radiocarbon dates summarized by Bernal (1965) also seemed to suggest a correlation considerably earlier than the G-M-T. While I feel that arguments for a correlation close to the Spinden have been effectively countered (Wolfman 1973:123–137), about a decade ago Andrews (1978) argued that there was still some evidence in support of such a correlation. Recently, as was also discussed above, several correlations later than the G-M-T have been proposed. Among these new correlations are those of Schove (1977; about 83 years later than the G-M-T), Kaucher (n.d.; about 30 years later than Schove), and Kelley (1983; about 216 years later than the G-M-T or about 475 years later than the Spinden correlation). In addition, Chase (1985) and Lincoln (1985) have revived interest in the so-called Vaillant correlation, about 260 years later than the G-M-T.

Unfortunately, no archaeomagnetic samples have been collected in the Petén where the greatest number of Long Count dates have been found. However, Long Count dates have been found outside of the Petén. Fortunately, it has been possible to correlate the ceramic sequence at Copán, which is substantially different from that found in the Petén, with the many Long Count dates found at that site (Longyear 1952:67–75). The results from six samples (CO100, CO102, CO183, CO185, CO186, and CO188) collected at Copán, which were measured in 1979 and 1983 (see Table 15.4 and the Appendix, Table A-4) using the calibration of the curve developed using conventional radiocarbon dates, are consistent with the G-M-T correlation. In the same manner, the results from the five archaeomagnetic samples collected at San Andrés (766 and 767, see Tables 15.1 and Appendix, Table A-4; SA158 and SA159, see Tables 15.4 and A-4) and Tazumal (787; Tables 15.1 and A-4) in western El Salvador, where there are ceramics similar to Copán, are consistent with the G-M-T correlation. Sample 570 from the site of Chachi, in Chiapas, was collected in a room in which a large portion of a Tepeu 3 bowl was found. The archaeomagnetic date of A.D. 885–930 is within the expected range using the G-M-T correlation. In addition, the Classic Maya hiatus, from A.D. 534 through 593 (G-M-T correlation), has been attributed to a decline in the power of the Teotihuacán. Archaeomagnetic evidence for a great fire there, quite possibly related to such a decline, at ca. A.D. 475–500, is also consistent with the G-M-T correlation or one close to it.

Perhaps the strongest archaeomagnetic evidence in favor of the G-M-T correlation, or one close to it, comes from sample AL85, which was collected from a baked-clay feature apparently located directly under five meters of volcanic ash deposited by the great Ilopango eruption. Unfortunately, since it was uncovered by a bulldozer during the construction of the new Altamira suburban development at the south edge of San Salvador, there is a slight chance that the feature is not contemporaneous with the eruption (Stanley Boggs, personal communication, 1976). While at least one other archaeomagnetic date (A.D. 520–560) is possible (and other possibilities earlier than A.D. 1 and later than A.D. 1170 may also exist), the most probable archaeomagnetic date of A.D. 75–135 for this baked feature is in almost perfect agreement with the A.D. 119 date for the Ilopango eruption suggested on the basis of frost-damaged tree rings (LaMarche and Hirshboeck 1984). The A.D. 119 date, of course, is not tied to either the conventional or corrected radiocarbon time scale. The Floral Park sphere in the Petén is thought by some (e.g., Culbert 1977:28; Lowe 1978:336) to be due to migrants from El Salvador displaced by the Ilopango eruption. While a date of A.D. 119 for the Ilopango eruption and the presumed migration from El Salvador at this time is consistent with the G-M-T, other correlations somewhat later and perhaps even a little earlier could also be accommodated.

THE RADIOCARBON TIME SCALE

Prior to this point, conventional ^{14}C dates have been used in all the discussions. These dates and ceramic cross-dating strongly support the G-M-T correlation or one fairly close to it. However, the recent calibrations of the radiocarbon time scale in the A.D. 1–1170 period shift conventional radiocarbon dates about 50 to 100 years later (see Fig. 15.3) and consequently may suggest a correlation about this much later than the G-M-T. The eruption of Ilopango in A.D. 119 (as suggested by frost-damaged tree rings) is consistent with a correlation in this range. Two recently proposed correlations fit this requirement (Kaucher n.d.; Schove 1977), but neither fits nearly as many astronomical criteria as does the correlation proposed by Kelley (1983), which is about 216 years later than the G-M-T. As mentioned above, all three of the correlations assume a break in the Maya calendar between the end of the Classic and the conquest.

Due to the temporal distribution of the corrected radiocarbon dates in Mesoamerica and the 95% confidence intervals associated with them (see Klein et al. 1982), there is considerable latitude in recalibrating the Mesoamerican polar curve. While the new radiocarbon calibrations do not eliminate the G-M-T correlation from consideration, it now appears to be near the early end of acceptable alternatives. At this time I think an acceptable upper limit on the correlation, based on all independent chronometric information, is on the order of 150 years later than the G-M-T. Interestingly, as discussed above, this upper limit is in accord with David Kelley's latest estimation (personal communication, 1987) based on documentary sources.

Since many sources of error may not have been fully taken into account when the radiocarbon samples were processed, the implications of the new calibrations are not entirely clear. Calcium carbonate contamination, which may not be completely removed by "routine" pretreatment, is particularly likely to occur in the Maya Lowlands, with its limestone-derived soil and where lime plaster was commonly used in construction. This will cause a ^{14}C date to be earlier than the "true" age of the sample. Although I would be surprised to see either one validated, this suggests that correlations even as late as the one recently proposed by Kelley (1983) and the Vaillant correlation should still be given serious consideration. On the other hand, humic acid contamination, derived from recent plants, can cause ^{14}C dates to be too young. This might be a particularly serious problem in jungle areas of the Maya Lowlands. Errors of this type are more likely to occur in charcoal buried in the soil than in wood removed from standing buildings. If future work shows that errors of this type have occurred, this might provide additional support for the G-M-T correlation. I would expect that the effects of both sources of contamination are reflected in some of the reported radiocarbon dates from the Maya Lowlands and elsewhere in Mesoamerica. One effect or the other was probably dominant in some (many?) samples, but without careful reprocessing it is impossible to determine which.

CONCLUDING REMARKS

The general agreement of the data supplied by radiocarbon, cross-dating, and archaeomagnetic methods, with tentative support from frost-damaged tree rings and some interpretations of native documents with respect to the date of the abandonment of Tula, suggests that the broad outlines of Mesoamerican chronology are well understood for the A.D. 1–1200 time period.

However, some aspects of the broad outlines of Mesoamerican chronology in this period may be inaccurate. Seemingly consistent arguments about Mesoamerican chronology have been discarded in the past (e.g., Thompson 1941; Vaillant 1941), and it would not be very surprising if some arguments presented here will be discarded in the future. The variant opinions on this topic expressed in the past ten years should also caution against a blanket acceptance of all aspects of the broad outlines of the chronology suggested above. Also, the exact placement of the sequence in absolute time remains to be determined. My own feeling at this time is that the correct correlation of the Maya and Christian calendars is somewhere between a little earlier than the G-M-T correlation and about 150 years later. But even if the correlation problem is resolved, many important chronological problems and questions about their processual implications will remain. The temporal placement of the extensive burning in the central part of Teotihuacán is but one such problem. The chronological and processual relationships of this event to the Classic Maya hiatus, whatever the correct correlation may be, are also of consideral interest.

Since archaeomagnetic polar curves must be calibrated, accurate dating ultimately depends on other dating methods. At this time, almost all independent absolute dating in Mesoamerica has been accomplished using the radiocarbon method. Occasionally ice cores and frost-damaged tree rings may provide some important data, and someday dendrochronology may be applied in Mesoamerica. As suggested above, a comparison of Mesoamerican archaeomagnetic results with those obtained in the southwestern and southeastern United States may also assist in this endeavor. Chronometric advances will continue to be made, using carefully processed radiocarbon samples. There are limits, however, to what traditional approaches to this method can provide, but as discussed above, radiocarbon "wiggle matching" (Pearson 1986) may eventually provide at least a few very precise and accurate results.

While there are many important chronometric problems in the Preclassic period that archaeomagnetic dating will ultimately resolve, I believe the most important area of curve extension in the near future will be in the Postclassic and Colonial periods. Somewhat surprisingly, dating in the Postclassic, the latest of the pre-Columbian periods, is still subject to considerable confusion. The lack of good chronometric control in the Postclassic in the Maya area is amply illustrated by the recent statement in the introduction to a volume on this period in that area that the papers in the volume "raise a host of culture-historical and processual questions and problems that, owing to our relative lack of control of basic chronological data, are simply unanswerable" (Sabloff and Andrews 1985:3). There are two principal interrelated reasons for the existence of this problem throughout Mesoamerica. First, until recently, modern excavation of Postclassic sites was severely limited. Fortunately, during the past decade there has been an effort to remedy this situation. Perhaps more important, because of the abundance of documentary sources on the Postclassic the ethnohistorically derived chronology was often uncritically accepted without archaeological verification. In addition to greatly improving our understanding of the relative chronometrics of the Postclassic, extension of the curve through the Postclassic and Colonial periods will allow more extensive comparison of the archaeomagnetic results with those obtained elsewhere in the world, particularly the Western Hemisphere. Such comparisons will be of considerable geophysical interest and may assist in providing a more accurate calibration of the Mesoamerican polar curve, particularly through comparisons with results from the southwestern and southeastern United States.

Ongoing research will probably lead to the construction of an archaeomagnetic polar curve from 1500 B.C. to the present before too long. In addition, the precision and accuracy obtainable with archaeomagnetic dating will undoubtedly lead to the resolution of culture-historical problems in all periods. However, the greatest contribution of archaeomagnetic dating should be in processual studies. Since this method can determine contemporaneity and the sequence of use of baked features with a precision much greater than is possible with radiocarbon dating, previously unanswered questions about demography and social interaction can be resolved.

ACKNOWLEDGMENTS

To acknowledge properly all of the individuals who contributed to the success of my archaeomagnetic work in Mesoamerica over the past 20 years would be impossible. The majority of those archaeologists working in the area during that time contributed in one way or another.

Those archaeologists whose excavations uncovered the baked features that were sampled contributed in a fundamental way. Those who directed the projects that provided the samples reported in this chapter are Claude Baudez, Stanley Boggs, Ruben Cabrera, Richard Diehl, Kent Flannery, Norberto González, Gareth Lowe, Eduardo Matos, Joseph Michels, Joseph Mountjoy, John Paddock, William Sanders, Robert Sharer, Michael and Elizabeth Snow, Michael Whalen, and Marcus Winter. In addition, many other archaeologists, including (but not limited to) those archaeologists working at the sites visited during the course of the fieldwork, provided important information and scholarly interchange. Of these I would particularly like to thank Donald Brockington, Arlen Chase, Charles Cheek, David H. Kelley, Richard S. MacNeish, and John Paddock, with whom I have had lengthy and fruitful discussions about Mesoamerican chronology. Earlier drafts of this chapter were read by Marvin Jeter and the editors of this volume. I thank them for their comments and suggestions. While the above individuals have all contributed greatly to this chapter, we have not always agreed (nor do they all agree with each other). Consequently, I alone take full responsibility for all statements and any errors made in the chapter.

The government officials who provided permits and other courtesies made this research possible. For this I am indebted to them and thank them greatly. They are Ignacio Marquina (Director) and Eduardo Matos (Subdirector) of the Departamento de Monumentos Prehispánicos and later Joaquín García-Bárcena, Director of the Departamento de Prehistoria, and Angel García Cook, Director of the Departamento de Monumentos Prehispánicos in Mexico; Luis Lujan (Director) and later Edna Nuñez de Rodas (Directora) of the Instituto Nacional de Antropología e Historia in Guatemala, and Ricardo Agurcia Fasquelle, Director of the Instituto Hondureño de Antropología e Historia in Honduras. It is once again a pleasure to thank the directors, researchers, and assistants in the three laboratories where the samples were measured (the University of Oklahoma, Robert L. DuBois, Director; University of Pittsburgh, Victor Schmidt, Director; and the University of California at Santa Barbara, Michael Fuller, Director, and J. Robert Dunn, in charge of day-to-day operations) for allowing me to work in their laboratories, providing various types of assistance too numerous to mention, and scholarly interchange. I would particularly like to thank J. Robert Dunn, who wrote the programs and entered the data that allowed the determination of the archaeomagnetic dates in column 8 of Tables 15.1 and 15.4. The research was made possible by funds from the two institutions where I was employed during this period, the University of Oklahoma and the Arkansas Archeological Survey, as well as outside support from the National Science Foundation (Grants GS 29188 and GA 34110), the National Geographic Society (Grants 786 and 856), and the Academic Specialist Program of the United States Information Agency. I would also like to thank Jaime Litvak, Director of the Instituto de Investigaciones Antropológicas at the Universidad Nacional Autónoma de México for providing me with office space during part of a sabbatical in 1982. Finally, I would like to thank David Coffman for initial drafting of the figures and Mrs. G. G. Williams and Mrs. Mary Ann Long for typing several drafts of this chapter.

PART 5

Perspective

Introduction

To conclude this book, we have included a single chapter by Wolfman. He provides us with his personal evaluation of the progress of the method of archaeomagnetic dating and some prospects for further elaboration and improvement in the future.

We believe that the archaeomagnetic dating method is entering a second generation. The basic techniques are established, much has already been learned concerning archaeomagnetic secular variation, and well-documented archaeomagnetic dates are now being determined on a fairly routine basis. On the whole, these dates have been found to make sense in terms of other available chronological information. As we enter the second generation, the techniques will be further refined, additional experiments and analyses will provide additional insight into the archaeomagnetic method, still more will be learned about the behavior of the earth's magnetic field, and many additional archaeomagnetic dates will help to provide the chronometric framework for the interpretation of human prehistory.

CHAPTER 16

Retrospect and Prospect

DANIEL WOLFMAN

In most areas of the world, archaeomagnetic direction dating is the only hope for the precise dating that is needed to answer the processual and culture historical questions that archaeologists are asking today. In addition, the accurately dated archaeomagnetic record of recent geomagnetic secular variation is of fundamental importance in providing constraints on models of the manner in which the earth's magnetic field is generated. Other applications of archaeomagnetic data include (1) dating Holocene volcanic eruptions (Champion 1980), which is of considerable interest in earthquake and volcanic hazard reduction studies (e.g., Holcomb et al. 1986); (2) determining whether certain soils have been baked, which is very important in determining when early hominids were using fire (Barbetti et al. 1980); and (3) studying the history of the compass throughout the world (Carlson 1977; Fuson 1969; Hirooka 1983). Only recently has archaeomagnetic dating been used in anything approaching a routine fashion. The publication of this volume represents a great stride in this direction.

The late development of archaeomagnetic dating is somewhat surprising because the basic principles of the method were known about 200 years before radioactivity was discovered. In the 1690s, two famous British scientists published articles that, in a sense, laid the foundations of archaeomagnetic dating. Boyle (1691) conducted experiments that showed that bricks acquire a magnetic direction parallel to the ambient field after heating and cooling. A year later, Halley (1692) published a paper discussing secular variation and westward drift. The only paper on archaeomagnetism published in the next 200 years of which I am aware was Gheradi's 1862 article on the stability of remanent magnetism in pottery. In a series of papers in the late 1890s, Folgerhaiter (1896, 1897a, 1897b, 1899) discussed the potential of archaeomagnetic dating in a surprisingly thorough way. Folgerhaiter, and somewhat later Mercanton (1907, 1918a, 1918b), published some experimental results that, unfortunately, apparently suffered due to the rather poor equipment available at that time and perhaps also to the presence of anisotropy and secondary magnetism in the samples they measured.

The title of this chapter, "Retrospect and Prospect," indicates its main trajectory. Throughout, I seek to answer the questions, Where did it all begin? Why has archaeomagnetic dating taken this long to develop? What is its place in the broad field of paleomagnetism? Where are we today? What are the current problems in archaeomagnetic dating? and Where are we going in the future? With respect to the last three questions, particular attention is paid to the papers in this volume. Following the theme of this volume, I pay considerably more attention to research carried out in the United States than elsewhere in the world. To achieve these objectives this chapter is organized in the following manner: (1) several short sections discussing early studies on the history of the geomagnetic field using both archaeomagnetism and direct observations (this portion of the chapter includes a short discussion about "an opportunity missed"); (2) a discussion of important developments in paleomagnetism between 1950 and the early 1970s and how they affected the development of archaeomagnetism; (3) a history of archaeomagnetism from 1960 to 1975 and archaeomagnetic dating from 1975 to 1986; (4) a discussion of current problems in archaeomagnetic dating; (5) a discussion of why archaeomagnetic dating developed slowly; and (6) concluding remarks.

EARLY DEVELOPMENTS IN ARCHAEOMAGNETISM

The first secular variation curve using paleomagnetic methods was developed by Chevallier (1925) on a stratigraphic series of historically dated lavas from Mount Etna in Sicily ranging in age from A.D. 1284 to 1911. While this early work was of great importance, the methodological advances made between about 1930 and 1960 mark the beginning of modern studies not only in archaeomagnetism but also in the broader field of paleomagnetism. Almost all of the methodological work in archaeomagnetism during these years was carried out under the guidance of one scholar, Emile Thellier. He and his students developed collecting techniques (Thellier 1936), laboratory equipment (Thellier 1933; Thellier 1938:163–216; Pozzi and Thellier 1963), alternating field (AF) (Thellier and Rimbert 1954, 1955; Rimbert 1959) and thermal (Thellier 1938; Thellier and Thellier 1942; Thellier and Thellier 1959a:318–320) cleaning procedures to eliminate secondary components, and the most widely used method of determining paleointensity (Thellier and Thellier 1959a). They also discovered basic magnetic properties of fired clay (Thellier 1951; Roquet 1954) and published the first archaeomagnetic direction measurements on samples collected from baked clay features at archaeological sites (Thellier and Thellier 1951, 1952). Thellier (1938:291) even suggested the possibility of a correlation between the strength of remanence and the cooling rate about 11 years before Néel (1949) predicted it theoretically and more than 35 years before the implications of cooling rate dependence in paleointensity studies were generally appreciated (Pullaiah et al. 1975; Dodson and McClelland-Brown 1980; Fox and Aitken 1980; Halgedahl et al. 1980). In addition, Néel (1949, 1955) built on the experimental results of Thellier to develop a comprehensive theory of how rocks and fired clay acquire remanent magnetism. While Thellier made very significant advances in both paleointensity and archaeomagnetic direction studies, he undertook this work not to develop an archaeological dating method but to learn about the history of the geomagnetic field.

There were, of course, important related advances in other areas of paleomagnetism during this 30-year period. Early rock magnetic studies begun by Koenigsberger (1938) in Germany and the United States were later advanced by Nagata (e.g., 1943, 1953) working in Japan. Following the initial studies of Chevallier, major attempts to determine past secular variation were made using varved and unvarved sediments by Ising (1942) in Sweden and by McNish, Johnson, and others (McNish and Johnson 1938, 1940; Johnson et al. 1948) working at the Carnegie Institution of Washington (CIW) in the United States. As part of the work at the CIW, Johnson (1938) developed one of the earliest spinner magnetometers.

The decade of the 1950s was a crucial transitional period in paleomagnetism. During this period, major technical advances were made in the design of astatic (Blackett 1952; Collinson and Creer 1960) and spinner (Graham 1955; Collinson and Creer 1960; Gough 1964) magnetometers. While an important paper on AF demagnetization appeared as early as 1937 (Von Schmidlin 1937), this technique was not used in paleomagnetic studies prior to the late 1950s. The work of Thellier and his student Rimbert (Thellier and Rimbert 1954, 1955) introduced this technique to paleomagnetists. Rimbert's (1959) thesis research provided the first thorough study of this technique. Brynjolfsson (1957), in his excellent study of secular variation using Icelandic lavas, was the first to use AF demagnetization routinely in paleomagnetism. In the next few years this technique was rapidly adopted by others (e.g., As and Zijderveld 1958; Creer 1959). Also at this time the famous British statistician R. A. Fisher (1953) developed the basic statistical model for dealing with directional data that is still used today. The development during the 1950s of high-speed computers, which are crucial in paleomagnetic calculations, should also be noted.

It was during this decade that, for the first time, other groups following Thellier's lead began working with baked-clay samples from archaeological sites. Cook and Belshé (1958) at Cambridge and Aitken and his co-workers at Oxford in England, Watanabe (1959) in Japan, and Burlatskaya and Petrova (1961a, 1961b, 1961c, 1961d) in the Soviet Union all entered the field at this time. Unfortunately, their programs were relatively short-lived. With the exception of Watanabe's work, more emphasis was placed on determining the history of the geomagnetic field than on archaeological dating.

While the introduction of AF and thermal demagnetization had a tremendous impact on many paleomagnetic studies in the late 1950s and early 1960s, these techniques were not routinely used in archaeomagnetism until somewhat later. No demagnetization was undertaken in the earliest studies reported in the 1950s (i.e., Cook and Belshé 1958; Thellier and Thellier 1951, 1952; Watanabe 1959). However, storage tests, a time-consuming technique to check for and, perhaps in some cases, to eliminate the effects of secondary magnetism, were used to some extent in archaeomagnetism during the late 1950s and early 1960s (Aitken and Weaver 1962; Thellier 1981). The first archaeomagnetic study of which I am aware in which AF demagnetization was used routinely was undertaken by Kawai et al. (1964). However, in this study all specimens in the samples measured were demagnetized only at 15 mT (150 oe) rather than the stepwise demagnetization procedure used today.

The decades of the 1950s and 1960s also saw a shift in emphasis in paleomagnetic studies from secular variation to reversals and continental drift. A discussion of this shift and an outline of further developments in paleomagnetism continue after the following two sections.

THE DIRECT MEASUREMENT
OF GEOMAGNETIC FIELD DIRECTION

While the early paleomagnetic research on secular variation using baked clays, lavas, and sediments laid the foundation for future archaeomagnetic work, very few reliable secular variation data had been published using this approach before 1959 (see Watanabe 1959). Prior to this time, almost all of the reliable secular variation data came from direct measurements. These early direct measurements are of great importance in archaeomagnetic studies. They provide incontrovertible data on rates of secular variation, about which there is some disagreement (see below).

Declination and, later, inclination readings were made at geophysical observatories, by ships' captains as they sailed the world, and occasionally on scientific expeditions. The earliest known declination data were recorded in China as early as the eighth century, with a few additional readings known from the 9th through the 13th centuries (Smith and Needham 1967). The earliest long, fairly continuous records of declination and inclination are available for London since 1580, with long records also available for Rome (earliest declination, 1508; earliest inclination, 1640), Paris (earliest declination, 1540; earliest inclination, 1680) and Boston (earliest declination, 1700; earliest inclination, 1722) (Bauer 1896). The scientific expeditions undertaken on the *Paramour* between 1698 and 1701 under the direction of Edmund Halley were particularly notable for the tremendous number of geomagnetic readings made at many locations around the globe at such an early date (Thrower 1981).

Beginning in the last century, a number of publications have catalogued many early readings. A particularly important early catalogue of geomagnetic direction readings was compiled by Hansen in 1819. In the United States, the U.S. Coast and Geodetic Survey, beginning in the latter half of the 19th century, and the CIW's Department of Terrestrial Magnetism, beginning in the early part of this century, were heavily involved in making observations and reporting their results. Both organizations published extensive catalogues of their observations (e.g., Schott 1883a, 1883b; Bauer 1908; Vestine, LaPorte, Cooper, et al. 1947; Johnson et al. 1948). L. A. Bauer, who worked for both organizations, was particularly active. His 1896 summary of historically recorded data was a major study that is still referred to today. His plots of the pattern of declination versus inclination data, which are now so familiar in archaeomagnetic studies, were the first of this type and are still sometimes referred to as "Bauer Loops." In addition, Bauer directed both departments when a tremendous number of instrument measurements were made. The Coast and Geodetic Survey worked primarily in the United States, while the CIW relentlessly made measurements around the globe, including a very extensive series made at sea on a specially constructed non-magnetic vessel. In addition to making new measurements, the Coast and Geodetic Survey compiled catalogues of earlier measurements made throughout the United States and to a lesser extent elsewhere in the hemisphere (e.g., Schott 1883a, 1883b, 1886, 1889, 1896; Bauer 1908). In the 1940s a large CIW project summarized and analyzed many of the numerous direct measurements made throughout the world (Vestine, LaPorte, Cooper, et al. 1947; Vestine, LaPorte, Lange, and Scott 1947).

AN OPPORTUNITY MISSED

In addition to the CIW's important work on direct measurement of the geomagnetic field, this institution, as noted above, was also very active in paleomagnetic secular variation studies using sediments. This work began in the 1930s and continued until the mid-1950s. If there was ever a chance that archaeomagnetic dating might have developed earlier than it did, it was at the CIW during this period. The CIW was then sponsoring research in many disciplines (including archaeology, particularly in the Maya area), and interdisciplinary cooperation was an important aspect of research undertaken by the institution (Bunker 1938:725). A. V. Kidder, who directed the CIW's archaeological research program, is well known for his interest in such studies (Woodbury 1973). In 1938 the CIW published a volume called *Cooperation in Research* (Staff Members and Research Associates of the CIW 1938), which specifically discussed collaborative research across institutional and disciplinary boundaries in which the CIW had been involved. In this volume, Kidder and J. Eric Thompson (1938) addressed the problem of absolute dating in the Maya area. They specifically discussed the possibility of cross-dating to the Southwest, where tree-ring dating was being used. Had Kidder and

Thompson been aware of the possibilities of archaeomagnetic dating and had they known that the CIW had one of the few laboratories in the world capable of making the necessary measurements, the history of this dating method might have been quite different. The fact that the Division of American History, in which archaeological research was pursued, was located in Cambridge, Massachusetts, while many of the other CIW laboratories (including those of the Department of Terrestrial Magnetism) were in or near Washington, D.C., may have limited the flow of interdisciplinary communication. However, at least one American archaeologist, Robert Heizer, was aware of the potential for collaboration in this area. He discussed it in an excellent article on absolute dating published in the mid-century summary *Anthropology Today* (Heizer 1951). He not only discussed archaeomagnetic dating as a real possibility but he also mentioned that the CIW geophysicists were the ones who should be contacted by archaeologists for this type of work. Since radiocarbon dating had not been developed at that time, it would not have been possible to calibrate reference curves in many areas. However, Heizer, whose thoughts on the matter were well ahead of his time, even discussed the importance of precise relative dating using the then undeveloped archaeomagnetic method (1951:21).

The geophysicists in the Department of Terrestrial Magnetism were certainly aware of archaeomagnetism and Thellier's work in France, even though their research was concerned with sediments. However, as far as I am aware, there was no contact between the CIW geophysicists in Washington and the archaeologists in Cambridge. Since the CIW archaeologists had worked extensively at Kaminaljuyu in Guatemala City, where baked features are very abundant, if a collaboration had been initiated, it would have led to the collection of many samples. Due to the volcanic soil in this region, the samples from Kaminaljuyu are very strongly magnetized and therefore could have been easily measured with the equipment available at that time. Even though demagnetization procedures were not then in use, in most cases the results obtained would have been sufficiently accurate for archaeomagnetic dating (see Wolfman, this volume, chap. 15). In addition, the Maya area was one of the few New World areas where good independent chronometric information was available (through the Long Count calendar). Had archaeomagnetic dating developed prior to radiocarbon dating, the development of archaeology in some areas might have been somewhat different.

It is unfortunate that, after more than half a century of eminence and seminal research in these disciplines, the CIW is no longer involved in archaeology or terrestrial magnetism. The Division of American History, under whose auspices archaeological research was carried out at the CIW, was terminated in the late 1950s. Although the Department of Terrestrial Magnetism still exists, research in the department now focuses on such topics as seismology, astrophysics, geochemistry, and volcanology, to the complete exclusion of studies of geomagnetism.

STUDIES IN REVERSALS
AND CONTINENTAL DRIFT, 1950–1970

Had the pre-1955 trajectory of paleomagnetism been followed, archaeomagnetism would certainly have been investigated with considerably more vigor during the past quarter century. However, during the crucial decade of the 1950s, two major problems—continental drift and field reversals—became of central concern in paleomagnetism. Both of these topics, which had been researched briefly in the past, were extremely controversial. Eventually, paleomagnetic studies on these topics provided the crucial data that led to the major revolution that occurred in the science of geology in the 1960s. Numerous summaries of these developments have appeared in recent years. Among these I have found two to be particularly useful: William Glen's (1982) book *The Road to Jaramillo*, written from the point of view of an historian of science, and *Plate Tectonics and Geomagnetic Reversals* (Cox 1973), a book that contains reprints of many of the major papers, with comments by Allan Cox.

The theory of continental drift, which had been proposed and developed by the geographer Alfred Wegener in the early part of the 20th century (1912, 1915, 1924), was strenuously opposed by many leading geologists (e.g., Chamberlin 1928; Jeffreys 1929). In the 1950s and early 1960s, the paleomagnetic data obtained by Runcorn (1956a, 1956b) and others (e.g., Creer et al. 1958), most of whom were working at British universities, strongly supported the existence of continental drift. Once drift was established, there were an extremely large number of research projects to be undertaken. These projects, which involved determining the history of past continental positions and configurations, have kept many paleomagnetists busy since that time, and they will continue to do so for many years to come. The recognition of continental drift may have had a secondary dampening effect on secular variation studies, because it was then clear that the problems related to tracing the secular variation of geomagnetic direction far into the past were going to be considerably more difficult than previously imagined.

The second controversial topic at this time was that of field reversals. Although important and (in retrospect) persuasive work on reversals had been accomplished by Matuyama (1929) and Mercanton (1926a, 1926b) in the 1920s and by Roche (1951, 1953, 1956), Hospers (1953, 1954), and Einarsson and Sigurgeirsson (1955) in the early 1950s, considerable resistance still existed to the idea that the geomagnetic field could, in fact, reverse itself. The discovery in 1952 of a self-reversing rock, the Haruna dacite (Nagata et al. 1952), and the publication of a theoretical paper by Néel (1951), which showed five possible mechanisms for self-reversal, strengthened the position that all the reversely magnetized rocks in the world were due to their peculiar mineralogy, not to the field. The great improvements in potassium-argon dating during the 1950s, coupled with two very ambitious collecting programs, strongly indicated that throughout the world, contemporaneous volcanic rocks almost always have the same polarity (e.g., Cox et al. 1963, 1964; McDougall and Tarling 1963, 1964) and this settled the question. As with continental drift studies, once the field reversal phenomenon was established, the extension of the reversal sequence, the use of the sequence as an ancillary dating technique, and the study of reversal processes have kept, and continue to keep, many paleomagnetists extremely busy.

The theory of sea floor spreading was, in a sense, the culmination and coalescing of the two research programs. This theory, which provides a mechanism for continental drift, was in part verified by the alternately magnetized strips of basalt that expanded outward from spreading centers under the oceans (Vine and Matthews 1963). Consequently, both the energy developed by the advent of modern paleomagnetic methods in the late 1950s and early 1960s and the growing number of practitioners were channeled into studies other than archaeomagnetism.

SECULAR VARIATION FROM SEDIMENTS

The 1970s saw renewed attention to questions of secular variation. Instead of turning to baked-clay archaeological features, however, there was a great rush to extract sediment samples from lake beds to obtain the crucially needed data. Sediments have one great advantage over baked clays: cores spanning very long periods of time can be collected rapidly. The rapid expansion of the use of data obtained from sediments during the 1970s was made possible by the development of two new generations of sensitive magnetometers: fluxgate spinners (Foster 1966; Molyneaux 1971) and cryogenic rock magnetometers (Goree and Fuller 1976). However, the ease and speed with which these measurements can now be made has been a mixed blessing. While the lake cores have the great advantage of providing data over a lengthy period, the quality of the data, in terms of both initial faithful recording of the past field and of magnetic stability, is generally far below that obtained from the more strongly magnetized baked clay (see Kent and Lowrie 1974; Thompson 1977; Verosub 1977). In addition, lake cores are notoriously difficult to date, whereas archaeomagnetic samples can be placed in time using a variety of methods. Not surprisingly, the more slowly obtained archaeomagnetic data are becoming the standard used to test the reliability of the data obtained from sediments (e.g., Wolfman et al. 1982; Verosub and Mehringer 1984). In addition, the interest in secular variation sparked by all of the sediment data has led to an increased interest in modeling secular variation (e.g., Creer 1977; Creer and Tucholka 1983). Recognition of the tentative nature of the lake data and the need for better-quality data to test recent models will, I believe, lead to increased interest in archaeomagnetic and volcanic data on the part of geophysicists.

ARCHAEOMAGNETISM, 1960–1975

While paleomagnetism really took off in the 1960s, archaeomagnetism declined in most areas of the world. As noted above, important advances were made in archaeomagnetism prior to 1960, when this topic occupied a central place in paleomagnetic studies. Significantly, the Thelliers' research seems to have culminated in their 1959 publication on paleointensity. While Thellier did not publish his archaeomagnetic direction data until 1981, he apparently collected (and perhaps measured) most of the samples much earlier (Aitken 1961b:148; Thellier 1971). Watanabe's major work on the samples he collected in Japan was also published in 1959. While archaeomagnetic research in Japan has continued sporadically since the publication of

Watanabe's major study in 1959, only Hirooka's (1971) dissertation project came close to Watanabe's in scope. The early archaeomagnetic work begun at Cambridge in the mid-1950s was discontinued at about the same time. The Oxford lab, which had made very significant contributions to archaeomagnetic direction studies, discontinued its program in this field in the mid-1960s, apparently due to the shape anisotropy problems they encountered in samples collected from large, strongly magnetized kilns (Aitken and Hawley 1967). However, very significant research on paleointensity using archaeological material has been undertaken at Oxford during the past decade (Walton 1977; Rogers et al. 1979; Fox and Aitken 1980; Aitken et al. 1984). It is encouraging that research in eastern Europe begun by Burlatskaya and Petrova (1961a, 1961b, 1961c, 1961d) in the Soviet Union has continued, most notably with the extensive work of Kovacheva and co-workers in Bulgaria (Kovacheva 1969, 1980; Kovacheva and Veljovich 1977; Kovacheva and Zagniy 1985).

In the early 1960s the focus of archaeomagnetic research shifted to the United States. In 1963 Norman Watkins (1963), a British geophysicist, left molds with archaeologists working in the Southwest. Although a few other researchers and I were involved in collecting samples using those molds, Watkins went back to England, and the samples collected were turned over to Robert L. DuBois for measurement. Beginning in 1962 or 1963, DuBois, a geophysicist at the University of Arizona, began collecting archaeomagnetic samples in the American Southwest. Since that time, workers in his laboratories at the Universities of Arizona and Oklahoma (where he went in 1967) have collected thousands of samples at many locations in the Western Hemisphere. The only data ever to appear from this lab, however, were those included in my dissertation on Mesoamerica (Wolfman 1973). These data are also included in my paper on this topic earlier in this volume. The rest of the data are unavailable to archaeologists and geophysicists. In this volume (chaps. 12, 13) and elsewhere (e.g., Tarling 1978) the lack of availability of the data from DuBois's laboratories has been deplored. While it should be noted that DuBois has informally reported "dates" on the telephone, in letters, and in lists submitted to the National Park Service (e.g., DuBois 1977a, 1977b), as Eighmy (this volume) forcefully notes this is not sufficient. Also, see Winter and Levine (1987:744) for a particularly strong comment on the situation. Certainly, the lack of publication of these data has had a serious effect on the development of archaeomagnetism, particularly because for more than 10 years (ca. 1963–1975) almost all of the archaeomagnetic samples collected in the Western Hemisphere were measured in DuBois's labs.

ARCHAEOMAGNETIC DATING, 1975–1986

The papers in this volume, as well as several published elsewhere (e.g., Wolfman 1977, 1978a, 1978b, 1979, 1982, 1984; Eighmy et al. 1980; Hathaway and Eighmy 1982; Sternberg 1982, 1983; Hathaway et al. 1983), indicate that there has been a greatly expanded interest in archaeomagnetic dating in the United States in recent years. A particularly healthy aspect of this activity is that archaeologists are taking increasing responsibility for this work. While geophysicists are concerned with the history of geomagnetic secular variation, very large numbers of individual results covering time periods for which a curve has already been developed are generally not of great interest in their discipline. Such data, which from the geophysicists' point of view are repetitive, are at the heart of archaeomagnetic dating.

Unfortunately, there has not been a parallel expansion recently in other parts of the world. The limited amount of work that has taken place in other countries has been oriented more toward geophysical aspects than archaeological dating. Several laboratories in Japan have made measurements on samples in that country (e.g., Shibuya 1984; Shibuya and Nakajima 1979). There has been some interest in Germany, principally at the Institut für Allgemeine und Angewandte Geophysik at the University of Munich. Helmut Becker (1979) has measured some samples he collected in Turkey, and more recently, Schurr et al. (1984) reported some results from fireplaces and ovens in southern Germany. The most ambitious program in eastern Europe continues to be centered at the Institute of Geophysics in Bulgaria (Kovacheva 1980; Kovacheva and Zagniy 1985). Some archaeomagnetic direction work is also being undertaken on samples collected in France at the Laboratoire de Geomagnetisme (e.g., Bucur 1984), which was established by Thellier, and at the Université de Rennes (Goulpeau and Langouet 1980, 1982; see also Langouet et al. 1983). In England, however, the main work on secular variation of direction (undertaken in the 1970s) was begun as a collaborative project between geophysicists at the University of Newcastle-upon-Tyne and archaeologists at the Ancient Monuments Laboratory in London (Clark et al. 1988). In addition, geophysicists at the University of

Newcastle have recently published some results from the Mediterranean (Downey and Tarling 1984).

While archaeomagnetic direction studies have been somewhat limited outside the United States in recent years, several ambitious paleointensity programs have been undertaken. The most important were those of Walton (1983) at McMaster University in Canada, Aitken and co-workers (e.g., Aitken et al. 1984) at Oxford University, and Thomas (Liritzis and Thomas 1980; Thomas 1981, 1983) at Edinburgh University. Special mention should be made of the important methodological research undertaken at the University of Liverpool (e.g., Shaw 1974, 1979; Games 1977, 1979, 1980, 1983). In addition, it is of considerable interest that the Oxford group now reports that, in some situations, paleointensity can be used for dating (Aitken et al. 1984).

Much of the direction and intensity work undertaken outside the United States is summarized in the volume *Geomagnetism of Baked Clays and Recent Sediments* (Creer et al. 1983). This volume has several chapters on secular variation data from many locations. In addition, there are chapters on the acquisition of remanence and theoretical discussions of secular variation. Two recent review articles are also of importance. The first discusses developments in secular variation studies of all types from 1978 to 1982 (Barton and Merrill 1983); the second (Wolfman 1984), written more for archaeologists, includes a comprehensive discussion of the history, method, and theory of all the geomagnetic dating methods.

The papers in this volume summarize much of the archaeomagnetic research undertaken at laboratories in the United States in recent years, with the notable exception of the work undertaken by R. L. DuBois and his co-workers at the University of Oklahoma. In addition, a few measurements made by Shuey at the University of Utah more than 10 years ago (Shuey 1974; Shuey and Reed 1972) are not discussed in this volume. Ongoing projects that have not yet been published include Sternberg's work in Israel, investigations by Eighmy and his co-workers on the Plains, and my work with Richard Dodson in Peru (Dodson and Wolfman 1983a, 1983b; Wolfman and Dodson 1984, 1986) and with Kean and Fowler at Modoc Rock Shelter in southern Illinois (Wolfman et al. 1982). This last study is of considerable importance because it demonstrates that good archaeomagnetic sequences can be developed prior to the beginning of settled life and suggests that eventually it may be possible to develop curves for the entire Holocene in many areas.

CURRENT PROBLEMS IN ARCHAEOMAGNETIC DATING

I believe we are now entering a major period of expansion in archaeomagnetic studies, and the publication of this volume is an important
part of this new thrust. This volume contains the largest quantity of
archaeomagnetic data thus far published anywhere in the world. In
addition, a number of significant questions are asked (with, perhaps,
a few answers) and some experimental results are reported. The recent book edited by Creer et al. (1983) and two review articles mentioned above, Barton and Merrill (1983) and Wolfman (1984), give
further evidence of an increasing interest in archaeomagnetic dating.
With this new flurry of activity, it is now appropriate to take stock
of the major problems confronting archaeomagnetic dating today.
Many of these problems were addressed earlier in this volume as
well as earlier papers published elsewhere.

As I see it, the main questions in archaeomagnetic dating today,
starting with the particular and moving toward the general, are:

1. How widely spread in time and space are samples likely to be
found?

2. How rapidly does secular variation occur?

3. How well do baked clays record the ambient geomagnetic
field at the time of firing?

4. Why is the ambient field at the time of firing sometimes not
accurately recorded by baked clay?

5. What mineral or minerals carry the primary remanence in
baked clay?

6. What secondary components are found in baked clay, how severely do they affect the final results, and what are the carriers of
such secondary components?

7. How accurate are the field procedures used today?

8. How accurate are the laboratory procedures used today?

9. How should archaeomagnetic curves be constructed?

10. How should archaeomagnetic dates be determined, and how
precise and accurate is archaeomagnetic dating?

11. What role should paleointensity measurements play in archaeomagnetic direction studies?

12. Who should undertake archaeomagnetic dating?

Researchers were aware of all of the questions prior to the appearance of this volume, but never have so many of them been discussed

in one place. The authors who have taken it upon themselves to address these fundamental questions in this volume are to be congratulated for bringing attention to them, undertaking experimental work, and suggesting some solutions. I have not tried, in the manner of too many concluding papers for volumes such as this, to summarize and criticize each paper. However, where portions of the papers in this volume are pertinent, I compare and contrast the different approaches used by some of the other authors and me. I also add some fundamental points not specifically mentioned by the other authors (in many cases drawing upon the extant literature in the field) which I believe are fundamental.

At this stage in the development of archaeomagnetic dating, many of our views about proper procedures are supported by heuristic arguments, limited experimental data, and general experience with the dating method. As such, many statements presented in this volume should be taken as hypotheses for future testing. In addition, at this stage of the development of research, many statements are still couched in semiquantitative or qualitative terms, whereas additional work will eventually allow stricter quantitative evaluation. Some of the recent work discussed in this volume is clearly moving in this direction, but in this still-young field much remains to be accomplished. In this paper I call attention to some very different views that some of the other contributors and I have about the nature of archaeomagnetic dating and what it is that makes this dating method so important (see, in particular, questions 9 and 10 below). It is in part because of these explicitly stated disagreements that this volume takes an important stride toward making archaeomagnetic dating a routinely applied method with tremendous potential for resolving major chronometric problems.

Due to the fact that the twelve questions are interrelated, it is not always possible to deal with them individually. However, the following discussion proceeds in the general order in which the questions are listed.

1. How widely spread in time and space are samples likely to be found? Baked archaeological features are found throughout the world. The archaeological literature and my personal experience suggest that Holocene-long secular variation records obtained from baked-clay features can be obtained in many areas. While the collection of archaeomagnetic samples in some areas and time periods currently is not possible due to the lack of ongoing excavations, far more

opportunities to collect crucial series of samples have been and continue to be missed due to the paucity of active collecting programs.

In almost all areas of the world an abundance of baked features can be found at least as early as the beginning of settled village life. In some areas, permanent habitation sites appeared near the end of the Pleistocene (e.g., Perrot 1966). In addition, many samples have been collected from early sites occupied seasonally by hunting and gathering peoples. The most notable example of samples collected from a site of this type in the United States is the long sequence from Modoc Rock Shelter in southern Illinois (Wolfman et al. 1982). To date, a total of 44 samples in three stratigraphic sequences have been collected. Most of them vary in age from ca. 9000 to 7000 B.P.

Underestimation of the widespread temporal and spatial occurrence of baked features, particularly by some geophysicists (e.g., Creer and Tucholka 1983:273), has been a continuing stumbling block in the development of archaeomagnetic studies. This misconception has, in part, been used by some as a justification for pursuing poor-quality lake sediment data in preference to the much better secular variation data obtained from baked clay. While it is certainly true that developing a secular variation record from samples collected from individual baked features is considerably more time-consuming than the "records" for periods of 12,000 years or more that can be developed from rapidly collected lake cores, this should not have led to the nearly exclusive concentration on the latter, at the expense of the former, on the part of almost all geophysicists interested in secular variation during the 1970s.

2. How rapidly does secular variation occur? An examination of observatory records and other reports of geomagnetic direction extending in some areas as far back as ca. A.D. 1500 reveals a wide range of rates of secular variation in the past several hundred years (Bauer 1896). Rates on the order of about 0.3°/10 yr from much of the Western Hemisphere during the past 130 years (Wolfman 1973:177–180; Wolfman 1984:406) contrast significantly with about 1.5°/10 yr in Europe during the 17th century. In this regard it is important to note that dipole wobble (MacDonald and Gunst 1967) and secular variation in general have been slower during the past 150 years than during the preceding approximately 300 years for which historical data are available (Barraclough 1974:510; Yukutake 1979:84–85).

The available archaeomagnetic data seem to me and most others who have previously worked with them to suggest strongly that rates of about 1°/10 yr *predominate* during the past 2,000 years (Watanabe

1959; DuBois and Wolfman 1970a, 1970b; Hirooka 1971; Rusakov and Zagniy 1973; Wolfman 1973, 1982; Aitken 1974:157; DuBois 1975c; Thellier 1981; Wolfman and Dodson 1985). Nonetheless, there were also some periods of considerably slower secular variation during the last two millennia (e.g., the American Southwest, 1851–present [Wolfman 1984:406]; Japan, 1600–1900 [Hirooka 1971:190]). The curve-fitting method developed by Sternberg (1982, 1983) suggests a slower rate of secular variation than those obtained by other investigators using methods similar to that discussed in connection with question 9 below. Answering the question of how rapidly secular variation occurs is crucial in assessing the ability of archaeomagnetic dating to resolve many of the chronometric questions that archaeologists are asking today. The fundamental disagreement about rates of secular variation is, I believe, related to the questions of how well baked clays record the ambient field at the time of firing (see question 3 below) and how archaeomagnetic curves should be constructed (see question 9 below). In addition, I think that the samples with which Sternberg and I have worked and what we believe that archaeologists most need from archaeomagnetic dating have influenced our thinking on this matter.

Finally, it should be noted that *extremely* rapid secular variation (referred to as an *excursion*) for short periods during the pre-Holocene Quaternary and perhaps earlier is suggested by data obtained from sediments, lavas, and a few archaeomagnetic samples (Barbetti and McElhinny 1976; Negrini et al. 1984; Verosub and Banerjee 1977; Wolfman 1981; Wolfman 1984:374–375).

3. How well do baked clays record the ambient geomagnetic field at the time of firing? A direct approach to this question would be to measure samples collected from modern and historic hearths for which the ambient geomagnetic field at the time of baking is known. While such a direct approach is certainly of great importance, ultimately the reasons why, in some possibly rare situations, the ambient field is imperfectly recorded by baked clay at the time of firing must be explored. Such related questions as, What are the magnetic carriers? What are the types of primary remanence? What temperatures are needed to "lock in" the ambient field? and, Is baked clay isotropic? which are part of the field of rock magnetism, are considered at various points later in this chapter.

Prior to this volume there were few reported measurements of the remanent direction of samples collected from modern and historic baked features where the direction of the ambient field in which the firing took place was known (e.g., Weaver 1961, 1962; Wolfman 1978a). In the cited early studies, the VGPs based on direct instrument measurement (referred to as the reference VGP) all fall within the 95% oval of confidence around the measured mean VGPs from the baked-clay samples. The 15 new results obtained by Hathaway and Krause (Hathaway et al., this volume, chap. 10) are important because of the quantity of new data and the high level of agreement between the reference VGP and the results obtained from the measurements on samples collected from the baked-clay hearths. The four additional results obtained by Smith (reported in Hathaway et al., this volume) are aberrant. Smith obtained the three largest arc distances (of the 19 reported by all three investigators) between the VGPs obtained from baked-clay samples and the reference VGP. Smith also obtained the two poorest α_{95} values (both well in excess of 4.0°). For a variety of reasons, samples with α_{95}s greater than or equal to 4.0° often provide very inaccurate VGPs. (I routinely reject all results with such poor precision. Eighmy and his co-workers prefer to reject samples with an α_{95} greater than 3.5°. In practice, the difference between the two cutoff points is minor.) Smith's poor results may have something to do with the movable frame on which his baked material rested and/or refiring of the material after rotating the frame 90°. In a second paper, Smith (this volume, chap. 8) reports the results from 12 samples (including the four reported in chap. 10) collected from baked clay on this movable frame. The α_{95} values range up to 7.88°, with only two of them less than 4.0°. In any case, the 15 results reported by Hathaway and Krause (this volume, chap. 13) are of much higher quality. Fourteen of them have α_{95} values less than 4.0°. Only one of these is more than 3° (i.e., 3.39°) away from the reference VGP, only two additional sample VGPs are more than 2.54° away from the reference value, and 67% of the VGPs fall within 2.15° of the reference value. These results indicate that *with proper selection of baked features in the field* and the rejection of results with α_{95} values greater than or equal to 4.0°, samples collected from modern hearths (and by inference, from baked clays in archaeological sites) usually give very accurate VGPs. While recognizing that aberrant results occasionally do occur, I am very encouraged by these results.

Eighmy et al. (this volume) have a considerably more pessimistic view. They use the data obtained by Hathaway et al. (unfortunately, relying heavily on Smith's results) to support their belief that a rather large spread of nearly contemporaneous VGPs with good precision is possible. They then use these data to justify their contention that a large spread of VGPs (up to 5° from the reference value) could have come from what they believe to be nearly contemporaneous samples (A.D. 880–900) from the Dolores project area. Based on Hathaway's and Krause's data, this seems unlikely. It should be noted that some of these samples were collected from walls that apparently moved after firing. Elimination of the results from such samples strongly suggests that the Dolores samples thought to date from A.D. 880 to 900 in fact cover a greater time span. This in turn suggests that the loop in the curve between about A.D. 700 and 900 is broader than that shown in Figure 13.1. This curve is discussed further under question 9 below.

4. Why is the ambient field at the time of firing sometimes not accurately recorded by baked clay? As discussed above, the measurements Hathaway and Krause made on modern samples (this volume, chap. 13) showed that when α_{95} is less than 3.5°, the average distance of sample VGPs from reference VGPs is less than the average α_{95} value and that this distance is rarely ever larger than the α_{95} value. When these results are added to the many measurements I have made on contemporaneous and stratigraphically related prehistoric samples (Wolfman 1973, 1982; and this volume, chaps. 14, 15), there is strong support for the conclusion that this is almost always the case. Occasionally, however, inaccurate directions are obtained from individual specimens or the sample as a whole. It is often difficult, and sometimes impossible, to distinguish between those sources that are inherent in the material and those that are due to imperfections in field and laboratory procedures. The former are considered here, and the latter in a later section.

As noted above, the reasons for the imperfect recording of field direction by baked clay include incomplete firing, small magnetic inclusions, and anisotropy. The question of the temperature needed to record the ambient field accurately has been discussed by several authors in this volume (e.g., Hathaway et al.), but it remains to be properly answered. Test firings with thermocouples embedded in hearths is an important first step in understanding this problem. The only early experiment of this type of which I am aware was reported by Roberts (1961) on a kiln. The numerous experimental firings reported in this volume by Hathaway, Krause, and Smith indicate that good results can be obtained even if the firing temperature is considerably below the Curie temperature of magnetite (580° C). Clearly, the question of what portion of the remanence in typical baked clays is TRM, PTRM, CRM, and/or high-temperature VRM needs further investigation. Regardless of the outcome of such studies, it seems that errors due to incomplete firing are sometimes caused by unbaked or poorly baked material in the specimen cube that was farthest from the source of heat. A strongly magnetized pebble in material that is not heated to a high enough temperature to remagnetize the pebble completely often also leads to an incorrect remanent direction.

Shape anisotropy and fabric anisotropy are both of concern in archaeomagnetic studies. Shape anisotropy (also referred to as magnetic refraction) is found only in highly magnetized baked features. Archaeomagnetists have been aware of this problem for many years (e.g., Thellier 1977:342; Thellier and Thellier 1959a:312). Aitken and Hawley (1967) gave this problem considerable attention and suggested sampling procedures to minimize its effect. Recent theoretical and experimental work by Dunlop and Zinn (1980) suggests that shape anisotropy is not a significant problem when baked clays have a magnetization less than about $10 \, A/m$ (1×10^{-2} emu/cc; 1 emu/cc = 1 gauss).

In addition, highly magnetized baked features may distort magnetic compass readings taken in or near them and thus further compound the error. A sun compass or a true magnetic alignment established with a transit or theodolite set up at some distance from the baked feature can eliminate this second source of error but cannot remedy the effects of shape anisotropy itself.

Both of these problems were discussed in this volume by Krause and Hathaway. However, since the experiments were undertaken on material with a magnetization of about $1 \, A/m$ (1×10^{-3} emu/cc), the fact that they observed no anisotropy or distortion of the compass reading is hardly surprising. While baked clay with a magnetization in excess of $10 \, A/m$ (1×10^{-2} emu/cc) is not common, based on the theoretical and experimental work mentioned above, there are hearths that may exhibit some shape anisotropy. In higher latitudes, where the vertical component of the geomagnetic field is stronger than the horizontal component, we should expect the anisotropy to be more pronounced in the vertical direction, especially on flat surfaces. Krause and Hathaway's experiments were concerned only with errors of declination.

Another possible source of error is fabric anisotropy. Fabric anisotropy has been found in pottery (particularly that made on a wheel)
used in paleointensity studies (Rogers et al. 1979). However, the susceptibility experiments undertaken by Baumgartner (1973) and
Schurr et al. (1984) and the studies on samples fired in a known field
discussed in this volume and elsewhere strongly suggest that this
source of error is minimal in baked archaeological features.

5. What mineral or minerals carry the primary remanence in
baked clay? There is considerable evidence that in most situations
the primary remanence (whether it be TRM, PTRM, high-temperature VRM, or perhaps some CRM) is carried by magnetite. In the
earliest work on this topic of which I am aware, Hopwood (1913)
extracted and optically recognized magnetite particles from baked
clay. Consequently, he attributed the remanence of baked clays to
this mineral. Later investigations on this topic (Thellier 1951; Roquet
1954; Baumgartner 1973; Hathaway, this volume, chap. 11) indicate
(due, for example, to the Curie temperature, strength of natural remanence, saturation remanence, etc.) that magnetite is generally the
major carrier of remanence. Despite the fact that magnetite is the
principal source of remanence, the possibility that other carriers of
the primary remanence are present and the effect this may have on
the long-term stability of the remanent magnetism of baked clays
need to be considered. While it has often been suggested that hematite is, or may be, a significant carrier of TRM in baked clay, the
numerous published demagnetization curves in paleointensity
studies have failed to reveal any significant portion of the Curie temperature spectrum in excess of about 580° (Bucha 1967; Kitazawa
and Kobayashi 1968; Nagata et al. 1965; Sasajima and Maenaka 1966;
Schwarz and Christie 1967).

6. What secondary components are found in baked clay, how severely do they affect the final results, and what are the carriers of
such secondary components? Early research on secondary magnetism in baked clay and methods that can be used to remove it was
undertaken by Thellier and his students (Thellier 1938; Thellier and
Rimbert 1954, 1955; Rimbert 1959). While considerable work on
other materials has been undertaken since then, little additional attention has been paid specifically to this problem for baked clays. It
does seem clear, however, that in most cases secondary remanence
appears to be due to VRM in magnetite. This is inferred from the

small magnitude of most secondary components and the ease with which they are apparently removed with AF demagnetization. It should be noted that, due to the very young age of most archaeomagnetic samples, the VRM is small compared to such secondary components usually encountered in paleomagnetic studies. Secondary remanence due to lightning strikes (usually an IRM, although the possibility of an ARM has also been suggested [Aitken 1961b:132]) also seems to be carried by magnetite. Once again, AF demagnetization seems to be effective in removing this source of secondary magnetism, which suggests that ARM effects are minimal. A third source of secondary remanence is CRM. The formation of iron oxyhydroxides due to the weathering of baked clay and the further alteration of these minerals are potential sources of error (Barbetti et al. 1977). Since this phenomenon is not well understood, its contribution to the total NRM may be underestimated. This problem is particularly significant because CRM may not be eliminated by ordinary demagnetization techniques.

7. How accurate are the field procedures used today? The studies undertaken by Smith (this volume) and Hathaway and Krause (this volume) show that, at least for modern material, fairly accurate results can be obtained by collecting specimens using commonly accepted field procedures (Eighmy 1980 and this volume, chap. 2; Windes 1978; Wolfman 1978b). Nonetheless, it is reasonable to ask whether other procedures would improve the results obtained.

A. What are the relative advantages of magnetic and celestial methods of orientation? The experimental work undertaken by Hathaway and Krause (this volume) in conjunction with their work on shape anisotropy suggests that magnetic declination charts in parts of Colorado are in error on the order of 1.5°. Since similar errors may exist in declination charts elsewhere, archaeomagnetists should undertake sun compass or theodolite measurements to determine whether they are present in the areas in which they are working. A theodolite (or transit) can be used to establish a true alignment with reference to the sun, Polaris, or other celestial objects at a known time. True alignments can also be established with a theodolite by shooting a line to a prominent distant landmark and determining the true azimuth of this line. In some cases, accurately placed bench marks can also assist in determining a "true" azimuth. Such caution was suggested and was employed in early archaeomagnetic studies (Aitken 1961b:134; Watkins 1963), but it has been absent until recently in the Western Hemisphere. The need to use a sun compass or other nonmagnetic method of orientation in highly magnetized baked features is discussed above. The same precaution, of course, applies to situations in which other highly magnetic objects are near the feature sampled. This problem is particularly acute in urban areas and in some igneous terrains.

B. What are the relative advantages of smaller vs. larger specimens? Since the earliest studies, the preferred method of orienting and protecting archaeomagnetic baked-clay specimens has been to encase them in plaster. A variety of cubic and rectangular solid sizes has been used throughout the history of archaeomagnetic dating to accomplish this task. The general trend, which continues today, has been toward smaller-volume containers. In determining optimum container size, a variety of variables must be considered. As with many problems in archaeomagnetism, it is important to consider the work of Thellier (1977). He argued that due to inhomogeneity in baked material, the larger the specimen, the more accurate the reading. This led him to measure baked-clay specimens encased in large rectangular blocks (Thellier 1967). The higher total moment of the larger specimens may also contribute to more accurate measurements. However, the natural remanent magnetism of most baked clays is sufficiently strong (ca. 0.01 to 1 A/m $[10^{-5}$ to 10^{-3} emu/cc]) so that even after considerable AF demagnetization the smaller specimens can usually be measured to acceptable accuracy with commercially available cryogenic and fluxgate sensor spinner magnetometers. The 1.7-inch cubes DuBois introduced were the standard in North America for many years, but in about 1975 I began using 1.05-inch cubes because most commercial magnetometers and demagnetizers can accept the 1.05-inch but not the 1.7-inch cubes. Recently I have begun collecting samples using small plastic boxes with external dimensions of about 1" × 1" × 3/4", with walls about 1/32-inch thick. Due to the shallowness of the specimen, unbaked material is rarely included in the plastic box, and collection is very rapid. The plastic box is filled about half full with plaster and inverted over the top of the baked-clay column. The bottom of the box (now facing up) is leveled with an accurate bull's-eye level, and a compass reading is taken in the usual manner. While the small cubes can be oriented accurately, the small specimen size may present some problems with weakly magnetized material. An additional advantage of collecting with these small boxes is that epoxy can be used in place of plaster. For baked material with a low magnetization (less than about 10^{-2} A/m [1×10^{-5} emu/cc]), epoxies that have virtually no remanence are an advantage over even the best plaster, which has a remanence of about 6×10^{-4} A/m (6×10^{-7} emu/cc).

However, the best α_{95} values I have ever seen were obtained from samples in which the specimens were encased in 1.7-inch cubes (Wolfman 1973; Wolfman, this volume, chap. 15). As Thellier has argued, this suggests that, in some (perhaps many) circumstances, larger specimens of baked clay give better results, at least up to a point. However, I question whether the small improvement is worth the effort. Among the advantages of specimens encased in smaller cubes are that (1) more specimens can be collected per unit area (this is particularly important when there is a limited amount of baked material), (2) often a more uniformly magnetized specimen is collected, particularly when the baked material is thin (consequently, in some situations a better measurement may be obtained from a smaller specimen), (3) transporting samples is much easier (this is particularly important when working in foreign countries and when the return trip is by airplane), and (4) as noted above, the larger cubes and rectangular solids do not fit in most magnetometers and demagnetizers.

Earlier in this volume, Smith (chap. 8) presented some results that superficially seem at variance with the preceding discussion. He found that there was only a small variation between the results obtained with 1-inch and with 1.7-inch cubes. As discussed above, his work must be regarded as very tentative at best. The α_{95} values of 10 of the 12 samples measured ranged between 4.00° and 7.88°. Therefore, using the criteria that DuBois, Eighmy and his co-workers, and I apply, no conclusions should be drawn from Smith's results. He also failed to discuss the more germane question of how much baked material is in the encasing plaster cubes. In many baked features (particularly small hearths), the baking may not be very deep. Consequently, when small hearths are sampled, although some increase in the amount of baked material is found in the large cubes, there may also be an increase in poorly fired or unfired material in the lower portion of the cube, which probably does not record the geomagnetic field direction at the time of firing very well and perhaps not at all. It should be recalled that Thellier collected most of his samples from deeply baked kilns.

Smith also neglected to consider the effect of measuring 1.7-inch cubes with a Schonstedt spinner magnetometer. Due to the way measurements are made using the Schonstedt spinner (i.e., essentially on each face of the cube), it might be expected that inhomogeneity in magnetization would be a more serious problem in the larger cubes than in the smaller (Collinson 1975, 1977; also, see below). Theoretically, the integrating effect of a pickup coil system would eliminate or considerably reduce errors due to inhomogeneity (Collinson 1975, 1977). More work on this point should be undertaken.

C. What effect, if any, does the use of magnetic cutting tools have on the results? The fact that steel cutting tools have been used with apparent success for many years is no reason to be complacent about this matter. Two potential sources of error seem to exist. First, small particles rub off a cutting tool, particularly a saw blade. Probably many fewer particles rub off when a knife (especially one made of stainless steel) is used. Second, the magnetic field strength close to a saw blade or knife may be considerably higher than the geomagnetic field intensity. The possibility of imparting an IRM (easily removed by AF demagnetization) or an ARM (less easily erased) should be considered. I plan to carry out straightforward comparative studies on the problem in the near future and encourage others to do so as well. The larger specimens (with a lower surface-to-volume ratio) might, in some situations, have smaller errors from both of the potential sources mentioned.

D. What is worth collecting, and are some baked materials likely to produce better results than others, based on visual characteristics? The question of whether visual characteristics of baked clay and earth exist that might help in selecting material to be sampled is raised by Hathaway et al. in this volume. I agree with Eighmy (this volume) that the most crucial variables are usually color, thickness, and texture. Well-oxidized baked material (red, yellow, or orange) at least a quarter inch thick (and preferably thicker) usually gives good results. Truly baked black (reduced) material also gives good results, but care must be taken not to collect samples from dirt that is merely blackened due to carbonized organic material. I choose fine-grained over coarse-grained material whenever possible, in part because the coarse-grained material in baked clay is often quartz. Other things being equal, baked material with more quartz has a smaller amount of ferromagnetic minerals than material with less quartz, which tends to decrease the precision of the results. This seems to apply to both modern hearths and those found in archaeological sites. Nonetheless, in some situations I have obtained very good results from coarse-grained material. For example, in Peru many coarse-grained samples (typical of baked material in the coastal desert) had low magnetization but excellent precision (Wolfman and Dodson 1984). I think an additional characteristic—a lack of soil moisture, presumably leading to less secondary magnetism due to weathering—is important here. I expect that samples collected from other arid areas of the world, other things being equal, would provide similar results.

The work of Hathaway et al. (this volume) on visual characteristics is concerned with soil texture. The three authors independently fired experimental hearths, and all three determined the percentages of silt, clay, and sand in the baked material. Smith also determined the percentage of gravel, but the other two authors (Hathaway and Krause) ignored this constituent and calculated silt, clay, and sand percentages after removing the gravel. They then compared the percentages of sand and clay in the baked material with three measures of sample quality: accuracy, precision, and strength of magnetization.

The results the three authors obtained are not entirely consistent, perhaps due to the small number of samples measured. Nonetheless, all three found a positive correlation between the α_{95} value and the clay percentage, and a negative correlation between the α_{95} value and the sand percentage. This is contrary to what Hathaway and Eighmy (1982) found in similar experiments on prehistoric hearths and what, in at least some situations, other researchers and I have noted informally.

The apparent contradiction may well be due to the fact that their experiments did not take into account other significant variables. Clearly, grain size, chemistry, and mineralogy of the ferromagnetic minerals in baked clay, as well as firing temperature and length of firing in relationship to the size ranges of those magnetic minerals that contribute to TRM and DRM, are important variables, and further study of the effects of all of them on sample quality is needed. Perhaps of greatest importance, Hathaway et al. (this volume) do not differentiate between ferromagnetic and nonferromagnetic (principally quartz) grains. This is particularly important because the principal source of remanent magnetism is probably magnetite in the pseudo–single domain size range (McElhinny 1973). Silt (2–50 microns in diameter) overlaps the upper end of the grain size of pseudo–single domain magnetite (0.05–15 μ in diameter; Dunlop 1975:59). While I think that the size of ferromagnetic grains is of greater importance, Hathaway's (1982) suggestion (repeated in Hathaway et al., this volume) that grain size (regardless of mineralogy) is related to heat conduction and therefore also to sample quality should be investigated further. Ignoring the gravel fraction, as they did, may also cause difficulties in the analysis. Although this fraction often does not contribute significantly to total remanence, there are situations in which it does. In Mesoamerica, I have occasionally seen gravel-sized chips of basalt included in baked clay. Finally, the contribution of secondary components often added to baked material that has been in the ground for hundreds or thousands of years must, of course, be explored.

In the future, multivariate statistical analyses rather than pairwise regressions should be undertaken to determine the interactions of all of the variables that affect the precision and strength of magnetization. Such studies may be of considerable importance not only in selecting material to be sampled in the field but also in refining laboratory procedures.

Until future work indicates otherwise, I still think that the best procedure is to collect thick, well-oxidized, fine-grained baked material *where there is a choice*. At the same time, it should be noted that good results have been obtained in some situations from rather thin, reduced (i.e., black), coarse-grained material.

Another subjective element in field collecting is the need to recognize a small displacement of baked material in the field. While it is usually possible to recognize a large displacement, small movements, particularly those due to differential settling, may be a source of error of unknown magnitude. Judging from the great quantity of precise and accurate archaeomagnetic results apparently obtained thus far, sufficient care has been applied in the field to keep such errors to a minimum. As discussed in the following section and as indicated in a comparative study undertaken by Lange and Murphy (this volume), experience is an important factor in selecting material for collection.

E. Who collects samples and how should they be trained? Until fairly recently, sample collection was carried out almost exclusively by individuals either directly involved in archaeomagnetic research or employed by someone who was. A few specialists traveled around an area, making collections of samples from features that archaeologists had "saved." In part this was the case because sample collection requires some training, special equipment, and subjective judgments of what is worth collecting. Improperly collected samples and collection of inadequately baked material or material which has moved not only waste valuable laboratory time but also might lead to some serious errors in the early stages of curve construction.

During the past 10 to 15 years, increasing numbers of archaeologists have become involved in sample collection, with mixed results (see, e.g., Lange and Murphy, this volume). While most archaeologists are initially interested in the collection procedure, they rapidly find it to be time-consuming, repetitious, and, to many, rather dull. The procedure is certainly too time-consuming to be the responsibility of a project field director. While I recognize the need for the involvement of field archaeologists in the collection process, I think some restraint is needed. Individuals who make collections should be trained by someone directly involved in archaeomagnetic research. Currently a number of collecting manuals are in use (Eighmy 1980; Windes 1978; Wolfman 1978b), but learning *solely* from a printed manual or from individuals at second- or third-hand should be strongly discouraged. The subjective elements of what to collect and how to collect specimens from difficult material strongly argue for personal instruction in conjunction with a manual and for fewer, rather than more, collectors. A smaller number of individuals would gain considerable experience and produce a higher percentage of useful samples over time. I am currently pursuing this approach in my work in Latin America, the American Southwest, and Arkansas.

8. How accurate are the laboratory procedures used today? Three areas need to be addressed to answer this question:

A. Measurement, a comparison of magnetometers. While it has not been discussed previously in this volume, some attention has been paid to this problem elsewhere (Collinson 1975, 1977; Wolfman 1984:383–385). The potential for error while using magnetometers that measure along one face of the specimen has been discussed theoretically (Collinson 1975) and shown to exist experimentally for a specimen that was both very weak and very asymmetrical (Collinson 1977). Unfortunately, only four specimens were measured in this study. Generally, the effects of an inhomogeneously magnetized specimen can be minimized by using magnetometers that measure magnetism with pickup coils (Collinson 1975, 1977). Such coils are found in ballistic magnetometers, some spinner magnetometers (e.g., those previously manufactured by Princeton Applied Research), and the cryogenic magnetometers available since the early 1970s (Goree and Fuller 1976). Thellier, who measured very large specimens, also discussed this problem (1977:242), but as far as I am aware, he never published any comparative data. He specifically avoided using an astatic magnetometer, which was commonly used at the time he began his work. Instead, he first used a ballistic magnetometer and later a spinner magnetometer with very large pickup coils set at a considerable distance from the spinning specimen. In Collinson's (1977) study results intermediate between those obtained with pickup coil magnetometers and fluxgate spinner magnetometers which measured along one face were obtained using a spinner magnetometer with a ring fluxgate. Comparative studies on a statistically significant number of archaeomagnetic samples measured with different magnetometers have yet to be undertaken.

B. Demagnetization. The natural remanent magnetism of archaeomagnetic samples is far more likely to record the ancient field accurately than all other types of palcomagnetic samples. This is due to their young age, a preponderance of magnetically stable minerals, the acquisition of their primary remanence in a very short period of time, a relatively low rate of alteration of magnetic minerals (particularly when compared to lacustrine and marine sediments), and magnetization in a nearly ideal range (neither too weak nor too strong). With regard to the final point, because the magnetization of baked clays rarely exceeds 10 A/m (1×10^{-2} emu/cc), shape anisotropy is rare. Consequently, while some individual results may be inaccurate, curves derived from many NRM results (e.g., Hirooka 1971; Thellier 1981; Watanabe 1959; Wolfman 1973 and this volume, chap. 15) are apparently quite reliable. In this regard, it should be noted that the configuration of the Southwest curve for the A.D. 900–1500 period originally reported by DuBois and Wolfman (1970b) based on NRM results did not change following an extensive program of AF demagnetization (DuBois 1975c). This is quite fortunate, because the great majority of the early published archaeomagnetic data were NRM results. Nonetheless, there is now ample evidence that demagnetization can improve the results of a great many samples. In the future, some sort of sample, or at least specimen, selection procedure, accompanied by demagnetization, should be mandatory.

In the early days of archaeomagnetic research, some researchers used a selection technique referred to as a storage test (Aitken

1961b: 135–136; Thellier 1981). While it is unlikely that many investigators will return to the storage test, a very stringent requirement of using only very stable samples (as indicated by demagnetization) in curve construction might be worth the effort.

Today, the attempt to eliminate secondary magnetic components is one of the most crucial steps in archaeomagnetic dating. Discussions of the sources of secondary magnetism and the methods used for their removal can be found in standard paleomagnetism textbooks (e.g., McElhinny 1973), as well as in my recent review paper (Wolfman 1984:377–380, 386–387, 393–394). The two most common methods are alternating field (AF) and thermal demagnetization. While investigators in the United States have used AF demagnetization almost exclusively, researchers elsewhere have used thermal demagnetization (e.g., Kovacheva 1969; Kovacheva and Veljovich 1977; Rusakov and Zagniy 1973). Thermal demagnetization can more effectively remove secondary VRM, which is fairly common, but not secondary IRM, which is apparently less common (McElhinny 1973:89–101). Experimental work comparing AF and thermal demagnetization on archaeomagnetic samples, particularly comparing their effects on secondary VRM, should be undertaken in the near future.

Since demagnetization and remeasurement are time-consuming, it has become common practice to stepwise demagnetize one or more pilot specimens to determine the "best" level of demagnetization (Wolfman 1984:393–394). Experience suggests that in most cases secondary magnetism (especially VRM) is effectively removed using AF demagnetization, with a peak field somewhere between 5 and 20 mT (50 and 200 oersteds). The determination of the "best" level in the pilot group is somewhat subjective, with two criteria— least dispersion (Irving et al. 1961) and the level at which stability occurs (As and Zijderveld 1958)—the most commonly used. Three pilot specimens should be the minimum number to determine this "best" level. The more time-consuming process of step demagnetizing all the specimens in a sample may have advantages in some situations (see below). Comparisons of the results from demagnetizing pilot groups compared to whole samples should be undertaken to see if the considerable extra work is worth the effort.

C. Specimen and sample selection. Occasionally, one or even two specimen directions in a sample of eight are radically different from the majority. Most of the reasons for such aberrant results were discussed under questions 3 and 4. Recognition of such outliers is usually done on a statistical basis. I have chosen the 95% confidence level as the basis for rejecting outliers, whereas Sternberg (1982) prefers the 99.5% level. One reason for preferring the 95% level is that there is a strong possibility that some outliers—perhaps a significant proportion—are due to incorrect compass readings of about 1° to 10°. I have caught students and myself making such errors numerous times. For that reason, I always take two nearly independent compass readings on each specimen, but I believe that, despite such precautions, errors due to this source occur. Often, the rejection of outliers at the 95%, but not the 99.5%, level eliminates specimens for which incorrect compass readings have been made. Another method of rejecting aberrant specimen results is to examine the behavior of the specimens during demagnetization. Magnetically unstable specimens can be identified by plotting Zijderveld (1967) diagrams. However, this would require demagnetizing the entire sample, which, as discussed above, is considerably more time-consuming.

Despite the fact that precision does not imply accuracy, mean sample directions are generally considered acceptable if the results are reasonably precise. Experience, as well as the experimental results reported by Hathaway et al. (this volume), suggests that less precise samples are on the average less accurate, with a fairly sharp increase of inaccurate results occurring in samples with α_{95} values larger than about 3.5° or 4.0°. I strongly believe that the precision criterion for accuracy is valid when qualified individuals collect the samples. However, great care should be used before collecting samples from walls or accepting the results from such samples. A carefully documented study comparing the precision and accuracy of mean directions, using stratigraphic and/or tree-ring or historically dated samples to obtain some control, is needed.

While inaccurate mean directions from samples with high precision (where the inaccuracy is not due to feature movement after firing) are rare, they do occur. Thus far, no work has been done to identify such samples in the laboratory. Such work would be of considerable practical and theoretical importance to archaeomagnetism.

9. How should archaeomagnetic curves be constructed? There is considerable difference of opinion between Sternberg and McGuire (this volume, chap. 6; see also Sternberg 1982, 1983) and me on the best way to fit curves to data and how to estimate archaeomagnetic dates. Eighmy and his co-workers (this volume) have also adopted

the statistical curve-fitting procedure developed by Sternberg. These differences arise from a difference of opinion about the way in which archaeomagnetic dating can be used most profitably in archaeology. This difference of opinion is related to three more fundamental disagreements (A, B, and C) discussed below.

A. What is it that archaeologists need most from archaeological dating? I would strongly argue, at least within the time frames covered in this volume, that very precise relative dating with only a rough idea of absolute time is usually of much greater importance than absolute dating per se. Archaeomagnetic dating can often provide this more important information, and furthermore, the *precision* parameters obtainable in this manner are considerably smaller than the error figures (which are a combination of precision and accuracy) reported by Sternberg and McGuire (this volume, chap. 6; see also Sternberg 1982, 1983; for a discussion of the terms *precision, accuracy,* and *error,* see below and also Wolfman 1984:395–399). Sternberg's procedure is designed to provide an estimate of the absolute or "true" date. My very strong preference for an alternative approach in the great majority of cases should not be taken as a severe criticism of Sternberg, because in some situations—perhaps many or even most situations—archaeologists seem to want only an absolute *date.* This is because in large part it is the model that archaeologists have come to expect from other dating methods. It is the responsibility of the archaeomagnetist to let the archaeologist know that archaeomagnetic dating can provide what may be crucial relative chronometric information. Consequently, I would like to emphasize that archaeomagnetism can provide precise relative dating with considerably smaller error than the absolute dates determined by Sternberg's procedure.

As with many such arguments in science, our differences are not absolute. At the end of chapter 6, Sternberg and McGuire do mention the possible importance of relative dating with archaeomagnetism, and I in turn think that in many situations archaeomagnetic dating can provide important *absolute* results. However, our primary objectives and fundamental disagreements have clearly determined our curve-fitting and date-estimation procedures.

B. Fidelity of magnetic direction in baked clays and rates of secular variation. Questions related to the fidelity with which baked clays record the ambient field direction and the rates of secular variation are discussed above (questions 2 through 6 and elsewhere in this volume). Hathaway et al. (this volume) come down on the side of rather poor fidelity, and Eighmy et al. (this volume) accept that point of view. Sternberg and McGuire (this volume) argue for relatively slow secular variation. In contrast, I take the opposing views.

C. Reliability of independent (i.e., nonarchaeomagnetic) age estimates. In this regard I think that some of our disagreements may be due in part to working with samples from different areas. First, and perhaps most important, tree-ring dating is applicable in the Southwest but not in most of the rest of the world. In most areas and time periods, it is not possible to apply Sternberg's procedure of assigning absolute date ranges of reasonable length to samples beforehand. Recent analyses of absolute dating in Mesoamerica have led to suggestions that have varied by at least 260 years and perhaps as much as 520 years within the past 1500 years (see chap. 15 for a discussion of this problem and other pertinent references). In Peru there are differences of opinion about North Coast chronology on the order of 300 years within the past 1200 years (Watson 1985; Wolfman and Dodson 1984, 1985). Other disagreements about earlier time periods in these two areas and elsewhere in the world abound. Even in the Southwest there are drastically different opinions about chronology. The arguments about the Snaketown chronology are perhaps the best known. Basically there are long and short chronologies, with some schemes differing in places by more than 600 years (for discussions of the problem and additional references, see Haury 1976 and Schiffer 1982). While the short chronology is more widely accepted today, there are some strikingly different versions (e.g., Plog 1980; Schiffer 1982).

These examples suggest that the age-range estimates that the archaeologist gives to the archaeomagnetist, even when supported by *some* radiocarbon dates, often cannot be trusted. Furthermore, there are numerous disagreements about the *relative* chronologies within subareas (e.g., Yucatan in the late Classic; see Lincoln 1985) or even at a single site (e.g., Schiffer and Plog's differences on the Snaketown sequence). Consequently, there are situations in which an *independent relative* chronology (i.e., one based on chronological information aside from archaeomagnetism) *alone* cannot be used to construct a curve. In contrast, the great precision and accuracy of archaeomagnetically determined pole positions are demonstrated by the stratigraphic series of samples I have worked with from Mesoamerica (particularly from Kaminaljuyu; see Wolfman 1973 and this volume, chap. 15), Peru (particularly from Huaca del Pueblo Batán Grande;

see Wolfman and Dodson 1986), Modoc Rock Shelter (Wolfman et al. 1982), and Arkansas (Wolfman 1982 and this volume, chap. 14). In almost every case, the sample VGPs lie on or close to the curve in the correct stratigraphic order. This is true even in situations in which the time between the samples is apparently quite small. (Parenthetically, these data support my contention that in many situations a precision of ±20 to ±40 years at the 95% confidence level can be obtained.) In addition, these results strongly suggest that archaeomagnetic direction *measurements* are usually far more accurate and precise than the age estimates of an *event* made by archaeologists on the basis of other chronometric methods, including, in some cases, tree-ring dating. An archaeomagnetic measurement (and ultimately a date) refers to a specific event of cultural importance, while problems of association often create difficulties when interpreting radiocarbon and tree-ring dates (see, e.g., Dean 1978). Additionally, in the future, samples collected from contemporaneous stratigraphic series will provide crucial tests of the alternative approaches to archaeomagnetic dating discussed below. Unfortunately, stratigraphic samples are apparently rare in the southwestern United States, where the authors of the other data-oriented papers in this volume have worked.

D. Comparison of curve-fitting procedures. The papers by Eighmy et al. and Sternberg and McGuire (chap. 12) in this volume provide further examples of some of our differences. The curve Eighmy et al. have drawn using Sternberg's procedure for the A.D. 700–900 period is very tight and crosses over itself several times. This contrasts with the much rounder curve for this area drawn earlier (DuBois and Wolfman 1970b; Wolfman 1979), using the approach advocated here (see below). I would argue that the Eighmy et al. curve is probably incorrect because their independent dating within a 20-year range (A.D. 880–900) for VGPs that are as much as 10° apart seems very unlikely, for the reasons discussed above (see particularly question 3). A free-hand curve drawn through the 14 VGPs that they independently date between 880 and 900 is at least a little rounder than the curve produced using the Sternberg statistical approach. In addition, the small number of samples thus far measured by Eighmy et al. (this volume) dating between A.D. 700 and 840 may also account for some of the discrepancy.

The slow average rate of secular variation (ca. 0.57°/10 years) found by Sternberg and McGuire (chap. 12; see also Sternberg 1982) for the Southwest in the A.D. 750–1425 interval, using Sternberg's procedure, is apparently due primarily to the small number of high-precision samples used to construct the curve in the A.D. 700–950 and 1300–1450 time periods. In addition, the few samples used are not evenly distributed in these intervals. The problems with the Sternberg and McGuire curve and their derived rate of secular variation are indicated by comparison with other curves developed in the Southwest. The curves presented by Eighmy et al. in this volume for the A.D. 700–900 interval (see Fig. 13.1, which was also derived using the Sternberg statistical procedure) and DuBois and Wolfman for the A.D. 600–1500 interval (DuBois and Wolfman 1970b; see also Wolfman 1984:406), both based on more data, suggest rates of secular variation approximately double that found by Sternberg and McGuire.

We can now compare the fundamental differences between Sternberg's procedure and mine. He starts by assigning an independent age range to the sample and then fits the curve, whereas I often fit the curve with only a vague notion of absolute age. In my procedure, assigning calibration points along the curve is a second, nearly independent step. In constructing polar curves, I let the archaeomagnetic data speak for themselves. Because I strongly believe that the independent age estimates are less exact than the archaeomagnetic data, I look for patterns (i.e., the curve) in fairly long intervals of VGPs, assisted by stratigraphy, seriation, cross-dating, good radiocarbon dating, and, when available, tree-ring dating. Throughout the process I cross-check back and forth between preliminary versions of the curve and all the other data. This procedure allows me to compare the consistency (and I hope the validity) of the radiocarbon dates across an area. Not surprisingly from the above discussion, I give precedence to the archaeomagnetic results, and often archaeological cross-dating, over radiocarbon results. In this manner it is sometimes possible to spot aberrant (presumably incorrect) radiocarbon dates and erroneous inferences about cross-dating while examining the archaeomagnetic results. Some attention is, of course, paid to the precision of the results. I reject all results with α_{95} values greater than 4° and give greater weight to VGPs with small α_{95}s as opposed to those with large values. Where possible, I work only with samples with α_{95} values somewhat smaller than 4°. As time goes on and more results become available, I hope to use only those samples with α_{95}s less than 2.5° in curve construction.

Once the curve is drawn, I review all the chronometric data and attempt to place absolute age calibration points at about 100-year intervals along the curve, and in some situations at 50-year intervals.

Because I consider all chronometric evidence throughout a period of several hundred years and compare these results with the sequential series of archaeomagnetic results, I can obtain calibration points (at 100- or 50-year intervals) with much better precision and accuracy than is possible with individual radiocarbon dates. In some situations, phase boundaries can be very important here. I usually interpolate by assuming a uniform rate in the intervals between the calibration points. I always regard all curves as preliminary and subject to further refinement as more information is obtained. While this procedure has not yet been formalized in a manner that can be written in a computer program, it probably could be, with the derivation of parameters giving the 95% confidence interval around the curve.

As a consequence of the above discussion, I regard the construction of polar curves as an exercise in archaeological inference rather than straightforward statistical inference. I demonstrated this lengthy procedure in my Mesoamerican paper in this volume. Inferring dates (see below, question 10) analogously requires a consideration of all the archaeological data (see chap. 15). It is in part because of these considerations that I believe that archaeologically trained archaeomagnetists will make the greatest contributions in these areas in the future. Furthermore, I believe that the former lack of such individuals contributed to the slow development of archaeomagnetic dating (see below, question 12).

An additional advantage that my curve-fitting procedure has over that proposed by Sternberg is that because his procedure requires a reasonably good estimate of the age of a sample, many good (i.e., low α_{95}) data are not used when constructing a curve. For example, 44 samples with α_{95} values less than 4.0° originally reported in Sternberg's 1982 dissertation were not used by Sternberg and McGuire (this volume, chap. 12) to fit the Southwest curve because they were not tightly dated. While the ages of samples may not have been known with good precision and accuracy, it is hard to believe that their ages could not be estimated within 200- to 300-year ranges or that at least some of them could not have been seriated approximately based on ceramic style alone. The deletion of these 44 samples is significant because they constitute nearly half of the 94 samples with such high precision. While Sternberg and McGuire have difficulty in using results with such uncertain independent dating, I welcome such data.

Further potential problems with the curve-fitting procedure reported by Sternberg and McGuire in this volume may be due to their acceptance of sample results with α_{95} values up to 10°. They used 23 results (out of a total of 73) with α_{95} values between 4.0° and 10.0°, which others, working in the United States, would have rejected. Several additional factors—including averaging over intervals, incorrect age estimates, and situations in which the true age of a sample is at one end of the independently estimated age range (especially when this range is large)—can also lead to problems when using Sternberg's procedure.

Several of the points discussed above give rise to the hairpin character of the curves derived by Sternberg and McGuire (this volume, chap. 12) and Eighmy et al. (this volume). In contrast, sweeping curves predominate in the freehand curves drawn for other parts of the world by various investigators (Aitken 1974:156; Hirooka 1971; Thellier 1981; Watanabe 1959; Wolfman 1982; Wolfman, this volume, chaps. 14, 15; see also Wolfman 1984:401–411). In addition, such curves are indicated by many historic data (e.g., Bauer 1896; Hirooka 1971; Thellier 1981). This is not to deny that hairpin curves exist but merely to point out that some aspects of Sternberg's procedure may introduce or accentuate such features or other distortions due to the use of running averages. In this context it should be emphasized that since the procedure I use does not average over independently estimated time intervals, removal of detail is minimized.

E. A proposed test. In the preceding paragraphs I have registered several objections to Sternberg's curve-fitting procedure. As a test I propose a simulation starting with a series of VGPs closely adhering to the freehand version of the Southwest curves from 900 to 1500 (DuBois and Wolfman 1970b; DuBois 1975c). Each VGP has a small α_{95} value and an independent date of the closest position along the curve with 95% confidence intervals of ±50 years. It would be interesting to see if the simulation reproduces the sweeping freehand curve or one that is tighter and more hairpinlike. The conditions could later be relaxed somewhat to see what effects such variables as incorrect dates, larger or smaller confidence intervals, independent "true" dates skewed toward one end of the estimated confidence interval, and larger or smaller numbers of samples have on the resulting curve.

The above discussion should not be construed to suggest that I am necessarily opposed to statistical or formalized methods of curve fitting. I merely state that Sternberg's procedure does not fit the bill, and I have indicated the lines along which such a program might be developed.

10. How should archaeomagnetic dates be determined, and how precise and accurate is archaeomagnetic dating? Sternberg (1982; Sternberg and McGuire, this volume, chap. 6) has proposed a strict procedure for calculating an archaeomagnetic date with a 95% confidence interval that develops naturally from his statistical approach to curve fitting. This procedure provides dates with an error parameter which is a combination of precision and accuracy. The few dates thus far published (Sternberg 1989b:543) have an error range on the order of 200 years (i.e., ca. ±100 years). In the preceding section I argued that some advantages can be obtained by developing the curve and determining the dates by separating errors related to precision from errors related to accuracy. Of particular importance in this regard are the more precise relative dates that are obtained, which I believe are usually of greater importance than absolute dates per se. In this regard, Dean (1978:223) has emphasized the great importance of determining contemporaneity. Dates determined in this manner in Arkansas and Mesoamerica (Wolfman, this volume, chaps. 14, 15) usually have a precision parameter range, at the 95% confidence level, on the order of 20 to 100 years (i.e., ca. ±10 to ±50 years). I have discussed my approach to obtaining an archaeomagnetic date elsewhere (Wolfman 1973:160–161; Wolfman 1982:279–284; Wolfman 1984:395–399). Essentially, ovals of confidence are compared to a curve drawn according to the procedure I outlined above. When I report dates, the confidence interval is a measure only of precision. I arbitrarily add five years to each end of the confidence interval of the age determined in this fashion to allow for nondipole variation across an archaeomagnetic area about 800 km in diameter.

I usually make some sort of estimate of the error involved in calibrating the curve separately. Since possible errors of accuracy often exceed the precision error, a combined estimate gives an unnecessarily skewed view of the usefulness of the archaeomagnetic result. Since I acknowledge that the dates I report are not necessarily "true," it may be best to use terms like "archaeomagnetic dates" or "archaeomagnetic ages," as I suggested more than 15 years ago (Wolfman 1973:235–236). In a general way these terms are analogous to "radiocarbon years" in the ^{14}C dating method. At the same time, I think that the calibration error for curves developed in this manner for about the past 3,000 years can, in those areas in which I have worked, be kept under ±50 years.

Other problems in archaeomagnetic dating require special care. Crossover points and the fact that different sections of a curve pass close together often present problems. However, there is often information in both the archaeological and archaeomagnetic data that can resolve these important problems. Stratigraphic samples that provide an indication of the proper order of the VGPs can often be very useful in this regard (Wolfman 1988). In addition, independent chronological information, including artifactual associations and paleointensity data, can further enhance the chronometric information inherent in the archaeomagnetic direction data.

While obtaining a date or an archaeomagnetic date (in the sense defined above) is certainly important and it is the model archaeologists have come to expect from other dating methods, archaeomagnetic dating also makes another major contribution. A well-constructed curve provides a chronological sequence of events across an area about 800 km in diameter. As I have argued above, I believe this is uniquely possible with archaeomagnetic data because of their high precision and accuracy and because events or objects of cultural importance are dated directly. With a sufficient number of samples across an area, it is possible to see the sweep of events dated. When such a sequence includes one or more stratigraphic series, it is even more valuable. This provides, within very tight limits, an overview of what was going on at the same time and what events preceded and succeeded others, both within a site and at widely separated sites. Where such data are available, archaeomagnetic dating provides new insights into cultural developments.

11. What role should paleointensity measurements play in archaeomagnetic direction studies? As Sternberg has pointed out in the introduction, paleointensity studies have been specifically excluded from this volume. Nonetheless, because of the potential importance of such data in improving archaeomagnetic direction dating and because of recent methodological advances (e.g., Walton 1987), a brief discussion is included here. For more complete coverage of paleointensity in archaeology, the reader is referred to my review article "Geomagnetic Dating Methods in Archaeology" (Wolfman 1984), which includes numerous references.

One of the weak links in archaeomagnetic direction dating is that curves cross over themselves, and sometimes sections of curve of different ages pass close together. Consequently, often a unique age cannot be determined from direction data alone. This also causes problems in constructing curves. Since three variables are measured simultaneously, the use of paleointensity measurements in conjunction with direction data can, at least in theory, significantly reduce problems related to the nonuniqueness of geomagnetic direction. This is particularly the case when paleointensity measurements are made on baked clay from the same baked feature that provides the archaeomagnetic direction sample.

While the potential use of paleointensity measurements in this regard has been suggested previously, to my knowledge actual applications of this approach have been rare (e.g., Kovacheva 1988). Reasons for this include time-consuming paleointensity laboratory procedures, the unsuitability for paleointensity measurements of clay from most baked features (and many ceramics), and considerable difference of opinion about the accuracy of such measurements. Recent research, including improvements in instrumentation and experimental procedures, is making the goal of using paleointensity both alone and in conjunction with direction measurements for archaeological dating more realistic.

12. Who should undertake archaeomagnetic dating? The answer to this question is crucial for the development of archaeomagnetic dating. Currently, the very few archaeomagnetists in the United States are either archaeologists who know something about geophysics or geophysicists who know something about archaeology. Why are they so few, how are they to be trained in the future, and how does this relate to the central question of why archaeomagnetic dating has proceeded so slowly? This discussion is part of the broader question of who does the various archaeometric analyses. This has been argued at several meetings of the International Symposium on Archaeometry without any consensus being reached (see, e.g., Olin 1982). There are physicists who claim that archaeometry should be the work of physical scientists, and there are young (and a few not so young) archaeometrists who obtained their degrees in anthropology and archaeology who maintain that this is nonsense. In addition, nonarchaeometric archaeologists have complained that the archaeometrists trained in the physical sciences are often finding answers for which there are no questions (e.g., Hole 1982).

I think something can be learned by looking at the history of the application of the natural sciences to disciplines other than archaeology. Important lessons can also be learned from the development of other dating methods, particularly what Sternberg (this volume) calls the pattern-matching methods. Furthermore, I think there may be an important distinction to be made about who does what in the three stages of development of archaeometric methods: initial idea, development, and application.

A. A comparison with geology. The history of the application of various physical science techniques to geology provides a good parallel to the situation of archaeometry with respect to archaeology. In the first half of this century it was primarily the physicists and chemists who developed the various age-dating and stable-isotope methods and laid the foundations of paleomagnetism, which are so important in modern geology. In part this was because the geology curriculum at that time did not include much training in the physical sciences. Also, the equipment needed to be custom-built, and the physicists and chemists were trained to do this and had access to the technicians and machine shops needed to accomplish the task.

As time went on, it became apparent to some geologists that very important questions could be answered with these techniques. They further realized that in many situations, extensive field sampling would be needed, and most of the problems were of much greater geological than physical interest. The training of geophysicists and geochemists soon followed, so that today geological problems that can be solved using physical-science methods are usually explored by scientists whose graduate degrees are in geology or geophysics. Nonetheless, despite a general shift toward geologically trained geophysicists and geochemists, some scientists trained in physics and chemistry continue to make important contributions both individually and in collaboration with geologists. Such individuals have both contributed to solving basic geological problems and acted in a service capacity.

Since anthropology and archaeology are much further removed from physics and chemistry than is geology (which is usually classified as a physical science), interdisciplinary collaboration and training is somewhat more difficult. Certainly until recently most archaeologists had a perhaps healthy fear of touching seemingly esoteric instruments about which they knew little or nothing. The advent of the computer and later the microcomputer has had far-reaching effects on society in general and on archaeologists in particular. The hands-on approach to computers will shortly spread to other pieces of seemingly forbidding equipment (e.g., magnetometers and demagnetizers).

In addition, as happened a generation ago in geology, more archaeologists are beginning to accept the fact that effective solutions of many of the most crucial problems in the discipline will require their greater participation in a wide range of natural-science applications. It was therefore perhaps inevitable that until these recent changes in archaeological perspective came about, archaeologically trained archaeometrists would be few in number. Within the past ten years, such individuals have begun to appear, and I expect their numbers to increase significantly in the next decade.

B. Training. A discussion of the details of training these individuals would require a considerable digression. Suffice it to say that basic course work in the natural sciences would be desirable. In addition, a few courses on the advanced level in the areas of an individual's specialization would certainly help. Of equal or greater importance is active participation in a research laboratory. In this regard, individuals who come to archaeology with an undergraduate degree or a background in one of the natural sciences would be in a position to make important contributions. Active recruiting of talented individuals with undergraduate majors in the natural sciences or mathematics (my undergraduate major) should be explored. A program of postdoctoral fellowships for archaeologists in scientific laboratories would also be helpful.

A brief look at my, and to a lesser extent Eighmy's, training illustrates the importance of hands-on laboratory training and interdisciplinary interaction. In retrospect, much of our training was haphazard and fortuitous. I first collected samples in 1963, using molds left in the Southwest by the British geophysicist Norman Watkins. Unfortunately, Watkins did not continue this work. Had he done so, we would have many more published data for this area. Later, both Eighmy and I worked in DuBois's lab at the University of Oklahoma, and we both learned a great deal there about the method. As mentioned above, I undertook research in that laboratory that provided the data for a portion of my doctoral dissertation research.

Starting in the mid 1970s and continuing to the present, I have had the opportunity to learn from a variety of paleomagnetists when visiting their laboratories to measure samples. Repeated and occasionally lengthy visits to the rock magnetism laboratories at the University of Pittsburgh and the University of California at Santa Barbara were particularly beneficial. These visits allowed me to interact with laboratory directors, postdocs, and graduate students; attend and present seminars; and become thoroughly familiar with the most advanced equipment, the latest computer programs, and the day-to-day operation of the laboratories. In addition, I have interacted more directly in collaborative projects with Richard Dodson of the University of California at Santa Barbara (e.g., Wolfman and Dodson 1986) and William Kean of the University of Wisconsin at Milwaukee (e.g., Wolfman et al. 1982). Starting just a bit later, the collaboration between Eighmy and Sternberg (and to a lesser extent Robert Butler, the director of the University of Arizona paleomagnetism laboratory and Sternberg's major professor) when they were graduate students has been particularly fruitful. Interaction has taken place both in the field and in the laboratory. More recently, Eighmy and his students have benefited from their close proximity to the University of Colorado, where there is an active paleomagnetism program under the direction of Edwin Larson (who, incidentally, was a member of my dissertation committee). All of these interactions have broadened the knowledge of those involved and been very beneficial to specific projects.

C. A brief review of several dating methods. In order to gain a better understanding of why archaeomagnetism took so long to develop and where we go from here, a quick review of the history of a few other dating methods is needed. Sternberg's very useful fourfold classification of dating methods in this volume provides a convenient framework for presenting such a review. He divides dating methods into regional and global, patterns and clocks. The pattern-matching methods, which include archaeomagnetic dating, have led to the greatest interdisciplinary research. This is because the underlying natural phenomena that cause the patterns that are useful for dating are also of fundamental interest in one, and sometimes several, other disciplines.

One of the most successful examples of interdisciplinary collaboration in the development and application of a pattern-matching method has been in dendrochronology. This method, which is of importance in many disciplines, was, as far as I am aware, first discussed by Charles Babbage (1838), an individual with very broad interests.

Subsequently it was first successfully applied by an astronomer, A. E. Douglass (1909, 1914, 1919). Since then, dendrochronology has been explored by meteorologists, climatologists, archaeologists, botanists, astronomers, and other researchers, very often in a truly interdisciplinary fashion. Despite the great difficulty of coordinating interdisciplinary research, the Laboratory of Tree-Ring Research at the University of Arizona stands as a model that others can only try to emulate. It should be noted that archaeologists have played an important role in the research and administration of this laboratory.

Radiocarbon dating is another topic that has been explored by scientists in a variety of disciplines. This is not surprising, because the pattern-matching aspect of radiocarbon dating due to fluctuation in carbon 14 in the atmosphere and other aspects of the method (e.g., isotopic fractionation) are of considerable interest in a variety of disciplines. However, there are several striking differences between the implementation of radiocarbon dating and that of tree-ring dating, including the number of laboratories, the nature of interdisciplinary interaction, and the very small number of archaeologists directing or working in radiocarbon laboratories. In part, the important role of archaeologists in tree-ring dating as opposed to radiocarbon dating is due to the simplicity of instrumentation in the former method. The fact that the routine dating of tree-ring samples was so important in the development of Southwest archaeology, and that there was nobody else to do this work, also contributed to the participation of archaeologists. Finally, and of considerable importance, some archaeologists recognized the unique contribution tree-ring results could make to understanding prehistoric cultures (e.g., Dean 1969).

Regional pattern-matching studies have generally been dominated by a single individual or a small group working together in an area. This is particularly true in the early years of development, when the basic patterns are being worked out. DeGeer dominated varve studies for many years, particularly in Scandinavia, with Antevs working alone in the United States. Various tree-ring chronologies were also worked out by individuals or small groups. It is particularly noteworthy that Watanabe (1959), who received his doctorate in anthropology, working alone, developed the first archaeomagnetic curve anywhere in the world. While some refinements were subsequently made in the curve he developed for Japan, his early work stands as a major contribution and presages the current wave of archaeomagnetic development in the United States, where archaeologists are playing a major role in field and laboratory work. In contrast, global pattern-matching in radiocarbon research was undertaken by a larger number of labs because a worldwide phenomenon was being studied and samples were abundant.

Looking more broadly at the development of dating methods in general, a pattern can be seen in who does what at various stages. The initial ideas and early development have come from natural scientists—radiocarbon (Libby 1949; Libby et al. 1949), archaeomagnetism (Boyle 1691; Halley 1692; Chevallier 1925; Thellier 1938); tree-ring dating (Babbage 1838; Douglass 1909, 1914, 1919), obsidian hydration (Friedman and Smith 1958, 1960); thermoluminescence (Daniels et al. 1953); and α-recoil tracks (Huang and Walker 1967). Where natural scientists did not take up the challenge, a few archaeologists have gotten involved in methodological and occasionally theoretical developments (e.g., obsidian hydration [Clark 1961, 1964; Erickson 1981; Michels 1967; Michels et al. 1983; Suzuki 1973] and α-recoil tracks [Garrison 1973; Garrison et al. 1978; Wolfman and Rolniak 1979; Wolfman and Stahle 1979]).

In the application stage in archaeometry in general and dating methods in particular, more archaeologists are taking on major portions of the operation, including laboratory work. Within chronometric methods this began many years ago with tree-ring dating. While also true of obsidian hydration and archaeomagnetism, archaeologists have undertaken only limited laboratory work in radiocarbon and thermoluminescence. The participation of archaeologists in working in and directing laboratories remains in part related to the difficulties in constructing and maintaining equipment.

In this brief discussion, along with that presented in the first part of this chapter, certain patterns are emerging in the history of archaeological dating methods. This suggests something about the future of these methods, particularly archaeomagnetism. As with tree-ring dating, archaeomagnetic dating had an early history in which the potential of the method was recognized but not utilized. As with most methods, the basic ideas, conceptual and methodological advances, and, with the notable exception of Watanabe's work in Japan, initial applications were carried out by physical scientists. As with other regional pattern-matching methods, single individuals continue to dominate specific geographic areas. In archaeomagnetism the restricted number of baked features excavated in an area in a particular year seems to require an individual or small groups working together in the curve construction phase.

In Europe and Asia the application of archaeomagnetism has been almost exclusively undertaken by physical scientists. In contrast, in the United States there have been fruitful collaborations of geophysicists and archaeologists, and in recent years a few individuals with graduate degrees in anthropology (archaeology) have taken on the sole responsibility for entire projects. In addition, these individuals are beginning to make methodological refinements.

D. Reasons for expected greater involvement of archaeologically trained archaeomagnetists in the future. In recent years, Eighmy and I have taken charge of our own projects. The implementation of archaeomagnetic projects by archaeologically trained archaeomagnetists in the United States, while a major departure from previous practices, is similar to past developments in geophysics and geochemistry, and other regional pattern-matching dating methods, particularly dendrochronology. I expect that a greater involvement of archaeologically trained archaeomagnetists, with or without geophysical collaborators and with relatively few geophysicists working alone on the day-to-day procedures of sample collection and measurement, will be the trend of the future. On the other hand, I expect that certain areas, particularly the rock magnetism of baked clay and the construction and utilization of models of the geomagnetic field, will be handled primarily by the geophysically trained archaeomagnetists.

The reasons for an increased involvement by archaeologists include the following:

1. Sample collecting is a major aspect of the work. In contrast to most other dating methods, archaeomagnetic sample collection is almost as time-consuming as sample measurement, and it often requires archaeomagnetists to visit sites to collect samples. This is particularly important in the curve construction phase in an area. Not only does it insure accurate collection of the best material but, just as important, it also allows interaction with those in charge of excavations. Very often much more chronometric information than a mere estimate of age can and should be obtained at this time. This is where archaeological expertise is crucial, because this information is needed, particularly in constructing curves but only slightly less so in estimating dates (see below). On the other hand, archaeomag-

netists trained in geophysics are more likely to be sensitive to physical problems in the field. Nonetheless, it will be far easier to train archaeologists in the mechanics of field collecting than to teach geophysicists about archaeological chronology and all its attendant problems.

2. Very reliable equipment is commonly available. Until about 20 years ago, each lab had to build most of its own equipment. Consequently, the earliest archaeomagnetism and paleomagnetism labs were generally managed by physicists. Geologically trained geophysicists soon followed, with their number increasing as manufactured equipment became available. Archaeologists can now do the same.

3. The repetitious data are of much greater interest to archaeologists. This is not to deny that geophysicists might direct laboratories with a service function, measuring samples for archaeological dating, but in contrast to the case of ^{14}C dating, service labs in paleomagnetism have not been successful.

4. Paleomagnetists have not shown a strong interest in becoming involved in archaeomagnetic studies. This provides a strong incentive, of course, for archaeologically trained archaeomagnetists to set up labs. This is in part a repetition of the conditions that led to the development of the subdisciplines of geophysics and geochemistry and what happened in dendrochronology.

5. Curve construction requires great familiarity with the archaeology of the area. The development of master curves (i.e., the discovery of the patterns) in archaeomagnetism is very different from that in radiocarbon dating or dendrochronology. In the latter methods the pattern that emerges does not rely on the independent dating of archaeological material. In contrast, a thorough knowledge of the archaeological chronology of an area, the methods used to develop the chronology, the history of the development of that chronology, and the current major problems is needed to develop an archaeomagnetic master curve. Recent improvements in radiocarbon dating and the very precise and accurate VGPs obtained from archaeomagnetism can often help resolve such problems but only when all the pertinent archaeological data are also understood. Basically, curve construction is a problem in archaeological inference.

6. The increasing interest of archaeologists in archaeomagnetic dating is part of a widening trend. This has been brought on in part by an absence of specialists from other disciplines willing to take on the chores of specialized analyses on a service or research basis. Of

greater importance is the fact that archaeologists are recognizing the need to develop a greater variety of primary data in order to understand fully their anthropological implications. This is perhaps nowhere more true than in the application of statistical methods and computer modeling, and it also accounts for the recent increased participation by archaeologists in such areas as dating, trace element analysis, paleoethnobotany, and archaeozoology.

The above discussion should not be construed to suggest that I think geophysicists will or should be absent from routine archaeomagnetic studies. But, for the reasons stated above, I believe that when geophysicists are involved, most of the work will be undertaken with an archaeological collaborator. Archaeologists should welcome and encourage the cooperation of geophysicists. Archaeomagnetism is of great importance in geophysics, and I strongly believe that a lively interaction between disciplines remains the most fruitful way to carry out interdisciplinary research. The great success of interdisciplinary research at the Laboratory of Tree-Ring Research at the University of Arizona indicates the value of such an approach.

I expect to see geophysicists taking greater interest in archaeomagnetism because of its importance in the investigation of secular variation and what such data reveal about the nature of the geomagnetic field. In the past 20 years, sediment studies have generated a renewed interest in secular variation. Geophysicists have recently realized, however, that data obtained from sediments are often not reliable enough to answer crucial questions about secular variation. I strongly suspect that this will lead to useful collaboration with archaeologists, as well as greater use of the data generated by archaeologically trained archaeomagnetists. As noted above, I believe that the erroneous statements made by Creer and his colleagues (e.g., Creer and Tucholka 1983:273) that long, continuous secular variation sequences cannot be obtained from baked clays and the suggestions by others that many years will pass before enough useful data can be obtained has deterred some geophysicists from devoting more time to archaeomagnetism. The long time it took for Thellier (1981) to publish his results and the fact that DuBois has yet to publish any basic data after more than 25 years of work have contributed to this erroneous notion. I hope that as more data become available (notably in this volume) these ideas will be dispelled, if this has not in fact already occurred.

The increasing interest in the use of data obtained from lavas to aid in the reconstruction of past secular variation (e.g., Champion 1980), as well as volcanic hazard reduction studies (Holcomb et al. 1986), will also attract more geophysicists to archaeomagnetic studies. In addition, I expect that they will contribute important work on the rock magnetism of baked clay which may lead to refinements of laboratory procedures and perhaps ultimately to even more reliable dating. Modeling of the geomagnetic field is another area in which the geophysicists and physicists will be working, with little input from archaeologists.

Finally, while some archaeomagnetists may contribute to all areas of archaeomagnetic research, I believe that there will be considerable division of labor along the lines of the principal discipline of the archaeomagnetist.

WHY DID ARCHAEOMAGNETIC DATING DEVELOP SLOWLY?

One of the initial questions I asked was why archaeomagnetic dating developed as slowly as it did. I think the above discussion suggests the answer. Archaeomagnetic dating is a subject in which the fieldwork and chronometric data analysis are best undertaken by archaeologists, but archaeologists never had the training to construct labs or, when equipment first became commercially available, to manage them. Perhaps even more important, until very recently archaeologists did not conceive of themselves as archaeometrists. The few physicists and geophysicists involved in early archaeomagnetic studies were interested almost exclusively in the history of the geomagnetic field, not archaeological dating. Clearly, until recently what was needed was collaboration between geophysicists and archaeologists. For a variety of reasons, early collaborations either did not take place, even in favorable institutional settings (e.g., the CIW in the 1930s and 1940s), or when they did occur did not lead to published results (e.g., DuBois with several archaeologists). Perhaps it was necessary for archaeologists to conceive of themselves as archaeometrists before successful collaboration could take place. Now that a few archaeologists have gotten sufficient training to manage labs and, more important, to conceive of themselves as archaeometrists, I expect we will see tremendous advances. This volume reports some studies that have been made in recent years and provides an indication of what can be expected in the future. I expect that advances similar to those recently made in the United States will not be made in Europe and Asia until the archaeologists on those continents become much more involved in archaeomagnetic dating.

CONCLUDING REMARKS

This volume marks a milestone in archaeomagnetic dating. It contains the first publication of a large quantity of archaeomagnetic data for North America and Mesoamerica. Important basic questions are asked and some experimental results are reported. Other researchers will build on some of the ideas presented here to achieve further refinement of archaeomagnetic dating and to increase its potential. Most important, this volume demonstrates that archaeomagnetic dating will advance more rapidly only when more archaeologists take part in sample collection and measurement. As noted above, in no other dating method are the establishment of the master curves (or chronologies) and the estimation of dates nearly as dependent on independent archaeological data as they are in archaeomagnetic studies. At the same time, I expect that there will be an increased interest in archaeomagnetism on the part of geophysicists. This is in part due to the increased interest in secular variation generated by the many studies on lacustrine sediments and to a lesser extent marine sediments, and the subsequently noted failure of this material to record the ambient geomagnetic field with sufficient precision and accuracy for very detailed secular variation studies. While I expect that much of the geophysicists' routine fieldwork, and probably routine laboratory work as well, will be conducted in close collaboration with archaeologists, they will probably make most of their advances in the rock magnetism of baked clay and in modeling the field while working alone.

While archaeomagnetic dating is making significant contributions today, research in the next decade should serve to refine the method. A considerable portion of this chapter has been devoted to a discussion of twelve broad questions about archaeomagnetic dating. This section has included an identification of problem areas, short reviews of previous research, suggestions on the direction of future research, and a discussion of some conflicting points of view. Also, I mentioned that I expect the greatest advancements to be made in laboratory procedures (particularly cleaning and the criteria of acceptance and rejection of individual specimen results). Important advances may also be made in curve fitting and date estimation.

Archaeomagnetic dating can contribute to archaeological chronometrics in a variety of ways. Archaeomagnetic dating that is characterized by an age estimate within a confidence interval of precision (or in some cases a combination of precision and accuracy) will assist archaeologists with traditional and new chronometric problems. I believe that the high precision of this method and the fact that it directly dates an event or object of cultural importance are its great strengths. Consequently, in many instances archaeomagnetic dates will be far more useful than dates obtained by other methods. Furthermore, I believe that the greatest contribution of archaeomagnetic dating will be its ability to provide a view of the sequence of events within a single site, throughout a restricted region, or over an area up to about 1,000 km in diameter. In this regard, the ability to provide information about the stability and change of various cultural and natural parameters through time will be particularly important. In addition, such tight dating may suggest new types of cultural analyses.

The thrust of processual archaeology is to understand how and why things happened in prehistory. In order to understand how and why events took place, it is necessary to know when they did (or at least the sequence in which they occurred). Furthermore, in some instances a knowledge of the sequence of events provides strong suggestions about how and why the events occurred. I believe archaeomagnetic dating will make important contributions to answering these questions in the years ahead.

ACKNOWLEDGMENTS

This chapter is the result of the interaction of a number of scholars in several disciplines. This is the nature of archaeometric research in general, but is probably nowhere more true than in archaeomagnetic dating. To some extent this interaction has been discussed in the preceding pages. Above all, I would like to thank the authors of the other chapters in this book and, more particularly, the editors. Without them there would have been no book and consequently no final chapter. In the acknowledgments to my chapters on Mesoamerica and Arkansas I thanked numerous archaeologists and the directors of the laboratories where I have worked. I thank them once again for their contributions to this chapter. I would also like to thank the many other archaeologists, geophysicists, and other scholars—too numerous to mention in a list of reasonable length—who have also contributed in various ways. For the most part, they know who they are, and I hope they will excuse me for not mentioning them specifically. As with the other two chapters I contributed to this volume, the editors and Marvin D. Jeter read earlier drafts of this chapter. Their comments are greatly appreciated. While all of these individuals have, in one way or another, contributed significantly to the summary view I have presented here, I alone take responsibility for the contents of the chapter and any errors it may contain. The several drafts of this chapter were typed by Mrs. G. G. Williams and Mrs. Mary Ann Long. I once again thank them for what at times seemed to be a never-ending chore.

Appendix

Introduction

The five tables in this appendix contain the raw data for the independently dated archaeomagnetic samples constituting the four studies of Part 3. These tables have been placed as an appendix for the sake of the continuity of those articles, but we consider their publication here a significant contribution in itself. Because archaeomagnetists are still using these data in different ways to derive secular variation curves, it is essential for the comparison and alternative treatment of these data to have the raw results readily available. A standard format for these data has been used in reporting the sample location, significant paleomagnetic parameters, and the age assigned to the sample. Given their importance in deriving the secular variation curves, these age assignments should be periodically reevaluated as new chronological information becomes available.

In the appendix tables, the VGPs are defined in terms of the following characteristics:

N_1	number of specimens collected from the features
N_2	number of specimens used in the final results
Demag	demagnetization level in milliteslas (mT)
I	sample mean inclination
D	sample mean declination
α_{95}	size in degrees of the 95% confidence interval
Plat	latitude of the VGP
Plong	longitude of the VGP
dp	semiminor axis (degrees) of the oval of confidence about the VGP
dm	semimajor axis (degrees) of the oval of confidence about the VGP
Age Range	independent age range of the pole position.

Table A-1. Archaeomagnetic Data from the American Southwest

Sample ID	Location	N_1/N_2	Demag	I	D	α_{95}
FL004	AZ:BB:9:14(ASM), Hs. 13A	8/8	15.0	45.85	5.01	11.2
FL001	AZ:BB:9:14(ASM), Hs. 4	8/8	10.0	47.67	352.59	13.6
MV005	Twin Tree Site, Ph. 1	9/9	20.0	55.44	0.04	3.2
PN001	NA13785, Str. 8, Feat. 26	8/8	15.0	59.87	333.22	20.6
PN002	NA13875, Str. 1, Feat. 20	9/7	15.0	56.21	357.59	3.5
LU001	AZ:K:12:3(ASM), Feat. 20	8/8	15.0	49.73	355.31	4.0
LU002	AZ:K:12:3(ASM), Feat. 13	8/8	15.0	49.50	0.53	2.0
FL003	AZ:BB:9:14(ASM), Hs. 12	9/8	15.0	55.95	350.76	3.6
NR005	Nan Ranch, Rm. 43, Feat. 2	9/8	15.0	54.56	355.09	6.4
NR006	Nan Ranch, Rm. 52	11/8	30.0	45.73	358.96	1.8
PN004	NA14002, Str. 2	8/7	15.0	53.80	354.19	17.3
MT001	LA676, Unit 286, Lev. 7F	9/8	15.0	51.65	357.25	1.8
MT002	LA676, Unit 286, Lev. 4	9/9	15.0	58.77	358.07	2.0
AM001	NA15909, Feat. 34	15/14	20.0	58.07	349.27	6.2
NR003	Nan Ranch, Rm. 51, Lev. 14	12/10	20.0	46.87	3.08	5.8
QR001	Q Ranch, APS-CS-245	8/5	15.0	57.32	343.78	7.7
MT003	LA676, Unit 410, Lev. 5S	9/8	15.0	60.98	346.82	3.3
MF001	NA862, Rm. 1	10/9	20.0	69.75	331.65	3.1
NR004	Nan Ranch, Rm. 46, Lev. 3	12/12	20.0	56.14	354.85	12.4
NR007	Nan Ranch, Rm. 47	12/10	30.0	49.99	336.37	12.5
WV001	NA3644M, Lower Floor	10/8	20.0	62.04	340.25	2.8
WV003	NA2133A	10/10	15.0	61.73	348.30	5.4
FL002	AZ:BB:9:14(ASM), Hs. 5	9/9	15.0	57.81	1.70	8.3
FL005	AZ:BB:9:14(ASM), Hs. 1	9/9	15.0	58.53	346.93	1.7
CH004	AZ:P:14:24(ASM)	8/7	15.0	66.40	354.88	7.4
GB001	AZ:U:13:24(ASU), Feat. 6	8/7	10.0	59.95	349.86	2.1
GB002	AZ:U:13:24(ASU), Feat. 1	9/8	10.0	55.53	353.73	1.1
WV004	NA2133D, Later Hearth	9/9	15.0	61.17	343.39	2.9
WV002	NA3644P	8/6	15.0	61.53	344.51	4.6
NR001	Nan Ranch, Area D, Rm. 41	12/8	30.0	45.02	357.39	10.8
NR002	Nan Ranch, Area D, Rm. 41	10/10	30.0	58.55	340.80	2.1
PN003	NA13767, Str. 1	10/9	15.0	57.02	345.01	5.0
PN005	NA13767, Str. 1	8/8	15.0	54.25	358.54	10.9

NOTE: The results are listed in terms of the number of specimens collected from the features (N_1) and the number of specimens used in the final results (N_2), the demagnetization level in milliteslas (mT), sample mean inclination (I) and sample mean declination (D), the size in degrees of the 95% confidence interval (α_{95}), latitude of the VGP (Plat), longitude of the VGP (Plong), error along the great circle in estimating the VGP (dp), error perpendicular to the great circle in estimating the VGP (dm), and expected age range of the pole position.

VGP				
Plat	Plong	*dp*	*dm*	Age Range (Years A.D.)
83.37	26.83	9.14	14.32	500–800
82.73	132.41	11.53	17.72	600–800
88.69	70.16	3.26	4.57	674–700
68.65	180.07	23.45	31.07	750–875
87.99	175.45	3.60	5.00	750–875
83.81	111.78	3.57	5.37	785–820
84.99	65.72	1.75	2.63	785–820
81.28	190.79	3.72	5.18	800–1100
85.24	193.66	6.36	9.01	850–1000
84.45	80.81	1.49	2.33	850–1000
84.89	139.50	16.95	24.25	875–900
87.62	149.18	1.72	2.52	936–1000
83.16	239.45	2.21	2.97	936–1000
79.97	191.33	6.72	9.12	950–1150
84.74	40.01	4.81	7.46	1000–1080
76.31	180.68	8.17	11.18	1000–1250
76.11	207.15	3.84	5.01	1020–1050
63.18	209.75	4.49	5.23	1060–1150
84.13	206.38	12.88	17.90	1080–1150
69.85	162.65	11.12	16.65	1080–1150
72.76	192.53	3.32	4.28	1088–1097
78.10	202.57	6.42	8.30	1095–1130
83.64	261.23	9.02	12.27	1100–1200
77.32	196.23	1.83	2.47	1100–1200
74.76	236.47	9.94	12.09	1100–1270
78.86	204.54	2.41	3.18	1100–1300
84.17	187.59	1.10	1.55	1100–1300
76.63	194.84	3.42	4.45	1101–1130
75.86	195.18	5.51	7.15	1107–1130
83.54	92.43	8.67	13.71	1107–1150
73.14	189.77	2.30	3.10	1107–1150
77.95	170.74	5.32	7.30	1130–1180
88.11	109.05	10.74	15.28	1130–1180

Table A-1 (Continued)

Sample ID	Location	N_1/N_2	Demag	I	D	α_{95}
GN002	Kiva 2, Bench	10/10	10.0	66.31	341.91	37.3
EP001	Elden Pueblo, Rm. 7	9/8	15.0	56.16	347.82	3.8
LM001	Los Morteros, Trench 84	12/11	20.0	57.86	345.54	1.2
NS001	AZ:BB:13:74(ASM), Feat. 3	8/7	15.0	56.04	346.94	1.4
NS002	AZ:BB:13:74(ASM), Feat. 4	8/8	20.0	57.11	344.03	4.5
NS003	AZ:BB:13:74(ASM)	10/10	15.0	56.17	347.20	3.3
NS004	AZ:BB:13:74(ASM), Feat. 8	10/9	15.0	58.18	346.52	1.5
NS005	AZ:BB:13:74(ASM), Feat. 9	9/9	10.0	58.65	345.79	2.6
LM002	Los Morteros, Trench 40	9/9	15.0	55.82	349.56	1.2
WL001	Z:5:80, 18-4-13H	9/9	15.0	58.15	354.64	1.9
WO002	Z:5:80, 18-4-14H	9/7	15.0	52.01	347.34	3.5
WL003	Z:5:80, 18-3F-3H	8/6	15.0	56.03	355.25	1.4
WL007	Z:5:80, 10-5S-15H	9/8	15.0	55.74	351.98	1.7
WL005	Z:5:80, 10-4F-5H	10/10	15.0	57.45	353.31	1.5
WL006	Z:5:80, 10-4F-6H	9/9	15.0	54.96	350.35	2.0
MV002	Long House, Kiva 1	8/8	15.0	62.86	351.69	3.6
MV004	Long House, Kiva 2	9/9	20.0	64.23	354.26	4.1
CS004	AZ:U:9:105(ASM), Rm. 2	12/12	10.0	60.34	344.92	3.2
CS001	AZ:U:5:14(ASM), Str. 4	9/6	15.0	69.44	345.22	2.0
CS002	AZ:U:5:14(ASM), Str. 4	8/8	15.0	62.02	341.48	2.1
CS003	AZ:U:5:14(ASM), Str. 5	10/9	15.0	54.03	352.93	4.8
GN001	Grinnell College Site, Kiva 1, Bench	9/9	15.0	52.18	354.58	16.6
CH007	AZ:P:14:24(ASM), Feat. 1	11/10	10.0	59.52	353.15	3.7
CH008	AZ:P:14:24(ASM), Feat. 7	9/8	10.0	56.34	357.69	3.2
CH009	AZ:P:14:24(ASM), Feat. 3	11/9	15.0	56.89	354.68	4.3
CH005	AZ:P:14:24(ASM), Feat. 1	8/7	15.0	59.60	348.39	3.7
CH006	AZ:P:14:24(ASM), Feat. 2	10/8	15.0	60.70	352.34	6.4
GR008	AZ:P:14:8(ASM), Rm. 1	8/8	15.0	53.66	355.91	1.9
CH001	AZ:P:14:24(ASM), Feat. 1	9/9	15.0	58.76	351.32	2.3
MV003	Long House, Kiva H	11/9	15.0	64.12	349.61	2.1
GR002	Rm. 68, Feat. 12, Hearth 4	8/8	15.0	57.13	355.31	3.2
MV001	Long House, Kiva H	8/7	10.0	64.12	352.78	3.0
CH002	AZ:P:14:24(ASM), Rm. 2	9/9	15.0	59.53	352.94	2.3
CH003	AZ:P:14:24(ASM), Feat. 3	8/8	15.0	57.86	348.59	3.3
GR010	Grasshopper Pueblo, Rm. 113, Feat. 7	10/8	15.0	52.75	352.07	4.7
GR011	Grasshopper Pueblo, Rm. 113	8/8	10.0	56.32	357.40	4.3
GR012	Grasshopper Pueblo, Rm. 113, Feat. 12	10/10	20.0	60.37	352.27	3.2

VGP				
Plat	Plong	*dp*	*dm*	Age Range (Years A.D.)
72.56	208.20	50.20	61.15	1135–1300
80.04	170.50	3.98	5.53	1150–1200
76.72	190.77	1.34	1.82	1150–1250
78.35	185.11	1.48	2.05	1150–1250
75.79	186.52	4.76	6.53	1150–1250
78.50	186.04	3.46	4.81	1150–1250
77.14	194.34	1.65	2.23	1150–1250
76.41	195.16	2.89	3.89	1150–1250
80.50	186.93	1.24	1.74	1150–1350
82.35	218.91	2.05	2.77	1175–1275
79.34	166.02	3.32	4.85	1175–1275
84.37	209.39	1.41	1.96	1175–1275
82.39	193.86	1.74	2.43	1175–1300
82.23	209.39	1.63	2.23	1200–1300
81.47	185.04	2.03	2.87	1200–1300
80.59	212.17	4.39	5.60	1202–1300
80.29	227.13	5.28	6.61	1202–1300
75.74	196.57	3.67	4.84	1225–1350
67.89	225.16	2.90	3.39	1240–1300
72.68	198.18	2.51	3.23	1240–1300
84.08	169.72	4.68	6.68	1240–1300
83.71	117.75	15.64	22.82	1244–1300
81.72	210.27	4.19	5.58	1250–1272
86.62	216.26	3.31	4.58	1250–1272
84.52	198.95	4.49	6.18	1250–1272
78.81	197.28	4.17	5.54	1270–1300
80.30	213.16	7.45	9.77	1270–1300
86.61	162.90	1.90	2.72	1270–1300
81.21	199.75	2.58	3.46	1271–1300
78.44	212.66	2.71	3.40	1272–1300
84.72	204.73	3.39	4.65	1275–1325
79.87	211.60	3.38	4.81	1280–1300
81.59	209.55	2.56	3.41	1285–1300
79.81	188.36	3.53	4.81	1285–1300
83.36	155.09	4.45	6.45	1300–1325
86.48	213.16	4.48	6.21	1300–1325
80.52	211.55	3.68	4.85	1300–1325

Table A-1 (Continued)

Sample ID	Location	N_1/N_2	Demag	I	D	α_{95}
GR004	Grasshopper Pueblo, Rm. 115, Feat. 11	9/12	15.0	63.28	353.19	2.5
GR003	Grasshopper Pueblo, Rm. 68, Feat. 11, Hearth 2	9/9	15.0	60.50	1.24	2.3
RR001	AZ:AA:12:46(ASM), Ph. 3	9/9	15.0	54.68	2.32	2.7
CC001	AZ:V:2:1(ASM), Rm. 24A	8/6	10.0	56.75	358.61	3.6
CC002	AZ:V:2:1(ASM), Rm. 24B	8/9	15.0	56.10	354.61	4.5
CC004	AZ:V:2:1(ASM), Rm. 24A	8/7	15.0	50.55	14.36	14.2
CC003	AZ:V:2:1(ASM), Rm. 22B	11/10	15.0	57.04	350.87	4.7
GR001	Grasshopper Pueblo, Rm. Blk. 2, Oven 2	10/10	15.0	57.74	355.13	2.1
GR005	Grasshopper Pueblo, Rm. 25, Feat. 1	10/8	10.0	59.60	358.39	2.9
GR006	Grasshopper Pueblo, Rm. 309, Feat. 2	9/8	30.0	59.85	357.54	2.6
GR007	Grasshopper Pueblo, Rm. 25, Feat. 5	10/9	15.0	55.01	347.59	5.6
GR009	Grasshopper Pueblo, Rm. 312, Feat. 2	5/5	10.0	61.31	11.00	20.5
GP001	Gila Pueblo, Rm. 108A	11/8	15.0	57.02	357.93	1.3
CV001	NA15769, Str. 1, Feat. 1	8/8	15.0	61.16	1.90	3.9
SX001	AZ:BB:13:56(ASM), N Rm.	10/9	20.0	54.80	11.84	4.1

VGP				
Plat	Plong	*dp*	*dm*	Age Range (Years A.D.)
78.05	225.38	3.17	4.02	1300–1350
82.53	256.55	2.69	3.54	1300–1375
86.55	282.32	2.72	3.85	1300–1450
86.46	231.09	3.74	5.16	1334–1375
84.85	192.16	4.67	6.49	1334–1375
77.62	347.96	12.87	19.14	1334–1375
81.75	188.28	4.99	6.85	1335–1375
84.17	208.42	2.21	3.02	1350–1375
83.50	238.45	3.28	4.36	1350–1400
83.06	233.73	2.99	3.97	1350–1400
79.71	171.10	5.64	7.95	1350–1400
78.01	292.04	24.25	31.54	1350–1400
85.43	228.19	1.36	1.87	1385–1450
82.19	258.64	4.62	6.02	1400–1450
79.65	317.77	4.11	5.80	1906–1910

Table A-2. Archaeomagnetic Data from the Dolores Archaeological Program, 1978–1983

Sample ID	Location	N_1/N_2	Demag	I	D	α_{95}
5MT4545-2	Rm. 1, NNW wall	12/9	2.5	63.56	358.75	2.21
5MT4545-6	Rm. 3, floor	12/12	10.0	58.94	349.94	1.92
5MT4684-5	Ph. 5, hearth	12/11	5.0	55.92	4.48	1.93
5MT4684-1	Ph. 1, hearth	12/12	12.5	50.87	4.84	1.96
5MT4614-1	Ph. 1, hearth	12/12	2.5	54.96	1.26	1.72
5MT2151-13	Ph. 2, hearth	12/12	2.5	50.16	2.72	2.03
5MT4614-2	Ph. 2, hearth	12/9	2.5	50.47	2.23	2.38
5MT2853-1	Ph. 1, hearth	12/10	2.5	47.82	1.40	1.52
5MT4671-3	Ph. 2, hearth	12/11	5.0	46.73	2.11	2.04
5MT4644-8	Ph. 3, hearth	12/10	5.0	46.32	1.87	2.20
5MT4644-7	Feat. 126, hearth	12/12	5.0	64.35	4.26	3.24
5MT4644-9	Rm. 5, hearth	12/11	7.5	59.42	1.61	3.37
5MT0023-20	Ph. 19, hearth	12/12	5.0	53.57	0.20	2.99
5MT2193-18	Ph. 1, SE wall	12/12	2.5	53.51	5.94	3.46
5MT2193-2	Rm. 1, floor	12/12	15.0	53.10	359.49	2.15
5MT0023-102	Ph. 90, hearth	12/12	17.5	49.65	1.65	1.53
5MT4671-1	Rm. 1, Feat. 7	12/10	5.0	51.41	2.83	2.07
5MT4671-2	Rm. 2, Feat. 9	12/11	5.0	50.34	3.63	2.49
5MT2236-2	Ph. 1, hearth	12/12	2.5	55.68	2.98	2.25
5MT2192-4	Rm. 1, hearth	12/12	10.0	63.91	4.03	3.13
5MT4644-6	Ph. 2, hearth	12/12	10.0	55.74	3.39	3.46
5MT2181-1	Ph. 1, hearth	12/12	5.0	47.46	1.10	1.88
5MT4644-2	Ph. 2, hearth	12/11	10.0	46.46	6.04	1.32
5MT4644-3	Ph. 2, N wall	12/12	10.0	44.64	2.91	2.55
5MT2182-3	Ph. 1, E wall	12/12	5.0	43.68	1.57	2.51
5MT2848-2	Ph. 1, floor	12/12	7.5	45.12	5.91	1.28
5MT4644-1	Ph. 1, W wall	12/12	7.5	42.52	4.54	1.40
5MT4644-5	Ph. 1, N wall	12/12	7.5	40.59	3.89	1.65
5MT4512-3	Feat. 45, hearth	12/12	2.5	68.37	4.44	2.23
5MT4671-4	Ph. 1, hearth	12/11	5.0	48.60	3.38	2.12
5MT4671-5	Ph. 4, hearth	12/10	5.0	52.90	3.08	2.53
5MT4725-2	Ph. 1, hearth	12/12	5.0	52.22	3.66	2.19
5MT2182-2003	Rm. 202, hearth	12/12	5.0	55.54	3.89	2.47
5MT4650-1	Ph. 1, hearth	12/11	5.0	52.55	356.50	2.59
5MT4725-3	Ph. 2, hearth	12/12	5.0	52.01	8.54	3.48
5MT0023-14	Ph. 3, hearth 312	12/10	5.0	58.08	1.83	1.82
5MT4725-6	Ph. 5, hearth	12/11	5.0	55.65	4.45	2.28
5MT0023-13	Ph. 3, hearth 100	12/11	5.0	56.02	2.85	2.21
5MT0023-79	Ph. 65, hearth	12/12	10.0	53.63	5.42	1.74
5MT4480-1	Ph. 4, hearth	12/11	5.0	53.43	3.96	2.54

*An asterisk indicates a sample for which tree-ring dating is available.

VGP				
Plat	Plong	*dp*	*dm*	Age Range (Years A.D.)
82.30	244.94	2.77	3.50	620–680*
81.85	180.06	2.14	2.86	620–680*
86.27	356.49	1.99	2.78	670–730*
82.84	36.20	1.79	2.65	675–705*
87.73	44.62	1.73	2.44	695–755
82.94	52.13	1.82	2.71	720–780*
83.43	54.62	2.15	3.20	720–780
81.29	63.12	1.29	1.97	725–825
80.26	60.39	1.70	2.63	725–825
79.98	61.88	1.81	2.82	730–790*
80.81	270.24	4.14	5.18	750–820
87.02	275.92	3.79	5.05	750–820
86.54	68.72	2.91	4.17	750–850
84.03	15.90	3.36	4.82	760–785*
86.12	77.67	2.06	2.98	760–800*
82.78	60.09	1.35	2.03	760–800*
84.04	47.78	1.91	2.81	760–825
82.88	45.55	2.24	3.34	760–825
87.29	8.97	2.30	3.21	770–790*
81.38	270.56	3.96	4.97	775–825
87.02	5.06	3.55	4.95	780–800*
81.00	65.29	1.59	2.44	780–800*
78.98	42.30	1.09	1.69	780–800*
78.48	58.25	2.02	3.21	780–800*
76.94	96.20	1.57	2.51	790–810*
78.05	45.05	1.02	1.61	790–810*
76.53	53.45	1.07	1.73	800–840*
75.28	57.24	1.21	2.00	800–840*
75.59	262.55	3.17	3.76	800–860
81.53	51.03	1.83	2.79	800–860
85.21	38.94	2.42	3.50	825–910
84.43	37.83	2.06	3.00	845–875*
86.56	5.44	2.52	3.52	850–910*
84.72	105.18	2.46	3.57	850–910
81.47	13.91	3.25	4.76	850–910*
88.14	301.40	1.98	2.69	855–875*
86.20	0.53	2.33	3.26	855–910*
87.52	4.29	2.28	3.17	860–880*
84.45	17.53	1.69	2.42	860–890*
85.21	28.16	2.46	3.53	860–890*

Table A-2 (Continued)

Sample ID	Location	N_1/N_2	Demag	I	D	α_{95}
5MT0023-7	Ph. 6, hearth	12/12	2.5	56.85	2.28	2.34
5MT0023-8	Ph. 4, hearth	12/12	2.5	57.10	0.84	1.48
5MT0023-61	Ph. 39, E and S walls	12/12	5.0	57.13	4.21	1.87
5MT4479-3	Rm. 7, hearth	12/12	5.0	55.88	6.56	3.14
5MT4725-5	Ph. 6, hearth	12/12	5.0	48.58	5.21	2.77
5MT4480-4	Rm. 8, hearth	12/12	5.0	51.22	1.62	2.09
5MT2182-2004	Ph. 201, E wall	12/11	5.0	50.91	12.60	3.54
5MT4475-20	Ph. 5, hearth	12/11	5.0	52.31	4.68	1.71
5MT0023-4	Rm. 12, hearth	12/11	2.5	55.20	3.42	2.23
5MT0023-21	Ph. 10, N wall	12/12	5.0	49.54	2.67	1.39
5MT2320-1	Ph. 1, hearth	12/9	2.5	57.88	3.31	1.44
5MT4475-27	Ph. 7, hearth	12/12	5.0	51.00	5.62	3.02
5MT0023-18	Ph. 16, hearth	12/11	10.0	55.83	2.69	3.53
5MT0023-36	Ph. 51, hearth	12/12	10.0	54.85	3.37	2.69
5MT0023-9	Ph. 2, hearth	12/12	2.5	54.75	5.35	3.01
5MT5107-7	Ph. 2, W wall	12/11	5.0	56.20	359.50	2.19
5MT5107-8	Ph. 2, hearth	12/12	7.5	53.24	7.11	2.37
5MT0023-46	Ph. 27, N and E walls	16/16	10.0	53.27	6.99	2.23
5MT2182-2	Rm. 3, hearth	12/12	7.5	50.72	10.73	3.03
5MT0023-40	Ph. 45, hearth	12/11	10.0	57.46	359.53	2.98
5MT4479-1	Ph. 1, hearth	12/12	5.0	56.13	4.87	1.49
5MT4479-2	Ph. 2, hearth	12/12	15.0	52.47	3.45	2.30
5MT4475-14	Ph. 3, hearth	12/9	5.0	55.17	3.98	2.33
5MT4475-15	Ph. 3, hearth	12/10	10.0	54.06	2.87	1.12
5MT4475-16	Ph. 3, wing wall	12/12	15.0	47.57	9.30	1.73
5MT4475-18	Ph. 3, N wall	12/11	5.0	49.73	6.05	1.43
5MT4477-2	Ph. 2, W wall	12/12	7.5	52.16	6.63	1.72
5MT4475-28	Ph. 7, N wall	12/12	7.5	51.91	4.19	1.94
5MT0023-15	Ph. 13, floor	12/12	5.0	53.37	4.12	1.00
5MT0023-16	Ph. 13, W wall	12/12	5.0	54.22	12.77	3.18
5MT0023-68	Rm. 95, Feat. 1654	12/12	10.0	51.15	7.67	1.59
5MT0023-70	Rm. 95, Feat. 5711	12/12	10.0	48.50	7.35	1.71
5MT0023-90	Ph. 70, hearth	12/12	10.0	50.95	5.58	2.05
5MT4475-3	Ph. 3, S wall	10/8	15.0	53.73	3.82	3.01
5MT0023-24	Ph. 13, hearth	12/12	10.0	54.13	4.39	3.04
5MT4475-26	Ph. 7, hearth	12/12	10.0	49.67	3.61	2.89
5MT0023-19	Ph. 17, W wall	12/12	10.0	59.94	353.19	2.34
5MT0023-12	Ph. 11, hearth	12/10	5.0	58.81	4.60	1.73
5MT0023-29	Ph. 32, N wall	12/12	10.0	48.79	5.33	2.57
5MT0023-73	Ph. 32, W wall	8/8	10.0	51.32	6.21	1.42
5MT0023-2	Ph. 1, hearth	12/11	10.0	57.50	358.75	3.25
5MT0023-3	Ph. 1, W wall	12/12	12.5	55.20	356.14	1.50

| VGP | | | | Age Range |
Plat	Plong	*dp*	*dm*	(Years A.D.)
88.19	344.94	2.47	3.40	860–900*
89.32	330.15	1.57	2.16	860–900*
86.66	337.49	1.99	2.73	860–910*
84.65	351.32	3.23	4.50	860–910
80.91	41.45	2.40	3.65	860–910*
84.21	57.63	1.92	2.83	860–925*
78.07	7.50	3.23	4.80	865–885*
84.01	30.35	1.62	2.35	865–895*
86.69	14.30	2.26	3.17	865–915
82.48	53.58	1.23	1.85	870–890*
87.20	319.19	1.56	2.12	870–890
82.57	31.37	2.76	4.08	870–890*
87.54	9.74	3.63	5.06	870–900*
86.51	19.37	2.70	3.81	870–900*
85.12	7.92	3.02	4.26	870–910*
89.09	97.65	2.27	3.15	870–910*
83.10	12.25	2.29	3.30	870–910*
83.20	12.76	2.15	3.10	870–910*
79.27	12.93	2.75	4.08	870–910
89.36	215.86	3.19	4.36	870–910*
86.03	352.07	1.55	2.15	875–910
84.73	38.14	2.17	3.16	875–910
86.32	9.94	2.35	3.31	880–900*
86.27	32.18	1.10	1.58	880–900*
78.23	27.42	1.47	2.25	880–900*
81.42	33.99	1.27	1.91	800–900*
82.79	20.74	1.62	2.36	880–900*
83.95	35.67	1.81	2.65	880–900*
85.05	27.66	0.97	1.40	880–900*
79.32	352.93	3.14	4.47	880–900*
81.48	21.50	1.46	2.15	880–900*
79.85	32.24	1.47	2.24	880–900*
82.51	32.05	1.87	2.77	880–900*
85.52	26.59	2.94	4.20	880–900*
85.42	19.49	3.00	4.27	880–900*
82.37	47.37	2.56	3.84	880–900*
83.80	195.20	2.67	3.35	880–900*
85.89	311.11	1.91	2.57	880–900
80.99	40.46	2.23	3.38	890–910*
82.45	27.23	1.31	1.93	890–910*
88.86	191.39	3.49	4.76	890–920*
86.40	131.97	1.50	2.11	890–920*

Table A-3. Archaeomagnetic Data from Arkansas and Adjacent Areas

Sample ID	Location[a]	N_1/N_2	Demag	I	D	α_{95}
Archaeomagnetic data reported in Wolfman (1982)						
BM61	3CA9, Md. 3, hearth 1	8/7	5.0	58.6	2.6	2.4
ZB48	3MS20, Feat. 280	7/7	15.0	61.1	354.2	2.5
HZ50	3PO6, Stat. C, lower baked fl.	7/6	NRM	56.0	345.5	1.9
HZ51	3PO6, Stat. C, upper baked fl.	8/8	15.0	58.1	344.9	1.5
HZ53	3PO6, Stat. G, lower baked fl.	8/8	NRM	55.8	355.8	2.0
HZ54	3PO6, Stat. D, upper baked fl.	8/8	20.0	53.9	346.9	2.7
HZ56	3PO6, Stat. D, mid baked fl.	8/8	20.0	52.8	345.7	0.9
HZ58	3PO6, Stat. D, lower baked fl.	8/7	10.0	52.3	345.1	2.7
ZB49	3MS20, Feat. 282	9/8	30.0	56.2	345.9	3.2
EA89	3CL21, Feat. 1, Md. D	8/8	5.0	55.1	350.4	1.5
EA90	3CL21, Feat. 2, Md. B	8/8	10.0	57.7	357.1	1.6
HZ55	3PO6, Stat. G, lower hearth	5/5	20.0	58.0	356.7	2.5
HZ57	3PO6, Stat. B, baked fl.	8/6	NRM	53.2	346.7	1.4
HZ59	3PO6, Stat. E, baked fl.	8/8	NRM	54.2	346.5	3.2
BO94	3AS58, Feat. 2	8/8	80.0	44.8	334.6	5.5
FE02	3HE63, Feat. 49, Md. A	7/6	20.0	54.6	349.6	1.6
FE03	3HE63, Feat. 222, Md. A	8/7	15.0	53.6	352.9	1.7
GL20	3DR17, fl. at 74 cm	7/7	NRM	54.3	347.9	2.1
SL38	3UN52, Feat. 6	6/6	NRM	54.1	352.3	8.7
SL39	3UN52, Feat. 7	8/8	NRM	49.6	349.4	4.9
SL40	3UN52, Feat. 9	6/6	NRM	60.2	340.2	10.2
SL42	3UN52, Feat. 12	8/8	NRM	50.4	353.2	2.3
WF36	3UN18, Md. D, floor 1	6/6	NRM	54.2	349.9	5.5
LI64	23MN38, Area B, Str. B	8/7	20.0	59.8	355.1	2.1
BS28	3CL27, Feat. 7	8/8	NRM	57.6	22.3	22.3
ST43	3MN53, Feat. 8	8/8	30.0	56.6	358.8	2.4
ST45	3MN53, Feat. 12	8/7	30.0	59.7	353.0	2.5
ST67	3MN53, Feat. 17	6/6	15.0	59.0	358.1	2.8
ST68	3MN53, Feat. 12	8/7	20.0	52.4	349.3	1.8
ST70	3MN53, Feat. 17	8/8	NRM	58.4	352.4	1.6
MM91	3CL56, Feat. 1	7/7	5.0	56.9	356.0	1.4
AN93	3CL60, Feat. 1	8/8	NRM	57.9	356.6	3.4
HZ52	3PO6, Stat. G, upper baked fl.	8/8	NRM	55.9	357.7	3.6
HZ60	3PO6, Stat. G, upper hearth	8/7	NRM	46.2	0.3	5.5
AR05	3MS23, Feat. 28	6/6	15.0	57.4	349.6	3.4
AR06	3MS23, Feat. 27	8/8	NRM	41.6	10.0	15.8

[a]Provenience information is given in greater detail in Tables 14.1 and 14.2.
[b]The letter *p* following a stated age range indicates that the range is probable.

VGP				Estimated Date
Plat	Plong	*dp*	*dm*	(Years A.D.)
83.8	284.5	2.7	3.6	650–800
82.4	235.2	2.5	3.3	800–1000
78.2	188.9	2.0	2.7	1100–1350(p)[b]
77.5	199.5	1.6	2.2	1100–1350(p)
86.5	195.2	2.1	1.9	1100–1350(p)
79.2	177.7	2.6	3.8	1100–1350(p)
78.0	173.6	0.9	1.2	1100–1350(p)
77.4	172.2	2.6	3.7	1100–1350(p)
78.6	188.1	3.3	4.6	1100–1350
82.0	190.8	1.5	2.1	1100–1450
85.1	238.9	1.8	2.4	1100–1450
85.9	230.2	2.7	3.7	1100–1500
78.9	174.4	1.3	1.9	1100–1500
78.9	179.5	3.2	4.5	1100–1500
78.7	168.0	4.9	7.3	1200–1300
81.3	189.2	1.6	2.2	1200–1300
84.1	182.8	1.7	2.4	1200–1300
79.9	189.5	2.1	3.0	1200–1300
83.4	193.1	8.6	12.2	1200–1300
80.6	163.9	4.3	6.5	1200–1300
72.3	210.5	11.7	15.5	1200–1300
83.9	161.0	2.1	3.1	1200–1300
81.5	191.1	5.4	7.7	1200–1350
84.3	229.5	2.4	3.2	1200–1350(p)
71.6	337.6	24.0	32.7	1300–1400
87.1	246.8	2.5	3.5	1300–1400
81.7	226.8	2.9	3.8	1300–1400
84.4	251.6	3.1	4.2	1300–1400?
81.0	170.4	1.7	2.5	1300–1400?
82.3	216.3	1.8	2.4	1300–1400?
85.3	224.3	1.5	2.0	1300–1700
84.8	235.9	3.7	5.0	ca. 1350?
87.9	205.7	3.7	5.2	1350–1500(p)
82.0	87.7	4.5	7.0	1350–1500?
81.4	197.7	3.6	5.0	1350–1700
75.3	51.7	11.8	19.3	1350–1700

Table A-3 (Continued)

Sample ID	Location[a]	N_1/N_2	Demag	I	D	α_{95}
NA07	3MS23, Feat. 7	6/6	20.0	53.9	356.2	1.6
AM69	3MN62, Feat. 3	7/6	10.0	56.9	359.7	3.4
ST41	3MN53, Feat. 1	8/8	NRM	53.7	4.2	7.2
ST72	3MN53, Feat. 1	7/7	NRM	64.6	349.9	1.0
CH09	40SY1, Unit 5, Str. 1	8/8	30.0	55.5	1.6	2.7
HE25	3HS60, Unit 62:40, Feat. 5	8/7	15.0	54.1	6.3	3.0
BM21	3CA9, Md. 6, fl.	6/6	30.0	53.7	353.7	2.1
BS27	3CL27, Feat. 1	8/8	NRM	60.9	22.8	16.9
BS29	3CL27, Feat. 3	5/5	NRM	62.1	358.3	10.0
BS30	3CL27, Stat. 4, Feat. 3	7/7	NRM	58.1	0.4	7.0
BS31	3CL27, Feat. 3	7/7	NRM	52.2	359.9	7.6
BS32	3CL27, Strat. 5	7/6	NRM	56.8	352.3	2.7
BS33	3CL27, Strat. 5	6/6	NRM	57.7	2.7	4.5
BE92	3CL51, Feat. 1	7/7	NRM	57.9	354.1	1.9
KI14	3PI13, Temple Md.	8/7	NRM	57.8	349.0	3.5
BS37	3CL27, arroyo S of site	7/7	NRM	36.5	18.6	24.1

Archaeomagnetic data reported in this volume, chap. 14

CO125	16BI19, Sq. N20 W110	8/8	NRM	53.0	1.3	3.6
PM143	40MD1, Sq. N1000 E998	8/8	50.0	58.0	3.7	1.5
CT201	3CT50, Feat. 376	8/8	NRM	52.9	356.7	3.5
CT202	3CT50, Feat. 28 (Seg. B)	8/8	50.0	45.6	3.4	5.8
CT203	3CT50, Feat. 295	6/6	50.0	47.6	354.3	6.8
CT204	3CT50, Feat. 294	6/6	NRM	50.5	350.1	10.6
CT205	3CT50, Feat. 316	8/8	10.0	54.3	345.5	5.6
CT206	3CT50, Feat. 317	8/8	50.0	40.1	345.1	7.8
CT207	3CT50, Feat. 300	8/7	10.0	47.8	352.6	3.7
BL129	3CT98, Feat. 83	8/8	15.0	51.3	335.2	1.2
TO106	3LN42, Md. D	9/9	15.0	43.3	5.0	3.6
RM124	3AR30, Feat. 7	8/8	10.0	50.8	339.4	1.1
WA130	3CN117, Unit 9, Feat. 2	8/8	NRM	61.3	29.6	22.5
AL157	3CN117, Trench E, Feat. 20	8/8	30.0	45.2	4.7	0.9
HM131	3MA122, N42W0, Feat. 4	8/7	15.0	59.7	335.7	2.1
LI62	23NM38, Area A, Str. 1	8/8	70.0	55.2	346.8	1.2
HM151	3MA22, Units N42E0, N44E0	8/8	15.0	50.1	334.0	3.0
BM22	3CA9, Md. 1, Fl. 1	8/8	10.0	54.3	338.3	1.5
FE13	3HE63, Md. A, Feat. 345	8/8	NRM	54.1	350.8	2.3
LI63	23MN38, Area B, Str. 3	8/8	NRM	53.0	347.1	1.0
SL39	3UN52, Sq. 27, Feat. 7	8/7	50.0	51.2	354.0	2.6
CA19	3CL156, fl. at 71 cm	9/8	NRM	51.7	356.2	1.8

| VGP | | | | |
Plat	Plong	*dp*	*dm*	Estimated Date (Years A.D.)
86.6	156.0	1.6	2.2	1350–1700?
86.9	262.4	3.6	5.0	ca. 1450?
86.5	357.2	7.1	10.0	ca. 1450
75.7	237.2	1.3	1.6	ca. 1450
88.4	326.2	2.7	3.8	1450–1550
84.8	351.9	3.0	4.3	1450–1700
84.7	188.4	2.0	2.9	1500+
70.5	326.8	19.8	25.9	1500+?
80.6	259.5	12.1	15.5	1500+?
85.3	270.8	7.6	10.3	1500+?
88.7	92.0	7.1	10.4	1500+?
82.9	207.2	2.8	3.9	1500+?
85.2	293.6	4.8	6.6	1500+?
83.5	221.7	2.1	2.8	?
80.1	205.7	3.7	5.1	?
68.5	32.1	16.4	28.1	?
88.3	307.3	3.5	5.0	ca. 3000 B.C.?
85.4	310.1	1.7	2.2	100 B.C.–A.D. 400
86.7	146.0	3.3	4.8	400–700
81.2	69.0	4.7	7.4	400–700
81.8	127.4	5.8	8.9	400–700
80.8	156.3	9.6	14.2	400–700
78.1	181.8	5.6	7.9	400–700
72.0	139.8	5.7	9.5	400–700
81.0	136.2	3.1	4.8	400–700
69.2	178.0	1.1	1.6	700–900 or later
79.6	62.0	2.8	4.5	700–900
72.5	175.3	1.0	1.4	700–1000
66.0	330.9	26.5	34.5	700–900
80.6	60.4	0.8	1.2	700–900
70.1	196.5	2.4	3.2	ca. 1100
79.3	179.9	1.2	1.7	1100–1250
67.8	169.9	2.7	4.0	1125–1250
72.0	172.1	1.5	2.1	ca. 1150
82.3	185.7	2.3	3.3	1200–1300
79.0	168.6	1.0	1.4	1200–1300
84.8	165.3	2.4	3.6	1200–1300
86.3	149.3	1.6	2.4	1200–1450

Table A-3 (Continued)

Sample ID	Location[a]	N_1/N_2	Demag	I	D	α_{95}
TN17	Fl. at 81 cm	8/8	5.0	52.8	346.9	0.9
GS189	3BE245, Strat. VB	8/8	30.0	56.3	345.4	2.5
HM152	3MA22, Units N46W2, N48W2	8/8	15.0	58.1	354.8	1.5
MY110	3MI19, Feat. 3A	10/10	10.0	53.0	356.0	2.0
ST47	3MN53, Feat. 18	10/9	30.0	60.7	353.6	3.2
CH154	40SY1, Unit 6, House 3	8/8	40.0	54.2	0.5	2.1
SS95	3BR40, Feat. 1	8/8	5.0	52.1	345.8	4.6
AM71	3MN62, Feat. 6, Sq. N19W46	8/8	NRM	53.4	0.2	4.2
BS34	3CL27, Strat. 6A	8/8	50.0	56.7	357.7	2.4
ST44	3MN53, Feat. 1, N wall	10/10	5.0	62.5	358.2	4.5
BL66	3YE15, House 2, N Md.	8/8	NRM	54.7	351.1	5.3

VGP				Estimated Date
Plat	Plong	*dp*	*dm*	(Years A.D.)
79.1	177.0	0.9	1.3	1200–1500
78.3	181.6	2.6	3.6	ca. 1250
85.1	210.4	1.7	2.3	1250–1350
86.6	180.6	1.9	2.8	ca. 1300
81.1	233.8	3.7	4.8	1300–1350
89.4	49.2	2.1	3.0	1300–1600
78.1	177.4	4.3	6.3	1400–1500
89.5	63.1	4.1	5.9	ca. 1450
86.3	236.8	2.6	3.5	1400–1600
80.4	244.9	5.5	7.1	1450–1500
82.7	184.0	5.3	7.5	?

Table A-4. Archaeomagnetic Data from Mesoamerica

Sample ID	Location/Site[a]	N_1/N_2	Demag	I	D	α_{95}
Samples collected 1969–1972						
408	Feat. 69-27 Brawbehl	8/6	NRM	36.0	357.3	2.9
749	Feat. 3 Tomaltepec	8/8	NRM	39.2	0.2	2.5
754	Floor A5 Tomaltepec	8/6	NRM	35.1	359.4	1.7
587	46-33-358, Test pit ext. Kaminaljuyu	8/8	NRM	29.5	358.3	2.8
776	EP-1-1-4/4 El Portón	8/8	NRM	23.6	358.2	1.3
458	46-12-189, Lot 01 Kaminaljuyu	7/7	NRM	25.1	358.4	1.9
777	46-23-210, Md. D-III-6 Kaminaljuyu	8/8	NRM	42.8	9.2	2.5
778	46-23-210, Md. D-III-6 Kaminaljuyu	8/7	NRM	36.7	6.0	0.7
569	45 cm below top of md. Panteón	8/8	NRM	17.9	356.3	1.5
768	Lg quebrada at 4–5 m Tronconera 3	8/6	NRM	29.0	357.5	0.8
770	Lg quebrada at 4–5 m Tronconera 1	8/8	NRM	29.1	359.6	2.1
771	E of hacienda bldgs. Mango	8/8	NRM	27.6	357.9	1.6
478	46-23-103, Feat. 247 Kaminaljuyu	9/8	NRM	27.2	275.6	2.9
480	46-23-103, Feat. 261A Kaminaljuyu	9/9	NRM	38.8	305.9	3.5
482	46-23-103, Feat. 278 Kaminaljuyu	8/8	NRM	30.2	352.1	0.8
787	N rm. of Str. I-D Tazumál	8/7	NRM	24.9	357.6	0.6
783	N milpa, Sec. 2 Manzanillo	8/7	NRM	38.5	359.8	2.6
784	Sq. 55AA Manzanillo	8/8	NRM	39.0	2.8	0.8

[a]Provenience information is given in greater detail in Tables 15.1 and 15.4.
[b]The estimated date is the date range suggested by all chronological evidence aside from archaeomagnetic data.

VGP				Estimated
Plat	Plong	*dp*	*dm*	Date[b]
86.0	224.2	1.9	3.3	250 B.C.–A.D. 200
84.8	265.8	1.8	2.9	250 B.C.–A.D. 200
87.6	250.5	1.1	1.9	250 B.C.–A.D. 200
88.0	212.1	1.7	3.1	200 B.C.–A.D. 100
86.7	122.6	0.7	1.4	200 B.C.–A.D. 200
87.8	136.4	1.1	2.1	200 B.C.–A.D. 400
86.7	308.5	1.9	3.1	200 B.C.–A.D. 400 or A.D. 600–900
81.9	313.3	0.5	0.8	200 B.C.–A.D. 400 or A.D. 600–900
81.9	114.3	0.8	1.6	125 B.C.–A.D. 1 or 400–125 B.C.
86.7	224.2	0.5	0.9	100 B.C.–A.D. 100
87.7	262.1	1.3	2.3	100 B.C.–A.D. 100
87.6	215.2	0.9	1.7	100 B.C.–A.D. 100
8.9	192.2	1.7	3.2	A.D. 100–400
38.4	196.0	2.5	4.2	A.D. 100–400
82.2	192.0	0.5	0.9	A.D. 100–600
87.5	159.2	0.3	0.6	A.D. 300–600
87.3	258.6	1.8	3.1	A.D. 350–500
86.0	302.5	0.6	1.0	A.D. 350–500

Table A-4 (Continued)

Sample ID	Location/Site[a]	N_1/N_2	Demag	I	D	α_{95}
471	46-23-103, Feat. 255 Kaminaljuyu	9/9	NRM	34.8	300.6	9.8
476	46-23-103, Feat. 246B Kaminaljuyu	8/7	NRM	32.0	263.3	1.8
580	46-23-103, Feat. 246B Kaminaljuyu	6/6	NRM	22.1	278.2	1.5
541	Md. 88, Baked area No. 11 Monte Albán	16/14	NRM	30.4	354.6	2.6
744	Cerro Atzompa, Patio E Monte Albán	8/8	NRM	34.2	354.9	3.0
773	46-23-103, Md. C-II-14 Kaminaljuyu	12/12	NRM	27.2	341.2	3.0
317	Teopancaxco (TE-20) Teotihuacán	9/9	NRM	50.0	7.0	3.0
540	Viking Group Teotihuacán	9/9	NRM	40.2	3.9	3.3
564	Palace 3, Rm. 7 Teotihuacán	8/8	NRM	42.7	2.4	3.0
786	Viking Group Teotihuacán	8/8	NRM	41.1	2.1	3.1
584	46-23-000, Md. C-II-4 Kaminaljuyu	8/8	NRM	32.3	358.5	1.9
772	46-23-000, Md. C-II-4 Kaminaljuyu	8/7	NRM	32.3	358.6	0.7
470	46-23-103, Feat. 238 Kaminaljuyu	8/8	NRM	32.7	354.6	1.1
474	46-23-103, Feat. 30 Kaminaljuyu	8/7	NRM	28.4	354.4	0.6
477	46-23-103, Feat. 68 Kaminaljuyu	9/9	NRM	30.5	356.5	0.3
481	46-23-103, Feat. 279 Kaminaljuyu	7/7	NRM	24.7	344.2	2.6
483	46-23-103, Feat. 280 Kaminaljuyu	8/6	NRM	30.0	355.1	0.8
585	46-23-020, Md. C-II-4 Kaminaljuyu	8/7	NRM	22.7	353.8	2.0
596	Md. 2, Excav. A, Lev. 6 Cerro Zapotecas	8/8	NRM	30.4	0.7	1.9
766	Md. N side of S plaza San Andrés	8/7	NRM	8.9	3.3	1.2

VGP				Estimated
Plat	Plong	*dp*	*dm*	Date[b]
33.3	193.0	6.5	11.3	A.D. 400–500
−1.9	198.0	1.2	2.1	A.D. 400–500
10.7	188.7	0.8	1.6	A.D. 400–500
84.8	166.7	1.6	2.9	A.D. 400–700?
84.8	193.9	1.9	3.4	A.D. 400–700
71.8	181.0	1.8	3.3	A.D. 400–900
79.4	296.9	2.5	3.8	A.D. 425–600
85.2	309.1	2.4	4.0	A.D. 425–725
84.5	284.1	2.3	3.7	A.D. 425–725
85.7	287.4	2.3	3.8	A.D. 425–725
86.8	242.4	1.2	2.2	A.D. 500–550
86.9	244.2	0.4	0.8	A.D. 500–550
84.0	211.1	0.7	1.2	A.D. 500–600
84.6	184.7	0.3	0.6	A.D. 500–600
86.2	206.8	0.2	0.3	A.D. 500–600
74.6	175.0	1.5	2.8	A.D. 500–600
85.1	196.5	0.5	0.9	A.D. 500–600?
83.3	154.6	1.1	2.1	A.D. 500–600
87.3	66.9	1.2	2.1	A.D. 500–900
80.1	70.8	0.6	1.3	A.D. 600–800

Table A-4 (Continued)

Sample ID	Location/Site[a]	N_1/N_2	Demag	I	D	α_{95}
767	E platform of Str. 1 San Andrés	8/8	NRM	8.9	4.2	2.4
469	Md. B-V-11, top of md. Kaminaljuyu	10/9	NRM	8.7	358.9	0.6
472	46-23-103, Sq. 24N-41E Kaminaljuyu	9/9	NRM	19.6	348.1	2.9
473	46-23-103, Sq. 24N-41E Kaminaljuyu	8/8	NRM	30.0	331.8	3.7
479	46-23-103, Feat. 36 Kaminaljuyu	8/7	NRM	19.9	357.5	0.5
583	46-23-102, Feat. 273 Kaminaljuyu	11/11	NRM	12.6	1.6	1.6
586	46-23-020, Str. L, Feat. 1 Kaminaljuyu	8/8	NRM	16.7	358.8	3.9
774	46-23-103, Md. C-II-14 Kaminaljuyu	8/8	NRM	28.7	2.8	1.5
775	46-23-020, Str. L, Feat. 2 Kaminaljuyu	8/7	NRM	18.8	353.0	1.7
318	Feat. 68-24, Bldg. 195 sub Lambityeco	8/7	NRM	15.2	1.0	1.2
527	Area A, Feat. 11 Tierras Largas	8/8	NRM	15.3	355.4	2.1
529	Feat. 2, Hearth 1 Tierras Largas	8/8	NRM	16.9	354.8	1.9
539	Feat. 30, Rm. 2 Huapalcalco	8/8	NRM	24.2	358.8	1.9
563	Feat. 30, Wall 1 Huapalcalco	9/9	NRM	25.9	1.7	2.5
570	Wall in small md. Chachi	8/8	NRM	10.9	356.3	1.9
319	Feat. 69-2, Md. 190 Lambityeco	8/7	NRM	27.7	348.9	2.9
321	Mound 190 Lambityeco	8/7	NRM	29.8	348.3	2.7
407	Mound 190, Zone B Lambityeco	8/8	NRM	32.6	348.0	3.4
488	Tula 70, Test Pit 1 Tula	8/8	NRM	40.8	346.4	1.9
598	Tula 70, Unit 3, Feat. 3 Tula	9/9	NRM	34.6	344.1	2.4
415	Palacio Quemado, E Wall Tula	8/8	NRM	50.5	322.4	3.9

VGP				Estimated
Plat	Plong	*dp*	*dm*	Date[b]
79.8	66.3	1.2	2.4	A.D. 600–800
79.6	95.6	0.3	0.6	A.D. 600–900
77.5	159.2	1.6	3.0	A.D. 600–900
62.8	186.2	2.3	4.1	A.D. 600–900
84.9	118.8	0.2	0.5	A.D. 600–900
81.5	78.8	0.8	1.6	A.D. 600–900
83.7	100.1	2.1	4.0	A.D. 600–900
87.2	346.4	0.9	1.7	A.D. 600–900
81.5	144.0	0.9	1.8	A.D. 600–900
80.8	77.5	0.7	1.3	A.D. 700–800
79.7	109.4	1.1	2.1	A.D. 700–1200
80.2	114.9	1.0	2.0	A.D. 700–1200
82.5	90.4	1.1	2.1	A.D. 750–950
83.4	67.1	1.4	2.7	A.D. 750–950
78.5	105.9	1.0	1.9	A.D. 800–1000
79.1	163.8	1.7	3.1	A.D. 900–1200
78.7	170.7	1.6	3.0	A.D. 900–1200
78.5	179.6	2.1	3.8	A.D. 900–1200
76.9	188.0	1.4	2.3	A.D. 950–1200
74.9	170.2	1.6	2.8	A.D. 950–1200
54.5	194.8	3.5	5.2	A.D. 1150–1200

Table A-4 (Continued)

Sample ID	Location/Site[a]	N_1/N_2	Demag	I	D	α_{95}
440	Palacio Quemado, E Wall Tula	8/8	NRM	30.4	345.5	1.5
611	Palacio Quemado, E Wall Tula	8/8	NRM	34.4	345.0	1.2
612	Palacio Quemado, E Wall Tula	8/8	NRM	36.1	347.3	1.1
613	Palacio Quemado, E Wall Tula	9/7	NRM	35.7	346.4	2.5
785	Palacio Quemado, E Wall Tula	9/9	NRM	42.4	342.2	3.4
Samples collected since 1973						
AL85	Below Ilopango ash Altamira	10/10	20.0	32.5	354.7	2.1
CO186	CV30, Op. IX, Str. 191 Copán	8/8	NRM	32.7	0.9	1.9
CO102	PAC 78, Op. IV, Str. 71 Copán	6/6	NRM	24.6	357.3	1.7
TE170	Ciudadela, Conjunto 1D Teotihuacán	8/8	5.0	40.8	2.4	1.6
TE171	Ciudadela, Conjunto 1D Teotihuacán	8/8	5.0	39.1	3.0	0.6
TE172	Ciudadela, Conjunto 1D Teotihuacán	8/8	10.0	40.0	1.0	1.0
TE173	Unidad 11, Cuadro 85 Teotihuacán	8/8	15.0	40.6	2.2	0.9
TE176	Unidad Punto 36 Teotihuacán	6/6	NRM	43.3	5.4	3.6
CO188	CV30, Op. IX, Str. 191 Copán	8/8	10.0	25.6	354.0	2.6
SA158	Str. 7, near center San Andrés	9/9	30.0	22.6	357.0	2.7
CO100	PAC 78, Op. IV, Str. 99 Copán	5/5	15.0	30.8	357.6	2.0
CO183	CV36, Op. XV, Str. 95 Copán	8/7	15.0	17.1	359.3	1.4
CO185	CV36, Op. XV, Feat. 1 Copán	8/8	NRM	34.4	357.0	2.5
SA159	Str. 7, SW corner San Andrés	10/10	20.0	13.7	1.0	1.4

| VGP | | | | |
Plat	Plong	*dp*	*dm*	Estimated Date[h]
75.8	158.2	0.9	1.6	A.D. 1150–1200
75.8	169.4	0.8	1.4	A.D. 1150–1200
78.0	173.5	0.8	1.3	A.D. 1150–1200
77.2	172.5	1.7	2.9	A.D. 1150–1200
72.9	189.4	2.6	4.2	A.D. 1150–1200
83.5	219.4	1.3	2.4	ca. A.D. 119?
86.9	287.4	1.2	2.1	ca. A.D. 300
86.8	144.7	1.0	1.8	A.D. 300–600
85.7	291.9	1.1	1.9	A.D. 425–725
86.3	309.3	0.4	0.7	A.D. 425–725
86.8	277.9	0.7	1.2	A.D. 425–725
85.9	291.5	0.7	1.1	A.D. 425–725
82.5	302.0	2.8	4.5	A.D. 425–725
84.0	168.0	1.5	2.8	ca. A.D. 600
86.4	146.6	1.5	2.8	ca. A.D. 600
87.1	219.1	1.2	2.2	A.D. 600–740
83.8	96.5	0.8	1.5	A.D. 600–800
85.0	235.4	1.7	2.9	A.D. 600–800
83.1	82.2	0.7	1.4	A.D. 600–800

Table A-5. Directional Data and Pole Positions from Experimental Hearths

Sample ID	Location Lat (N)	Long (E)	N_1/N_2	Demag	I	D
Samples reported in Krause (1980)						
K1	40.58	254.86	12/12	NRM	69.29	14.46
K2	40.58	254.86	12/12	NRM	69.08	13.05
K3	40.58	254.86	12/12	NRM	68.44	13.17
Samples reported in Hathaway (1982)						
H1	37.53	251.45	12/12	NRM	64.47	12.57
H2	37.53	251.45	12/12	NRM	65.54	10.05
H3	37.53	251.45	12/12	NRM	64.53	8.78
H4	37.52	251.43	12/12	NRM	64.28	11.99
H5	37.52	251.43	12/12	NRM	66.06	9.87
H6	37.52	251.43	12/12	NRM	64.47	12.90
H7	37.55	251.46	12/12	NRM	62.43	10.14
H8	37.55	251.46	12/12	NRM	64.92	11.92
H9	37.55	251.46	12/12	NRM	63.67	11.12
H10	37.52	251.45	12/12	NRM	65.24	13.25
H11	37.52	251.45	12/12	NRM	65.88	15.22
H12	37.52	251.45	12/12	NRM	65.00	7.79
Samples reported in Smith (1981)						
S1	40.35	255.35	12/12	NRM	64.37	24.78
S2	40.35	255.35	12/12	NRM	64.84	29.75
S3	40.35	255.35	12/12	NRM	62.39	20.00
S4	40.35	255.35	12/12	NRM	68.04	13.40
S5	40.35	255.35	11/11	NRM	59.11	18.38
S6	40.35	255.35	12/12	NRM	65.78	20.12
S7	40.35	255.35	10/10	NRM	65.22	15.34
S8	40.35	255.35	10/10	NRM	61.71	15.09
S9	40.35	255.35	9/9	NRM	66.66	14.69
S10	40.35	255.35	12/12	NRM	65.76	16.69
S11	40.35	255.35	12/12	NRM	62.58	14.19
S12	40.35	255.35	12/12	NRM	71.19	15.20

α_{95}	VGP		dp	dm
	Plat	Plong		
3.87	74.25	288.56	5.63	6.60
2.35	75.05	286.97	3.40	4.00
3.30	75.68	289.69	4.70	5.57
1.57	77.20	294.17	2.01	2.51
1.38	77.44	284.15	1.82	2.24
2.16	79.01	284.96	2.77	3.46
1.32	77.66	293.83	1.68	2.11
3.27	76.97	281.76	2.61	3.19
2.16	77.02	294.77	2.78	3.47
2.05	80.13	299.33	2.49	3.19
2.89	77.17	290.94	3.75	4.65
2.70	78.64	294.98	3.39	4.28
3.08	76.20	292.11	4.04	4.99
3.09	74.64	292.85	4.12	5.05
4.09	78.92	280.22	5.32	6.60
7.88	71.13	319.15	10.09	12.61
5.13	67.66	318.68	6.65	8.26
7.47	74.81	325.99	9.09	11.65
4.88	75.78	291.69	6.87	8.18
6.41	75.96	341.26	7.16	9.58
4.00	73.73	310.53	5.31	6.51
6.78	76.98	308.12	8.87	10.97
6.12	78.45	327.67	7.31	9.46
5.74	76.36	300.00	7.81	9.47
2.91	75.84	307.12	3.87	4.75
2.03	78.90	321.84	2.48	3.17
4.66	71.64	283.30	7.10	8.13

References Cited

Acosta, J. R.
  1967   Una Clasificación Tentativa de los Monumentos Arqueológicos de Teotihuacán. In *Teotihuacán: XI Mesa Redonda*, 1:45–55. Sociedad de Antropología Mexicana, Mexico City.
  1972   El Epílogo de Teotihuacán. In *Teotihuacán: XI Mesa Redonda*, 2:149–156. Sociedad Mexicana de Antropología, Mexico City.

Adams, R. M.
  1966.   *The Evolution of Urban Society*. Aldine, Chicago.

Aitken, M. J.
  1961a   Measurement of the Magnetic Anomaly. *Archaeometry* 4:28–30.
  1961b   *Physics and Archaeology*. Interscience, New York.
  1970   Dating by Archaeomagnetic and Thermoluminescent Methods. *Philosophical Transactions of the Royal Society of London* 269:77–88.
  1974   *Physics and Archaeology*. 2d ed. Clarendon Press, Oxford.

Aitken, M. J., P. A. Alcock, G. D. Bussell, V. Jones, and C. J. Shaw
  1981   Geomagnetic Intensity as a Dating Parameter for Pottery. Paper presented at the 10th Congress, International Union of Prehistoric and Protohistoric Sciences, Oct. 19–24. Mexico City.

Aitken, M. J., A. L. Allsop, G. D. Bussell, and M. B. Winter
  1984   Geomagnetic Intensity in Egypt and Western Asia During the Second Millennium B.C. *Nature* 310:305–306.

Aitken, M. J., M. R. Harold, and G. H. Weaver
  1964   Some Archaeomagnetic Evidence Concerning the Secular Variation in Britain. *Nature* 201:659–660.

Aitken, M. J., and H. N. Hawley
  1966   Magnetic Dating—III: Further Archaeomagnetic Measurements in Britain. *Archaeometry* 9:187–197.
  1967   Magnetic Dating—IV: Further Archaeomagnetic Measurements in Britain. *Archaeometry* 10:129–135.
  1971   Archaeomagnetism: Evidence for Magnetic Refraction in Kiln Structures. *Archaeometry* 13:83–85.

Aitken, M. J., and G. H. Weaver
  1962   Magnetic Dating: Some Archaeomagnetic Measurements in Britain. *Archaeometry* 5:4–22.

Andrews, E. W.
  1965   Archaeology and Prehistory in the Northern Maya Lowlands: An
          Introduction. In *Handbook of Middle American Indians*, vol. 2,
          edited by G. R. Willey, 288–330. University of Texas Press, Austin.
Andrews V, E. W.
  1978   Endnote: The Northern Maya Lowlands Sequence. In *Chronolo-
          gies in New World Archaeology*, edited by R. E. Taylor and C. W.
          Meighan, 377–381. Academic Press, New York.
Anthropology Newsletter
  1978   NSF Funding for Anthropology October 1, 1976, to September 30,
          1977. *Anthropology Newsletter* 19(3): 9–11.
Aramaki, S., and S. Akimoto
  1957   Temperature Estimation of Pyroclastic Deposits by Natural Rem-
          anent Magnetism. *American Journal of Science* 255:619–627.
Armillas, P.
  1944   Exploraciones Recientes en Teotihuacán, México. *Cuadernos
          Americanos* 16(4): 121–136.
  1950   Teotihuacán, Tula, y Los Toltecas: Las Culturas Post-Arcaicas y
          Pre-Aztecas del Centro de México: Excavaciones y Estudios,
          1922–1950. *RUNA* 3:37–70.
As, J. A., and J.D.A. Zijderveld
  1958   Magnetic Cleaning of Rocks in Paleomagnetic Research. *Geophys-
          ical Journal of the Royal Astronomical Society* 1:308–319.
Asami, E., K. Tokieda, and T. Kishi
  1972   Archaeomagnetic Study of Kilns in San-in and Kyushu, Japan.
          *Memoirs of the Faculty of Literature and Science, Shimane Uni-
          versity, Natural Sciences* 5:18–22.
Babbage, C.
  1838   On the Age of Strata, as Inferred from the Rings of Trees Embedded
          in Them. In *The Ninth Bridge-Water Treatise: A Fragment*. Note
          M, pp. 256–264. J. Murray, London. Reprinted in *Man's Discovery
          of His Past: Literary Landmarks in Archaeology*, edited by R. F.
          Heizer, 48–51. Prentice-Hall, Englewood Cliffs, N.J., 1962.
Barbetti, M.
  1976   Archaeomagnetic Analyses of Six Glozelian Ceramic Artifacts.
          Journal of Archaeological Science 3:137–151.
  1977   Measurements of Recent Geomagnetic Secular Variation in
          Southeastern Australia and the Question of Dipole Wobble. *Earth
          and Planetary Science Letters* 36:207–218.
Barbetti, M., J. D. Clark, F. M. Williams, and M.A.J. Williams
  1980   Palaeomagnetism and the Search for Very Ancient Fireplaces in
          Africa. *Anthropologie* 18 (2–3): 299–304.
Barbetti, M., and M. W. McElhinny
  1976   The Lake Mungo Geomagnetic Excursion. *Philosophical Transac-
          tions of the Royal Society of London* A281:515–542.
Barbetti, M. F., M. W. McElhinny, D. J. Edwards, and P. W. Schmidt
  1977   Weathering Processes in Baked Sediments and Their Effects on

Archaeomagnetic Field Intensity Measurements. *Physics of the Earth and Planetary Interiors* 13:346–354.

Barraclough, D. R.
1974   Spherical Harmonic Analyses of the Geomagnetic Field for Eight Epochs Between 1600 and 1910. *Geophysical Journal of the Royal Astronomical Society* 36:497–513.

Barton, C. E., and R. T. Merrill
1983   Archaeo- and Paleosecular Variation, and Long-Term Asymmetries of the Geomagnetic Field. *Reviews of Geophysics and Space Physics* 21:603–614.

Bauer, L. A.
1896   On the Secular Motion of a Free Magnetic Needle, II. *Physical Review* 3:34–48.
1908   *U.S. Magnetic Tables and Magnetic Charts for 1905.* U.S. Department of Commerce and Labor, Coast and Geodetic Survey, Washington, D.C.

Baumgartner, E. P.
1973   Magnetic Properties of Archeomagnetic Materials. Master's thesis, University of Oklahoma, Norman.

Beck, M. E., Jr.
1983   Comment on "Determination of the Angle of a Fisher Distribution Which Will Be Exceeded with a Given Probability," by P. L. McFadden. *Geophysical Journal of the Royal Astronomical Society* 75:847–849.
1985   Reply to Comments of McFadden and Fisher. *Geophysical Journal of the Royal Astronomical Society* 80:285–286.

Becker, H.
1979   Archaeomagnetic Investigations in Anatolia from Prehistoric and Hittite Sites (First Preliminary Results). *Archaeo-Physika* 10:382–387.

Bell, R. E. (ed.)
1984   *Prehistory of Oklahoma.* Academic Press, New York.

Belmont, J. S.
1982   The Troyville Concept and the Gold Mine Site. In *The Troyville-Baytown Period in Lower Mississippi Valley Prehistory: A Memorial to Robert Stuart Neitzel*, edited by J. L. Gibson. *Louisiana Archaeology* 9:65–98.

Belshé, J. C., K. Cook, and R. M. Cook
1963   Some Archaeomagnetic Results from Greece. *Annual of the British School at Athens* 58:8–13.

Bennett, W. C.
1948   The Peruvian Co-tradition. In *A Reappraisal of Peruvian Archaeology*, edited by W. C. Bennett. Society for American Archaeology Memoir, no. 4, pp. 1–7. Menasha, Wis.

Bennyhoff, J. A.
1967   Chronology and Periodization: Continuity and Change in the Teotihuacán Ceramic Tradition. In *Teotihuacán: XI Mesa Redonda*,

1:19–27. Sociedad de Antropología Mexicana, Mexico City.

Berlin, H.
1947 Ensayo Sincronológico. In *Historia Tolteca-Chichimeca: Anales de Quauhtinchan*, prepared and annotated by H. Berlin and S. Rendon. Fuentes para la Historia de México, no. 1. Mexico City.

Bernal, I.
1965 Teotihuacán: Nuevas Fechas de Radiocarbono y su Posible Significado. *Anales de Antropología* 2:27–35.

Berry, K. J., P. W. Mielke, and K. L. Kvamme
1982 Efficient Permutation Procedures for Analyses of Artifact Distributions. In *Intrasite Spatial Analyses in Archaeology*, edited by H. Hietala and P. Larson, 54–74. Cambridge University Press, London.

Blackett, P.M.S.
1952 A Negative Experiment Relating to Magnetism and the Earth's Rotation. *Philosophical Transactions of the Royal Society of London* A250:309–370.

Blanton, R. E.
1978 *Monte Albán Settlement Patterns at the Ancient Zapotec Capital.* Academic Press, New York.

Blinman, E.
1984 *Dolores Archaeological Program Dating Justification and Procedures.* Dolores Archaeological Program Technical Report DAP-144. U.S. Bureau of Reclamation, Upper Colorado Region, Salt Lake City, Utah.

Boas, F.
1913 Archaeological Investigations in the Valley of Mexico by the International School, 1911–1912. *Proceedings of the 18th International Congress of Americanists*, pt. 2, pp. 176–179. London.

Boggs, S. H.
1972 Preclassic Underground Ovens of Usulután, El Salvador. Paper presented at the 37th Annual Meeting of the Society for American Archaeology, Bal Harbour, Fla.

Boyle, R.
1691 *Experimenta & Observationes Physicae.* Printed for J. Taylor and J. Wyat, London.

Breternitz, D. A.
1967 The Eruption(s) of Sunset Crater: Dating and Effects. *Plateau* 40:72–76.

Browman, D. L.
1981 Isotopic Discrimination and Correction Factors in Radiocarbon Dating. In *Advances in Archaeological Method and Theory*, edited by M. B. Schiffer, 4:241–295. Academic Press, New York.

Brown, F. H., and R. T. Shuey
1976 Magnetostratigraphy of the Shungura and Usno Formations, Lower Omo Valley, Ethiopia. In *Earliest Man and Environments in the Lake Rudolf Basin*, edited by Y. Coppens, F. Clark Howell, G. L.

Isaac, and R.E.F. Leakey. University of Chicago Press, Chicago.

Brown, J. A.
1984   *Prehistoric Southern Ozark Marginality: A Myth Exposed*. Missouri Archaeological Society Special Publications, no. 6. Columbia, Mo.

Bryant, V. M.
1974   The Role of Coprolite Analysis in Archeology. *Bulletin of the Texas Archaeological Society* 45:311–342.

Brynjolfsson, A.
1957   Studies of Remanent Magnetism and Viscous Magnetism in the Basalts of Iceland. *Advances in Physics* 6:247–254.

Bryson, R. A., and W. M. Wendland
1967   Tentative Climatic Patterns for Some Late Glacial and Postglacial Episodes in Central North America. In *Life, Land, and Water*, edited by W. J. Mayer-Oakes, 271–298. University of Manitoba Press, Winnipeg.

Bucha, V.
1967   Intensity of the Earth's Magnetic Field During Archaeological Times in Czechoslovakia. *Archaeometry* 10:12–22.
1971   Archaeomagnetic Dating. In *Dating Techniques for the Archaeologist*, edited by H. N. Michael and E. K. Ralph, 57–117. MIT Press, Cambridge, Mass.

Bucur, I.
1984   XIVth Century Archaeomagnetic Field Directions from Geographically Distributed Sites in France. Paper presented at the 1984 Archaeometry Symposium, Washington, D.C.

Bunker, F. F.
1938   Cooperative Research, Its Conduct and Interpretation. In *Cooperation in Research*, by Staff Members and Research Associates of the Carnegie Institution of Washington, 713–752. Carnegie Institution of Washington Publication, no. 501. Washington, D.C.

Burlatskaya, S. P.
1972   Secular Geomagnetic Field Variations, According to Archaeomagnetic and Paleomagnetic Data. *Geomagnetism and Aeronomy* 12:582–592. English translation.

Burlatskaya, S. P., and I. Ye. Nachasova
1978   Reliability of the Periods of Secular Geomagnetic Field Variations According to Archaeomagnetic Data. *Geomagnetism and Aeronomy* 18:488–490. English translation.

Burlatskaya, S. P., I. Ye. Nachasova, and K. S. Burakov
1977   New Determinations of the Parameters of the Ancient Geomagnetic Field for Mongolia, Soviet Central Asia, and Abkhasia. *Geomagnetism and Aeronomy* 16:447–450. English translation.

Burlatskaya, S. P., and G. N. Petrova
1961a   The Archaeomagnetic Method of Studying Changes of the Geomagnetic Field of the Past. *Geomagnetism and Aeronomy* 1:104–112. English translation.

1961b   First Results from an Archaeomagnetic Study of the Past Geomagnetic Field. _Geomagnetism and Aeronomy_ 1:262–267. English translation.

1961c   First Results of a Study of the Geomagnetic Field in the Past by the "Archeomagnetic" Method. _Geomagnetism and Aeronomy_ 1:233–236. English translation.

1961d   Restoration of the Past Secular Variations of the Geomagnetic Field by the Archeomagnetic Method. _Geomagnetism and Aeronomy_ 1:383–386. English translation.

Burns, P. K.
1981   Magnetic Reconnaissance in the Dolores Archaeological Program. Master's thesis, Department of Anthropology, University of Nebraska, Lincoln.

Butzer, K. W.
1982   _Archaeology as Human Ecology._ Cambridge University Press, Cambridge.

Cabrera, R., I. Rodriguez, and N. Morelos (comps.)
1982   _Memoria del Proyecto Arqueológico Teotihuacán 80–82._ Colección Científica 132, vol. 1. Instituto Nacional de Antropología e Historia. Mexico City.

Carlson, J. B.
1977   The Case for Geomagnetic Alignments of Pre-Columbian Mesoamerican Sites: The Maya. _Katunob_ 10(2): 67–88.

Caso, A.
1949   El Mapa de Teozacoalco. _Cuadernos Americanos_ 7(5): 3–40.

Chamberlin, R. T.
1928   Some of the Objections to Wegener's Theory [abs.]. Paper presented to the American Association of Petroleum Geologists, Tulsa, Okla.

Champion, D. E.
1980   _Holocene Geomagnetic Secular Variation in the Western United States: Implications for the Global Geomagnetic Field._ U.S. Geological Survey Open-File Report 80-824. Washington, D.C.

Chapman, C. H.
1975   _The Archaeology of Missouri, I._ University of Missouri Press, Columbia.

1980   _The Archaeology of Missouri, II._ University of Missouri Press, Columbia.

Chase, A. F.
1985   Time Depth or Vacuum: The 11.3.0.0.0 Correlation and the Lowland Maya Post Classic. In _Late Lowland Maya Civilization: Classic to Postclassic,_ edited by J. A. Sabloff and E. W. Andrews V, 99–140. University of New Mexico Press, Albuquerque.

Cheek, C. D.
1977a   Excavations at the Palangana and the Acropolis, Kaminaljuyu. In _Teotihuacán and Kaminaljuyu: A Study in Prehistoric Culture_

Contact, edited by W. T. Sanders and J. W. Michels, 1–204. Pennsylvania State University Press, University Park.

1977b   Teotihuacán Influence at Kaminaljuyu. In *Teotihuacán and Kaminaljuyu: A Study in Prehistoric Culture Contact,* edited by W. T. Sanders and J. W. Michels, 441–452. Pennsylvania State University Press, University Park.

Chelidze, Z. A.
1966   Some Results of a Study of the Past Geomagnetic Field in the Georgian SSR by the Archeomagnetic Method. *Geomagnetism and Aeronomy* 6:744–746. English translation.

Chelishvili, M. L.
1971   Some Archeomagnetic Problems. *Geomagnetism and Aeronomy* 11:321–323. English translation.

Chevallier, R.
1925   L'Aimantation des Laves de l'Etna et l'Orientation du Champ Terrestre en Sicile du XIIe au XVIIe Siècle. *Annales de Physique,* ser. 10, 4:5–162.

Clark, A. J., D. H. Tarling, and M. Noel
1988   Developments in Archaeomagnetic Dating in Britain. *Journal of Archaeological Sciences* 15:645–667.

Clark, D. L.
1961   The Application of the Obsidian Dating Method to the Archaeology of Central California. Ph.D. diss., Stanford University, Stanford, California.

1964   Archaeological Chronology in California and the Obsidian Hydration Method. In *Annual Report of the Archaeological Survey,* 143–211. University of California, Los Angeles.

Clark, R. M.
1975   A Calibration Curve for Radiocarbon Dates. *Antiquity* 49:251–266.

Clark, R. M., and R. Thompson
1978   An Objective Method for Smoothing Paleomagnetic Data. *Geophysical Journal of the Royal Astronomical Society* 52:205–213.

Coe, R. S.
1979   The Effect of Shape Anisotropy on TRM Direction. *Geophysical Journal of the Royal Astronomical Society* 56:369–383.

Collinson, D. W.
1967   Chemical Demagnetization. In *Methods in Palaeomagnetism,* edited by D. W. Collinson, K. M. Creer, and S. K. Runcorn, 306–310. Elsevier, Amsterdam.

1975   Instruments and Techniques in Paleomagnetism and Rock Magnetism. *Reviews of Geophysics and Space Physics* 13:659–686.

1977   Experiments Relating to the Measurement of Inhomogeneous Remanent Magnetism in Rock Samples. *Geophysical Journal of the Royal Astronomical Society* 48:271–275.

1983   *Methods and Techniques in Palaeomagnetism.* Chapman and Hall, New York.

Collinson, D. W., and K. M. Creer
1960   Measurements in Palaeomagnetism. In *Methods and Techniques in Geophysics,* edited by S. K. Runcorn, 1:168–210. Interscience, New York.
1983   *Methods in Rock Magnetism and Paleomagnetism.* Chapman and Hall, London.

Collinson, D. W., K. M. Creer, and S. K. Runcorn (eds.)
1967   *Methods in Palaeomagnetism.* Developments in Solid Earth Geophysics. Elsevier, Amsterdam.

Cook, R. M., and J. C. Belshé
1958   Archaeomagnetism: A Preliminary Report on Britain. *Antiquity* 32:167–178.

Cox, A.
1961   *Anomalous Remanent Magnetization of Basalts.* U.S. Geological Survey Bulletin, no. 1083E, pp. 131–160.

Cox, A. (ed.)
1973   *Plate Tectonics and Geomagnetic Reversals.* W. H. Freeman, San Francisco.

Cox, A., and R. R. Doell
1960   *Review of Paleomagnetism.* Geological Society of America Bulletin, no. 71, pp. 645–768.

Cox, A., R. R. Doell, and G. B. Dalrymple
1963   Geomagnetic Polarity Epochs and Pleistocene Geochronometry. *Nature* 198:1049–1051.
1964   Reversals of the Earth's Magnetic Field. *Science* 144:1537–1543.

Creer, K. M.
1959   A.C. Demagnetization of Unstable Triassic Keuper Marls from S.W. England. *Journal of Geophysics* 2:216–275.
1977   Geomagnetic Secular Variations During the Last 25,000 Years: An Interpretation of Data Obtained from Rapidly Deposited Sediments. *Geophysical Journal of the Royal Astronomical Society* 48:91–109.

Creer, K. M., E. Irving, A.E.M. Nairn, and S. K. Runcorn
1958   Palaeomagnetic Results from Different Continents and Their Relation to the Problem of Continental Drift. *Annual of Geophysics* 15:492–501.
1959   Palaeomagnetic Results from Different Continents and Their Relation to the Problem of Continental Drift. In *Paleomagnetism et Variation Séculaire,* IAGA Bulletin, no. 16a. Paris.

Creer, K. M., and P. Tucholka
1983   Epilogue. In *Geomagnetism of Baked Clays and Recent Sediments,* edited by K. M. Creer, P. Tucholka, and C. E. Barton, 273–306. Elsevier, Amsterdam.

Creer, M., P. Tucholka, and C. E. Barton (eds.)
1983   *Geomagnetism of Baked Clays and Recent Sediments.* Elsevier, Amsterdam.

Culbert, T. P.
1977   Early Maya Development at Tikal, Guatemala. In *The Origins of Maya Civilization*, edited by R.E.W. Adams, 27–43. University of New Mexico Press, Albuquerque.

Damon, P. E.
1968   Radiocarbon and Climate. *Meteorological Monographs* 8:151–154.

Damon, P. E., C. W. Ferguson, A. Long, and E. I. Wallick
1974   Dendrochronologic Calibration of the Radiocarbon Time Scale. *American Antiquity* 39:350–366.

Daniels, F., C. A. Boyd, and D. F. Saunders
1953   Thermoluminescence as a Research Tool. *Science* 117:343–349.

Davies, N.
1977   *The Toltecs Until the Fall of Tula.* University of Oklahoma Press, Norman.

Davis, H. (ed.)
1982   *A State Plan for the Conservation of Archeological Resources in Arkansas.* Arkansas Archeological Survey Research Series, no. 21. Fayetteville.

Dean, J. S.
1969   *Chronological Analysis of Tsegi Phase Sites in Northeastern Arizona.* Papers of the Laboratory of Tree-Ring Research, no. 3. University of Arizona, Tucson.

1978   Independent Dating in Archaeological Analysis. In *Advances in Archaeological Method and Theory*, vol. 1, edited by M. B. Schiffer, pp. 223–255. Academic Press, New York.

Dicks, A. M., and C. S. Weed
1986   Radiocarbon Dates. In *Archaeological Investigations of the Little Cypress Bayou Site (3CT50), Crittenden County, Arkansas*, edited by A. M. Dicks and C. S. Weed, Appendix 15. New World Research, Inc., Report of Investigations, no. 82-21.

Diehl, R. A.
1981   Tula. In *Supplement to the Handbook of Middle American Indians.* Vol. 1: *Archaeology*, edited by J. A. Sabloff, 277–295. University of Texas Press, Austin.

Diehl, R. A. (ed.)
1974   *Studies of Ancient Tollan: A Report of the University of Missouri Tula Archaeological Project.* University of Missouri Monographs in Anthropology, no. 1. Columbia.

Dodson, M. H., and E. McClelland-Brown
1980   Magnetic Blocking Temperatures of Single-Domain Grains During Slow Cooling. *Journal of Geophysical Research* 85:2625–2637.

Dodson, R. E.
   1979   Counterclockwise Precession of the Geomagnetic Field Vector and Westward Drift of the Non-dipole Field. *Journal of Geophysical Research* 84:637–644.
Dodson, R. E., and D. Wolfman
   1983a   Archeomagnetic Secular Variation in Peru. Paper presented at the American Geophysical Union Fall Meeting, San Francisco, December 5–9.
   1983b   Los Resultados Arqueomagnéticos de las Muestras Recogidas en el Perú en 1982. Report submitted to the Instituto Nacional de Cultura, Lima, Peru.
Doell, R. R., and A. Cox
   1963   The Accuracy of the Paleomagnetic Method as Evaluated from Historical Hawaiian Lava Flows. *Journal of Geophysical Research* 68:1997–2009.
Douglass, A. E.
   1909   Weather Cycles in the Growth of Big Trees. *Monthly Weather Review* 37:225–237.
   1914   A Method of Estimating Rainfall by the Growth of Trees. In *The Climatic Factor*, edited by E. Huntington, 101–122. Carnegie Institution of Washington Publication, no. 192. Washington, D.C.
   1919   *Climatic Cycles and Tree Growth.* Carnegie Institution of Washington Publication, no. 289. Washington, D.C.
Downey, W. S., and D. H. Tarling
   1984   Archaeomagnetic Dating of Santorini Volcanic Eruptions and Fired Destruction Levels of Late Minoan Civilization. *Nature* 309:519–523.
Drennan, R. D.
   1983   Radiocarbon Dates from the Oaxaca Region. In *The Cloud People: Divergent Evolution of the Zapotec and Mixtec Civilizations*, edited by K. V. Flannery and J. Marcus, 363–370. Academic Press, New York.
DuBois, P. M.
   1962   Paleomagnetism and Correlation of Keweenawan Rocks. *Geological Survey Canada Bulletin*, no. 71, p. 75.
DuBois, R. L.
   1975a   *Development of an Archeomagnetic Chronology.* Research proposal submitted to the National Science Foundation.
   1975b   Recent developments in the Archaeomagnetic Dating Program. Paper presented at the 40th Annual Meeting of the Society for American Archaeology, Dallas.
   1975c   Secular Variation in Southwestern U.S.A. as Suggested by Archaeomagnetic Results. In *Proceedings of the Takesi Nagata Conference: Magnetic Fields, Past and Present*, edited by R. M. Fisher, M. Fuller, V. A. Schmidt, and P. J. Wasilewski, 133–144. Goddard Space Flight Center, Greenbelt, Md.

1977a   Archeomagnetic Dating of Archeological Sites. Final Report (Contract No. CX-1595-4-0194), 1974–75. Interagency Archeological Services, Denver.

1977b   Dating of Archeological Sites by Archeomagnetic Methods. Final Report (Contract No. CX-1494-4-0430), 1975–76. Interagency Archeological Services, Denver.

1982   Some Archaeomagnetic Results and Their Analysis: Southwestern United States and Mesoamerica [abs.]. *EOS: Transactions of the American Geophysical Union* 63:650.

1989   Archaeomagnetic Results from the Southwest United States and Mesoamerica, and Comparison with Some Other Areas. *Physics of the Earth and Planetary Interiors* 56:18–33.

DuBois, R. L., and D. Wolfman

1970a   Archaeomagnetic Dating in Mesoamerica and Peru. Paper presented at the 39th Meeting of the International Congress of Americanists, Lima, Peru.

1970b   Archeomagnetic Dating in the New World. Paper presented at the 35th Annual Meeting of the Society for American Archaeology, Mexico City.

1971   Recent Archeomagnetic Results for the United States. Paper presented at the 36th Annual Meeting of the Society for American Archaeology, Norman, Okla.

Dunlop, D. J.

1972   Magnetic Mineralogy of Unheated and Heated Red Sediments by Coercivity Spectrum Analysis. *Geophysics* 27:37–55.

1975   Rock Magnetism: Basis of the Paleomagnetic Record. In *Proceedings of the Takesi Nagata Conference, Magnetic Fields: Past and Present*, edited by R. M. Fisher, M. Fuller, V. A. Schmidt, and P. J. Wasilewski, 58–80. Goddard Space Flight Center, Greenbelt, Md.

Dunlop, D. J., and M. B. Zinn

1980   Archeomagnetism of a 19th Century Pottery Kiln near Jordan, Ontario. *Canadian Journal of Earth Sciences* 17:1275–1285.

Eckstein, D., J. Ogden, G. C. Jacoby, and J. Ash

1981   Age and Growth Rate Determination in Tropical Trees: The Application of Dendrochronological Methods. In *Age and Growth Rate of Tropical Trees*, edited by F. H. Bormann and G. Berlyn, 83–106. Yale University, School of Forestry and Environmental Studies Bulletin, no. 94. New Haven, Conn.

Eighmy, J. L.

1980a   Archaeomagnetists Agree on Reporting Procedure. *Society for Archaeological Sciences Newsletter* 4(1): 1–2.

1980b   *Archaeomagnetism: A Handbook for the Archaeologist*. U.S. Department of the Interior, Interagency Archeological Services, Heritage Conservation and Recreation Service, no. 58, Washington, D.C.

Eighmy, J. L., and H. Hathaway
1987 Contemporary Archaeomagnetic Results and the Accuracy of Archaeomagnetic Dates. *Geoarchaeology* 2:49–61.
Eighmy, J. L., J. H. Hathaway, and A. E. Kane
1982 An Evaluation of the Dolores Modification of the Southwest Archaeomagnetic Curve. Paper presented at the 47th Annual Meeting of the Society for American Archaeology, Minneapolis.
Eighmy, J. L., R. S. Sternberg, and R. F. Butler
1978 Recent Archaeomagnetic Results from the Southwest. Paper presented at the 43d Annual Meeting of the Society for American Archaeology, Tucson, Arizona.
1980 Archaeomagnetic Dating in the American Southwest. *American Antiquity* 45:507–517.
Einarsson, Tr., and T. Sigurgeirsson
1955 Rock Magnetism in Iceland. *Nature* 197:892.
Engebretson, D. C., and M. E. Beck, Jr.
1978 On the Shape of Directional Data. *Journal of Geophysical Research* 83:5979–5982.
Erickson, J. E.
1981 *Exchange and Production Systems in California Prehistory.* British Archaeological Report, International Series, no. 110. Oxford.
Fabiano, E. B., and N. W. Peddie
1975 *Magnetic Declination in the United States: Epoch 1975.* U.S. Department of the Interior, Geological Survey. Reston, Va.
Fabiano, E. B., N. W. Peddie, D. R. Barraclough, and A. K. Zunde
1983 *International Geomagnetic Reference Field 1980: Charts and Grid Values.* IAGA Bulletin, no. 47; and U.S. Department of the Interior, Geological Survey Circular, no. 873. Washington, D.C.
Fisher, N. I.
1985 Comments on M. E. Beck's Comment on "Determination of the Angle in a Fisher's Distribution Which Will Be Exceeded with a Given Probability," by P. L. McFadden. *Geophysical Journal of the Royal Astronomical Society* 80:283–284.
Fisher, N. I., T. Lewis, and M. E. Wilcox
1981 Tests of Discordancy for Samples from Fisher's Distribution on the Sphere. *Journal of the Royal Statistical Society*, ser. C: Applied Statistics, 30:230–237.
1983 Comment on "Rejection of Paleomagnetic Observations," by P. L. McFadden. *Earth and Planetary Science Letters* 64:316–317.
Fisher, R. A.
1953 Dispersion on a Sphere. *Proceedings of the Royal Society of London* A217:295–305.
Flannery, K. V.
1965 The Ecology of Early Food Production in Mesopotamia. *Science* 147:1247–1255.
1977 Review of *The Valley of Mexico*, edited by E. R. Wolf. *Science* 196:759–761.

Fleming, S.
1976   *Dating in Archaeology.* J. M. Dent, London.
Folgerhaiter, G.
1896   Ricerche sull' Inclinazione Magnetica all' Epoca Etrusca. *Rendiconti della R. Accademia dei Lincei* 5:293–300.
1897a   Sulla Forza Coercitiva dei Vasi Etruschi. *Rendiconti della R. Accademia dei Lincei* 6:64–70.
1897b   La Magnetizzazione dell' Argilla Colla Cottura in Relazione Colle Ipotesi Sulla Fabbricazione del Vasellame Nero Estrusco. *Rendiconti della R. Accademia dei Lincei* 6:368–376.
1899   Sur les Variations Séculaires de l'Inclinaison Magnétique dans l'Antiquité. *Archives des Sciences Physiques et Naturelles* 8:5–16.
Foster, J. H.
1966   A Paleomagnetic Spinner Magnetometer Using a Fluxgate Gradiometer. *Earth and Planetary Science Letters* 1:463–466.
Fox, J.M.W., and M. J. Aitken
1980   Cooling-Rate Dependence of Thermoremanent Magnetisation. *Nature* 283:462–463.
Freidman, L., and R. L. Smith
1958   The Deuterium Content of Water in Some Volcanic Glasses. *Geochimica et Cosmochimica Acta* 15:218–228.
1960   A New Dating Method Using Obsidian; Part I: The Development of the Technique. *American Antiquity* 25:476–522.
Fritz, G. J.
1979   Mounds in the Ozarks of Northwest Arkansas. Paper presented at the 21st Annual Caddo Conference, Arkadelphia, Ark.
1986   Mounds in Northwest Arkansas: A More Positive Approach to the Late Prehistoric in the Ozarks. In *Contributions to Ozark Prehistory*, edited by G. Sabo III, 49–54. Arkansas Archeological Survey Research Series, no. 27.
Fuson, R. H.
1969   The Orientation of Mayan Ceremonial Centers. *Annual of the Association of American Geographers* 59:494–511.
Games, K. P.
1977   The Magnitude of the Palaeomagnetic Field: A New Non-thermal, Non-detrital Method Using Sun-Dried Bricks. *Geophysical Journal of the Royal Astronomical Society* 48:315–329.
1979   Short Period Fluctuations in the Earth's Magnetic Field. *Nature* 277:600–601.
1980   The Magnitude of the Archaeomagnetic Field in Egypt Between 3000 and 0 BC. *Geophysical Journal of the Royal Astronomical Society* 63:45–56.
1983   Magnetization of Adobe Bricks. In *Geomagnetism of Baked Clays and Recent Sediments*, edited by K. M. Creer, P. Tucholka, and C. E. Barton, 22–28. Elsevier, Amsterdam.
Gamio, M.
1913   Arqueología de Azcapotzalco, D.F., México. *Proceedings of the*

18th International Congress of Americanists, pt. 2, pp. 180–193. London.

Garrison, E. G.
  1973   Alpha-Recoil Track Dating and Its Potential Application to Archeological Age Determination. Master's thesis, University of Arkansas, Fayetteville.

Garrison, E. G., C. R. McGimsey, and O. H. Zinke
  1978   Alpha-Recoil Tracks in Archeological Ceramic Dating. *Archaeometry* 20:39–46.

Gheradi, S.
  1862   Sul Magnetismo Polare de Palazzi ed Altri Edifizi in Torino. *Il Nuovo Cimento* 16:384–404.

Gifford, J. C., and R. J. Sharer
  1970   Preclassic Ceramics from Chalchuapa, El Salvador, and Their Relationships with the Maya Lowlands. *American Antiquity* 35:441–462.

Gilbert, W.
  1958   *De Magnete.* Translated by P. F. Mottely, 1893. Dover, New York. Originally published 1600.

Glen, W.
  1982   *The Road to Jaramillo.* Stanford University Press, Stanford, Calif.

Goree, W. S., and M. Fuller
  1976   Magnetometers Using RF-driven Squids and Their Applications in Rock Magnetism and Palaeomagnetism. *Reviews of Geophysics and Space Physics* 14:591–608.

Gough, D. I.
  1964   A Spinner Magnetometer. *Journal of Geophysical Research* 69:2455–2463.

Goulpeau, L., and L. Langouet
  1980   Datations d'Apports de Tuiles et Briques sur des Sites Galloromains à l'Aide de Mesures Archaéomagnétiques Opérées sur d'Abondants Échantillonnages. *Revue d'Archéométrie* 4:153–164.
  1982   Étude Archéomagnétique du Grand Caldarium du Champ Mulon à Corseul. *Dossiers du Centre Regional Archéologique d'Alet* 10:41–46.

Gowlett, J.A.J., R.E.M. Hedges, I. A. Law, and C. Perry
  1987   Radiocarbon Dates from the Oxford AMS System: Archaeometry Date List 5. *Archaeometry* 29:125–155.

Graham, J. W.
  1955   Evidence of Polar Shift Since Triassic Time. *Journal of Geophysical Research* 60:329–347.

Graham, J. W., A. F. Buddington, and J. R. Balsley
  1957   Stress-induced Magnetizations of Some Rocks with Analyzed Magnetic Minerals. *Journal of Geophysical Research* 62:465–474.

Graham, K.W.T.
  1961   The Re-magnetization of a Surface Outcrop by Lightning Cur-

rents. *Geophysical Journal of the Royal Astronomical Society* 6:85–102.

Grisso, J. M.
1978   An Analysis of Some Secondary Magnetizations of Baked Clay. Master's thesis, University of Oklahoma, Norman.

Grubbs, F. E.
1969   Procedures for Detecting Outlying Observations in Samples. *Technometrics* 11:27–58.

Halgedahl, S. L., R. Day, and M. Fuller
1980   The Effect of Cooling Rate on the Intensity of Weak-Field TRM in Single-Domain Magnetite. *Journal of Geophysical Research* 85:3690–3698.

Halley, E.
1692   An Account of the Cause of the Change of the Variation of the Magnetic Needle; With an Hypothesis of the Structure of the Internal Part of the Earth. *Philosophical Transactions of the Royal Society of London* 17:563–578.

Hallimond, A. F., and E. F. Herroun
1933   Laboratory Determinations of the Magnetic Properties of Certain Igneous Rocks. *Proceedings of the Royal Society of London* A141:302–314.

Hammer, C. U., H. B. Clausen, and W. Dansgaard
1980   Greenland Ice Sheet Evidence of Post-glacial Volcanism and Its Climatic Impact. *Nature* 288:230–235.

Hargrave, M. L., G. A. Oetelaar, N. H. Lopinot, B. M. Butler, and D. A. Billings
1983   *The Bridges Site (11-Mr-11): A Late Prehistoric Settlement in the Central Kaskaskia Valley.* Southern Illinois University at Carbondale Center for Archaeological Investigations Research Paper, no. 38.

Harold, M. R.
1960   Magnetic Dating: Kiln Wall Fallout. *Archaeometry* 24:45–46.

Harrison, C.G.A., and T. B. Lindh
1981   Comparison of Paleomagnetic and Sea Floor Spreading Data. *EOS: Transactions of the American Geophysical Union* 62:853.

1982   A Polar Wandering Curve for North America During the Mesozoic and Cenozoic. *Journal of Geophysical Research* 87:1903–1920.

Hathaway, J. H.
1982a   Archaeomagnetic Sampling Program. In *Analysis*, vol. 6. Dolores Archaeological Program Technical Reports. U.S. Department of the Interior, Bureau of Reclamation, Salt Lake City.

1982b   Simulated Hearth Experiments: An Archaeomagnetic Approach. Master's thesis, Colorado State University, Fort Collins.

Hathaway, J. H., and J. L. Eighmy
1982   Analysis—1979: Archaeomagnetism. In *Analysis*, vol. 6. Dolores Archaeological Program Technical Reports. U.S. Department of the Interior, Bureau of Reclamation, Salt Lake City.

Hathaway, J. H., J. L. Eighmy, and A. E. Kane
    1983   Preliminary Modification of the Southwest Virtual Geomagnetic
            Pole Path, A.D. 700 to A.D. 900: Dolores Archaeological Program
            Results. *Journal of Archaeological Science* 10:51–59.
Haury, E. W.
    1976   *The Hohokam: Desert Farmers and Craftsmen.* University of Ari-
            zona Press, Tucson.
Heizer, R. F.
    1951   Long-Range Dating in Archeology. In *Anthropology Today*, edited
            by S. Tax, 3–42. University of Chicago Press, Chicago.
Hester, T., R. F. Heizer, and J. A. Graham
    1975   *Field Methods in Archaeology.* Mayfield Publishing Co., Palo
            Alto, Calif.
Hewitt, N. J.
    1983   Excavation at Sagehill Hamlet (Site 5MT2198), a Basketmaker III-
            Pueblo I Habitation Site. In *Dolores Archaeological Program:
            Field Investigations and Analysis, 1978*, 103–138. U.S. Depart-
            ment of the Interior, Bureau of Reclamation, Salt Lake City.
Hirooka, K.
    1971   Archaeomagnetic Study for the Past 2,000 Years in Southwest
            Japan. *Memoirs of the Faculty of Science, Kyoto University, Series
            on Geology and Mineralogy* 38:167–207.
    1983   Results from Japan. In *Geomagnetism of Baked Clays and Recent
            Sediments*, edited by K. M. Creer, P. Tucholka, and C. E. Barton,
            150–157. Elsevier, Amsterdam.
Holcombe, R., D. E. Champion, and M. McWilliams
    1986   Dating Recent Hawaiian Lava Flows Using Paleomagnetic Secular
            Variation. *Geological Society of America Bulletin* 7:829–839.
Hole, F.
    1982   Finding Problems for All the Solutions. In *Future Directions in
            Archaeometry: A Round Table*, edited by J. S. Olin, 80–84. Smith-
            sonian Institution, Washington, D.C.
Hopwood, A.
    1913   The Magnetic Materials in Claywares. *Proceedings of the Royal
            Society of London* A89:21–30.
Hospers, J.
    1953   Reversals of the Main Geomagnetic Field, I, II. *Koninklijke Neder-
            landse Akademie van Wetenschappen, Proceedings*, ser. B,
            56:457–491.
    1954   Reversals of the Main Geomagnetic Field, III. *Koninklijke Neder-
            landse Akademie van Wetenschappen, Proceedings*, ser. B,
            57:112–121.
House, J. H.
    1985   Summary and Conclusions. In *The Alexander Site*, edited by E. T.
            Hemmings and J. H. House, 99–110. Arkansas Archeological Sur-
            vey Research Series, no. 24.

Hoye, G. S.
1981   Archaeomagnetic Secular Variation Record of Mount Vesuvius. *Nature* 291:216–218.
1982   A Magnetic Investigation of Kiln Wall Distortion. *Archaeometry* 24:80–84.

Huang, W. H., and R. M. Walker
1967   Fossil Alpha-Particle Recoil Tracks: A New Method of Age Determination. *Science* 155:1103–1106.

Hunt, C. B.
1972   *Geology of Soils: Their Evolution, Classification, and Uses.* W. H. Freeman and Co., San Francisco.

Irving, E.
1964   *Palaeomagnetism and Its Application to Geological and Geophysical Problems.* John Wiley, New York.

Irving, E., W. A. Robertson, P. M. Stott, D. H. Tarling, and M. A. Ward
1961   Treatment of Partially Stable Sedimentary Rocks Showing Planar Distribution of Directions of Magnetization. *Journal of Geophysical Research* 66:1927–1933.

Irving, E., P. M. Stott, and M. A. Ward
1961   Demagnetization of Igneous Rocks by Alternating Magnetic Fields. *Philosophical Magazine* 6:225–241.

Ising, G.
1942   On the Magnetic Properties of Varved Clay. *Arkiv fer Matematik, Astronomi och Fysik* 29A(5): 1–37.

Jacoby, G. D.
1981   Case Study 3: Dating High-Altitude Tropical Conifers. In *Age and Growth Rate of Tropical Trees,* edited by F. H. Bormann and G. Berlyn, 92–97. Yale University, School of Forestry and Environmental Studies, Bulletin No. 94. New Haven, Conn.

Jeffreys, H.
1924   *The Earth: Its Origin, History and Physical Constitution.* Cambridge University Press, Cambridge.
1929   *The Earth: Its Origin, History and Physical Constitution.* 2d ed. Cambridge University Press, Cambridge.

Jiménez Moreno, W.
1941   Tula y los Toltecas Según las Fuentes Históricas. *Revista Mexicana de Estudios Antropológicos* 5:79–83.
1954–   Síntesis de la Historia Precolonial del Valle de México. *Revista*
1955   *Mexicana de Estudios Antropológicos* 14:219–236.

Johnsen, S. J., W. Dansgaard, H. B. Clausen, and C. C. Langway, Jr.
1972   Oxygen Isotope Profiles Through the Antarctic and Greenland Ice Sheets. *Nature* 235:429–434.

Johnson, E. A.
1938   The Limiting Sensitivity of an Alternating-Current Method of Measuring Small Magnetic Moments. *Review of Scientific Instruments* 9:263–266.

Johnson, E. A., T. Murphy, and O. W. Torreson
  1948   Pre-history of the Earth's Magnetic Field. *Terrestrial Magnetism and Atmospheric Electricity* 53:359–372.
Johnson, F., and R. S. MacNeish
  1972   Chronometric Dating. In *The Prehistory of the Tehuacan Valley*, edited by R. S. MacNeish, 4:3–55. University of Texas Press, Austin.
Johnson, F., and E. S. Willis
  1970   Reconciliation of Radiocarbon and Sidereal Years in Meso-American Chronology. In *Radiocarbon Variations and Absolute Chronology*, edited by I. U. Olsson, 93–104. John Wiley and Sons, New York.
Kane, A. E.
  1984   The Prehistory of the Dolores Project Area. In *Dolores Archaeological Program: Synthetic Report, 1978–1981*, 21–51. U.S. Department of the Interior, Bureau of Reclamation, Salt Lake City.
Kaucher, C. D.
  n.d.   Maya Chronology and the Conjunction of Mars. Unpublished manuscript in possession of the author; referred to in Kelley 1983.
Kawai, N., K. Hirooka, S. Sasajima, K. Yaskawa, H. Ito, and S. Kume
  1964   Archaeomagnetic Studies in Southwestern Japan. *1964 Annual Progress Report of the Rock Magnetism Research Group in Japan*, 39–43.
Kawai, N., K. Hirooka, and K. Tokieda
  1967   A Vibration of Geomagnetic Axis Around the Geographic North Pole in the Historic Time. *Earth and Planetary Science Letters* 3:48–50.
Kelley, D. H.
  1950   A History of Pre-Spanish Meso-America: A Brief Summary and Analysis of Available Documentary Materials. Senior honors thesis, Harvard University, Cambridge, Mass.
  1976   *Deciphering the Maya Script*. University of Texas Press, Austin.
  1983   The Maya Calendar Correlation Problem. In *Civilization in the Ancient Americas*, edited by R. M. Leventhal and A. L. Kolata, 157–208. University of New Mexico Press, Albuquerque.
Kelley, D. H., and K. A. Kerr
  1973   Mayan Astronomy and Astronomical Glyphs. In *Mesoamerican Writing Systems*, edited by E. P. Benson, 179–215. Dumbarton Oaks, Washington, D.C.
Kent, D. V., and W. Lowrie
  1974   Origin of Magnetic Instability in Sediment Cores from the Central North Pacific. *Journal of Geophysical Research* 79:2987–3000.
Kern, J. W.
  1961   Effects of Moderate Stresses on Directions of Thermoremanent Magnetization. *Journal of Geophysical Research* 66:3802–3806.

Kidder, A. V., J. D. Jennings, and E. M. Shook
1946   *Excavations at Kaminaljuyu, Guatemala.* Carnegie Institution of Washington Publication, no. 561. Washington, D.C.

Kidder, A. V., and J. E. Thompson
1938   The Correlation of Maya and Christian Chronologies. In *Cooperation in Research*, by Staff Members and Research Associates of the Carnegie Institution of Washington. Carnegie Institution of Washington Publication, no. 501, pp. 493–510. Washington, D.C.

King, R. F., and A. E. Rees
1962   The Measurement of the Anisotropy of Magnetic Susceptibility of Rocks by the Torque Method. *Journal of Geophysical Research* 67:1565–1572.

Kirchoff, P.
1943   Mesoamérica. *Acta Americana* 1:92–107.
1950   The Mexican Calendar and the Founding of Tenochtitlan-Tlaltelolco. *Transactions of the New York Academy of Sciences* 12:126–132.
1954–   Calendarios Tenochca, Tlaltelolco y Otros. *Revista Mexicana de*
1955   *Estudios Antropológicos* 14:257–267.
1955   Quetzalcoatl, Huemac y el Fin de Tula. *Cuadernos Americanos* 14:163–196.

Kirschvink, J. L.
1981   A Quick, Non-acidic Chemical Demagnetization Technique for Dissolving Ferric Minerals. *EOS: Transactions of the American Geophysical Union* 62:84.

Kitazawa, K., and K. Kobayashi
1968   Intensity Variation of the Geomagnetic Field During the Past 4000 Years in South America. *Journal of Geomagnetism and Geoelectricity* 20:7–19.

Klein, J., J. C. Lerman, P. E. Damon, and E. K. Ralph
1982   Calibration of Radiocarbon Dates: Tables Based on the Consensus Data of the Workshop on Calibrating the Radiocarbon Time Scale. *Radiocarbon* 24:103–150.

Klinger, T. C., S. M. Imhoff, and R. J. Cochran, Jr.
1983   *Brougham Lake.* Historic Preservation Associates Reports 83-7. Fayetteville, Ark.

Kobayashi, K.
1959   Chemical Remanent Magnetization of Ferromagnetic Minerals and Its Application to Rock Magnetism. *Journal of Geomagnetism and Geoelectricity* 90:99–117.

Koenigsberger, J. G.
1938   Natural Residual Magnetism of Eruptive Rocks, Parts I and II. *Terrestrial Magnetism and Atmospheric Electricity* 43:119–127, 299–330.

Kovacheva, M.
1969   Inclination of the Earth's Magnetic Field During the Last 2000

Years in Bulgaria. *Journal of Geomagnetism and Geoelectricity* 21:573–578.

1980   Summarized Results of the Archaeomagnetic Investigation of the Geomagnetic Field Variation in the Last 8000 Years in Southeastern Europe. *Geophysical Journal of the Royal Astronomical Society* 61:57–64.

1988   Archaeomagnetism as a Dating Method. Paper presented at the 1988 International Symposium on Archaeometry, May 1988. Toronto.

Kovacheva, M., and D. Veljovich
1977   Geomagnetic Field Variations in Southeastern Europe Between 6500 and 100 Years B.C. *Earth and Planetary Science Letters* 37:131–138.

Kovacheva, M., and G. Zagniy
1985   Archaeomagnetic Results from Some Prehistoric Sites in Bulgaria. *Archaeometry* 27:179–184.

Krause, G. J.
1980   An Experimental Approach Toward Refining Archaeomagnetic Dating Techniques. Master's thesis, Colorado State University, Fort Collins.

Kuhn, T. S.
1962   *The Structure of Scientific Revolutions.* University of Chicago Press, Chicago.

Kulp, J. L., H. W. Feely, and L. E. Tryon
1951   Lamont Natural Radiocarbon Measurements, I. *Science* 114:565–568.

LaMarche, V. C., Jr., and K. K. Hirschboeck
1984   Frost Rings in Trees as Records of Major Volcanic Eruptions. *Nature* 304:121–126.

Lange, R. C., and B. A. Murphy
1989   *Project Data for 312 Archaeomagnetic Samples.* Colorado State University Archaeometric Laboratory, Technical Series, no. 2. Colorado State University, Fort Collins.

Langouet, L., I. Bucur, and L. Goulpeau
1983   Les Problemes de l'Allure de la Courbe de Variation Séculaire du Champ Magnétique Terrestre en France: Nouveaux Resultats Archéomagnétiques. *Revue d'Archéométrie* 7:37–43.

Larochelle, A.
1967a   *A Re-examination of Certain Statistical Methods in Palaeomagnetism.* Geological Survey of Canada, paper 67-17. Ottawa.

1967b   *Further Considerations on Certain Statistical Methods in Palaeomagnetism.* Geological Survey of Canada, paper 67-26. Ottawa.

Lee, S.
1975   Secular Variation of the Intensity of the Geomagnetic Field During the Past 3000 Years in North, Central, and South America. Ph.D. diss., University of Oklahoma.

Leng, J.
1955   Thermal Demagnetization of Triassic New Red Sandstone. Master's thesis, University of London.

Lentner, M.
1972   *Elementary Applied Statistics*. Bogden and Quigley, Tarrytown-on-Hudson, N. Y.

Lewis, T., and N. I. Fisher
1982   Graphical Methods for Investigating the Fit of a Fisher Distribution to a Sample of Spherical Data. *Geophysical Journal of the Royal Astronomical Society* 69:1–13.

Libby, W. F.
1949   *Radiocarbon Dating*. University of Chicago Press, Chicago.
1955   *Radiocarbon Dating*. 2d ed. University of Chicago Press, Chicago.

Libby, W. F., E. C. Anderson, and J. R. Arnold
1949   Age Determination by Radiocarbon Content: World-wide Assay of Natural Radiocarbon. *Science* 109:227–228.

Liebermann, R. C., and S. K. Banerjee
1971   Magnetoelastic Interactions in Hematite: Implications for Geophysics. *Journal of Geophysical Research* 75:2735–2756.

Limbrey, S.
1975   *Soil Science and Archaeology*. Academic Press, New York.

Lincoln, C. E.
1985   The Chronology of Chichen Itza: A Review of the Literature. In *Late Lowland Maya Civilization: Classic to Postclassic*, edited by J. A. Sabloff and E. W. Andrews V, 141–196. University of New Mexico Press, Albuquerque.

Linné, S.
1942   *Mexican Highland Cultures, Archaeological Researches at Teotihuacán, Calpulalpán and Chalchicomula in 1934–35*. Ethnographical Museum of Sweden Publication, no. 7. Stockholm.

Liritzis, Y., and R. Thomas
1980   Palaeointensity and Thermoluminescence Measurements on Cretan Kilns from 1300 to 2000 B.C. *Nature* 283:54–55.

Longyear, J. M.
1952   *Copán Ceramics: A Study of Southeastern Maya Pottery*. Carnegie Institution of Washington Publication, no. 597. Washington, D.C.

Lothrop, S. K.
1952   *Metals from the Cenote of Sacrifice, Chichen Itza, Yucatan*. Memoirs of the Peabody Museum of Archaeology and Ethnology, vol. 10, no. 2. Harvard University, Cambridge, Mass.

Lounsbury, F. G.
1983   The Base of the Venus Table of the Dresden Codex, and Its Significance for the Calendar-Correlation Problem. In *Calendars in Mesoamerica and Peru Native American Computations of Time*, edited by A. F. Aveni and G. Brotherston, series 174, pp. 1–27. Proceedings of the 44th International Congress of Americanists. General editor, H. Hammond.

Lowe, G. W.
   1978   Eastern Mesoamerica. In *Chronologies in New World Archaeology*, edited by R. E. Taylor and C. W. Meighan, 331–393. Academic Press, New York.

McDonald, K. L., and R. H. Gunst
   1967   *An Analysis of the Earth's Magnetic Field from 1835 to 1965.* Environmental Science Services Administration Technical Report IER 46-IES. Washington, D.C.

McDougall, I., and D. H. Tarling
   1963   Dating of Polarity Zones in the Hawaiian Islands. *Nature* 200:54–56.

   1964   Dating Geomagnetic Polarity Zones. *Nature* 202:171–172.

McElhinny, M. W.
   1973   *Palaeomagnetism and Plate Tectonics.* Cambridge University Press, London.

McFadden, P. L.
   1982   Rejection of Paleomagnetic Observations. *Earth and Planetary Science Letters* 61:392–395.

   1984   A Time Constant for the Geodynamo? *Physics of the Earth and Planetary Interiors* 34:117–125.

   1985   Comment on M. E. Beck's Comment on "Determination of the Angle of a Fisher Distribution Which Will Be Exceeded with a Given Probability," by P. L. McFadden. *Geophysical Journal of the Royal Astronomical Society* 80:281–282.

McFadden, P. L., and F. J. Lowes
   1981   The Discrimination of Mean Directions Drawn from Fisher Distributions. *Geophysical Journal of the Royal Astronomical Society* 34:163–189.

McGimsey, C. R., and H. A. Davis
   1977   *The Management of Archeological Resources: The Airlie House Report.* Special Publication of the Society for American Archaeology.

McGuire, R. H., R. S. Sternberg, and R. F. Butler
   1980   Exchange of Archaeomagnetic Information Between the Archaeologist and Geophysicist. Paper presented at the 45th Annual Meeting of the Society for American Archaeology, Philadelphia.

MacNeish, R. S.
   1964   Ancient Mesoamerican Civilization. *Science* 143:531–537.

   1976   Early Man in the New World. *American Scientist* 64:316–327.

MacNeish, R. S., F. A. Peterson, and K. V. Flannery
   1970   *Ceramics.* Vol. 3 of *The Prehistory of the Tehuacan Valley.* University of Texas Press, Austin.

McNish, A. G., and E. A. Johnson
   1938   Magnetization of Unmetamorphosed Varves and Marine Sediments. *Terrestrial Magnetism and Atmospheric Electricity* 43:401–407.

   1940   *Determination of the Secular Variation in Declination in New*

England from Magnetic Polarization of Glacial Varves. IUGG, Section of Terrestrial Magnetism and Electricity Bulletin, no. 2, pp. 339–347.

Malin, S.R.C., and E. Bullard
1981 The Direction of the Earth's Magnetic Field at London, 1570–1975. *Philosophical Transactions of the Royal Society of London* A299:357–423.

Manley, H.
1956 The Effects of Weathering and Alteration on the Magnetic Properties of a Doleritic Basalt. *Geofisica Pura e Applicata* 33:86–90.

Mason, B., and L. G. Berry
1959 *Elements of Mineralogy.* W. H. Freeman, San Francisco.

Matson, F. R.
1971 A Study of Temperatures Used in Firing Ancient Mesopotamian Pottery. In *Science and Archaeology*, edited by R. H. Brill, 65–79. MIT Press, Cambridge, Mass.

Matsuzaki, H., K. Kobayashi, and K. Momose
1954 On the Anomalously Strong Natural Remanent Magnetization of the Lava of Mt. Utsukushi-ga-hara. *Journal of Geomagnetism and Geoelectricity* 6:54–56.

Matuyama, M.
1929 On the Direction of Magnetization of Basalt in Japan, Tyosen and Manchuria. *Proceedings of the Imperial Academy of Japan* 5:203–205.

Mercanton, P. L.
1907 La Méthode de Folgerhaiter et son Rôle en Géophysique. *Archives des Sciences Physiques et Naturelles*, Per. 4, 23:467–482.
1918a État Magnétique de Quelques Terres Cuites Préhistoriques. *Comptes Rendus des Seances de l'Academie des Sciences* 166:681–685.
1918b État Magnétique de Quelques Terres Cuites Préhistoriques. *Comptes Rendus des Seances de l'Academie des Sciences* 166:949.
1918c État Magnétique de Quelques Terres Cuites Préhistoriques. *Bulletin de la Société Vaudoise des Sciences Naturelles*, ser. 5, 52:9–15.
1926a Aimantation de Basaltes Groenlandais. *Comptes Rendus des Seances de l'Academie des Sciences* 180:859–860.
1926b Inversion de l'Inclinaison Magnétique Terrestre aux Ages Géologiques. *Archives des Sciences Physiques et Naturelles*, Per. 5, 8:345–349.

Merrill, R. T., and M. W. McElhinny
1983 *The Earth's Magnetic Field.* Academic Press, New York.

Michels, J. W.
1967 Archaeology and Dating by Hydration of Obsidian. *Science* 158:211–214.
1973 *Dating Methods in Archaeology.* Seminar Press, New York.

Michels, J. W., I.S.T. Tsong, and C. M. Nelson
   1983   Obsidian Dating and East African Archeology. *Science* 219:361–366.
Mielke, P. W.
   1984   Meteorological Applications of Permutation Techniques Based on Distance Functions. In *Handbook of Statistics*, vol. 4, edited by P. R. Krishnaiah and P. K. Sen, 813–830. North-Holland, Amsterdam.
   1986   Non-metric Statistical Analyses: Some Metric Alternatives. *Journal of Statistical Planning and Inference* 13:377–387.
Mielke, P. W., and K. J. Berry
   1982   An Extended Class of Permutation Techniques for Matched Pairs. *Communications in Statistics: Theory and Methods* 11:1197–1207.
Mielke, P. W., K. J. Berry, and G. W. Brier
   1981   Application of Multi-response Permutation Procedures for Examining Seasonal Changes in Monthly Mean Sea-Level Pressure Patterns. *Monthly Weather Review* 109:120–126.
Mielke, P. W., K. J. Berry, and E. S. Johnson
   1976   Multi-response Permutation Procedures for A Priori Classifications. *Communications in Statistics: Theory and Methods* 5:1409–1424.
Millon, R.
   1973   *Urbanization at Teotihuacan, Mexico.* Vol. 1. University of Texas Press, Austin.
   1976   Chronological and Developmental Terminology: Why They Must Be Divorced. In *The Valley of Mexico*, edited by E. R. Wolf, 23–27. University of New Mexico Press, Albuquerque.
   1981   Teotihuacan: City, State, and Civilization. In *Supplement to the Handbook of Middle American Indians.* Vol. 1: *Archaeology*, edited by V. R. Bricker and J. A. Sabloff, 198–243. University of Texas Press, Austin.
   1988   The Last Years of Teotihuacan Dominance. In *The Collapse of Ancient States and Civilizations*, edited by N. Yoffee and G. L. Cowgill, 102–164. University of Arizona Press, Tucson.
Molloy, J. P.
   1983   Dynasts and Revolutionists: A Synthesis of Toltec Chronology and History. Ph.D. diss., University of Arizona.
Molloy, J., and D. H. Kelley
   n.d.   A Toltec Dynastic Sequence. Manuscript in possession of authors.
Molyneux, L.
   1971   A Complete Result Magnetometer for Measuring the Remanent Magnetization of Rocks. *Geophysical Journal of the Royal Astronomical Society* 24:429–433.
Morse, D. F., and P. A. Morse
   1983   *Archaeology of the Central Mississippi Valley.* Academic Press, New York.

Muto, G. R.
1978   *The Habiukut of Eastern Oklahoma: Parris Mound.* Part 1, Phase
        1: *An Archaeological Report.* Oklahoma Historical Society Series
        in Anthropology, no. 3. Oklahoma City.
Nachasova, I. Ye.
1972   Magnetic Field in the Moscow Area from 1480 to 1840. *Geomag-
        netism and Aeronomy* 12:277–280. English translation.
Nagata, T.
1943   The Natural Remanent Magnetism of Volcanic Rocks. *Bulletin of
        the Earthquake Research Institute* 21:1–196.
1953   *Rock Magnetism.* Maruzen, Tokyo.
1961   *Rock Magnetism.* Rev. ed. Maruzen, Tokyo.
Nagata, T., K. Kobayashi, and E. J. Schwarz
1965   Archaeomagnetic Intensity Studies of South and Central
        America. *Journal of Geomagnetism and Geoelectricity* 17:399–
        405.
Nagata, T., S. Uyeda, and S. Akimoto
1952   Self-reversal of Thermo-remanent Magnetism of Igneous Rocks.
        Journal of Geomagnetism and Geoelectricity 4:22–38.
Néel, L.
1949   Théorie du Traînage Magnétique des Ferromagnétiques aux
        Grains Fins avec Applications aux Terres Cuites. *Annales de
        Géophysique* 5:99–136.
1951   L'Inversion de l'Aimantation Permanente des Roches. *Annales de
        Géophysique* 7:90–102.
1955   Some Theoretical Aspects of Rock Magnetism. *Advances in
        Physics: A Quarterly Supplement of the Philosophical Magazine*
        4:191–243.
Negrini, R. M., J. O. Davis, and K. L. Verosub
1984   Mono Lake Geomagnetic Excursion Found at Summer Lake, Ore-
        gon. *Geology* 12:643–646.
Nichols, R. F.
1975   Archaeomagnetic Study of Anasazi-related Sediments of Chaco
        Canyon, New Mexico. M.S. thesis, School of Geology and Geo-
        physics, University of Oklahoma.
Olin, J. S. (ed.)
1982   *Future Directions in Archaeometry: A Round Table.* The Twenty-
        first Symposium for Archaeometry, Smithsonian Institution,
        Washington, D.C.
Onstott, T. C.
1980   Application of the Bingham Distribution Function in Paleomag-
        netic Studies. *Journal of Geophysical Research* 85:1500–1510.
O'Reilly, W.
1984   *Rock and Mineral Magnetism.* Chapman and Hall, London.
Ottaway, B. S.
1986   Is Radiocarbon Dating Obsolescent for Archaeologists? *Radiocar-
        bon* 28:732–738.

Paddock, J.
  1967   Current Research: Western Mesoamerica. *American Antiquity* 32:422–427.
  1983   The Oaxaca Barrio at Teotihuacán. In *The Cloud People*, edited by K. Flannery and J. Marcus, 170–175. Academic Press, New York.
Paddock, J., J. R. Mogor, and M. D. Lind
  1968   *Lambityeco Tomb 2: A Preliminary Report.* Boletín de Estudios Oaxaqueños, no. 25. Instituto de Estudios Oaxaqueños, Mitla, Mexico.
Parkes, P. A.
  1987   *Current Scientific Techniques in Archaeology.* St. Martin's Press, New York.
Parkinson, W. D.
  1983   *Introduction to Geomagnetism.* Elsevier, Amsterdam.
Parsons, L. A.
  1969   *Bilbao, Guatemala.* Vol. 2. Milwaukee Public Museum, Publications in Anthropology, vol. 12. Milwaukee.
Payne, M. A.
  1981   SI and Gaussian Units: Conversions and Equations for Use in Geomagnetism. *Physics of the Earth and Planetary Interiors* 26:10–16.
Pearson, G. W.
  1986   Precise Calendrical Dating of Known Growth-Period Samples Using a "Curve Fitting" Technique. *Radiocarbon* 28(2A): 292–299.
Perrot, J.
  1966   Le Gisement Natufien de Mallaha (Eynan), Israel. *L'Anthropologie* 70:437–484.
Peterson, F. A.
  1959   *Ancient Mexico.* Ruskin House/George Allen and Unwin, London.
Phillips, P.
  1970   *Archaeological Survey in the Lower Yazoo Basin, Mississippi, 1949–1955.* Harvard University, Papers of the Peabody Museum of Archaeology and Ethnology, vol. 60. Cambridge, Mass.
Plog, F.
  1980   Explaining Culture Change in the Hohokam Preclassic. In *Current Issues in Hohokam Prehistory*, edited by D. Doyel and F. Plog, 4–23. Arizona State University, Anthropological Research Papers, no. 23. Tempe.
Polach, H. A.
  1976   Radiocarbon Dating as a Research Tool in Archaeology: Hopes and Limitations. In *The Proceedings of a Symposium on Scientific Methods of Research in the Study of Ancient Chinese Bronzes and Southeast Asian Metal and Other Archaeological Artifacts*, 255–298. National Gallery of Victoria, Melbourne.
Powell, D. W.
  1960   Stress Dependent Magnetization in Some Quartz-Dolerites. *Nature* 187:225.

Pozzi, J. P., and E. Thellier
1963   Sur des Perfectionnements Recents Apportes aux Magnétometres à Tres Haute Sensibilité Utilises en Minéralogie Magnétique et en Paleomagnétisme. *Comptes Rendus des Seances de l'Academie des Sciences* 257:1037–1040.
Price, B. J.
1976   A Chronological Framework for Cultural Development in Mesoamerica. In *The Valley of Mexico*, edited by E. R. Wolf, 13–21. University of New Mexico Press, Albuquerque.
Pullaiah, G., E. Irving, K. L. Buchan, and D. J. Dunlop
1975   Magnetization Changes Caused by Burial and Uplift. *Earth and Planetary Science Letters* 28:133–145.
Raab, L. M., G. Fritz, D. Wolfman, R. H. Ray, and G. Sabo III
1982   The Arkansas Ozarks. In *A State Plan for the Conservation of Archeological Resources in Arkansas*, edited by H. A. Davis, pp. NW1–24. Arkansas Archeological Survey Research Series, no. 21. Fayetteville.
Rabin, E.
1970   Appendix on C_{14} Dates. In *The Lambityeco Friezes: Notes on Their Content, with an Appendix on C_{14} Dates*, by J. Paddock, 14–15. Boletín de Estudios Oaxaqueños, no. 33. Mitla, Mexico.
Ralph, E. K., and H. N. Michael
1967   Problems of the Radiocarbon Calendar. *Archaeometry* 9:3–11.
Ralph, E. K., H. N. Michael, and M. C. Han
1973   Radiocarbon Dates and Reality. *Masca Newsletter* 9(1).
Rands, R. L.
1954   Artistic Connections Between the Chichen Itza Toltec and the Classic Maya. *American Antiquity* 19:281–282.
Redman, C. C., W. T. Langhorne, Jr., M. J. Berman, N. M. Versaggi, V. Edward, and J. C. Wanser (eds.)
1978   *Social Archaeology: Beyond Subsistence and Dating*. Academic Press, New York.
Renfrew, C.
1968   Wessex Without Mycenae. *Annual of the British School of Archaeology at Athens* 63:277–285.
1973   *Before Civilization*. Alfred A. Knopf, New York.
Rikitake, T., and Y. Honkura
1985   *Solid Earth Geomagnetism*. Terra Scientific Publishing, Tokyo.
Rimbert, F.
1959   Contribution à l'Étude de l'Action de Champs Alternatifs Sur Les Aimantations Remanentes des Roches, Applications Géophysiques. *Revue de l'Institut Francais du Pétrole* 14:17–54, 123–155.
Roberts, J. P.
1961   Temperature Measurements. *Archaeometry* 4:19–21.
Robertson, W. A., and L. Hastie
1962   A Paleomagnetic Study of the Cygnet Alkaline Complex of Tasmania. *Journal of the Geological Society of Australia* 8:259–268.

Roche, A.
1951   Sur les Inversions de l'Aimantation Remanente des Roches Vol-
        caniques dans les Monts d'Auvergne. *Comptes Rendus des Se-
        ances de l'Academie des Sciences* 233:1132–1134.
1953   Sur l'Origine des Inversions de l'Aimantation Constantees dans
        les Roches d'Auvergne. *Comptes Rendus des Seances de l'Aca-
        demie des Sciences* 236:107–109.
1956   Sur la Date de la Derniere Inversion du Champ Magnétique Ter-
        restre. *Comptes Rendus des Seances de l'Academie des Sciences*
        243:812–814.
Rodgers, J. B.
1978.   *Archaeomagnetic Sampling: A Procedural Primer.* Center for An-
        thropological Studies, Albuquerque, New Mexico.
Rogers, J., J.M.W. Fox, and M. J. Aitken
1979   Magnetic Anisotropy in Ancient Pottery. *Nature* 277:644–646.
Rolingson, M. A.
1982   Emerging Cultural Patterns at the Toltec Mounds Site. In *Emerg-
        ing Patterns of Plum Bayou Culture*, edited by M. A. Rolingson,
        60–63. Arkansas Archeological Survey Research Series, no. 18.
        Fayetteville.
Roquet, J.
1954   Sur les Rémanences Magnétiques des Oxydes de Fer et Leur In-
        térêt en Géomagnétisme. *Annales de Géophysique* 10:226–247,
        282–325.
Rowe, J. H.
1960   Cultural Unity and Diversification in Peruvian Archaeology. In
        *Men and Cultures: Selected Papers of the Fifth International
        Congress of Anthropological and Ethnological Sciences*, edited
        by A. Wallace, 627–631. University of Pennsylvania Press, Phila-
        delphia.
Roy, J. L., and J. K. Park
1974   The Magnetization Process of Certain Red Beds: Vector Analysis
        of Chemical and Thermal Results. *Canadian Journal of Earth Sci-
        ences* 11:437–471.
Runcorn, S. K.
1956a   Palaeomagnetic Survey in Arizona and Utah: Preliminary Re-
        sults. *Bulletin of the Geological Society of America* 67:301–316.
1956b   Palaeomagnetic Comparisons Between Europe and North Amer-
        ica. *Proceedings of the Canadian Association of Geology* 8:77–85.
Rusakov, O. M., and G. F. Zagniy
1973   Archaeomagnetic Secular Variation Study of the Ukraine and Mol-
        davia. *Archaeometry* 15:153–157.
Sabloff, J. A., and E. W. Andrews V
1985   Introduction. In *Late Lowland Maya Civilization: Classic to Post-
        classic*, edited by J. A. Sabloff and E. W. Andrews V. University of
        New Mexico Press, Albuquerque.

Sabo III, G., ed.
1986a   *Contributions to Ozark Prehistory.* Arkansas Archeological Survey Research Series, no. 27.

Sabo III, G.
1986b   Preliminary Excavations at the Huntsville Site. In *Contributions to Ozark Prehistory*, edited by G. Sabo III, pp. 55–76. Arkansas Archeological Survey Research Series, no. 27.

Sabo III, G., D. B. Waddell, and J. H. House
1982   *A Cultural Resource Overview of the Ozark–St. Francis National Forests, Arkansas.* Arkansas Archeological Survey. Fayetteville.

Sanders, W. T.
1977   Ethnographic Analogy and the Teotihuacán Horizon Style. In *Teotihuacán and Kaminaljuyu: A Study in Prehistoric Culture Contact*, edited by W. T. Sanders and J. W. Michels, 397–410. Pennsylvania State University, University Park.

Sanders, W. T., J. R. Parsons, and R. S. Santley
1979   *The Basin of Mexico.* Academic Press, New York.

Sasajima, S., and K. Maenaka
1966   Intensity Studies of the Archaeo-secular Variation in West Japan, with Special Reference to the Hypothesis of the Dipole Axis Rotation. *Memoirs of the College of Science, University of Kyoto*, ser. B: *Geology and Mineralogy*, 33:53–67.

Satterthwaite, L., and E. K. Ralph
1960   New Radiocarbon Dates and the Maya Correlation Problem. *American Antiquity* 26:165–184.

Schambach, F. F.
1982   The Archeology of the Great Bend Region in Arkansas. In *Contributions to the Archeology of the Great Bend Region*, edited by F. F. Schambach and F. Rackerby, 1–11. Arkansas Archeological Survey Research Series, no. 22. Fayetteville.

Schiffer, M. B.
1976   *Behavioral Archeology.* Academic Press, New York.
1982   Hohokam Chronology: An Essay on History and Method. In *Hohokam and Patayan Prehistory of Southwestern Arizona*, edited by R. H. McGuire and M. B. Schiffer, 299–344. Academic Press, New York.

Schlanger, S. H.
1983   Excavations at Sheep Skull Camp (Site 5MT2202), a Multiple-Occupation Site. In *Dolores Archaeological Program: Field Investigations and Analysis, 1978*, 79–101. U.S. Department of the Interior, Bureau of Reclamation, Salt Lake City.

Schott, C. A.
1883a   On the Secular Variation of the Magnetic Declination in the United States and at Some Foreign Stations. In *U.S. Coast and Geodetic Survey: Fiscal Year Ending with June, 1882*, 211–276. Washington, D.C.

1883b   Distribution of the Magnetic Declination in the United States at the Epoch January, 1885. _U.S. Coast and Geodetic Survey: Fiscal Year Ending with June 1882,_ 277–328. Washington, D.C.

1886   The Geographical Distribution and Secular Variation of the Magnetic Dip and Intensity in the United States. In _U.S. Coast and Geodetic Survey: Fiscal Year Ending with June, 1885,_ 129–274. Washington, D.C.

1889   The Secular Variation of the Magnetic Declination in the United States and at Some Foreign Stations. In _U.S. Coast and Geodetic Survey: Fiscal Year Ending with June, 1888,_ 177–312. Washington, D.C.

1896   The Secular Variation in Direction and Intensity of the Earth's Magnetic Force in the United States and in Some Adjacent Foreign Countries. In _U.S. Coast and Geodetic Survey: Fiscal Year Ending with June 1895,_ 167–320. Washington, D.C.

Schove, D. J.
1977   Maya Dates, A.D. 352–1296. _Nature_ 263:670.

Schurr, K., H. Becker, and H. C. Soffel
1984   Archaeomagnetic Study of Medieval Fireplaces at Mannheim-Wallstadt and Ovens from Herrenchiemsee (Southern Germany) and the Problem of Magnetic Refraction. _Journal of Geophysics_ 56:1–8.

Schwarz, E. J., and K. W. Christie
1967   Original Remanent Magnetization of Ontario Potsherds. _Journal of Geophysical Research_ 72:3263–3269.

Scott, S. D.
1966   _Dendrochronology in Mexico._ Papers of the Laboratory of Tree-Ring Research, no. 2. University of Arizona, Tucson.

Sharer, R. J.
1978   Conclusions. In _The Prehistory of Chalchuapa, El Salvador,_ vol. 3, edited by R. J. Sharer, 205–217. University of Pennsylvania Press, Philadelphia.

Shaw, J.
1974   A New Method of Determining the Magnitude of the Palaeomagnetic Field Application to Five Historic Lavas and Five Archaeological Samples. _Geophysical Journal of the Royal Astronomical Society_ 39:133–141.

1979   Rapid Changes in the Magnitude of the Archaeomagnetic Field. _Geophysical Journal of the Royal Astronomical Society_ 58:107–116.

Sheets, P. D.
1979   Environmental and Cultural Effects of the Ilopango Eruption in Central America. In _Volcanic Activity and Human Ecology,_ edited by P. D. Sheets and D. K. Grayson, 525–564. Academic Press, New York.

Shepard, A. O.
1954   *Ceramics for the Archaeologist.* Carnegie Institution of Washington Publication, no. 609. Washington, D.C.

Shibuya, H.
1984   Several Archeomagnetic Measurements on Baked Earths in Kyoto Prefecture. *Rock Magnetism and Paleogeophysics* 11:1–9.

Shibuya, H., and T. Nakajima
1979   Archaeomagnetism of Southwestern Japan Measured and Compiled in Osaka University. *Rock Magnetism and Paleogeophysics* 6:10–13.

Shive, P. N.
1986   Suggestions for the Use of SI Units in Magnetism. *EOS: Transactions of the American Geophysical Union* 67:25–26.

Shuey, R. T.
1974   Archaeomagnetic Chronology of U-95 Sites. In *Highway U-95 Archaeology,* vol. 2, edited by C. J. Wilson, 207–209. University of Utah, Salt Lake City.

Shuey, R. T., E. R. Cole, and M. J. Mikulich
1970   Geographic Correction of Archeomagnetic Data. *Journal of Geomagnetism and Geoelectricity* 22:485–489.

Shuey, R. T., and R. Reed
1972   Archaeomagnetism of Evans Mound. In *The Evans Site,* edited by M. S. Berry, 289–296. University of Utah, Salt Lake City.

Sigalas, I., N.H.J. Gangas, and J. Danon
1978   Weathering Model in Paleomagnetic Field Intensity Measurements on Ancient Fired Clays. *Physics of the Earth and Planetary Interiors* 16:15–19.

Smiley, T. L.
1958   The Geology and Dating of Sunset Crater, Flagstaff, Arizona. In *Guidebook of the Black Mesa Basin, Northeastern Arizona,* edited by R. Y. Anderson and J. W. Harshbarger, 186–190. New Mexico Geological Society, Socorro.

Smith, G. P.
1981   Clay Content, Cube Size, and Refiring as Factors in Archaeomagnetic Sample Quality. Master's thesis, Colorado State University, Department of Anthropology, Fort Collins.

Smith, P. J., and J. Needham
1967   Magnetic Declination in Medieval China. *Nature* 214:1213–1214.

Smith, R. E., and J. C. Gifford
1965   Pottery of the Maya Lowlands. In *Handbook of Middle American Indians,* vol. 2, edited by G. R. Willey, 498–534. University of Texas Press, Austin.

Spriggs, M. (ed.)
1984   *Marxist Perspectives in Archaeology.* Cambridge University Press, New York.

Stacey, F. D., and S. K. Banerjee
    1974   *The Physical Principles of Rock Magnetism*. Elsevier, Amsterdam.
Staff Members and Research Associates of the Carnegie Institution
of Washington
    1938   *Cooperation in Research*. Carnegie Institution of Washington
            Publications, No. 501. Washington, D.C.
Stahle, D. W., E. R. Cook, and J.W.C. White
    1985   Tree-Ring Dating of Bald Cypress and the Potential for Millennia-
            long Chronologies in the Southeast. *American Antiquity* 50:796–
            802.
Stahle, D. W., and D. Wolfman
    1985   The Potential for Archaeological Tree-Ring Dating in Eastern
            North America. In *Advances in Archaeological Method and
            Theory*, vol. 8, edited by M. B. Schiffer, 279–302. Academic Press,
            New York.
Stange, E.
    1984   On an Archaeological Battlefield, It's Scholars vs. 'Shovel Bums.'
            Chronicle of Higher Education 27(18): 5–8.
Sternberg, R. S.
    1982   Archaeomagnetic Secular Variation of Direction and Palaeoin-
            tensity in the American Southwest. Ph.D. diss., University of
            Arizona.
    1983   Archaeomagnetism in the Southwest of North America. In *Geo-
            magnetism of Baked Clays and Recent Sediments*, edited by
            K. M. Creer, P. Tucholka, and C. E. Barton, 158–167. Elsevier,
            Amsterdam.
    1989a   Archaeomagnetic Paleointensity in the American Southwest dur-
            ing the Past 2000 Years. *Physics of the Earth and Planetary In-
            teriors* 56:1–17.
    1989b   Secular Variation of Archaeomagnetic Direction in the American
            Southwest, A.D. 750–1425. *Journal of Geophysical Research*
            94:527–546.
Sternberg, R. S., R. F. Butler, and R. McGuire
    1980   Some Paleomagnetic Considerations for Archaeomagnetic Dat-
            ing. Paper presented at the Forty-fifth Annual Meeting of the Soci-
            ety of American Archaeology, Philadelphia.
Sternberg, R. S., and P. E. Damon
    1979   Sensitivity of Radiocarbon Fluctuations and Inventory to Geo-
            magnetic and Reservoir Parameters. In *Radiocarbon Dating*,
            edited by R. Berger and H. Suess, 691–717. University of Califor-
            nia Press, Berkeley.
Sternberg, R. S., and R. H. McGuire
    1981a   An Archaeomagnetic Paleointensity Test of Hohokam Chronolo-
            gies. Paper presented at the 21st Symposium for Archaeometry,
            Upton, N.Y.
    1981b   Archaeomagnetic Secular Variation in the American Southwest.

> *EOS: Transactions of the American Geophysical Union* 62:852.

Stewart-Abernathy, J. C.
  1982   Ceramic Studies at the Toltec Mounds Site: Basis for a Tentative
          Culture Sequence. In *Emerging Patterns of Plum Bayou Culture*,
          edited by M. A. Rolingson, 44–53. Arkansas Archeological Survey
          Research Series, no. 18. Fayetteville.

Stone, D. B.
  1963   Anisotropic Magnetic Susceptibility Measurements on a Phono-
          lite and on a Folded Metamorphic Rock. *Geophysical Journal of
          the Royal Astronomical Society* 7:375–390.

Stone, M.
  1974   Cross-validatory Choice and Assessment of Statistical Predic-
          tions. *Journal of the Royal Statistical Society*, ser. B, 36:111–147.

Stott, P. M., and F. D. Stacey
  1960   Magnetostriction and Paleomagnetism of Igneous Rocks. *Journal
          of Geophysical Research* 65:2419–2424.

Strangway, D. W.
  1970   *History of the Earth's Magnetic Field.* McGraw-Hill, New York.

Stuiver, M.
  1982   A High-Precision Calibration of the AD Radiocarbon Time Scale.
          Radiocarbon 24:1–26.

Stuiver, M., and R. Kra (eds.)
  1986   Proceedings of the Twelfth International Radiocarbon Confer-
          ence. *Radiocarbon* 28 (2).

Stuiver, M., and P. J. Reimer
  1986   A Computer Program for Radiocarbon Age Calibration. *Radiocar-
          bon* 28:1022–1030.

Suess, H. E.
  1968   Climatic Changes, Solar Activity, and the Cosmic Ray Production
          Rate of Natural Radiocarbon. *Meteorological Monographs* 8:146–
          150.
  1970   Bristlecone-Pine Calibration of the Radiocarbon Time-Scale, 5200
          B.C. to the Present. In *Radiocarbon Variations and Absolute
          Chronology*, edited by I. U. Olssen, 303–311. John Wiley, New York.

Suzuki, M.
  1973   Chronology of Prehistoric Human Activity in Kanto, Japan. Part I:
          Framework for Reconstructing Prehistoric Human Activity in Ob-
          sidian. *University of Tokyo Journal of the Faculty of Science*
          4:241–318.

Tanguy, J. C.
  1970   An Archaeomagnetic Study of Mount Etna: The Magnetic Direc-
          tion Recorded in Lava Flows Subsequent to the Twelfth Century.
          Archaeometry 12:115–128.

Tanguy, J. C., I. Bucur, and J. F. C. Thompson
  1985   Geomagnetic Secular Variation in Sicily and Revised Ages of His-
          toric Lavas from Mount Etna. *Nature* 318:453–455.

Tarkhov, Ye. N.
1964   Rules for the Construction of Archaeomagnetic Curves. *Geomagnetism and Aeronomy* 4:718–720. English translation.

Tarling, D. H.
1971   *Principles and Applications of Paleomagnetism*. Chapman and Hall, London.
1975   Archaeomagnetism: The Dating of Archaeological Materials by Their Magnetic Properties. *World Archaeology* 7(2): 185–197.
1978   UK Geophysics: Alive and Well? *Nature* 274:641–642.
1983   *Palaeomagnetism: Principles and Applications in Geology, Geophysics and Archaeology*. Chapman and Hall, London.

Teeple, J. E.
1930   Maya Astronomy. *Contributions to American Archaeology No. 2.* Carnegie Institution of Washington Publications, No. 403, pp. 29–115.

Thellier, E.
1933   Magnétomètre Insensible aux Champs Magnétiques Troubles des Grandes Villes. *Comptes Rendus des Seances de l'Academie des Sciences* 197:232–234.
1936   Aimantation des Briques et Inclinaison du Champ Magnétique Terrestre. *Annales de l'Institut de Physique du Globe* 14:65–70.
1938   Sur l'Aimantation des Terres Cuites et ses Applications Géophysiques. *Annales de l'Institut de Physique du Globe* 16:157–302.
1951   Propriétés Magnétiques des Terres Cuites et des Roches. *Journal de Physique et le Radium* 12:205–218.
1967   Methods of Sample Collection and Orientation for Archaeomagnetism. In *Methods in Paleomagnetism*, edited by W. Collinson, K. M. Creer, and S. K. Runcorn, 16–20. Elsevier, Amsterdam.
1971   Magnétisme Interne. *Encyclopédie de la Pléiade. Géophysique*, 235–376.
1977   Early Research on the Intensity of the Ancient Geomagnetic Field. *Physics of the Earth and Planetary Interiors* 13:241–244.
1981   Sur la Direction du Champ Magnétique Terrestre, en France, Durant les Deux Derniers Millénares. *Physics of the Earth and Planetary Interiors* 24:89–132.

Thellier, E., and F. Rimbert
1954   Sur l'Analyse d'Aimantations Fossiles par Action de Champs Magnétiques Alternatifs. *Comptes Rendus des Seances de l'Academie des Sciences* 239:1399–1401.
1955   Sur l'Utilisation en Paléomagnétisme de la Désaimantation par Champs Alternatif. *Comptes Rendus des Seances de l'Academie des Sciences* 240:1404–1406.

Thellier, E., and O. Thellier
1942   Sur l'Intensité du Champ Magnétique Terrestre, en France, Trois Siècles Avant les Premieres Mesures Directes: Application au Probleme de la Désaimantation du Globe. *Comptes Rendus des Seances de l'Academie des Sciences* 214:382–384.

1951   Magnétisme Terrestre: Sur la Direction du Champ Magnétique Terrestre, Retrouvée sur des Parois de Fours des Époques Punique et Romaine, à Carthage. *Comptes Rendus des Seances de l'Academie des Sciences* 233:1476–1479.

1952   Magnétisme Terrestre: Sur la Direction du Champ Magnétique Terrestre, dans la Région de Trèves, vers 380 Après J.-C. *Comptes Rendus des Seances de l'Academie des Sciences* 234:1464–1466.

1959a   Sur l'Intensité du Champ Magnétique Terrestre dans le Passé Historique et Géologique. *Annales de Géophysique* 15:285–376.

1959b   The Intensity of the Earth's Magnetic Field in the Historical and Geological Past. *Bulletin of the Academy of Science*, USSR Geophysics Series 9:929–949. English translation.

Thomas, R. C.
1981   Archaeomagnetism of Greek Pottery and Cretan Kilns. Ph.D. diss., University of Edinburgh.

1983a   Review of Archaeointensity Methods. *Geophysical Surveys* 5:381–393.

1983b   Summary of Prehistoric Archaeointensity Data from Greece and Eastern Europe. In *Geomagnetism of Baked Clays and Recent Sediments*, edited by K. M. Creer, P. Tucholka, and C. E. Barton, 117–122. Elsevier, Amsterdam.

Thompson, J.E.S.
1935   *Maya Chronology: The Correlation Question*. Carnegie Institution of Washington, Contributions to American Anthropology and History, no. 14. Washington, D.C.

1941   A Coordination of the History of Chichen Itza with Ceramic Sequences in Central Mexico. *Revista Mexicana de Estudios Antropológicos* 5:97–111.

1959   Review of *Chichen Itza and Its Cenote of Sacrifice*, by A. M. Tozzer. *American Journal of Archaeology* 63:119–120.

1960   *Maya Hieroglyphic Writing: An Introduction*. 2d ed. University of Oklahoma Press, Norman.

1970   Putun (Chontal Maya) Expansion in Yucatan and the Pasion Drainage. In *Maya History and Religion*, edited by J.E.S. Thompson. University of Oklahoma Press, Norman.

Thompson, L. G., S. Hastenrath, and B. M. Arnao
1979   Climatic Ice Core Records from the Tropical Quelccaya Ice Cap. *Science* 203:1240–1243.

Thompson, L. G., E. Mosley-Thompson, P. M. Grootes, M. Pourchet, and S. Hastenrath
1984   Tropical Glaciers: Potential for Ice Core Paleoclimatic Reconstructions. *Journal of Geophysical Research* D89:4638–4646.

Thompson, R.
1977   Stratigraphic Consequences of Palaeomagnetic Studies of Pleistocene and Recent Sediments. *Journal of the Geological Society of London* 133:51–59.

Thompson, R., and D. R. Barraclough
  1982   Geomagnetic Secular Variation Based on Spherical Harmonic and
          Cross Validation Analyses of Historical and Archaeomagnetic
          Data. _Journal of Geomagnetism and Geoelectricity_ 34:245–263.
Thompson, R., and R. M. Clark
  1981   Fitting Polar Wander Paths. _Physics of the Earth and Planetary
          Interiors_ 27:1–7.
Thrower, N.J.W. (ed.)
  1981   _The Three Voyages of Edmond Halley in the_ Paramour, _1698–
          1701._ Hakluyt Society, London.
Tite, M. S., and C. E. Mullins
  1971   Enhancement of the Magnetic Susceptibility of Soils on Archaeo-
          logical Sites. _Archaeometry_ 13:209–219.
Toll, H. W., T. C. Windes, and P. J. McKenna
  1980   Late Ceramic Patterns in Chaco Canyon: The Pragmatics of Mod-
          eling Ceramic Exchange. In _Models and Methods in Regional Ex-
          change,_ edited by R. E. Fry, 95–117. Washington, D.C.
Tolstoy, P.
  1978   Western Mesoamerica Before A.D. 900. In _Chronologies in New
          World Archaeology,_ edited by R. E. Taylor and C. W. Meighan,
          241–284. Academic Press, New York.
Townsend, W. N.
  1973   _An Introduction to the Scientific Study of the Soil._ St. Martin's
          Press, New York.
Tozzer, A. M.
  1921   _Excavations of a Site at Santiago Ahuitzotla, D.F., Mexico._ Smith-
          sonian Institution, Bureau of American Ethnology Bulletin, no.
          74. Washington, D.C.
Trubowitz, N. L., and M. D. Jeter (eds.)
  1982   _Arkansas Archeology in Review._ Arkansas Archeological Survey
          Research Series, no. 15. Fayetteville.
Tucker, P., and R. C. Thomas
  1983   Magnetization Processes in Baked Clays. In _Geomagnetism of
          Baked Clays and Recent Sediments,_ edited by K. M. Creer, P.
          Tucholka, and C. E. Barton, 2–9. Elsevier, Amsterdam.
Uyeda, S., M. D. Fuller, J. C. Belshé, and R. W. Girdler
  1963   Anisotropy of Magnetic Susceptibility of Rocks and Minerals.
          Journal of Geophysical Research 68:279–291.
Vaillant, G. C.
  1941   _Aztecs of Mexico._ Doubleday, New York.
Van Alstine, D. R.
  1980   Analysis of the Modes of Directional Data with Particular Refer-
          ence to Palaeomagnetism. _Geophysical Journal of the Royal As-
          tronomical Society_ 61:101–113.
Van Alstine, D. R., and J. de Boer
  1978   A New Technique for Constructing Apparent Polar Wander Paths

and the Revised Phanerozoic Path for North America. *Geology* 6:137–139.

Van der Waerden, B. L.
1969 *Mathematical Statistics*. Springer-Verlag, New York.

Verosub, K. L.
1977 Depositional and Postdepositional Processes in the Magnetization of Sediments. *Reviews of Geophysics and Space Physics* 15:129–143.

Verosub, K. L., and S. K. Banerjee
1977 Geomagnetic Excursions and Their Paleomagnetic Record. *Reviews of Geophysics and Space Physics* 15:145–155.

Verosub, K. L., and P. J. Mehringer, Jr.
1984 Congruent Paleomagnetic and Archeomagnetic Records from the Western United States, A.D. 750 to 1450. *Science* 224:387–389.

Verosub, K. L., P. J. Mehringer, Jr., and P. Waterstraat
1986 Holocene Secular Variation in Western North America: Paleomagnetic Record from Fish Lake, Harney County, Oregon. *Journal of Geophysical Research* 91:3609–3623.

Vestine, E. H., L. LaPorte, C. Cooper, I. Lange, and W. C. Hendrix
1947 *Description of the Earth's Main Magnetic Field and Its Secular Change, 1905–1945*. Carnegie Institution of Washington Publication, no. 578. Washington, D.C.

Vestine, E. H., L. LaPorte, I. Lange, and W. E. Scott
1947 *The Geomagnetic Field: Its Description and Analysis*. Carnegie Institution of Washington Publication, no. 580. Washington, D.C.

Vine, F. J., and D. H. Matthews
1963 Magnetic Anomalies Over Oceanic Ridges. *Nature* 199:947–949.

Von Schmidlin, H.
1937 Über Entmagnetisierende Wirkung der Anderungen des Magnetischen Erdfeldes. *Beitrage zur Angewandten Geophysik* 7:94–111.

Walton, D.
1977 Archaeomagnetic Intensity Measurements Using a Squid Magnetometer. *Archaeometry* 19:192–200.
1983 The Reliability of Ancient Intensities Obtained by Thermal Demagnetization. In *Geomagnetism of Baked Clays and Recent Sediments*, edited by K. M. Creer, P. Tucholka, and C. E. Barton, 88–97. Elsevier, Amsterdam.
1987 Improving the Accuracy of Geomagnetic Intensity Measurements. *Nature* 328:789–791.

Watanabe, N.
1959 The Direction of Remanent Magnetization of Baked Earth and Its Application to Chronology for Anthropology and Archaeology in Japan. *Journal of the Faculty of Science, University of Tokyo* 2:1–188.

Watanabe, N., and R. L. DuBois
1965 Some Results of an Archaeomagnetic Study on the Secular Varia-

tion in the Southwest of North America. *Journal of Geomagnetism and Geoelectricity* 17:395–397.

Watkins, N. D.
  1963   Magnetic Dating of Archeological Specimens. Manuscript on file in the library of the Laboratory of Anthropology of the Museum of New Mexico, Santa Fe.
  1972   Review of the Development of the Geomagnetic Time Scale and Discussion of Prospects for Its Finer Definition. *Bulletin of the Geological Society of America* 83:551–574.

Watson, G. S.
  1956   Analysis of Dispersion on a Sphere. *Monthly Notices of the Royal Astronomical Society, Geophysical Supplement* 7:153–159.

Watson, G. S., and E. Irving
  1957   Statistical Methods in Rock Magnetism. *Monthly Notices of the Royal Astronomical Society, Geophysical Supplement* 7:289–300.

Watson, G. S., and E. J. Williams
  1956   On the Construction of Significance Tests on the Circle and Sphere. *Biometrika* 43:344–352.

Watson, R. P.
  1985   C-14 and Cultural Chronology on the North Coast of Peru: Implications for a Regional Chronology. In *Andean Archaeology: Papers in Memory of Clifford Evans*, edited by R. Matos M., A. T. Solveig, and H. H. Eling, Jr., 83–129. University of California, Institute of Archaeology Monograph, no. 27.

Wauchope, R.
  1954   Implications of Radiocarbon Dates from Middle and South America. *Middle American Research Record* [Tulane University] 2:17–40.

Weaver, G. H.
  1961   Magnetic Dating Measurements. *Archaeometry* 4:23–28.
  1962   Archaeomagnetic Measurements on the Second Boston Experimental Kiln. *Archaeometry* 5:93–107.

Weaver, K. F.
  1967   Magnetic Clues Help Date the Past. *National Geographic* 131:696–701.

Wegner, A.
  1912   Die Entstehung der Kontinente. *Petermanns Geographische Mitteilungen* 58:185–195, 253–256, 350–408.
  1915   *Die Entstehung der Kontinente and Ozeane*. Braunschweiz, Vieweg.
  1924   *The Origin of Continents and Oceans*. Methuen, London.

Weymouth, J., and R. Huggins
  1983   Magnetometer Results. In *Dolores Archaeological Program: Field Investigations and Analysis, 1978*, 194–251. U.S. Department of the Interior, Bureau of Reclamation, Salt Lake City.

Willey, G. R.
  1966   *An Introduction to American Archaeology.* Vol. 1: *North and Middle America.* Prentice-Hall, Englewood Cliffs, N.J.
  1978   A Summary Scan. In *Chronologies in New World Archaeology,* edited by R. E. Taylor and C. W. Meighan, 241–284. Academic Press, New York.
Wilshusen, R.
  1986   Excavations at Periman Hamlet (Site 5MT4671), Area 1, A Pueblo I Habitation. In *Anasazi Communities at Dolores: Middle Canyon Area,* compiled by A. E. Kane and C. K. Robinson, 25–210. U.S. Department of the Interior, Bureau of Reclamation, Salt Lake City.
Wilson, R. L.
  1961   Paleomagnetism in Northern Ireland; Part 1: The Thermal Demagnetization of Natural Magnetic Moments of Rocks. *Geophysical Journal* 5:45–69.
Windes, T.
  1978   *Archaeomagnetic Sampling Field Procedures and Equipment.* National Park Service, Division of Chaco Research, Albuquerque, N.Mex.
  1980   *Archaeomagnetic Dating: Lessons from Chaco Canyon, New Mexico.* Paper presented at the Forty-fifth Annual Meeting of the Society for American Archaeology, Philadelphia.
Winter, J. C., and F. Levine
  1987   The Site 48 Chronology. In *Investigations at Sites 48 and 77, Santa Rosa Lake, Guadalupe County, New Mexico,* vol. 2, edited by J. C. Winter and F. Levine, 739–757. University of New Mexico, Office of Contract Archeology, Albuquerque.
Wolf, E.
  1959   *Sons of the Shaking Earth.* University of Chicago Press, Chicago.
Wolfman, D.
  1968   Review of *Dendrochronology in Mexico,* by S. D. Scott. *American Antiquity* 33:115–116.
  1973   A Re-evaluation of Mesoamerican Chronology, A.D. 1–1200. Ph.D. diss., University of Colorado.
  1977   Archaeomagnetic Dates from the Baca Float Sites. In *Excavations in the Middle Santa Cruz River Valley, Southeastern Arizona,* by D. E. Doyel, Appendix G. Contributions to Highway Salvage Archaeology in Arizona, no. 44, Arizona State Museum, Tucson.
  1978a   An Inundated Archeomagnetic Sample. In *The Mechanical and Chemical Effects of Inundation at Abiquiu Reservoir,* edited by C. F. Schaafsma, Appendix I, pp. 1–8. School of American Research, Sante Fe.
  1978b   *The Potential for Archeomagnetic Dating in the Knife River Indian Villages National Historic Site.* Report submitted to the National Park Service, Midwest Archeological Center, Purchase Order No. PX-6115-7-0158.

1978c   Recent Archaeomagnetic Results from Arkansas. Paper presented at the Forty-third Annual Meeting of the Society for American Archaeology, Tucson.

1979   Archaeomagnetic Dating in Arkansas. In Proceedings of the 18th International Symposium on Archaeometry and Archaeological Prospection. *Archaeo-Physika* 10:522–533.

1981   Looking for the Needle in a Haystack, When the Needle May Not Be There: The Possibility of Using Geomagnetic Excursions as a Basis for Archaeological Dating. Paper presented at the Twenty-first Symposium for Archaeometry, May 1981. Upton, N.Y.

1982   Archeomagnetic Dating in Arkansas and the Border Areas of Adjacent States. In *Arkansas Archeology in Review*, edited by N. Trubowitz and M. Jeter, 277–300. Arkansas Archeological Survey Research Series, no. 15. Fayetteville.

1983   Fechas Definidas por Arqueomagnetismo. In *Introducción a la Arqueología de Copán, Honduras*, 1:546–549. Instituto Hondureño de Antropología e Historia, Tegucigalpa.

1984   Geomagnetic Dating Methods in Archaeology. In *Advances in Archaeological Method and Theory*, vol. 7, edited by M. B. Schiffer, 363–458. Academic Press, New York.

1988   The Importance of Stratigraphic Samples in Archaeomagnetic Dating. Paper presented at the 1988 International Symposium on Archaeometry, May 1988. Toronto.

n.d.   Cautionary Notes on Radiocarbon Dating. In *Zebree Archeological Project: The Beginning of Mississippian Cultures in the Central Mississippi Valley*, edited by D. F. Morse and P. A. Morse. Arkansas Archeological Survey Research Series.

Wolfman, D., and R. E. Dodson
1984   Recent Archaeomagnetic Results from Peru. Paper presented at the 1984 International Symposium on Archaeometry, Washington, D.C.

1985   Archeomagnetic Dating on the North Coast of Peru. Paper presented at the Dumbarton Oaks Symposium, The Northern Dynasties: Kingship and Statecraft in Chimor, Washington, D.C.

1986   Los Resultados Arqueomagnéticos de las Muestras Recogidas en el Perú en 1983. Report submitted to Instituto Nacional de Cultura, Lima, Peru.

Wolfman, D., W. Kean, and M. Fowler
1982   Archeomagnetic Results from Modoc Rock Shelter. Paper presented at the American Geophysical Union Spring Meeting, Philadelphia, 1982.

Wolfman, D., and T. M. Rolniak
1979   Alpha-Recoil Track Dating: Problems and Prospects. *Archaeo-Physika* 10:512–521.

Wolfman, D., and D. Stahle
1979   Recent Advances and Results in Alpha-Recoil Track Dating. Paper

presented at the 44th Annual Meeting of the Society for American Archaeology, Vancouver.

Woodbury, R. B.
 1973   *Alfred V. Kidder*. Columbia University Press, New York.

Yarnell, R. W.
 1983   *Excavations at Areas 2, 3, 4, and 7, Periman Hamlet (Site 5MT4671), A Pueblo I–Pueblo II Habitation*. Dolores Archaeological Program Technical Report, DAP-091. U.S. Department of the Interior, Bureau of Reclamation, Salt Lake City.

Yu, J. H.
 1978   Some Thermal Magnetic Properties of Baked Clay. Master's thesis, University of Oklahoma, Norman.

Yukutake, T.
 1967   The Westward Drift of the Earth's Magnetic Field in Historic Times. *Journal of Geomagnetism and Geoelectricity* 19:103–116.
 1968   Free Decay of Non-dipole Components of the Geomagnetic Field. *Physics of the Earth and Planetary Interiors* 1:93–96.
 1979   Review of the Geomagnetic Secular Variations on the Historical Time Scale. *Physics of the Earth and Planetary Interiors* 20:83–95.

Zijderveld, J.D.A.
 1967   A.C. Demagnetization of Rocks: Analysis of Results. In *Methods in Paleomagnetism*, edited by D. W. Collinson, K. M. Creer, and S. K. Runcorn, 254–286. Elsevier, Amsterdam.

Index